WE
SHALL
NOT
BE
MOVED

WE SHALL NOT BE MOVED

The Jackson Woolworth's Sit-In and the Movement It Inspired

M. J. O'Brien

UNIVERSITY PRESS OF MISSISSIPPI • JACKSON

www.upress.state.ms.us

Designed by Peter D. Halverson

The University Press of Mississippi is a member of the Association of American University Presses.

Excerpt from "For A. D. Beittel, President, Tougaloo College, Mississippi" by Elizabeth Sewell, reprinted with the permission of UNCF

Cover photo and photo on page ii by Fred Blackwell

First printing 2013

∞

Library of Congress Cataloging-in-Publication Data

O'Brien, M. J., 1951–
   We shall not be moved : the Jackson Woolworth's sit-in and the movement it inspired / M. J. O'Brien.
      p. cm.
   Includes bibliographical references and index.
   ISBN 978-1-61703-743-6 (cloth : alk. paper) — ISBN 978-1-61703-744-3
(ebook) 1. Civil rights movements—Mississippi—History—20th century.
2. African Americans—Civil rights—Mississippi—History—20th century.
3. African Americans—Segregation—Mississippi—History—20th century. 4. Mississippi—Race relations—History—20th century. I. Title.
   E185.93.M6O25 2013
   323.1196'073076251—dc23   2012037943

British Library Cataloging-in-Publication Data available

For Medgar

For Myrlie

For Darrell

For Reena

For Van

Forever

To all those who participated in the Jackson Movement.

To Joan Harris Nelson Trumpauer Mulholland in appreciation for her enduring friendship and inspiration.

THEY GO WILD OVER ME

They go wild, simply wild over me
Every time I go downtown for tea.
They make up all sorts of rules
Even try to remove the stools.
They go wild, simply wild over me.

Civil rights parody of the equally satirical Industrial Workers of the World song "The Popular Wobbly,"
as noted in the sit-in display at the National Civil Rights Museum, Memphis, Tennessee.

CONTENTS

FOREWORD

Julian Bond

MICHAEL O'BRIEN HAS WRITTEN A DETAILED HISTORY AND FASCINATING study of one of the iconic moments of the modern civil rights movement and the powerful effect it had. The 1963 sit-in at a Jackson, Mississippi, Woolworth's lunch counter was captured by a local photographer, as were many other demonstrations, but this one captured the imagination as no other did.

The photograph, taken three years after the modern civil rights movement was stirred into action by a similar sit-in in Greensboro, North Carolina—and decades after similar protests in the 1950s, 1940s, and earlier—had greater significance and carried greater weight than those that went before.

In many ways, the important elements in this and the earlier protests were the same. The petty apartheid of lunch counter segregation grated at blacks' sensibilities. They knew whites did not mind closeness or intimacy when the blacks were maids or nurses, or subservient and servile. They did not mind blacks preparing food for white children and even nursing them. But something about eating side by side struck a strong nerve in many white southerners. One of the white high school students drawn to this scene said he had never seen whites and blacks sitting together in a public place—he thought it was wrong in 1963 and told the author he thinks it is wrong today.

The mechanics of most southern lunch counter sit-ins had become routine by 1963. Peaceful black and white protesters would calmly take seats at an eating facility reserved for whites only. Where laws forbade blacks to sit at eating facilities reserved for whites, as was true in most of the South until the Civil Rights Act of 1964 became law, the blacks were asked to leave. If they refused, police were called. Practicing what they understood to be Gandhian nonviolence, the protesters refused to strike back if struck.

In most places, that was it, but in Jackson, where racial protests of any kind had been infrequent and little noticed, an explosion occurred. This protest took place in the immediate aftermath of a Supreme Court decision legalizing sit-ins. Rather than acknowledging an obligation to protect the sit-inners, the Jackson police interpreted the decision as granting them the right to ignore the protesters if any but the most dangerous violence occurred. The result was that Jackson's finest stood outside the Woolworth's while as many as three hundred angry whites were allowed to attack the sit-inners at will, without any interference by the law.

The photo only hints at the level of violence that occurred. By looking at the faces of the three at the counter—John Salter, Joan Trumpauer, and Anne Moody—and their disheveled and soiled clothing, one can imagine the degree of anger their assailants expressed. But the photo does not show the beatings the sit-inners received, the blows that rained upon them, or the cuts they received.

The Woolworth's sit-in became the alarm that awakened black Jackson. A movement erupted where, despite decades of racist degradation, organizers with their best efforts had been unable to arouse a seemingly placid black population. With the sit-in as a catalyst for an activist movement in Jackson, the drama that followed for the next month occupies the rest of this absorbing story. Organizational jealousy threatened movement unity and harmony. Personal conflicts menaced movement cohesiveness.

This story doesn't have the happiest of endings. A promising movement was stymied by tragedy and backbiting and failed to deliver victories earlier enthusiasm had promised. The people we now know as heroes and heroines were people, after all, and often they acted like other human beings, revealing the same shortcomings.

But most of all, as the author shows them here, they were brave. Avoiding the triumphalism of most civil rights history, O'Brien shows the human weaknesses common to us all, analyzing the emotions and maneuvering that characterized some of civil rights history.

Readers will enjoy this behind-the-scenes look at an important event in movement history, and will see people as they are—at their best and worst.

Julian Bond is chairman emeritus of the NAACP Board of Directors. He is a Distinguished Scholar in the School of Government at American University in Washington, D.C., and a professor in the Department of History at the University of Virginia.

WE
SHALL
NOT
BE
MOVED

PROLOGUE

Start with the photograph, a striking image in black and white. The background features a phalanx of jeering young white men seemingly engaged in the kind of sophomoric prank every high school yearbook boasts. Their hairstyles date them somewhere post-Elvis but pre-Beatles: slicked-back, James Dean types, raising a little hell down at the after-school hangout. Their faces show glee, fascination, bemusement as they consider what the reaction will be to a canister of sugar one prankster has just dumped down a young woman's back.

The woman—white, thin, nonchalant—tries hard to ignore her predicament; she doesn't seem to get the joke. She sits at the lunch counter between a light-skinned man and a black woman, and the three must be wondering what might come next. Their outward calm gives no sign that they have been enduring the whims of these raucous teens for several hours. The evidence, however, is on their clothes and hair, which have been doused with mustard, catsup, pepper, sugar, and other condiments as the trio sit, outwardly serene, on steel-backed lunch counter stools.

In addition to the young rowdies and their prey, some adults appear in the photo: a weary-looking, middle-aged man at the far end of the counter; an older man in a hat and glasses watching intently behind the kid pouring the sugar; and some men toward the back sporting sunglasses.

The focus, however, is on the three seated in the foreground. Their inaction, their stoicism contrast sharply with the activity behind them and reveal that this scene is not an ordinary prank but is instead a battle—one moment, captured on film for posterity—in the war between oppression and freedom.

The photograph is of a sit-in, one stage of America's civil rights movement, which sought equality for African American citizens. The sit-in phase began on February 1, 1960, when four black college students in Greensboro, North Carolina, decided they had had enough of segregation and dared each other to take a stand. When they went down to the local Woolworth's store and sat in the whites-only section of the lunch counter, they sparked a nationwide student movement in support of better treatment of blacks in American society.

The sit-in captured by this photo is at another Woolworth's. The blurred sign in the top center, just behind the youth in sunglasses, can barely be made out: "F. W. _____H Co."—the Woolworth trademark. Another marker indicates the site of the demonstration is the "Hot Donut Department." A small U.S. flag flies high above the scene, an ironic reminder that this confrontation is taking place in the land that prides itself on being the home of individual freedom.

The date is May 28, 1963, just two weeks and a few hours before one of the first political assassinations would occur during that turbulent decade—the murder of Medgar Evers. And that killing will happen in this city, in part as a response to this sit-in and to the grassroots uprising it will ignite.

The city is Jackson, the capital of Mississippi—an unlikely venue for this kind of outbreak. Most of the sit-ins happened soon after the Greensboro demonstration. In the border states of Maryland, Virginia, Tennessee, and Kentucky, most lunch counters and movie houses were quickly opened up to people of color after a few well-staged, generally peaceful protests. Georgia, Alabama, Florida, the Carolinas, Louisiana, and Mississippi were less inclined to roll over after a bit of bad press. In fact, certain pockets in each of these states were hell-bent on maintaining the segregated "southern way of life," no matter what the human cost. In Mississippi, as in several of the other Deep South states, the resistance was so strong and the paranoia so deep that the state government formed its own network of spies to terrorize and attempt to thwart the efforts of those it called, but who seldom were, "outside" agitators. Only in Mississippi could a sit-in of this magnitude occur in 1963—nearly three years after many other southern cities had conceded the point—and break into a full-scale riot.

On this day, in this city, the battleground had been selected with great care, although the combatants on both sides somewhat haphazardly decided to join. The photo misrepresents the scope of battle: it appears to be three against twenty; in reality, the numbers are more like nine against three hundred—less than advantageous odds for those at the counter. Yet the three demonstrators in the photograph and the six others outside its frame wield their only weapon unflinchingly: their nonviolent insistence that they will not be moved. They have determined to react without anger to the indignities they suffer; they sit quietly and take whatever comes, insisting that there must be a better way.

Despite the odds, these young people will succeed in changing at least one heart this day. They will spark to life a movement that will shake up the city of Jackson and, in time, will have ramifications for the entire country. And the image that documents their courage will be passed on for generations as an enduring symbol of America's hard-fought struggle for civil rights.

What happened on that day to the people represented in the photo is the subject of this book. It is a "lifestyle story" of sorts, since it describes the participants' entire lives and what brought them to this moment of confrontation and danger as well as what became of them after their time in the spotlight had passed. It is a story of great tragedy but also of great hope. And it all begins with the tale of a central character, absent from the photo but crucial to the unfolding of the narrative—the story of Medgar Evers and his native state of Mississippi.

CHAPTER 1

MEDGAR'S MISSISSIPPI

Medgar Evers was not on the scene when violence erupted at the downtown Jackson Woolworth's. Instead, he was dutifully ensconced in his office, awaiting word of how the demonstration was going. He hoped, though, that this first direct action strike would force a breakthrough that would not only bring the whites in power to the bargaining table, but also shatter the seeming indifference of the local black community he was attempting to lead.

His whole life had been moving him toward this moment. Born in poverty in rural Mississippi, he had for years sought to fix the injustice of racial segregation. Now, with the backing of the most distinguished civil rights organization in the country, the NAACP, he was prepared for a long campaign of demonstrations and protests in Mississippi's capital city to finally crack the state's seemingly impenetrable barrier to black advancement.

Though he was not on site, Evers's presence hovered over the protesters as they endured hour after hour of abuse from the out-of-control mob at Woolworth's. He was considered by the sit-in participants the tenth demonstrator at the counter—the one who worked longest and hardest for the triumph this day would bring.

Medgar Evers would enjoy this sweet victory ever so briefly before his movement dissolved under the too-heavy crush of segregation's deadly response and his own organization's bureaucratic wavering. But this sit-in would count among his most memorable achievements and would set in motion the forces that would ultimately turn the tide in the battle for racial freedom in his beloved home state.

FROM THE TIME MEDGAR WILEY EVERS WAS BORN, ON JULY 2, 1925, THROUGH the time of the Jackson Woolworth's sit-in, Mississippi was trapped in a post–Civil War time warp in which most blacks were treated little better than slaves. A brief period of forced equanimity had settled over Mississippi just after that war, during which blacks and whites had the same political rights. Once the federal government lost its will to enforce the rights of blacks, however, whites found opportunities—generally through violent means—to ensure that blacks were kept from power and would live as whites decreed. By the 1890s, whites had begun to construct policies that completely shut blacks out from the political process and kept most from achieving even basic economic gains. Racial segregation became more than just an accepted practice: it was the law. Blacks were not allowed to use the same libraries or parks, swim in the same swimming pools, attend the same schools, or even be buried in the same cemeteries as whites. Every aspect of white/black interchange was carefully choreographed to ensure that blacks would feel inferior. Most whites believed that blacks *were* inferior, perhaps not even wholly human. With such rationalizations, it became easy for whites to deprive black Mississippians of their basic human and economic rights, to limit their citizenship status, and to react with violence when blacks asserted themselves.[1]

It was into this atmosphere that Medgar Evers was born.[2] His mother, Jessie Wright Evers, was descended from slaves, including a half–Native American maternal grandfather—Medgar Wright—after whom Evers was named. Jessie's paternal grandfather had been white—a case of "nighttime integration,"[3] as Evers's older brother, Charles, called such liaisons.

James Evers, Medgar's father, also had a mixed lineage; his mother had been half–Creole Indian. And James Evers's family knew well the difficulties of surviving in a harsh economic and political system. His father—Medgar's paternal grandfather, Mike Evers—had had his two-hundred-acre farm taken away when, during hard times, he was unable to come up with the funds to pay the taxes on the property.

From these two family lines, Medgar Evers absorbed lessons in both courage and civility. Jessie Evers was deeply religious, and the Evers children—two boys and two girls, plus two older half-siblings from a prior marriage—would spend all day Sunday in church. Jessie Evers also taught her children not to hate, no matter how poorly they were treated. "Hatred only breeds more hatred," she told them repeatedly. In addition, she instilled in her children the idea that they were every bit as good as the whites they interacted with. "White folks are not better than you," she insisted. "They just *think* they are."[4]

From their father, the Evers children learned the value of hard work and the courage to stand up to adversaries. James Evers was a man of many talents: he was a sawmill laborer, lumber contractor, railroad worker, and farmer, as well as a part-time funeral attendant. Still poor despite his resourcefulness, "Crazy James" remained unbowed in the face of white intimidation. He refused to step off the sidewalk when whites approached, a behavior expected of blacks under segregation. And he would challenge whites who tried to take advantage of him. Once, when young Medgar and Charles went with their father to pay the family's bill at the sawmill store, which extended credit to workers until payday, the boys witnessed a display of courage and daring unusual for any black man at the time. Though unschooled, James Evers knew enough to realize he was being cheated that day and challenged the white clerk over the bill. "Are you calling me a liar, nigger?" the clerk shouted. Even though the store was full of white patrons, James Evers did not back down, insisting that the bill was wrong. When the clerk became more enraged and headed behind the counter to get his gun, Evers blocked his path. He then grabbed a bottle, broke it off at its neck, and pointed the cut glass toward the clerk, yelling, "Move another step and I'll bust your damn brains in!"

Next, Evers told his sons to leave the store and, keeping his eyes on the grocer and the other whites, backed carefully out the door and into the street. No one followed. As the three walked home, James Evers told his sons, "Don't ever let anyone beat you." Stand toe-to-toe with whites, demand respect, and you'll get it; that was the lesson Medgar and Charles Evers learned from their father.[5]

But such respect was rare, while the daily realities of segregation were all encompassing. The Evers children walked to school and Medgar never forgot the taunting of white kids who rode the bus that passed by. Even the white bus driver joined in, careening the bus toward the black children as if he were about to run over them. But some white children who lived nearby befriended the Evers siblings, and they played together daily. Later in life, Medgar Evers spoke of one neighboring white boy from whom he was inseparable until "one day [he] stopped coming by. In a little while he began to get nasty. Finally, out in the street with a group of his friends, he called me a 'nigger'. . . . I guess at that moment I realized my status in Mississippi."[6]

There would be further lessons, as well. Perhaps the most alarming was the lynching of a family friend, Willie Tingle, for insulting a white woman. Tingle was tied to a wagon and dragged through the streets, then lynched and used for target practice near the fairgrounds. After his body had been removed, some of his torn clothing remained on the fairgrounds fence. "I can still see those clothes now in my mind's eye," Evers told a reporter years later. "Every Negro in town was supposed to get the message." But just as horrifying to Evers as the murder was the fact that no one in the black community complained about the outrage. "Nothing was said in public. No sermons in church. No news. No protest. It was as though this man just dissolved."[7]

When he graduated from the one-room schoolhouse in his hometown of Decatur, Medgar Evers entered high school in the neighboring town of Newton ten miles away. Attending a school so far from home—one to which, still, no school bus would carry him—made Evers resentful of the opportunities white Decatur children enjoyed. They had their own high school close to home and their own school buses to take them there. But instead of letting the resentment gnaw away at him, Evers found an innovative solution to his problem by earning enough money to buy a bicycle and then riding the ten miles each way.

Something of a bookworm, Medgar would often curl up with a book or newspaper on the Everses' back porch. He was a good student and well liked because of his easygoing demeanor. Charles called him the "saint"[8] of the Evers kids and used to tease him about how good he was.

While still in their early teens, the Evers brothers attempted their first boycott. It was targeted at the white peddlers who roamed the black sections of town selling fruit, vegetables, dairy products, and furniture. Because they thought the peddlers were a little too casual with their black customers, even walking into their homes without an invitation, and because blacks couldn't go through white neighborhoods selling products, Medgar and Charles started telling their neighbors to stop buying from the whites. Their effort didn't get very far. Most blacks told them, "You Evers boys gonna get in trouble messin' with these white folks. Y'all too biggity!"[9]

Despite the hardships of poverty and segregation, during his adolescence Medgar Evers fell in love with Mississippi. An avid outdoorsman, he would take long walks through the countryside and would regularly hunt and fish. He reveled in the area's natural beauty—its pine forests and clean lakes and streams. Years later, he would often describe "what a wonderful place Mississippi would be if it could only rid itself of racism."[10]

While Medgar was in high school, America entered World War II, and, as with the many other young, black Americans who served, the war had a defining effect on him. First Charles, then Medgar volunteered for the U.S. Army. Medgar enlisted in October 1943, just as his junior year was getting under way. After basic training and stints as a laborer at Fort Warren, Wyoming, and Fort Mead, New Jersey, he was sent to Europe as part of a segregated port battalion—the 657th Port Company—that initially was stationed in England. Once Allied troops invaded the Normandy beaches on D-Day, however, Evers's company geared up for action. He hit Omaha Beach less than a month after the invasion, witnessed the devastating losses of American lives, and served in the contingent supporting the Allied efforts in northern Europe at Le Havre, Liége, Antwerp, and Cherbourg. He also became part of the famed Red Ball Express: mostly black privates who raced equipment and supplies from the Normandy beachheads through France as Allied forces pushed German troops back toward their own borders in the late summer of 1944. Evers earned two bronze service stars for his participation in the Normandy and northern France campaigns.

While in the army, he developed two significant relationships. One was with a white lieutenant who befriended him and advised him to "make something of himself"[11] when he returned home. The other was with a white French woman, with whom Evers had a brief affair. Both experiences gave the impressionable youth a new perspective on how blacks and whites could live together amicably if race were not the overriding issue.

When the war ended, Evers stayed in France to assist with the U.S. withdrawal effort. He was honorably discharged in April 1946 and returned to Mississippi—one of many black men who had risked their lives in service to their country during a time of need and who expected things to be different for them when they returned home. When he discovered, however, that Mississippi's stance on segregation remained unchanged, Medgar Evers, along with his brother, Charles, decided to test the system by attempting to register to vote. They met with some harassment from local whites and discouragement from the Newton County clerk, but eventually were allowed to register. As Charles Evers pointed out, however, "registering was less than half the battle."[12] The real test came when the two tried to vote in a Democratic primary election later that year.

On July 2—Medgar's twenty-first birthday—he, Charles, and some other black veterans arrived at the polling place early to try and avoid trouble, but a gang of whites was waiting. The veterans managed to slip through the crowd, enter the courthouse, and get their ballots, but then learned that election officials had hidden the ballot box. Another gang of whites blocked entry to the room where the box was being held. Charles Evers wanted to force his way in, but Medgar measured the costs and convinced him to back down. While the Evers brothers were walking home, whites followed them in their cars, threatening them with guns. Medgar and Charles went home and got their own guns, hid them in their car, and returned to try and vote again—but were once again rebuffed. Furious over their inability to vote, Medgar Evers set his intention. "I made up my mind then that it would not be like that again, at least not for me."[13]

In September of 1946, with the help of the GI Bill, Medgar and Charles both entered Alcorn A&M College, now Alcorn State University. Located just south of Vicksburg in the southwestern part of the state, Alcorn was Mississippi's first state-sponsored black college. Medgar entered as a high school junior in Alcorn's lab school, part of the education department. Two years later, he received his high school diploma and enrolled in the college.

During his six years at Alcorn, Medgar distinguished himself academically and athletically. He was an all-star football player and editor of the school newspaper. He also ran track, sang with the glee club, and excelled on the debating team. Charles Evers, with whom Medgar roomed for most of his Alcorn years, says his younger brother was "studious [and] disciplined" and that he "followed current events and itched to get out in the world."[14]

The Evers brothers spent their summers together, as well. Once school was out, the two headed for Chicago, where they worked as construction laborers to earn money for the school year. Although he appreciated the good wages he could make in the North, Medgar never liked the way people lived there. He was always in a hurry to get back to Mississippi, where the pace was slower, the air was cleaner, and there was room to roam.

At the start of his junior year of college, Medgar met the woman who would become his wife. Eight years his junior, Myrlie Beasley had been raised by her grandmother and her maiden aunt in a highly disciplined household in nearby Vicksburg.

"You be a good girl and don't get involved with any of those veterans!"[15] her grandmother warned her as she dropped Myrlie off on campus the day she started at Alcorn. Two hours later, however, she was leaning against a lamp-post, talking with some other freshman girls, and watching the football team return from practice. "You shouldn't lean on that electric pole," Medgar flirted with Myrlie as he sauntered by. "You may get shocked!" "Oh, I'm not worried,"[16] Myrlie playfully responded. And so it began.

Though Medgar had a reputation as a ladies' man, within a few months the two were dating each other exclusively. The following summer they secretly became engaged, and on Christmas Eve of 1951 they married.

The following spring, Medgar graduated from Alcorn with a degree in business administration. Determined not to work for a white-owned business, he was thrilled to receive a job offer from one of the wealthiest black businessmen in the state, Dr. Theodore Roosevelt Mason (T. R. M.) Howard. Dr. Howard was a surgeon and general practitioner who had holdings in a variety of medical-related businesses.

Evers accepted a job as insurance salesman in Dr. Howard's Magnolia Mutual Insurance Company, and he and Myrlie moved to Mound Bayou, an all-black town in the heart of the state's Delta region, halfway between Vicksburg and Memphis. Traveling regularly through the Delta, Evers learned every part of this flat, richly soiled expanse, where raising cotton was a way of life and where conditions for blacks had, if anything, worsened in the nearly ninety years since Emancipation. Day after day, Evers would drive through the countryside and visit with poorly fed and shabbily clothed blacks living in run-down shacks. They were having a painfully difficult time making a living as sharecroppers in the most prosperous agricultural region of the state, on the most fertile land in the South.

Sharecropping was a system in which wealthy landowners kept their profits high by minimizing what they paid their agricultural workers. Ostensibly a land-lease deal, the landowner typically took half of the crop that the leasing family grew each year as payment for the use of the land. The rest of the crop would be sold at market prices by the leasing family and would constitute the family's annual income. Most of the time, however, the "croppers" didn't come close to breaking even. Their entire lives were in thrall to the landowner's system. They bought seed for planting from the landowner's store, were dependent on that same store for credit for the family's food and clothing, and ultimately were controlled—and often cheated—by the landowner when settlement time came at the end of each growing season. In the Delta, these practices were refined into an art form to ensure an enduring, nearly free labor supply while keeping blacks, as well as many whites, impoverished and dependent. "They might as well still be slaves,"[17] Medgar told his wife when discussing the plight of the sharecropping blacks he encountered.

Medgar Evers rose quickly in the ranks of Dr. Howard's company, from insurance agent to district supervisor to agency director. But constant exposure to the cruel poverty all around him convinced him that he needed to do more than sell insurance to people who could hardly afford it. In the evenings, Evers began organizing local branches of the National Association for the Advancement of Colored People (NAACP), a group that was anathema to southern whites because it asserted that blacks were equal to whites and had established a long list of legal precedents to ensure that they eventually would be treated that way.

THE IDEA BEHIND THE NAACP[18] CAME ABOUT IN 1909 WHEN, ON THE ONE hundredth anniversary of Abraham Lincoln's birth and in response to an increasing number of lynchings, a group of radical thinkers and activists issued a call for a conference on the status of blacks in America. "The Call," as it came to be known, was endorsed by sixty white and black leaders, and out of the conference came the organization that became the NAACP. Incorporated in New York City in 1911, the NAACP went to work on an expansive agenda that included halting lynching, extending full voting rights to blacks, ending segregation, and lobbying for federal aid to help educate black youth. These goals would occupy the greater part of the association's energies for the next sixty years.

To operate effectively at the local, state, and national levels, the NAACP's founders devised an ingenious system of branches that would work for social change locally while providing financial support and grassroots political muscle for the organization's statewide and national agendas.[19]

Medgar Evers began to organize NAACP branches in Mississippi in 1953. He helped revive Mound Bayou's dormant branch, then worked to start a branch in the town of Cleveland, ten miles away. For his efforts, Evers was invited to become a board member of the NAACP's Mississippi State Chapter.

At the same time, Evers's boss, Dr. Howard, became more politically active, creating the Regional Council of Negro Leadership (RCNL), a locally controlled black activist group. The RCNL focused primarily on voter registration drives and took early steps to confront discrimination wherever it appeared, including holding a breakthrough meeting with the state's police commissioner to protest the Mississippi Highway Patrol's harassment of blacks. Perhaps the RCNL's most visible campaign was its bumper sticker boycott of gas stations that maintained bathroom facilities only for whites. "Don't Buy Gas Where You Can't Use the Rest Room" the bright neon-colored banners read. Medgar Evers enthusiastically embraced this form of protest and distributed the eye-catching sticker to anyone brave enough to display it.

During this period, both Evers brothers became fascinated with the violent tactics employed by African rebel Jomo Kenyatta and his Mau Mau movement, which was attempting to overthrow British colonial rule in Kenya. Medgar and Charles considered whether similar violence could help abolish the system imposed on blacks in Mississippi. Charles Evers said he and Medgar even discussed specifics about how they might carry out such a campaign. Myrlie Evers recalled that Medgar "was an angry young man" during those days of political and economic awakening, "grasping at any solutions that might bring an end to the degradation he saw around him."[20] At the urging of their mother, however, the Evers brothers moved on to thinking about less violent methods of obtaining racial equality. Still, to memorialize the Kenyan leader's impact on his thinking, Medgar decided in June 1953 to name his first child Kenyatta after the charismatic leader. Myrlie protested and secretly put the name "Darrell" before "Kenyatta" on the boy's birth certificate—a decision her husband grudgingly went along with.

Medgar Evers's activism ratcheted up late in 1953 when he decided, at the suggestion of some NAACP regulars within the state, to be the first black man to attempt to enter the University of Mississippi's law school. Knowing the risks he was taking, Myrlie Evers wondered "what kind of dream world Medgar inhabited."[21] But Evers had been thinking of becoming a lawyer ever since meeting Thurgood Marshall, the legendary black civil rights attorney, at an event sponsored by Dr. Howard's RCNL. Evers submitted the required registration documents and asked Marshall to represent him in what would surely become a test case for school integration in the state. Myrlie was horrified by her husband's new plan, particularly since she was pregnant again. Medgar used this as further justification. "Now he had twice as much to fight for,"[22] she later recalled.

Evers had to wait until late August 1954 to receive a reaction from the school and the state. Then, he was invited to an interview with the executive secretary of the Board of Trustees of State Institutions of Higher Learning, E. R. Jobe, and Attorney General J. P. Coleman (who would later become governor of Mississippi). Coleman offered to pay Evers's tuition to an out-of-state school, a standard approach to keeping up the ruse of "separate but equal" opportunities for all races. But Evers said he wanted to go to school in the state where he was planning to practice law. Then Coleman asked whether Evers expected on-campus housing and food service. "Yes," Evers told the somewhat incredulous officials. "I plan to live on campus in a dormitory and to do all the things any other student of the law school might do: use the library, eat in the dining hall, attend classes. But I can assure you," he continued, "that I bathe regularly, that I wear clean clothes, and that none of the brown of my skin will rub off."[23]

On September 16, 1954—three days after Reena Denise Evers was born—the Mississippi board of higher education rejected Evers's application on a technicality. To enter the school, applicants had to provide letters of recommendation from two prominent citizens from the applicant's county. In an extraordinary twist, Medgar had, in fact, found two white men from his home jurisdiction of Newton County to vouch for him. But the board ruled that the recommendations had to come from Evers's current Mound Bayou jurisdiction of Bolivar County.

Disappointed but undeterred, Evers planned to fight the ruling through the courts. After all, just four months earlier the United States Supreme Court had issued its *Brown v. Board of Education* decision calling for the integration of the public secondary educational system nationwide. But when Evers asked the NAACP for help to use his application as a test case to extend the court's ruling to higher education, Executive Secretary Roy Wilkins—realizing the unlikely odds of winning such a case—decided instead to offer him the job of the NAACP's first Mississippi field secretary.

The decision was a calculated one. Wilkins apparently figured that such a test in the deepest bastion of segregation would serve little purpose but to inflame white rage. Since the *Brown* decision, whites in Mississippi already had initiated the Citizens' Council, a group of upper- and middle-class whites dedicated to maintaining the "southern way of life" and stopping integration at all costs—"the Klan without sheets,"[24] Charles Evers called it.

Medgar Evers reluctantly went along with Wilkins's decision not to press the case and agreed to go to work for the NAACP. By the time he officially joined the staff in mid-December 1954—at a starting annual salary of $4,500[25]—the Citizens' Council was claiming 110 active chapters within the state, with a reported membership of more than 25,000.[26] By contrast, that same month Evers reported to his superiors that the NAACP had only 32 active branches in Mississippi, with about 3,000 dues-paying members.[27] Though both sides were preparing for battle, the freedom brigade was vastly outnumbered.

Evers's resolve to fight racial oppression had solidified the prior year. Aside from his legal battle, Medgar experienced a deeply personal run-in with the dehumanizing impact of segregation. His father had a stroke and was hospitalized at the Newton County Hospital in Union, Mississippi, near Decatur. The hospital catered to whites, but had a section in the basement where they would admit blacks. Charles Evers recalled the scene: "It was freezing cold. Water was dribbling from the pipes. Rats and roaches were running around. A line of Negroes was stretched out on cots. There were no doctors or nurses anywhere."[28]

Medgar Evers regularly visited his dying father in that hospital. One night, as James Evers's condition worsened, Medgar left his bedside to get some fresh air and saw, just outside, a loud, angry white mob that had come to lynch a wounded black man in the emergency room. The man had just fought with a local white and been shot. For Medgar, the scene was just too much. "My Daddy was dying in the basement," he said, "a white mob was yelling to get at a wounded Negro, and it seemed that this would never change. It was that way for my Daddy, it was that way for me, and it looked as though it would be that way for my children."[29]

A shaken and tearful Medgar Evers returned to his father's bedside. "My dad died a short time later," he said, "and outside, these whites were demonstrating like animals. I've never forgotten that. . . . A Negro cannot live here or die here in peace as long as things remain the way they are."[30] It was after that night that Evers "really began organizing NAACP chapters," and later, "quit the insurance business and went to work full time for the N-Double-A."[31]

EVERS'S NEW JOB TOOK HIM AND HIS GROWING FAMILY TO JACKSON, THE political and commercial capital of the state. Myrlie Evers, a classically trained pianist, welcomed the change and looked forward to participating in the city's social and cultural opportunities, which were substantial, since Jackson had developed into a cultural and commercial mecca for the Magnolia State's residents. Mississippi's capital city had its beginnings as a late eighteenth-century trading post known as LeFleur's Bluff. Louis LeFleur, a French-Canadian, and his French-Choctaw wife, Rebecca Cravant, established the post in 1792 on a scenic rise just west of the Pearl River. Within thirty years, because of its accessibility to roads and waterways and its central location in the newly established state of Mississippi, the post had been chosen as the capital city. By 1839, an elegant limestone and brick structure with a stucco finish in the Greek Revival style had been built as the state capitol building. At the crest of the bluff and facing westward, it crowned the thoroughfare that would become known as Capitol Street. As the seat of state government—as well as that of surrounding Hinds County—and as a perfectly situated trade and distribution center, Jackson quickly grew to become Mississippi's largest city.[32]

During the Civil War, Jackson was ravaged three times by Union troops and garnered the nickname "Chimneyville," a reference to the brick chimneys that remained when fires burned most of the city's homes to the ground. Jackson rebounded after the war, however, and by 1903 a new state capitol a few blocks north and west of the old one had been built. The old capitol kept its grand placement, however, and the original Capitol Street kept its name.

By the end of World War II, downtown Capitol Street stretched for eight blocks and served much the same function the trader LeFleur had intended. Known as the best place to shop in the state, the street was where the finest stores were located and where white Jackson shopped. Aside from stores, Capitol Street boasted the finest hotels in Mississippi, the King Edward and the Heidelberg, which hosted state legislators, dignitaries, businesspeople, and tourists, many of whom arrived on daily trains from New Orleans and Chicago. In fact, the elevated railroad created a boundary that divided the eight-block business district from the rest of the city. The Governor's Mansion also stood on Capitol Street, just two blocks from the old capitol, along with churches, federal and state office buildings, restaurants, five-and-dime variety stores like Woolworth's and H. L. Green's, and other commercial establishments.

Blacks also shopped on Capitol Street, but a black man or woman who entered a white-run store could expect to be treated rudely and made to wait until all white customers were served, even if the black customer had entered first. Unlike their white counterparts, black shoppers were not allowed to try on clothes before buying them. As interested as Myrlie Evers was in Jackson's cultural offerings, she was appalled at how blacks were treated. She recounted how once she went shopping for a hat at a Capitol Street store and was initially ignored by the white clerks. Then, when she took matters into her own hands and tried on a hat without assistance, one clerk scolded her for not putting tissue inside it so her hair wouldn't ruin the merchandise. Evers curtly put the hat down and walked out.[33]

Since they were treated unfairly and made to feel unwelcome in the white business district, blacks created their own commercial district a few blocks north on Farish Street, which runs perpendicular to and intersects Capitol Street. Restaurants, bars, and movie theaters did a thriving business in that area; the prominent, black-owned Collins Funeral Home was also located there, as was the black-focused—though conservative—newspaper the *Jackson Advocate*.

Because of its strategic location within the black community, Farish Street seemed the obvious location in which to establish the NAACP's first state headquarters, so Medgar Evers set up shop there. His wife became his first secretary.

During their first year in Jackson, the Everses witnessed a reign of terror on the black population of Mississippi. Medgar investigated the murders of a number of blacks from all parts of the state and began, through the NAACP's press operation, to publicize the killings to a national audience.

The most prominent civil rights murder of the decade occurred just eight months into Evers's tenure as field secretary. Emmett Till, a fourteen-year-old black youth from Chicago, was visiting his great-uncle in the Delta during the summer of 1955. On a dare from some local black kids, young Till reportedly either whistled at or made suggestive comments to a young white female store clerk. For that, Till was taken from his great-uncle's home a few nights later, severely beaten until his body was nearly unrecognizable, shot, and then thrown into the Tallahatchie River with a cotton gin tied to his neck with barbed wire. His remains were soon discovered, and Medgar Evers was one of the first on the scene to investigate for the NAACP. Charles Evers reported that his brother "took a photo of [the corpse], then went home and cried."[34]

Had this been the murder of a black Mississippi youth, perhaps not much would have come of it, since white on black violence was culturally sanctioned and often went unreported in the white press. Till's mother, however, had his body shipped back to Chicago and insisted on an open casket at his funeral. Photographs of Till's mutilated and bloated body, initially published in *Jet* magazine, shocked the nation and called widespread attention to the atrocities that could happen in Mississippi.

By November 1955, the national NAACP office had published a brochure, "M Is for Mississippi and Murder," telling about three instances of white brutality against blacks. The pamphlet included press clippings from local Mississippi and nearby Tennessee newspapers, all of which provided the segregationist interpretation of the three events. About the Till murder, for instance, a Yazoo City (Mississippi) *Herald* editorial blamed "the nine ninnies who comprise the present U.S. Supreme Court" for the murder. By January 1956, the NAACP national office had reprinted the popular pamphlet, adding that two more racially motivated incidents had occurred since the first printing two months earlier.

Late in 1955, Evers moved the state NAACP office from Farish Street to the ironically named Lynch Street—so named to honor John R. Lynch, a black legislator from the Reconstruction era, not to memorialize the inhumane practice of lynching. The new office was about a mile further west of the black business district, and was part of the newly constructed tan brick structure that housed the black Masonic Temple—what some African Americans at the time called the "black capitol of Mississippi." Evers's choice of this site was prescient, giving the NAACP access to a large auditorium in which to hold mass meetings and fund-raising events, stage demonstrations, and coordinate citywide activities. The site was also near two of Jackson's historically black colleges, Jackson State and Campbell College, providing Evers continuous contact with the youth whom he believed would be a key to changing Mississippi's apartheid system. For the next eight years, Evers would enter the building almost daily, climb the stairs to the second floor, and make his way to his sparse offices that looked out over Lynch Street.

Evers attempted to get involved with other nascent civil rights groups just forming in the wake of the successful bus boycott in Montgomery, Alabama. He attended the organizational meeting of Martin Luther King's Southern Christian Leadership Conference (SCLC) in 1957 and was elected assistant secretary. The NAACP leadership looked unfavorably, however, on what they perceived as a competitive threat and asked Evers to quietly resign, which he grudgingly did.[35]

Most of Evers's efforts in the years leading up to the Woolworth's sit-in, therefore, focused on NAACP initiatives, primarily voter registration drives and the investigating and publicizing of instances of violence against blacks across the state. He took reports from those who had been beaten or otherwise brutalized, attempted to get charges dropped against blacks who had been framed, and spoke to local and national audiences about Mississippi's deplorable conditions and the NAACP's efforts to change the situation.

During this time, Evers was gaining a national following. Late in 1957, he was quoted in the *New York Times* as stating that "total racial integration will be accomplished in Mississippi by 1963"—a claim seen as so preposterous that it was worthy of note.[36] Little did anyone, not the least Evers, know then the tumultuous changes that 1963—the one hundredth anniversary of Lincoln's Emancipation Proclamation—would bring.

Evers also found a way to make his work a personal endeavor. He took time for many people who just dropped by his office looking for help, both financial and emotional. Robert Calhoun, who nearly lived in the Lynch Street offices as a boy, had fond memories of Evers during that period. Calhoun's mother, one of Jackson's first black female entrepreneurs, ran a small business on the first floor of the Masonic Temple building, just below the NAACP offices. She also operated a restaurant across the street where Evers often ate. Calhoun said that Evers was like a father to him, frequently stopping to offer a word of encouragement.[37] Myrlie Evers remembered that this type of personal involvement was typical of Medgar's outgoing, warmhearted approach. He would often offer money or shelter to those who were victims of segregation's cruelty. "Please help me" was a plea that Medgar couldn't resist.[38]

Evers's fight against segregation also meant putting himself and his family on the line when the situation warranted. He included his children on the list of petitioners to desegregate the Jackson school system, and he once staged his own personal sit-in. Early in 1958, while returning from an NAACP southeast regional meeting in North Carolina, Evers boarded a Trailways bus in Meridian, Mississippi, ninety miles east of Jackson. Rather than moving to the back, he sat down just behind the driver. When the driver told him to move, Evers refused. The driver then got off the bus to confer with the ticket agent and a police officer, who ordered Evers off the bus. He was taken across the street to the police station, strongly told to stop his protest, and then returned to the bus, which by that time was about forty-five minutes off schedule. When Evers again sat up front, the bus driver gave in and began driving out of Meridian. A few blocks from the station, however, the bus was stopped by a cab driver who had seen Evers's defiance at the station. The cabby banged on the bus door until he was admitted, then punched Evers in the face. The driver then ordered the cabby off the bus and headed to Jackson with a bruised but victorious Medgar Evers in a front seat.[39]

That same year, *Ebony* magazine ran a six-page, large-format feature on Medgar Evers titled "Why I Live in Mississippi." In it, Evers described the state's natural beauty, but he also delineated the harsh conditions faced by nearly half of the state's residents, simply because of the color of their skin. He also humorously chided the Mississippi power structure, saying, "We are doing our best to embarrass the whites to death . . . . Now, when a Negro is mistreated, we try to tell the world about it." He also stuck up for his organization, saying that "one of our strongest appeals to the conscience of Southern whites is that the NAACP has never been linked to violence." He concluded with a challenge: "I'll be damned if I'm going to let the white man lick me. There's something out here that I've got to do for my kids, and I'm not going to stop until I've done it."

Evers's bus protest and his outspokenness were unusual in the state at the time. The formation of the Citizens' Council movement, which quickly swept through other southern states, legitimized and politicized white repression against blacks. As Council numbers grew, so did their political power. As politicians catered to the Council's interests, more Mississippians joined, drowning out—and then literally driving out—most moderate white voices. In the mid-1950s, Mississippi even created its own state-sanctioned spy organization, the Mississippi State Sovereignty Commission, to infiltrate groups favoring integration, keep tabs on "suspicious" characters like Medgar Evers, and funnel funds to Citizens' Councils throughout the state.

In late 1959, Mississippi voters elected as their governor Ross Barnett, a reactionary Jackson attorney who had twice previously run unsuccessfully for the position. Barnett won on his third try largely because he played the race card at every gathering of his white constituency and publicly supported the Citizens' Council agenda. Barnett's election set the stage for what would become Mississippi's reign of terror—a time that would solidify the state's reputation as the most repressive and racist state in the country.

THE CITY OF JACKSON ITSELF, IN COMPARISON TO OTHER PARTS OF THE STATE, was a bastion of civility and—at least on the surface—racial harmony. In 1960, Jackson boasted a population of nearly one hundred fifty thousand, about one-third of whom were black. The city was run by the long-established mayor, Allen Cavett Thompson, and his appointed administrators, who had strong ties to the local business community and an interest in the city's economic well-being and reputation. Thompson himself was a native Jacksonian and hailed from a politically connected family.[40] His father had run unsuccessfully for mayor in 1907, and it was Thompson's "one ambition" to eventually secure the coveted position for himself. A graduate of Jackson's Central High School, Thompson attended Ole Miss and left with both a bachelor of arts and a law degree. He then began his political climb. He achieved his first elective office in 1940 when he was chosen to represent the people of Hinds County in the state legislature. His service was interrupted by World War II. The civic-minded Thompson enlisted as a commissioned officer in the navy. After the war, he served as legislative aide to Mississippi's governor, Thomas Bailey. That position led to an appointment as state excise tax commissioner. It was from this post that he launched his first successful bid for mayor of Jackson in 1948. Thompson was forty-two.

Some of Thompson's earliest challenges as mayor involved putting the city on firm fiscal footing. When he took office, the city, which had no tax base, was facing bankruptcy. Thompson formed close ties with the business community and together they forged a coalition that passed the city's first sales tax, thus securing the city's fiscal health. He then set about to enhance the city's economic base through a building campaign—floating bonds to build the city's Mississippi Coliseum, a new municipal facility to house the courts and police station, and to renovate city hall. He also negotiated with the state to increase the city's share of the state sales tax, was instrumental in securing the location of the University of Mississippi Medical Center within the city limits, and was largely responsible for the creation of the Jackson city airport.

With matinee idol good looks and an affable personality, Thompson charmed the city's business and political leaders and was on generally good terms with the black establishment. He was viewed as a progressive on racial matters and worked hard to keep an open channel of communication with the black business and religious communities. As a product of his culture, however, he was staunchly segregationist and did not condone the "mixing" of the races.

Thompson was so popular that he was habitually reelected with no real opposition throughout the 1950s and 1960s. As a result of that longevity, he had the opportunity to serve as president of the American Municipal Association and became a booster, of sorts, for the "southern way of life"—the code phrase for racial segregation. He was, in fact, invited to debate civil rights issues on national television in 1960 with none other than Dr. Martin Luther King, Jr., but coyly declined, citing "reaction by his constituents." He took the opportunity, however, to suggest that should the network offer him the opportunity to discuss the matter with a different (white) guest, he would accept, indicating that "we have a most wonderful story to tell about Jackson . . . and our wonderful race relations."[41] Several months later, Thompson accepted an invitation to be interviewed on national TV, indicating that "we believe segregation is better for us" and that he spoke for "the great majority of our Negro citizens" as well as for whites.[42] It was with this air of positivism, completely disconnected from reality, that Thompson would attempt to handle the most significant crisis of his tenure—the struggle for equal rights by one-third of Jackson's residents. Unfortunately for the citizens of Jackson, Thompson would not have the leadership skills nor the long-term vision necessary to negotiate the crisis without substantial upheaval.

DESPITE THE ARCHSEGREGATIONIST FORCES IN MISSISSIPPI AND OTHER southern states, a new wave of activism on the civil rights front emerged as the new decade dawned. On February 1, 1960, four young black college students walked into the Woolworth's variety store in Greensboro, North Carolina, sat down at the whites-only lunch counter, and asked for service. When the waitresses refused, the men sat there until the store closed. The next day they showed up again, this time with reinforcements. It was a simple yet brazen act that shocked the nation and sent southern politicians and segregationists reeling. Within weeks, more than seventy demonstrations followed in southern border states and even in such segregationist strongholds as Rock Hill, South Carolina, and Montgomery, Alabama.

Though it seemed completely spontaneous, in fact the idea for such a sit-in had been percolating for years in activist circles, particularly among members of the Congress of Racial Equality (CORE). An offshoot of the Fellowship of Reconciliation (FOR), which espoused Mohandas Gandhi's nonviolent approach to effecting social change, CORE had been formed in 1942 to focus specifically on America's race problem. In fact, CORE had used sit-ins as an effective tool for integrating northern lunch counters and other public facilities during the 1940s and 1950s. CORE leaders, especially James Lawson—who had studied with Gandhi's followers in India—had been working for several years to develop a cadre of student activists trained in the dynamics of nonviolence to lead just such a charge on public establishments in the South. When the four Greensboro students unexpectedly stepped out ahead of CORE's meticulously planned program, CORE's forces nonetheless were ready to follow the students' example in strategic southern locations. Soon, the sit-in became *the* tactic for demanding equal access to public facilities and, in effect, equal rights for America's black citizens.

The NAACP's response to the student-led demonstrations was swift and generally supportive. In fact, NAACP youth groups readily embraced the new technique and were active in many of the extended battles that soon emerged. But whereas CORE espoused Gandhi's technique of filling the jails with nonviolent resisters of morally questionable laws, a tactic known as "jail, no bail," the NAACP encouraged exactly the opposite approach, "bail, no jail," so as to further fight the battle for civil rights in the courts. This fundamental difference in tactics caused a substantial rift between the NAACP and the growing student movement.[43] After all, the students reasoned, had the NAACP's legal approach during the past fifty years been effective, they wouldn't need to be putting their lives on the front lines now.

In Jackson, Medgar Evers was generally supportive of the student protest movement, though like most NAACP stalwarts, he thought it should be led through the NAACP youth councils, which meant that the youth would be controlled by the adults who oversaw the youth activities. This approach, however, was soundly rejected by the students spearheading the demonstrations as well as by their adult advisors.

In April 1960, Ella Baker, a long-time civil rights activist who was then affiliated with Dr. King's SCLC, called a conference of student leaders to develop a nationwide approach to the sit-ins. The SCLC shared with the NAACP the goal of equality for African Americans, but its style of leadership and its tactics were more oriented toward grassroots mass movements. At the student conference, held in Raleigh, North Carolina, more than two hundred students who had participated in sit-ins and others interested in the burgeoning movement gathered to share their experiences and enthusiasm. Although the independent-minded Baker had planned the conference under the auspices of the SCLC, she encouraged the students in attendance to go their own way. Thus, the Student Nonviolent Coordinating Committee (SNCC) was formed. Sponsored by SCLC but with a completely separate organizational structure, SNCC became the leading voice of change for a new generation of freedom fighters.

All four organizations, however—NAACP, CORE, SCLC, and SNCC—were part of a loose affiliation that ebbed and flowed depending on local circumstances. Of the four, the NAACP was most territorial, at least at the national level, and nowhere did that register more acutely than in Jackson. Even Evers was not immune to the myopia of his organization. Despite the fact that nothing much was happening in the way of civil rights protests in Mississippi, Evers took a dim view of the SNCC and CORE students who entered the state in the summer of 1961 to establish beachheads for a student-led movement, but there was little he could do to stop them.[44]

Bob Moses, a mathematics teacher from New York City, was the first youthful leader to enter Mississippi not long after the student movement had taken off. At the suggestion of Baker and SNCC's first office manager, Jane Stembridge, Moses went on a bus tour of Mississippi in the summer of 1960, trying to round up recruits for SNCC's upcoming fall conference. One of the local NAACP leaders he met challenged him not to recruit youth *out* of Mississippi, but rather to bring outside activists into the state to orchestrate change. Moses promised to return after completing his teaching contract, and in 1961 he came back with a few other SNCC recruits and began to organize voter registration projects throughout the state.

Moses, however, was only one of many of a new breed of advocates for social change who converged on the state that summer because Mississippi became, by default, the final destination of the Freedom Riders. The Freedom Ride, a CORE initiative, sent an integrated group on public buses through the Deep South to test a recent Supreme Court decision banning segregated facilities for interstate travelers. Thirteen Freedom Riders left Washington, D.C., on May 4, 1961, and encountered only limited difficulty until they reached the city of Anniston, just inside the Alabama border. There, one of the two buses was attacked and firebombed. When the second bus reached Birmingham, another angry crowd was waiting. Many of the Riders were beaten and hospitalized; one was paralyzed for life. Because of the violence, the original Riders decided not to continue the experiment. But a group comprised primarily of Nashville

students who were aligned with SNCC and versed in CORE's nonviolent strategies, decided that a defeat of the Freedom Ride—which had captured national
headlines—would be a defeat for the movement. They sent more students to
take the place of those who couldn't go on and the Ride continued.

Trouble followed them throughout Alabama, however, until a deal was
struck to provide the Riders with safe passage out of the state and into Mississippi. At the state border, the buses were met by a Mississippi National Guard
unit, which protected them until they entered the state capital. In Jackson, the
authorities took a different tack: they arrested the Freedom Riders as soon as
they entered the whites-only section of the bus stations. Although New Orleans had been their intended destination, Jackson became the end of the road
for the Freedom Riders.

Once this second wave of Riders was arrested in Jackson, one might have
assumed that the Freedom Rides were over. CORE, though, in true Gandhian
style, wanted to fill the jails of Mississippi with political prisoners, so hundreds
of additional students, mostly from the North, soon traveled to Jackson to integrate bus and rail stations and even the airport. By summer's end, more than
three hundred Freedom Riders had been arrested and jailed.

Most Riders remained in jail for thirty-nine days—the maximum allowed
if an appeal was to be filed. Once out on bond, many young people decided
to stay and work for freedom in the South's most repressive state. They immediately set up a Freedom House in Jackson, opened up an office down the
street from the NAACP headquarters on Lynch Street, and settled in for what
they figured would be a long, hard siege. From this base, a loose configuration
of SNCC and CORE workers spread throughout the state, first causing a stir
with demonstrations (including a sit-in at a store on Capitol Street), but later
adopting Bob Moses's strategy of concentrating primarily on voter registration
as the best way to empower Mississippi's black citizens.

At first, Medgar Evers was extremely territorial and less than cordial to this
group of upstarts representing civil rights organizations that he and others in
the NAACP viewed as their competition. In a special report to Roy Wilkins
and his other NAACP superiors in October 1961, Evers took a derisive tone
when describing the activities of SNCC and CORE. He snidely told of how
little money they were raising despite the appearances of big-name leaders like
Dr. King and CORE leader James Farmer, and suggested that the presence of
the students constituted an intrusion into NAACP territory.[45]

It is hard to know now, however, how much Evers's report was influenced
by what his bosses wanted to hear. What is clear is that he soon came to see
the presence of other civil rights groups in the state as a help rather than a
hindrance. Just four months after that report, Evers participated with Moses
of SNCC, Tom Gaither of CORE, and his own NAACP state conference board
president, Aaron Henry, in establishing an umbrella group called the Council

of Federated Organizations (COFO) that for a time would assist in coordinating the activities of all three civil rights groups within the state.[46]

Even if Evers was at first resistant to the presence of external student groups, he certainly was in tune with the mood of African American youth and had already authorized some local demonstrations by NAACP youth councils and college branches. The most famous of these occurred just prior to the arrival of the Freedom Riders when, in the spring of 1961, Evers helped orchestrate a library sit-in by a group now known as the Tougaloo Nine.

IT IS NEARLY TEN MILES FROM THE OLD CAPITOL IN DOWNTOWN JACKSON TO Tougaloo College, just outside the city limits to the north. State Street, which runs perpendicular to Capitol Street, leads directly there.

Tougaloo is one of America's approximately one hundred surviving historically black colleges and universities (HBCU). Distinctive double-arched wrought-iron gates stand guard at its main entrance. Between the words "Tougaloo College" on the large arch, an ornamental cross indicates the school's religious foundations. The second, smaller arch, carries the acronyms "AMA" and "UCMS," additional clues to the college's rich history.[47] AMA refers to the American Missionary Association, a Christian organization with strong abolitionist leanings that was established in 1846 to educate whites on the evils of slavery while evangelizing and educating blacks in both Africa and America. After the Civil War, the AMA shifted its focus to educating the recently freed slaves, or freedmen. Initially nonsectarian and nondenominational, the AMA eventually became the vehicle through which several denominations fulfilled their charitable and evangelical missions.

With the financial support of the churches and the Freedmen's Bureau, a post–Civil War federal agency charged with helping former slaves, the AMA started more than five hundred schools in the South during Reconstruction. Tougaloo was founded in 1869 on the land of what was known as the old Boddie Plantation. Because Mississippi's Reconstruction constitution promised all citizens—white and black—a public education, for a time Tougaloo received state funds in addition to AMA support. The college also obtained a state charter in 1871, a significant political move that would shield it decades later from the attacks of conservative political leaders.

In its early days, the college's primary mission was to educate black teachers for the state's growing number of black schools. Initially named Tougaloo University, the school first created a "normal school" to train teachers and a "model school" where the developing teachers could get classroom experience by teaching local children.

The college was by tradition politically conservative—more in the Booker T. Washington mold than that of W. E. B. Du Bois. Advising its students to concentrate on education rather than activism as the best long-term strategy

for success, the institution's administrators seldom openly challenged segregation for nearly the first century of its existence. But Tougaloo's mere existence
challenged the established norms of Mississippi culture once Jim Crow laws
and a new segregationist constitution went into effect in 1890. At Tougaloo,
whites and blacks lived and worked together, while in the rest of the state the
two races rarely interacted other than in boss/servant relationships.

The UCMS initials on Tougaloo's arches are those of the United Christian
Ministry Society, an offshoot of the Disciples of Christ denomination that had,
like the AMA, sponsored schools for blacks during Reconstruction. One of
those schools, the nearby Southern Christian Institute, merged with Tougaloo
in the early 1950s.

The historical center of the campus is the Boddie Plantation house, a three-
story structure with wide porches and dramatic overhangs built in 1848. The
house, called "the Mansion" by modern students, sits atop the highest point on
campus and overlooks large oak and hickory trees covered with draping Span-
ish moss. The spiritual center of the college is Woodworth Chapel. Built at the
turn of the century and named for an early Tougaloo president, the chapel is
an elegant wood and brick structure with a tall bell tower that in earlier days
regularly called the students to prayer. With the onset of the civil rights era,
the bell also would beckon students to the chapel during moments of crisis or
celebration.

In the 1950s and '60s, Beard Hall was known as the intellectual center of the
campus thanks to the radical thinking of the college's lead sociology professor, Dr. Ernst Borinski.[48] Professor Borinski, nicknamed Bobo, was a Jewish
refugee from Nazi Germany. He had been a law clerk and law professor in his
native country, but once Hitler came to power, he became acutely aware of
the danger he and other Jews were risking by staying in the country. Unable
to convince his family of the coming catastrophe, he decided to save himself
and successfully bribed his way out of the country. He arrived in the United
States in 1939 and served in the U.S. Army during World War II. After the war,
with the help of the GI Bill, Borinski earned a master's degree in sociology at
the University of Chicago and a doctorate at the University of Pittsburgh. In
1947, he accepted a professorship at Tougaloo because, in the words of one of
his students, "He believed that the race question was at the heart of America's
problems, and he wanted to be where that problem would work itself out."[49]

Borinski created his now-legendary Social Science Lab in Beard Hall's basement, which for thirty-five years served as the radical heart of the college. One
feature of the Lab was Bobo's Social Science Forums—evenings when blacks
and whites from the Jackson area gathered to hear speakers and discuss topics
of local, national, and international significance. Among the speakers Borinski
hosted were U.S. diplomat and Nobel laureate Ralph Bunche, author James

Baldwin, and Dr. Otto Nathan, friend and confidante of Albert Einstein. It is said that the Lab was the only place in Mississippi where local blacks and whites could interact regularly as equals. Borinski insisted that food be served and that blacks and whites sit together as they ate, a clear violation of Jim Crow laws.

Bobo's forays into integration did not go unnoticed by the state's political establishment. As early as 1955, he was denounced as a communist by the *Jackson Daily News*, and he was described on the floor of the Mississippi legislature in 1957 as "that white radical professor at Tougaloo College"—a badge of honor he wore proudly. Borinski ruffled the conservative administrators at Tougaloo as well, but his ability to consistently attract lucrative foundation grants and to place promising students into well-regarded graduate schools helped to keep his on-campus critics at bay.

Tougaloo's window on political activism opened a bit wider with the accession of Dr. A. D. Beittel to the presidency of the college in 1960.[50] A native of Lancaster, Pennsylvania, Beittel was a United Church of Christ minister and had been a teacher of sociology and religion at a variety of religious schools. He had also served as president of Talladega College, another HBCU in neighboring Alabama in the late 1940s and early 1950s. Beittel brought with him liberal racial views that helped to galvanize activist segments of the student population—and later members of the faculty—into motion.

It is safe to say that without the existence of Tougaloo College and its proximity to Jackson, Medgar Evers would have never been able to get his local movement off the ground. Thanks to Borinski's radical focus and Beittel's liberal thinking, Tougaloo provided the fertile soil for Evers's civil rights agenda to take root in Jackson.

Evers was familiar with both Borinski and Beittel. In fact, one of his first public speaking engagements after being named to head the NAACP's Mississippi office was at one of Borinski's Social Science Forums.[51] He attended many forums after that and visited the campus often, attempting to organize students into an NAACP college chapter. After years of laying the groundwork, Evers finally had a committed, activist youth group there. In mid-March 1961, he wrote to an NAACP attorney in New York: "At long last we are about to commence direct protests against racial segregation in Mississippi, Jackson in particular."[52] He was referring to the nine Tougaloo students who had agreed to stage a sit-in at the whites-only public library.

LATE MONDAY MORNING, MARCH 27, 1961, THE NINE STUDENTS—ALL MEMBERS of the Tougaloo chapter of the NAACP Youth Council—entered the main branch of the Jackson Municipal Library system, located a few blocks north of the old state capitol building.[53] The students used the card catalogues, selected books that were unavailable at the black library in town, and sat down to read. When the police arrived, the students said they were attempting to re-search their school assignments. After a bit of wavering, the police arrested the students and held them without bond for more than thirty hours while an NAACP attorney was blocked from posting bail for them. Dr. Beittel visited them in jail and voiced his support for their actions—an unprecedented move for a Tougaloo president. Meanwhile, Evers, who had been involved in the planning of the sit-in, secured the attorney, publicized the students' actions, and did what he could to ensure their safety and secure their release.

Several days after their arrest, the students were tried at the Hinds County Courthouse in downtown Jackson. Throngs of local African Americans lined the street and crowded into the black section of the courtroom. When the defendants arrived, their supporters cheered loudly. For that, the crowd was subjected to brutal police beatings and attacks by police dogs. Evers himself was cursed at and beaten by a policeman with a billy club. He later called the scene "indescribable. Men and women were beaten with clubs and pistols. The Negroes had done nothing to provoke the attack."[54] At the trial, the Tougaloo Nine were convicted and fined one hundred dollars each. Their sentence of thirty days jail time was suspended, but they were required by the court to write a thousand-word essay on juvenile delinquency.

This use of what was referred to as "direct action" tactics had a spillover effect both in Jackson and throughout Mississippi as Evers and his statewide NAACP network orchestrated a slew of small demonstrations. Two weeks after the library sit-in, NAACP members staged a "wade-in" on the beaches and surf of Biloxi, Mississippi, where blacks were banned. On April 19, four black college students—all members of the Inter-Collegiate Chapter of the NAACP—were arrested for not moving to the back of a Jackson city bus. In June, six NAACP youth members were arrested for entering the Jackson City Zoo. Other protests against segregation were staged at city parks and swim-ming pools. Later that summer, three black businessmen, all NAACP mem-bers, sat in on a Jackson city bus. By October, the Tougaloo College chapter of the NAACP caused another stir when its members, along with the CORE and SNCC youth, participated in a boycott of the segregated Mississippi State Fair. All of these moves caught headlines at the time, but none had lasting impact.

In another part of Evers's operation, however, a small group of mostly high school students was just beginning to organize under a new youth advisor. John Salter, an incoming Tougaloo sociology professor and former labor orga-nizer, had agreed to serve as the advisor to the NAACP's North Jackson Youth Council, the most active of the five or so youth groups in and around Jackson. In November 1961, the group conducted a survey of Jackson's black communi-ty to gauge the level of interest in voter registration and school desegregation.

The Youth Council also supported a Christmas boycott of Capitol Street stores in December 1961, which Evers had called for the second year in a row to protest the business district's abysmal treatment of blacks.[55]

By this time, however, Evers's attention was diverted to another front. A young black college student named James Meredith had contacted him early in 1960—the same year his and Myrlie's third child, Van, was born—and asked for the NAACP's help in integrating the University of Mississippi. Evers encouraged Meredith in his efforts, but it wasn't until January 1961 that Meredith submitted his application. Evers enlisted the help of Thurgood Marshall and the NAACP Legal Defense and Educational Fund and the battle was on. It took more than eighteen months of legal wrangling to get Meredith accepted; only after a riot on campus, which resulted in two deaths, was Meredith enrolled on October 1, 1962. Through it all, Evers played a pivotal role in advising Meredith and securing NAACP legal assistance.

As a result of his close association with the Meredith case, Evers became a sought-after speaker. For the six months following Meredith's enrollment, the emerging NAACP leader traveled nonstop, speaking nationwide about the Meredith crisis and raising funds for the association. It was at this time, however, that Evers also came to the attention of Mississippi's virulent racist fringe. Myrlie Evers herself later wrote that as a result of his prominent role in the Meredith struggle, her husband earned "the formidable, ever-spiraling hatred of segregationists."[56]

Even so, Meredith's enrollment changed the equation of racial dynamics throughout the state. Hopeful that a crack had finally appeared in the segregationists' hard-line strategy, activists began to plan how to widen the opening that the Meredith success had created. Evers, despite his NAACP superiors' conservatism, was beginning to favor more forceful tactics in attempting to overturn Mississippi's racial codes. Just a few weeks after Meredith's enrollment at Ole Miss, Tougaloo students once again spearheaded the boycott of the Mississippi State Fair, this time with more effective support from Evers, Professor Salter, and the North Jackson Youth Council. Salter and the Youth Council also began to consider more seriously Evers's repeated calls for an economic boycott of Capitol Street stores. The Youth Council created its own newsletter, *North Jackson Action*, to share information with other civil rights groups, as well as with sympathetic individuals and institutions around the country. By Thanksgiving, they were fully prepared to support Evers in his third annual boycott announcement.

From early December 1962 through early May 1963, Salter—with Evers's blessing—organized the North Jackson Youth Council, Tougaloo's student activists, and representatives of SNCC and CORE into a loose affiliation that came to be known as the Jackson Movement. Together they staged a series of pickets outside Capitol Street stores, distributed thousands of leaflets in support of the boycott, created phone trees to communicate directly with local blacks, and spoke at some of Jackson's more liberal black churches.

By mid-May, an emboldened Medgar Evers and his statewide board issued a strong statement of support for the boycott, and the Jackson Movement began to catch fire. For the next two weeks, a media war was waged, with Evers, Salter, the Youth Council, the local and national NAACP on one side, and Jackson mayor Allen Thompson, his administrators, the city and county police forces, and Governor Ross Barnett on the other. Evers even petitioned and won from the Federal Communications Commission an opportunity to present his case on local TV.

It eventually came down to a key negotiating session at which the mayor invited black business leaders and ministers to discuss their grievances. Evers was excluded from the group because the mayor refused to negotiate with representatives of the NAACP. At Evers's direction, however, the black leadership took a strong stance against the mayor's policies, and when the mayor offered no substantial concessions, the majority of the black contingent walked out, setting the stage for full-scale demonstrations.

Evers and other Jackson Movement strategists planned two modest demonstrations on Capitol Street for the next day, including one at Woolworth's. They hoped that over the next several months they could build an effective grassroots campaign that would force the mayor to negotiate.

When Tuesday, May 28, 1963, arrived, Medgar Evers was in his office working out the details of the day's demonstrations and planning for the next phase of the Jackson Movement. He was fully aware that the actions they were taking had the potential to force a dramatic change in Mississippi's intractable system. He also knew—more so than did any of his advisors or collaborators—that such a change would not come without a price.

CHAPTER 2

SOME PEOPLE IN THE PHOTOGRAPH

THE SIT-IN PHOTOGRAPH IS SO STRIKING PRECISELY BECAUSE OF THE INTENSE human drama being played out within its frame. Who are these people? Why are some sitting idle at the counter while others, in a frenzy, find ways of tormenting them? Who are the others spying intently from behind? Before delving into the events leading up to this moment in Mississippi racial history, it is instructive first to meet a few of the individuals in the photo and discover how they came to be at Woolworth's on this tumultuous day.

Annie Moody

She is the focal point of the photograph, the point at which all lines converge. Even her fellow demonstrators look at her—the only dark-skinned face in a sea of white. It is her presence that is causing the commotion, her simple act of sitting down with friends at a lunch counter, that has forced all of Jackson to take notice.

Her name is Annie Moody, and she is a native Mississippian. Her family has begged her not to take part in this or any other civil rights demonstration in her home state. But she has been pushed once too often. Sweeping away the instinctive fear bred into generations of her forebears, she has decided to risk it all for freedom.[1]

ANNIE MOODY WAS BORN ON SEPTEMBER 15, 1940, INTO A FAMILY OF SHAREcroppers on the Carter Plantation, a tract of land just outside of Centreville, Mississippi, in the southwestern corner of the state. Her mother, nicknamed Toosweet, had grown up there, just ten miles from the Louisiana border, and her grandmother had worked on the plantation for more than twenty years. Moody's early life was full of privation and poverty as her mother scratched out a sharecropper's existence that would barely keep Annie and her younger brother and sister fed and clothed. Once she separated from her husband, Toosweet took a variety of domestic jobs that required that she move frequently— a pattern her eldest daughter would repeat in later life. "It seemed as though we were always moving," Moody complained. "Every time it was to a house on some white man's place and every time it was a room and a kitchen."[2]

But Toosweet's jobs afforded the family with the benefits of an improved diet. "Sometimes Mama would bring us the white family's leftovers," Moody reported. "It was the best food I had ever eaten. That was when I discovered that white folks ate different from us. They had all kinds of different food with meat and all. We always had just beans and bread."[3]

This simple realization caused Moody to begin questioning Mississippi's racial caste system. Why did whites have bigger homes with indoor plumbing while blacks lived in two-room shacks with outdoor toilets? Why were the white schools made of brick with sidewalks connecting the buildings while the black schools were rundown wood structures with dirt and mud all around? "It really bothered me that they had all these nice things and we had nothing," she later wrote.[4] Toosweet's defensiveness and anger would rear up anytime the topic came up, however, so Moody was left to ponder this conundrum on her own.

At Toosweet's suggestion, Moody got her first job at age nine sweeping the porch for a white woman who supplied the family with milk. Moody's earnings provided immediate benefit for the household and gave her a much-needed boost of self-esteem. "I got a good feeling out of earning three quarters and two gallons of milk a week," she confided. "It made me feel good to be able to give [siblings] Adline and Junior each a quarter and then have one for myself."[5]

Her job also brought the young girl into direct contact with sympathetic whites. At one point, Moody helped care for an elderly white woman, Miss Ola Claiborne, and even stayed overnight in the family's home. In return, the woman helped the budding student with her math and reading homework. Later, the Claiborne family invited Moody to sit down with them at dinner and encouraged her to take part in the conversation—a situation that appalled Toosweet. "Miss Claiborne and Miss Ola done ruined you!" she once complained.[6] But Moody was learning that friendship was possible between the races—even in Mississippi—at least with open-minded whites.

Moody recounted her early years—up to and including her time at the Woolworth's counter—in a powerful memoir that offers a gripping portrait of the near-slavery conditions that existed for southern blacks in the 1940s, '50s, and '60s. *Coming of Age in Mississippi* has been compared to the early slave narratives for its brutal clarity and its intimate rendering of the horrors of black life under segregation. Published in 1968, the book would make her an overnight sensation and an international celebrity. The stories she would tell—of fire bombings and torture and intimidation of her rural black community—are too horrendous to fathom. One story in particular stands out because of the deep impression it made on her and many others of her generation.

Moody had just entered high school in August 1955. She was walking home from school one afternoon late that month when she heard about the murder of Emmett Till. She was shocked by its brutality and seeming capriciousness. She was exactly the same age as Till, and—like many young black Mississippians—she traced her later activism to the day she realized that the lives of blacks could be taken on a whim. "Before Emmett Till's murder," she would write, "I had known the fear of hunger, hell and the Devil. But now there was a new fear known to me—the fear of being killed just because I was black."[7]

Despite this and other racial horrors of that time, the budding activist found ways of coping with her environment. She excelled in her studies and in sports, and she worked throughout her high school years to earn funds to pay for college. Moody's meager earnings, however, were not enough to pay for a full year's tuition at the college of her choice. Instead, she accepted a basketball scholarship to a small Baptist school, Natchez College. Unhappy with the school's limited academic offerings and the rigors of an athletic scholarship, Moody searched for other options. After two years at Natchez, she succeeded in transferring to Tougaloo on a full academic scholarship.

What she found there was nothing short of magical for her: "I could not believe it—this place was beautiful. It was large and spacious. There was evenly cut grass everywhere and huge old oak trees with lots of hanging moss. Birds were singing and the air was fresh and clean. I must have walked all over the campus in a trance."[8]

What Moody found at Tougaloo—for the first time in her life—was acceptance, scholarship, community, and activism. She worried at first that her rural education hadn't prepared her for the school's academic challenges, and she panicked when she heard that most of her teachers were white, assuming they were like most of the whites she had encountered back home. Her roommate helped calm her fears on both fronts, telling her that a majority of the white teachers were from the North and that even a rural education would be sufficient if she was willing to work hard.

One aspect of campus life that was completely foreign to Annie Moody was the open involvement by some students in civil rights activities. Back in Centreville, one of her teachers had been fired for merely talking to her about the NAACP. At Tougaloo, the movement was a regular topic of conversation.

Her first memory of Medgar Evers is when he came to campus before the first boycott of the Mississippi State Fair to give what she called "a big hearty speech about 'how Jackson was gonna move.'"[9] Moody's involvement in movement activities deepened the next summer when she had the opportunity to get more acquainted with Joan Trumpauer, a white transfer student deeply grounded in movement work. Each seemed taken with the other. Moody was intrigued by Trumpauer's firm belief that the South could really change if enough pressure were brought to bear. Trumpauer, for her part, appreciated that Moody was "a little more openly inquisitive with me than some other students . . . We just sort of hit it off."[10]

Moody was also a risk taker who once dared a friend to help her integrate the downtown Jackson bus terminal. After being accosted by several whites, including a drunk wielding a bottle as a weapon, the girls were rescued by a black bus station employee who drove up to them and commanded them to get into his car. He drove them back to campus, all the while upbraiding them for not having a better plan for their impromptu demonstration.

It was during this time that the Jackson Movement began to pick up steam, with Moody's sociology professor, John Salter, providing leadership to the boycott of white Jackson stores. Salter was an exceptional teacher and a charismatic leader. "He was our inspiration," she said of him. "He was brilliant. All the students loved him."[11]

Moody rapidly became one of Salter's most reliable boycott helpers. She started going into the black neighborhoods on weekends and handing out leaflets to urge blacks not to shop on Capitol Street. She also spoke about the boycott at sympathetic black churches around town. Salter said that Moody was "one hell of a canvasser. In the months preceding the sit-in, she was one of the best boycott people we had."[12]

Toward the end of the 1963 spring semester, Salter told Moody that the boycott might soon change tactics. He asked if she would be willing to participate in a sit-in at Woolworth's if the city leaders refused to negotiate over the demands of the boycott. Despite her mother's pleas to stay out of the movement, Moody told Salter that he could count on her. "He was the only one who could have talked me into it,"[13] she would later admit.

Within the week, Moody was walking into Woolworth's with two other Tougaloo students, none of them expecting the sit-in to be anything more than a symbolic gesture. Whatever was to come, however, Moody felt ready for the challenge. She'd been waiting for this moment her entire life.

Joan Trumpauer

The camera catches the back of her head as she faces her dark-skinned friend, bridging Mississippi's broad racial divide through the simple gesture of conversation. She seems unaware of the crowd behind her, of their taunting, of the sugar that cascades down the back of her neck and onto her beige, cap-sleeved dress with its dainty pink and yellow flowers. She tries to ignore the mustard dribbled on the crown of her head and the high school rebel about to pour another stream of sugar down her back, as if he were decorating her like a cake.

With her long blonde hair done up in a neat granny bun, she seems ageless. She could be fifteen. Or fifty. In fact, she is twenty-one and a junior at Tougaloo College— the first full-time white student to enroll there. Her name is Joan Trumpauer and she is, of all things, a southerner.[14]

JOAN HARRIS NELSON WAS BORN ON SEPTEMBER 14, 1941, INTO A NORTH-SOUTH hybrid of a family—the elder daughter of two enterprising individuals who came of age during the Great Depression of the 1930s. Ealton "Bud" Nelson was from Essex, Iowa, a second-generation Dane on his father's side and a descendent of colonial-era Americans on his mother's. Joan said all of her father's family were "staunch Democrats—the kind that stood up for what was right in spite of all opposition." If agitation can be inherited, then Nelson had some of it in her blood. Her great-grandmother had been one of a handful of suffragists who chained themselves to the steps of the Iowa statehouse in a demonstration for their right to vote.

But if Nelson's paternal roots tended to the radical, her maternal ones were white southern mainstream. Merle Chandler was a no-nonsense Georgia country girl from the little town of Nicholson, just north of Athens in the north-central part of the state, an area known for its lumber and its poverty. The couple met in Washington, D.C., during Roosevelt's New Deal and settled in northern Virginia where Bud pursued a career with the federal government and Merle would eventually become a successful real estate entrepreneur.

Young Joan Nelson's focus during the mid-1950s was primarily on the international scene, not domestic issues. She admitted that she accepted segregation as part of the norm. It was the Cold War instead that captured her imagination. She was transfixed by the 1956 revolt in Hungary, which helped her see that a small group of determined individuals could stand up, if only fleetingly, to a repressive state. She would draw upon the example of the courageous Hungarians and their passion for freedom during her own later battles on the civil rights front.

Nelson's parents differed substantially from each other on the race issue, but it was a subject about which they had agreed to disagree. Merle accepted southern norms and believed that segregation was part of the natural order for the races; Bud maintained a more moderate view of the subject. What Nelson herself remembered most about the racial attitudes she grew up with, however, is the blindness that whites would affect toward blacks. "You didn't speak to blacks; you didn't look at blacks directly," she said. "You sort of stared off. . . . If you were driving through a black neighborhood, you weren't supposed to look at the people on the street, no matter how interesting. You just acted like they weren't there."

Joan Nelson absorbed this racial myopia at an early age, yet one experience in particular opened her eyes to the stark reality of racial inequality in America. Her epiphany came around the age of nine, when she was visiting her mother's family in Oconee, Georgia, as she did every summer. When she and a friend sneaked off to take a daring walk through "Niggertown" to see how the other half lived, Nelson was astonished at the extreme poverty she encountered. When they reached the black school, her surprise turned to disbelief.

Compared to her school back home, or even to Oconee's new, well-built white school, the one-room black schoolhouse was "just a shack . . . a big shack," she said. The contrast hit her hard, and she never forgot it. She began to ask difficult questions back home about the discrepancies she had witnessed during that life-changing summer.

It was the Little Rock school integration crisis in 1957 that caused Nelson to realize that the civil rights issue was just as compelling as anything America faced abroad and forced her to make the startling connection between the international scene and her own backyard. In September 1957, hundreds of outraged whites gathered on the Central High School campus in downtown Little Rock to prevent nine young black students from entering the school. President Eisenhower reluctantly sent federal troops to maintain order, and the newspapers and TV reports were full of images of soldiers with bayoneted rifles protecting the nine students. Nelson was shocked. "I remember being surprised that things could turn that ugly," she said. "To see that real raw ugliness that came out and to see troops at school. I mean, you thought of troops marching around in the oppressive societies of Eastern Europe—not in the United States, which we considered the height of civilization."

The race issue came into sharper focus the following year when Virginia's governor closed schools in the southern part of the state rather than integrate them. Although no northern Virginia schools had been closed, the threat of school closings troubled Nelson and her classmates. "If the schools close and you don't graduate from high school," she reasoned, "what happens to you? You can't get into college!" The crisis, known as "massive resistance," never reached the more liberal northern Virginia school districts, but had a profound impact on various southern and central areas of the state, where schools were closed, in some cases for years. By the time the matter was resolved by the courts in favor of integration, Nelson had graduated and left for college.

Nelson's involvement in the civil rights movement seems to have happened almost by accident. She had wanted to go to a small, liberal Presbyterian college in Ohio, but her mother had insisted on a more prestigious institution: "Something with a name," Nelson recalled, "and preferably in the South, where it would be segregated." They settled on Duke University in Durham, North Carolina.

Nelson had been at Duke for less than six months when the first sit-in at Greensboro—just fifty miles west of the Duke campus—unleashed a torrent of energy within both the black and white student communities. Black students across the South immediately mirrored the example of the Greensboro demonstrators, but relatively few whites got involved at the beginning and fewer still were white students from the South. Nelson was one of those few.

At the invitation of the black students, Nelson and a few of her Duke classmates began attending mass meetings in Durham and volunteering on picket

lines in front of stores with segregated lunch counters. Eventually, they participated in two crucial sit-ins in early May at the S. H. Kress Co. lunch counter
in Durham.¹⁵ They were arrested and jailed for their actions, then bailed out
by the NAACP.

Nelson's role in the Durham sit-ins was pivotal. It was she who started the
integrated demonstrations by going to the counter alone, ordering a hot dog,
and then sharing it with a black demonstrator once the blacks joined her. Of
the more than one hundred arrested in Durham in early May, only Nelson
and six others—five blacks and one white male Duke student—had their cases
picked up by the NAACP as models for challenging the state's segregation laws.
Nelson thus became party to *Avent et al.* v. *North Carolina*,¹⁶ which eventually made its way to the U.S. Supreme Court, where the defendants won in a
landmark decision that would be announced just one week before the Jackson
Woolworth's sit-in.

Although the Durham demonstrations were Nelson's first experience with
radical direct action, she knew that participation meant saying good-bye to her
comfortable middle-class life. "There was a certain amount of fear," she said of
her early activism. "I was going against everything I had been brought up with.
And I had a feeling of no turning back. I was making a pretty strong break
with white society. It was a complete leap into the unknown."

On the Duke campus, although they weren't expelled, Nelson and the other
white demonstrators were put under surveillance and their psychological
stability was questioned. At home, her mother became grim and tight-lipped,
feeling that her daughter had brought shame on the family. Her father was a bit
more measured, wondering aloud how an arrest record would affect her future
employability. Both parents expressed concern for her safety.

Although she was one of the first white southern women to join the student
movement, Nelson did not attend the famous gathering of student activists in
Raleigh that spring at which the Student Nonviolent Coordinating Committee
(SNCC) was formed. The meeting took place just weeks before her first arrest,
but she considered it too dangerous to be part of a public integrated gathering
in the South. By October, however, when SNCC held its first full-blown conference on desegregation in Atlanta, Nelson attended as a delegate. By then she
was an old hand at civil disobedience.

AFTER HER FRESHMAN YEAR AT DUKE, NELSON HEADED HOME, DETERMINED
like many other movement students to get involved in direct action campaigns on her own turf. Early that summer, Nelson hooked up with a group
of mostly black student activists from Washington, D.C.'s Howard University
who formed the Non-Violent Action Group, or NAG. The group eventually
became a SNCC affiliate; their motto was: "NAG! NAG! NAG!" Nelson participated in a variety of demonstrations with NAG that summer, including the

one staged at Glen Echo, a segregated amusement park just over the Potomac River in Bethesda, Maryland. The Glen Echo picketing became one of the most newsworthy integration battles of the summer of 1960, attracting black leaders like A. Philip Randolph, Roy Wilkins, and Adam Clayton Powell, Jr., to the picket lines at various times. Despite all of the publicity, Glen Echo remained segregated throughout the summer. Thanks to NAG's consistent focus, though, the park finally integrated the following spring.

In addition to her burgeoning civil rights involvement, Nelson's personal life also blossomed. At the beginning of summer, she eloped with a high school sweetheart—a dark-skinned young man with some Native American ancestry. Although the marriage lasted only three months, Nelson kept her husband's last name after they broke up because she was aware of the possibility of backlash against her mother's family in Georgia if a connection with her were ever discovered. Later, she even changed her married name slightly to protect her estranged husband's family, which also had some southern roots. Thus, she became Joan Trumpauer, the name by which most of her movement friends would come to know her.

By the end of the summer, Trumpauer had decided not to return to Duke, but to continue working with NAG. The group expanded its operations and participated in demonstrations up and down the East Coast. By the spring of 1961, Trumpauer had moved close to the Howard University campus to facilitate her civil rights work, while also working full-time on the staff of Democratic Senator Claire Engle of California, who was modestly supportive of her efforts. She was tiring, however, of the low-level jobs she was able to get and had begun actively searching for ways to continue her education. Then came the Freedom Rides.

Many SNCC members initially saw the initiative as easy work: "going off on a vacation," Trumpauer joked. "Sort of the Club Med of its day for the movement." But NAG had a particular interest in the Freedom Rides since one of its members was among the original riders who left Washington, D.C., on May 4. When one bus was burned outside Anniston, Alabama, then the other was attacked in Birmingham, NAG members grew alarmed. Although it was the Nashville students, led by Diane Nash, who forced the rides to continue, NAG soon followed suit, sending a small contingent of experienced activists to help keep the faltering rides going. Trumpauer was at the heart of the NAG operation. Because her phone did not go through the Howard University switchboard, long-distance calls could be made and received through her line without difficulty, so her apartment became a primary communications link with the Freedom Riders. "For a while," she laughed, "it was Diane in Nashville and my apartment in Washington that were keeping the rides going!"[17]

Once the original cadre of NAG members had left for the Freedom Rides, Trumpauer closed up shop and joined them. By that point, the riders had moved on from Alabama and were being arrested en masse in Jackson, Mississippi. Trumpauer and her group hatched a new strategy. Rather than taking a bus, they were flown to New Orleans—where the original rides were to have ended—and then took the train to Jackson, integrating another public interstate transportation facility in the process. Trumpauer and her retinue, which included the activist Stokely Carmichael, entered Mississippi on June 8, 1961. Newsreel footage documents her first few steps in the state.[18] She walks with an integrated group of young women, moving rather quickly through the Jackson train station, down the stairs and into the lobby of the whites-only section, where she and her friends were whisked off in a paddy wagon to the Hinds County Courthouse a few blocks away in downtown Jackson. She looks calm, unfazed, as if out for a picnic with friends—laughing, smiling, joking—showing little comprehension that she has just entered a war zone.

Nor were the authorities quite ready for someone like Trumpauer—long strawberry blonde hair, light complexion, petite, and speaking with a charming southern drawl. As she stepped down from the paddy wagon, a white policeman extended his hand to her, a courtesy he did not offer to the black women: "I guess he lost it," Trumpauer recalled, "and said something like, 'Let me help you down, little lady.'" Even in such strained circumstances, some southern customs held steadfast.

After their arrest, Trumpauer and the others were charged with breach of the peace.[19] At their trial the next day, they were found guilty and sentenced to four months in jail (with two months suspended) and fined two hundred dollars. As part of the Gandhian strategy, Trumpauer was determined not to get bailed out but to serve out her entire jail sentence. She thus was one of the few Freedom Riders whom CORE did not bail out after thirty-nine days—the maximum allowable time in jail if an appeal were going to be filed.

Interestingly, Trumpauer kept a diary during her two weeks at the Hinds County Jail, prior to being moved to the more secure and more remote state penitentiary. She wrote on five small sheets of stationery, which she kept crumpled up and hidden in the hem of her skirt. The group was separated by race at the jail, and the document demonstrates both her deep spirituality and her intense—at times, humorous—identification with the southern blacks rather than the northern whites with whom she was locked up. "The food is plain, but better than some campuses," she wryly commented. "I think all of the girls here are gems, but I feel most in common with the Negro girls + wish I was locked with them instead of these atheist Yankees—particularly when they sing. They're trying to be nice, but as they jokingly said, I'm 'square.' By the time I get out I'll know how a minority feels."[20]

Her diary ends abruptly on June 23, the day her group was moved to the legendary Parchman penitentiary in the Mississippi Delta. Conditions at Parchman were much harsher than they had been in Jackson. Officials had literally cleared out death row to make room for the Freedom Riders, and the women were made to wear standard prison attire—black and white striped skirts and shirts—rather than their own clothing. Although the white women's block was less crowded than at the Hinds County Jail, there was no way to send messages back and forth between the men and women prisoners as there had been in Jackson. In addition, the white women were held far away from the black women, whereas in Jackson they had been in adjoining cell blocks. The prisoners were also kept guessing about their status and that of their friends in other parts of the penal compound. "You felt really isolated," Trumpauer remembered, "and you felt that they could do anything they wanted."

One bright spot during this period would be when the rabbi from Jackson's only synagogue would visit the young inmates, many of whom were Jewish. Most of the arrested riders would attend his service, no matter what their religious affiliation, to get word about the outside world. "He would start . . . chanting the prayers," Trumpauer recalled, "and right in the middle of chanting away in Hebrew, he would throw in, 'And, Mary, your mother says . . . this and that.' And then he'd go back to Hebrew or whatever and throw in another message along the way."[21]

After serving the two months of her sentence, Trumpauer began working off the two-hundred-dollar fine at three dollars a day. She might have stayed in Parchman until October, but another part of her long-term plan beckoned. She had earlier decided she wanted to go to an all-black southern college. She had been struck earlier in the year by the courage of Charlayne Hunter, who, along with Hamilton Holmes, had endured riots, mental distress, and physical threats in order to integrate the University of Georgia. Trumpauer observed that the burden of integration fell disproportionately on the black students and wanted to find a way to demonstrate her solidarity with them. Her rationale was simple: "I thought that if integration meant anything, it should be a two-way street. It shouldn't just be that blacks were allowed into white places, but that whites and blacks did things together."

When Trumpauer asked her friends in SNCC what they thought of her idea, they were supportive and suggested she consider Tougaloo College, particularly because of its growing liberal reputation. They also felt that if change was going to come to Mississippi, a strong SNCC presence would be needed there. From Trumpauer's perspective, Tougaloo was ideal; it was a small Christian college—the kind she had wanted to attend all along.

When she received an acceptance letter from the school chaplain just days before flying to New Orleans to join the Freedom Rides, the timing was perfect. CORE would pay her way to Mississippi, the state would provide her room and board for the summer, and once released from Parchman, she could head for campus. Once again, it turned out that Joan Trumpauer was in the right place at the right time.

ON SEPTEMBER 11, 1961, JOAN TRUMPAUER BECAME THE FIRST FULL-TIME white college student to enroll at Tougaloo.[22] For a while she became the darling of the black press. *Ebony* magazine did a five-page feature story on her, complete with a picture spread. *Jet* magazine heralded her presence on the Mississippi scene with the headline "Reverse Integration." She was also featured in some church-related publications, and even the *Washington Post* and the *New York Times* ran brief articles about her.[23]

But not everyone was delighted. The Mississippi state legislature considered revoking the school's charter. Fortunately, because Tougaloo's charter had been granted before segregation became institutionalized into law, the state could bring no claim against the school.

Not all Tougaloo students were thrilled with Trumpauer's arrival either. No one had told them that a white student would enter their formerly all-black college. Some thought her education in white schools gave her an unfair academic advantage. Eventually, she was viewed more as a curiosity than a threat since most black students had never before interacted with a white person on equal terms. When her classmates began to give her nicknames like "sistah baby" and "homegirl," Trumpauer knew she had arrived.

Two students who welcomed Joan because of her activist views were the Ladner sisters. Dorie Ladner and her younger sister, Joyce, had come to Tougaloo after being expelled from Jackson State College because of their civil rights activities. The three young women bonded over their SNCC connections, making Trumpauer's arrival somewhat more welcoming.

While adjusting to her new social and educational environment, Trumpauer also began to perform secretarial duties for the newly opened SNCC and CORE offices on Lynch Street. The SNCC office had been opened by Diane Nash and the Nashville SNCC contingent after they were bailed out of their Freedom Ride jail sentences. They had also set up a Freedom House on Rose Street, just a block away, where movement workers and their visitors were housed.[24]

CORE workers opened an office in a room adjacent to SNCC's once they realized they needed to coordinate the return court appearances of the more than three hundred people who had been bailed out and appealed their Freedom Ride convictions. With thousands of dollars tied up in the court system, someone had to make sure it was all recovered. Trumpauer, who would regularly catch a ride to the SNCC/CORE offices from some of Tougaloo's day students, began helping out with the retrieval effort by writing letters to Freedom Riders who had left the state and reminding them of their court dates.

Trumpauer met Medgar Evers within the first week of her release from Parchman. Her attitude toward him was typical of the student activists who had come to Mississippi: "[Medgar] represented the NAACP," she said, "and to those of us in SNCC and CORE, people from the NAACP were absolute fuddy duddies—useful for bond money and lawyers and not a whole lot else." Nevertheless, there was a general recognition that all three groups were working to advance the same cause and were "all in this together." Trumpauer occasionally would make the trek up Lynch Street when things were slow at the SNCC/CORE offices to see if Evers or his secretary needed any help.

Trumpauer kept connected to SNCC and CORE workers across the state through a creative newsletter she devised. Called "The Mixissippi News"[25]—a tongue-in-cheek variation on the word "mixers," the derogatory term segregationists used for integrationists—the monthly update was an amalgamation of excerpts from field reports along with other bits of gossip and creative writing. Through this vehicle, she came to the attention of the editor of the *Southern Patriot*, the publication of the Southern Conference Educational Fund (SCEF)—a liberal organization working for social justice, particularly in the South. Trumpauer became friends with Anne Braden, editor of the *Patriot*, and her husband, Carl, a long-time civil libertarian. In a letter from that period, Anne Braden assessed Trumpauer's skills as a budding journalist and also provided a telling glimpse into her state of mind during her first year in Mississippi. "She's a good reporter," Braden wrote, "the first I've come across in the civil rights movement." But she goes on to say that Trumpauer "is really in a pioneering position at Tougaloo—and it will be fine if she does not have a nervous breakdown in the process, which in my opinion she is on the verge of. She is really in an almost impossible situation—rejected by her family, rejected by the white world, and yet not accepted in the Negro world either. Has absolutely no social life—white or Negro—which can be devastating at that age. Terribly lonely and frustrated."[26]

Upon hearing Braden's assessment years later, Trumpauer took exception. "I was probably just expressing my frustrations to another white southerner and she caught me at a bad moment," Trumpauer said. "Yeah, things weren't easy, but I wasn't losing any sleep."[27]

Trumpauer's version seems closer to the truth. By the end of her first year at Tougaloo, she seemed to be thriving. Her freshman credits from Duke had been transferred, she was named the college's Outstanding Sophomore, and a campus fraternity had chosen her for their Outstanding Citizenship Award. She had also made the dean's list for academic scholarship—a feat she would repeat each of her three years at Tougaloo. In addition, Trumpauer was being considered for Delta Sigma Theta, a black sorority that she joined the following fall. She later would observe with gleeful irony, "I was doing everything my mother wanted—just not the way she expected."

During the fall of 1962 and the winter of 1963, while things were heating up with the NAACP's North Jackson Youth Council boycott of the downtown area, Trumpauer continued her work with SNCC and CORE. She also began helping out the Jackson Movement when she could, raising student awareness of the boycott and recruiting black students to deliver handbills door-to-door. She helped organize a campus-wide meeting to drum up support for the boy-cott after the first pickets were arrested in early December, and she also gained experience as a "spotter" during this and other demonstrations downtown. A spotter was a person who did not actually participate in the demonstration, but instead observed and reported on the event's progress to the strategists back at headquarters. Spotters were also trained to watch every aspect of the demonstration carefully in order to identify perpetrators of violence, should any occur.

As the boycott began to make an impact on the downtown business district, Trumpauer started to hope that an effective movement was finally taking hold in Jackson. But on the day of the Woolworth's sit-in, her participation was almost an afterthought. The school semester had just ended and most students had returned home two days earlier. Trumpauer and Lois Chaffee, a white Tou-galoo instructor, were recruited at the last minute as spotters for some picket-ing that was to occur just a few stores up the street from Woolworth's.

Trumpauer and Chaffee rode into town with the pickets, were dropped off a few blocks from Capitol Street, walked to their assigned spots, and tried to blend in with the crowd like everyday shoppers. But the demonstration they were spotting ended quickly as the police arrested all the pickets just seconds after they pulled out their signs and began marching.

After calling in their report to NAACP headquarters, the two white women were left to figure out what to do next. Because they had not seen any police cars rushing down the block, they figured that the other demonstrators were still sitting-in at Woolworth's. They decided to walk over and see what was happening there.

Trumpauer made a small purchase when she entered the store: "That made me a valid customer and also gave me time to get a sense of the crowd and what was going on at the lunch counter." After watching the growing turmoil around the first group of demonstrators, however, Trumpauer started to fear for her own safety when some people in the crowd began to realize that she was in sympathy with the black students. As the crowd became more agitated, she quickly conferred with a movement leader on hand and decided that, ironically, she would be safer at the counter than in the mob. "The idea was to support the sit-in, not to get killed in the crowd," she later recalled.

Annie Moody and another black Tougaloo student were sitting at the coun-ter in the midst of the mayhem, and without another thought, Trumpauer pushed her way through the rowdy crowd and joined her friends.

D. C. Sullivan

He faces the camera dead on—the only one in the photo to do so. Languid eyes, a drooped lower lip, and a tough guy stance suggest a Marlon Brando in the making. He frowns as he takes a drag from a newly lit Winston cigarette, somewhat oblivious to his rambunctious friends, unconcerned about the escalating tension in the air, unfazed by the noise and the hysteria. He just stares, right into the camera it seems, glad to be there at the heart of the action.

At the time of the sit-in, D. C. Sullivan was only days away from graduating from Jackson's Central High School, located just two blocks away from Woolworth's. The specter of Vietnam, which would claim the lives of many friends and leave him with a heart muscle sprinkled with shrapnel, had not yet entered his awareness. A restless rebel, always in search of a fight, he was excited to be defending his southern way of life on this crucial day in the Battle of Jackson.[28]

DORMAN CARROLL SULLIVAN WAS BORN ON OCTOBER 3, 1944, NEAR HIS parents' hometown of Ackerman, ninety miles east of Jackson and not far from Decatur where Medgar Evers grew up. His father, W. R. (Russell) Sullivan, worked the oil fields of Louisiana and commuted back and forth to see the family when he could. By the time the younger Sullivan was three, the family had moved to Jackson, where his father owned and operated automobile service stations and worked as a mechanic. As he grew older, Sullivan often spent time helping out at his father's businesses, and had a particularly strong memory of an older man named Red Hydrick who used to frequent the shop. A notorious bootlegger and strident racist with a pronounced stutter, Hydrick drove classic, antique cars and was quite particular about who touched them. "I was just a little squirt," Sullivan recalled, but even then he knew not to "mess" with Hydrick's cars. Ironically, Hydrick also would appear in the famous sit-in photo: he is the older man wearing glasses and a hat in the far left corner, intently watching the proceedings and cheering on the young rowdies.

Sullivan's adult recollections of race relations during his early years in Jackson harken back to some idealized version of pre–Civil War days. He claimed that blacks "had it real, real good" when he was growing up in the 1940s and 1950s. "In my eyes," he said, "blacks had it a lot better off before integration. If they ever needed any help or ever had problems, they always had somebody to help them." He told of how his mother would make "many, many meals" for blacks who came begging at the back door (with little appreciation of why they might have been in that condition to begin with). And he described how little crime there was then, how there was no need to be afraid when he walked out his front door, how all the neighborhoods were safe, and how people—blacks and whites—were willing to help one another. "Blacks treated white people with more respect," Sullivan recalled. "And the white people done for them and helped them out a whole bunch."

The civil rights movement first became real for Sullivan at about the same time as it did for Joan Trumpauer, during the siege of Little Rock's Central High School. By then he was almost thirteen and just entering Peeples Junior High in Jackson. He clearly understood that if integration could happen just over the state line in Arkansas, then it could eventually happen in Mississippi. He also knew intuitively that it would be a long time before Mississippi's schools would integrate. "They would have never made it in Mississippi when I was in school," he said of the Little Rock Nine. "The boys back then were too rough. I just don't think they would have ever made it."

Sullivan fit right into that rough crowd; from an early age he displayed a hot temper and a willingness to use his fists to settle any dispute. "I just loved to fight," he remembered jovially, and he proved the point time and again with his classmates. After he had spent two years at Peeples, his parents decided to send him to military school. There may have been other considerations, as well, since Sullivan's father was embarking upon a political career that required his family to have a more respectable public demeanor. Russell Sullivan had been elected constable for Hinds County's Fifth District, a position of considerable influence and respect within the community and one that would come into play during the three-week heyday of the Jackson Movement.

After just one year at Chamberlain-Hunt Military Academy in Port Gibson, Mississippi, though, D.C. Sullivan was sufficiently "reformed" to be able to return home. In the fall of 1960, he entered Central High School in the heart of the city.

The Central High School building, which rises like a nineteenth-century industrial castle in downtown Jackson, was completed in 1888, just as Jackson was becoming a regional trade center. Though no longer a school, the building, with its dark brown brick turrets and notched, flat roof, still gives the impression of an impregnable fortress. Although now overshadowed by high-rise hotels and office buildings, Central must have dominated the landscape when it first opened, fifteen years prior to the completion of the new state capitol just across the street. Jackson's city planners gave the public school system a full city block of prime downtown real estate on which to build the school, and the builders filled the entire site. The front entrance faces west towards the capitol, while the back doors exit to Lamar Street, which intersects Capitol Street two blocks away and just up from where the downtown Woolworth's once stood.

By the time Sullivan and his friends entered Central High, the school had seen its better days; by 1960 it had become the least favored of Jackson's three white senior high schools. One of Sullivan's friends from the period, Charlie Newell, described Central as the school for the "less fortunate," where kids from a "lower social class" would go. "Some of these kids came from some pretty tough, deprived backgrounds," he said. Two other schools—Murrah to the northeast and Provine to the southwest—catered to the upper and middle classes, respectively. "Murrah was for the kids from silk stocking row," Newell recalled, "while Provine took in the middle class. Both were college prep schools. Central was more of what you'd call today an industrial trade school."[29]

Central was the only school in the region to offer an ROTC program, which attracted Newell away from Provine where he could have gone. Since he was from south Jackson, Provine was closer to where Sullivan lived as well. But the scrappy Sullivan was happy to attend Central. "Central was the lower class and that was just where I wanted to go," he said.

Across Lamar Street and half a block closer to Capitol Street stands an old art deco building that once housed the Greyhound bus station. A long line of pink neon outlines nine white squares that once held the letters G-R-E-Y-H-O-U-N-D. A loping dog at the top, outlined in blinking blue neon, rushes eternally onward. It was here in May 1961 that some of the first Freedom Riders arrived in Jackson and were promptly arrested.

The station also served as an early-morning and late-afternoon hangout for wayward Central boys. Sullivan, Newell, and their other buddies, like Joe Johnston and Jimmy Madden, would congregate at "the Dog" in the mornings before school for a smoke, a Coke, and some pinball. Sometimes they would get into fights with other students; sometimes they'd just shoot the breeze or even do a little last-minute studying. But once the final morning school bell rang at 8:30 a.m., students were expected to be in class. "Instructors would go over and inspect the bus station," Newell recalled, "and if you were caught over there, you were in big trouble."[30] Surprisingly, Sullivan was rarely late. "I didn't skip classes too much," he claimed. "If I played hooky, my ole daddy would tear my tail up!"

One of Central's yearbooks remembers Sullivan for his "friendly trouble."[31] "I would fight," he repeated, "but I had the best friends in the world." In fact, Sullivan's tenure at Central was undistinguished, except for participating in "the biggest fight" the school had seen. Sullivan and his friend Jimmy Madden had taken on each other one night in the parking lot of a fast-food place in south Jackson after a fight by two lesser lights had ended. With a crowd eager to see another show of hand-to-hand combat, the two had it out for fun and to split the hundred dollars someone put up. The next day, when they decided to continue the fight on school grounds, Sullivan claimed that more than five hundred people showed up to watch.

A typical school day during his last year at Central High started with Sullivan driving himself and some buddies to school, spending at least half an hour hanging out at the Dog with Newell and other friends, then a full day of classes, followed by an evening working with Newell at the local drive-in. This part-time job provided him with only twenty-one dollars a week, but it was good gas and cigarette money. Newell remembered that it was not typical for Central students to leave campus during the school day. In fact, it was forbidden; besides, the school cafeteria provided a substantial hot lunch daily for about half of what Woolworth's charged. But the rules were relaxed somewhat during the last week of classes while students took final exams and cleaned out their lockers.[32]

It was during just such a week, his final week of high school, that Sullivan heard about the trouble over at Woolworth's. It was a little after the noon hour—perhaps over lunch—that he learned from friends that some blacks were trying to integrate the lunch counter. Sullivan, along with Madden, Johnston, and some other friends decided to go investigate.

As he entered the store, Sullivan immediately knew something unusual was happening. He spied the blacks at the counter and then, with amazement, saw the whites. He had never seen the two races seated together in a public place, so D. C. Sullivan pushed his way forward to have a ringside seat.

John Salter

He stares intently ahead, away from the camera, as sugar showers the woman beside him. His own light, cropped hair is white from the sugar poured onto it. Three small dabs of catsup—or is it blood?—dribble from the crown of his head, leading a viewer's eye to the oozing blobs of catsup, blood, mustard, salt, and vinegar that soak his tan summer jacket. A cigarette sits idly on the counter top no more than an inch or so from his clasped hands. A box of matches lies beside it, an indication he is a smoker, would love a puff of his unfiltered Pall Mall if only the mob would take a break. "Can't we just settle this calmly over a cigarette and a cup of coffee?" his quiet pose seems to suggest. Not on this day is the answer. Not in this city. Not on your life.

This was not the first time that John Salter faced an angry mob, nor would it be the last. He began his professional career as a rough-and-tumble union organizer in the West and would go on to become a champion of the poor and dispossessed in numerous struggles in the decades ahead. It was this moment, however, that would provide his most visible memento of a lifetime of agitation for social change—and it would come for sitting as peacefully as a monk and letting a mob have its way.[33]

FIRST AND FOREMOST, JOHN SALTER, LIKE HIS RADICAL LABOR HERO RALPH Chaplin, is a westerner: "where the country opens out instead of in," as Salter was fond of saying. Though he spent his early years in the Midwest, Salter preferred to recount the story of his life from the time his family reached its final western destination of Flagstaff, Arizona, where his father, John Salter, Sr.—after a lifetime of adventurous travel and wandering—settled down to a teaching career in the arts at Arizona State College and where the younger Salter became exposed to an interesting mix of Indian, Anglo, Mormon, Mexican, and black cultures. Salter recalled the discrimination his own father experienced when seeking lodgings when he first moved to Flagstaff—no white person would rent a room to him, so he rented from a Mexican family. Salter can even remember seeing signs that read "No Dogs or Indians Allowed."

The story is telling because John Salter, Sr., was a nearly full-blooded Indian from Massachusetts, born to two impoverished and unwed Native Americans of Mohawk, Micmac, and Abenaki extraction. The elder Salter was adopted at the age of seven by one of the most prominent and intellectually connected families in turn-of-the-century America. William Mackintire (Mack) Salter, Salter, Sr.'s adoptive father, was himself active in the Indian Rights Association, a group of mostly white men who advocated adopting and mainstreaming young and impoverished Native Americans as the best way to improve the lives of native peoples.[34] In addition, he helped found the Ethical Culture Movement,[35] an offshoot of Unitarian Universalism, and participated in the creation of a group that became the American Civil Liberties Union.

Mack Salter was also one of the sixty signatories to a 1909 document calling for a conference on the plight of African Americans, which led to the creation of the NAACP.[36] Thus, Mack Salter's adoptive grandson had a direct link back to the origins of the organization he would later attempt to serve in Jackson.

Mack Salter's wife was Mary Gibbens, whose sister, Alice, was married to the philosopher and social psychologist William James, the renowned Harvard professor and brother of novelist Henry James.[37] John Salter, Sr., spent his youth in a setting of extreme intellectual ferment, among the most free-thinking minds of the age. It was also a life free from material want.

John Salter's mother had a lineage every bit as colorful as his father's.[38] Josephine Senn was the granddaughter of Swiss-born abolitionist Michael Senn, who fought for the Union during the Civil War and was later elected to the Kansas legislature, where he introduced a bill calling for women's suffrage. Josephine was well connected to Kansas politicians and was herself a graduate of the University of Wisconsin at a time when such an accomplishment was still unusual for a woman. She later became a corporate trailblazer by serving as a public relations executive for the Quaker Oats Company.

John Salter clearly relished his extensive family tree and could go on for hours about his relatives' accomplishments, as if their deeds set the stage for his, in a long chain of evolutionary radical refinement. He was born on Valentine's Day 1934 in Chicago and spent his early years in the Midwest. But Salter's story really picks up once the family followed Salter, Sr., to Arizona when the younger Salter was fourteen. "I fell in love with the rugged country all around there," he said. He became an outdoorsman there and indulged his fascination with hunting and guns.

He also met an interesting mix of liberal thinkers and students whom his father would bring home for dinner from the college. One in particular, Frank Dolphin, had a singular influence on the impressionable youth. A former California labor organizer and a fighter pilot during World War II, the experienced Dolphin plied young Salter with the ideals of the early labor movement and the fighting spirit of the trade union known as the Wobblies—the Industrial Workers of the World—so much so that Salter adopted the IWW motto, "An injury to one is an injury to all," as his own.

Salter entered Arizona State College in 1951, but he was looking for a different experience. "I was beginning to chafe," he admitted. So in March 1953, he enlisted in the U.S. Army, hoping to fight in the Korean War. The war ended, however, just as Salter completed his basic training, so he filled out the rest of his two-year stint in the Pacific Northwest and experienced firsthand the new, integrated army that President Truman's executive order had created.

After receiving an honorable discharge, Salter stumbled upon his destiny while hanging around the old IWW haunts, listening to old Wobblies recount their glory days. "The IWW was fading, but the dream could certainly grip a person," Salter tellingly recounted. He joined what was left of the IWW, got his union card, and headed home to finish college with the help of the GI Bill. By his own telling, all Salter was interested in at this point was "hunting and saving the world."

Salter finished his bachelor's degree at Arizona State in Tempe and also began working for the unions part-time. In fact, nearly everywhere he went from this point onward, Salter would involve himself in one volatile situation after another—primarily organizing grassroots movements to protect the rights of ordinary citizens against bureaucratic or repressive institutions. And each experience taught him additional lessons on how to best take on entrenched power structures.

It was while still in Arizona and working part-time for the Union of Mine, Mill and Smelter Workers (known as Mine-Mill) that Salter came to the attention of J. Edgar Hoover's Federal Bureau of Investigation. Salter later estimated that his FBI file totals in excess of four thousand pages of reports that date back to his early involvement with Mine-Mill. One of the earliest entries notes that "Salter is a very determined, belligerent and confused young man." A later FBI observer wrote that his "subject's activities indicate that he seeks out controversial situations."[39]

Indeed, Salter did just that, moving from Arizona to Nebraska to teach high school, then returning to Arizona to obtain a master's degree in sociology, then moving to his mother's alma mater, the University of Wisconsin, to teach. At each stop he got tangled up in local issues and successfully led student uprisings against the authoritarian and repressive administrations that were prevalent during the later days of 1950s Eisenhower America.

It was in Wisconsin that Salter met the young woman who would become his wife: Eldri Johanson, a social worker and daughter of a Lutheran minister. "We formed an association that obviously lasted," Salter said dryly nearly forty years later. Salter also began to consider his next move and wondered if he could play a role in the developing student movement for civil rights by moving south. After discussing the idea with some of his radical acquaintances, he wrote to two historically black colleges seeking employment. Dr. Beittel at Tougaloo offered him a job, sight unseen. That summer, John and Eldri married in August 1961, and the two set out for a new set of adventures.

Salter described the drive from Flagstaff, where they had gone to visit his folks, to Mississippi as a trip to a "weird, alien, foreign country." As he and Eldri passed through central Texas and entered the hill country, the humidity increased, the landscape changed, and the people became more suspicious and visibly poorer. There were more black people than Salter had ever seen. In Louisiana, they stopped for gas, and the white owner greeted them with a riddle: "How in the hell can Kennedy get a man on the moon when he can't even get a busload of niggers across Mississippi?"[40] It was a sardonic reference to the Freedom Rides.

When the Salters reached the Mississippi River a little past midnight, they crossed the bridge at Vicksburg and were greeted by heavily armed officers who questioned them about their destination. "It occurred to me," Salter recalled, "that this was not the moment to say that I was coming to teach at a black college which you might have heard about." Instead, he made up a story about visiting relatives in Alabama (he had an uncle in Birmingham), and they were allowed to pass.

As much as they wanted to hide their shock, the Salters were not at all prepared for living in one of the South's most ardent strongholds of segregation. After spending their first nights at Dr. Beittel's home, they agreed to live in Jackson temporarily until the college could find accommodations for them on campus. They were "a little surprised" when a white couple visiting the school congratulated them for doing such a "brave thing" as coming to Tougaloo.[41]

Later, Salter was appalled when he greeted his black students on the streets of Jackson and they didn't answer out of fear. He had a hard time believing his students who told him their parents thought "blacks were inferior to whites, and that nothing could ever change that." And he was stunned when his students hardly commented on the murder of black Mississippi farmer Herbert Lee—the first casualty in the SNCC voter registration drive within the state. "They had lived in Mississippi all their lives," Salter recalled sadly. This type of treatment had become all too familiar to them.[42]

So, true to type, Salter got to work to try and change things. When one of his students, Colia Liddell,[43] one of the leaders of the North Jackson Youth

Council, invited him to become the adult advisor to the youth council, he jumped at the chance. As a result, he and Eldri were invited to attend the NAACP Freedom Fund Dinner that November in Jackson. The presence of John and Eldri (six months pregnant with their first child) as the only non-blacks created quite a stir—not only among the police watching from across the street, but also among the surprised NAACP regulars.

That night, Salter met two men who would have a significant impact on his future: police captain John L. Ray and NAACP field secretary Medgar Evers. Ray was the police force leader who had devised the city's instant arrest strategy for civil rights agitators. First employed during the 1961 Freedom Rides, the strategy proved ingenious, for by immediately arresting demonstrators, Ray could justifiably claim that he was protecting them from harm while at the same time denying them the kind of national publicity these confrontations often generated. Although Salter would come to consider Ray a "mortal adversary," he also granted Ray grudging respect for his basic human decency during unusually tense situations.

As the Salters made their way into the NAACP dinner that night, Ray stopped them and asked for some identification. "How about an Arizona driver's license?" Salter quipped. "I think you should show me a Mississippi driver's license one of these days," Ray shot back. "Well," Salter said, "I'll show you something else. I'll show you an NAACP [membership] card. Ever seen one?" "I don't think I have," Ray responded. After studying the card, Ray let the couple enter.

At the door of the auditorium, the Salters were greeted by an enthusiastic man taking tickets. He had "an optimism that contrasted sharply with the lines cut deeply into his face," Salter would later write in his autobiographical memoir of the period, *Jackson, Mississippi: An American Chronicle of Struggle and Schism.*[44] This was John Salter's first introduction to Medgar Evers.

These two giants of the Jackson Movement bonded over interests that might have been considered antithetical to a nonviolent movement—guns and the military—but which were part and parcel of their common experience. Both had served in the U.S. Army, and both were accomplished hunters and outdoorsmen. Evers carried a gun in his car, had one in his desk at the NAACP office, and had a small arsenal at home to protect his family.[45] In fact, Salter remembered that the first thing Evers did when the Salters came to visit the Everses' home was to show off his gun collection.

Salter respected Evers's courage as well as his friendly optimism against all odds. He also was impressed by Evers's refusal to hate. "He greeted every human being on an equal-to-equal basis," Salter stated emphatically. But Salter saw something else in Evers—something he believed he could help remedy. Evers, he said, was a "lone wolf"[46]—someone who after nine years of tireless, thankless work for the NAACP was in desperate need of help in taking the struggle to the next level. That's where Salter's organizing skills could be put to good service and where he hoped to have an impact.

At the NAACP Freedom Fund Dinner that night, Salter heard presentations from and visited with several NAACP luminaries from the state: board president Aaron Henry; state board member Amzie Moore, who had welcomed SNCC's Bob Moses to Mississippi that same year; and, of course, Evers himself. But Salter sensed that each speech was tinged with defeat. Not much was changing despite all of their heroic efforts. "Never before had we quite realized the oppression of Mississippi,"[47] he wrote. "[It] was absolutely awful."[48]

After hearing firsthand about these challenges, Salter reaffirmed his commitment to working with the NAACP's North Jackson Youth Council. Although at the time the council had only about a dozen active members, it did some important work during Salter's first year, including conducting a survey for the NAACP across a large part of Jackson's black community that measured grassroots support for voting rights and school desegregation initiatives. As a result of his work with the youth council, Salter was named to the Mississippi NAACP board of directors. At about the same time, in the early spring of 1962, he and Eldri finally moved into a campus apartment in what was known as Pope Cottage, just in time for the birth of their first daughter, Maria.

After the summer break, during which Salter did some organizing work for the International Chemical Workers Union of Akron, Ohio, he returned to Tougaloo ready for action. On his first free afternoon, Salter sat down at his Underwood typewriter and began creating the first edition of what would come to be the youth council's newsletter, *North Jackson Action*. Modeled after a similar newsletter he had developed during an earlier student struggle in Wisconsin, this mimeographed sheet would become a way for the youth council to publicize its activities, which Salter intended to increase significantly.

Aside from these activities and his teaching responsibilities, Salter found time to prepare an important sociological study for the NAACP about the devastating effects of poverty on blacks in rural Mississippi. At Evers's request and with a revolver for protection, Salter traveled to the Mississippi Delta early in 1963 to record conditions there. The national office believed that this information, gathered by a credentialed sociologist, could have an impact on federal policies. What Salter found while he interviewed more than 250 individuals was a poverty class kept in line "by police power and the Citizens' Council . . . virtually enslaving generation after generation through debt and fear."[49] He wrote an extensive report for the NAACP and testified before the U.S. Commission on Civil Rights about his findings. These experiences in rural Mississippi further convinced Salter that something more had to be done to change the racial balance of power in the state.

On campus, the Salters' home had become a mecca for student activists and sympathetic teachers, as well as de facto headquarters of the fledgling Jackson Movement. Every Saturday, student activists would pick up their leaflets and get their marching orders at Pope Cottage before spreading out into the black community. Salter was also becoming one of the most popular teachers at Tougaloo. In February 1963, he was presented with the Citizen of the Year Award for the faculty member who most embodied "the outstanding qualities of citizenship and interest in good government."[50]

Salter loved to repeat the old Micmac adage that "when you're fishing for trout, you have to expect to be bitten by mosquitoes." Even so, he was not fully prepared for the consequences when the direct action phase of the Jackson Movement began. On the morning of May 28, 1963, he was with Medgar Evers and the demonstrators at the NAACP office on Lynch Street attending to last-minute details. This was the moment he had planned for during the entire six-month boycott of Capitol Street—a full-blown demonstration supported by the NAACP and ready to be backed up by more demonstrations if the movement's demands were not met. But like most of those involved that day, Salter's expectations were low. The Woolworth's sit-in and picketing of other downtown stores were to be only the first in a series of events designed to gradually escalate and pressure the mayor and white business leaders to negotiate. "This was the beginning," Salter said. "We decided to start with smaller things that were symbolically important, then move on to bigger things like mass marches. Instant arrest was expected. No violence."

So on the day of the sit-in, instead of worrying about what might happen to the demonstrators, Salter and Evers were busy planning their next move. When the call came into the office that those sitting-in had not been arrested, Salter sensed something was wrong. When they heard next that one of the demonstrators had been knocked off his seat and violence had erupted, Salter knew where he belonged.

Knowing that Evers was already a "marked man," Salter urged him to stay at the office and serve as contact with the press—a role Evers typically played. Then Salter grabbed his tan summer jacket and headed to Woolworth's with two other activists. He slipped past the throng of police and onlookers without being noticed and stepped into the store. He quickly assessed the scene, surreptitiously communicated his plans to his colleagues, and then headed for the counter.

As he moved to take a seat next to Joan Trumpauer, an older man in the crowd—thinking Salter was another thug heading forward to hurt the women—urged him on. "Hit 'em, boy!"[51] he said. Never yet having backed away from his convictions, Salter simply growled at him and sat down.

CHAPTER 3

OTHERS AT THE COUNTER

A PHOTOGRAPH—ANY PHOTOGRAPH—IS INCOMPLETE. THE CAMERA ONLY captures whatever image is right in front of it. Other dramas may be unfolding all around, but if they are not within the optical span of the camera's lens, they are not recorded. In the case of the famous Jackson sit-in photograph, there were many other scenes that could have been documented—some of them happening at exactly the same time. But the photographer chose to point and shoot at a scene that his trained eye told him would stand the test of time. Many other demonstrators spent time at the counter that day. Here are some of their backstories, and what brought them there.

Memphis Norman

By the time the camera clicked the now-famous photograph, he was already absent from the scene, no longer quietly sitting hunched over the lunch counter between the two classmates he had accompanied there. He had become the demonstration's first casualty—the first to shed blood for what was escalating into a war in the Magnolia State's capital city.

Memphis Norman traveled a road of extreme deprivation to voluntarily place himself in such deadly danger—to "make my contribution," as he put it. He would later participate in another controversial war, fought on foreign shores, but he would always contend that he got his first and most fearsome dose of human brutality in his home state down at the local five-and-dime.[1]

MEMPHIS NORMAN WAS BORN JULY 23, 1942, TO A FAMILY OF SHARECROPPERS who had barely moved from the land their slave forebears had inhabited a century before. That area in southwestern Alabama is just at the rim of the rich black soil that had made cotton king. His family's circumstances were abysmal. In a good year his father, Judge Norman, would earn between $250 and $400 after a backbreaking spring and summer of chopping and picking cotton. Judge's wife, Elizabeth MacMillian Norman, worked in the landowner's house as a domestic—caring for her own five children along with those of the white household while also cleaning house and cooking meals. Judge labored twelve-hour days in the fields, giving half of everything he grew back to the landowner as payment. Only after settling that debt and others accumulated at the landowner's store could he think about his own needs or those of his family.

Unfortunately for the family, Judge Norman compulsively put his own needs ahead of theirs. He was a drinker and a gambler in a situation where there was money for neither. He often spent the family's meager funds on his own pursuits, leaving his wife and children with nothing beyond what Elizabeth earned or what they were given by their landlord or well-meaning but equally destitute neighbors.

At least they had the land, and Elizabeth planted a vegetable garden every spring. She canned produce to ensure a supply of food for the winter months, once the cotton money was gone. They grew melons and had fig and apple trees nearby. And there was corn, from which Elizabeth ground cornmeal for the family's staple, cornbread. They kept a few chickens and pigs for meat, and they hunted wild animals: raccoons, opossums, rabbits, and squirrels. Still, there was never enough to go around, even though only five of the dozen children to whom Elizabeth gave birth lived past infancy.

Memphis Norman's father often left his family for days at a time, sometimes, ironically, to attend classes on becoming a preacher. Judge Norman wanted to improve his lot, no doubt, and figured it would ultimately help the family if he could succeed in another profession. "It was crazy," Memphis said resentfully. "Here was a man with a third-grade education and he was trying to become a full-fledged minister. For what? To preach to the rural blacks of Alabama? How much money was there in that?" The younger Norman felt that the church exploited black men like his father, siphoning off precious funds from poor families while holding out the unrealistic promise of economic improvement down the road.

Judge Norman never realized his dream. Instead he uprooted his family time and again, always seeking a better farm to sharecrop, with larger acreage and better soil that would produce a more abundant crop so as to earn a few more dollars—all to be either gambled or drunk away or spent in the vain hope of climbing up a rung or two on the socioeconomic ladder.

Of the five surviving children—four boys and a girl—Memphis Norman was in the middle. Norman and his older brothers would often help their father in the field, as would Elizabeth when her housework was done. But Memphis displayed an uncanny ability with numbers. At an early age, his mother had taught him the alphabet and multiplication tables, and he delighted in reciting them. As a result, teachers admired him and convinced his parents to let the child attend school regularly rather than working in the fields. Although the family's moves often disrupted his education, Norman continued to excel at mathematics and reading. These positive developments helped him form a different opinion of himself and his abilities than his circumstances might otherwise have allowed.

The all-black schools he attended were mostly small and run-down structures, sometimes with only two rooms for six grades. The one lasting memory that Norman carried from those days was that he and his siblings would often have to attend school barefoot—a stigma no other children there had to endure. Even the poor have their pecking order; his family was at the very bottom. No land, no money, dependent on the landowner. Even other blacks looked down upon "those Normans." "A lot of days we dreaded going to school," Norman recalled. "We didn't want the experience of being less than other people—being openly without basic necessities. It led to a feeling of inadequacy and feeling that you don't belong. You'd rather be off by yourself."

Because they moved so often, the Normans also failed to establish ties to any one place or community. Their lives were similar to those of migrant farm workers who seasonally moved up and down the eastern and western seaboards. The memory of this constant moving haunted Norman during his adulthood. "There seems to be an urge to go back, to visit all of those places where we were sharecroppers," he said. "I suspect there were more than a dozen—maybe fifteen houses where we lived. Whenever I go there I'm looking for something. I'm not sure what it is."

When Norman was thirteen, his family moved to a more stable setting, away from the country and into the city of Pascagoula, a mid-sized city on the Mississippi coast along the Gulf of Mexico, just west of the Alabama border. His father had landed a job working in the shipyards, and the family moved into Carver Village, a segregated urban subdivision. For the Norman family, this was a dramatic and positive change. Here, for the first time, they had hot and cold running water, an indoor bathroom, electricity, a refrigerator, and a gas stove. Finally, Norman could attend a decent school and become part of a thriving community. "Suddenly there were all these people who had similar lives and backgrounds as ours, but who had been on the move earlier from rural Alabama and Mississippi." He joined a local Baptist church, attended Sunday school, and became integrated into the fabric of black society—something the family's previous migrant existence in the country had not allowed.

It was at the end of Norman's first summer in Pascagoula that Emmett Till was murdered. "That really struck hard at people—at black people," he recalled. "There was this feeling of anger and also a feeling of helplessness and vulnerability. There was this feeling of exposure, that it could happen to anybody, and that the law was not on our side. You could be invaded, violated," Norman continued. "I had an enormous fear when I walked to town and was walking down a sidewalk and a white person was walking toward me. I don't know what this person's going to do to me, and I can't do anything back."

Other events of the early civil rights movement didn't have as much impact on Norman's life. "All those things were happening far away," he said. "There was nothing happening in Mississippi."

After two years of relative stability, Judge Norman's erratic behavior again led to upheaval. His drinking and gambling steadily got worse after they came to the city; eventually he lost his job at the shipyards and the family's circumstances became increasingly dire. One night in January 1957, Judge awakened Memphis in the middle of the night and told him that the family was moving once again. "We went from a fairly good situation in Pascagoula," Norman remembered, "back to a poverty kind of environment that we had lived in in Alabama. We left a place with electricity and moved back to kerosene lamps and a wood stove."

They ended up in the Turpentine Quarters of Wiggins, Mississippi, a remote town in the southeast corner of the state, known as the Piney Woods region because of its ample, tall pine trees. If rural Alabama had been near slavery, this place was like a forced labor camp. The landowner, J. B. Newton, provided separate shacks and running water for the twenty or so individuals and families that worked the forests chipping trees and dipping turpentine, a labor-intensive process of harvesting the sap from pine trees—just like tapping maple trees for their syrup—for distillation into turpentine. On a good day, a man could fill maybe two barrels with sap, if it wasn't too hot and he was feeling strong. Newton also ran a country store, where the workers could order food and clothing on credit against future work. Like the coal miners of Appalachia, many families fell deeper and deeper into debt while providing the owner with cheap labor.

For the Normans, these conditions were the worst they had known. At least in Alabama they had had land to farm, had grown their own vegetables, and had animals around for meat. Here, they lived in close quarters with other families and had no available tillable land. With Newton paying just five dollars a barrel for sap, it didn't take long for families to rack up enormous bills at the store that took years, even decades, to pay off.

Education became key to Norman's hopes for the future, and his teachers offered substantial encouragement. Once, his high school principal took Norman to visit the principal's old homestead. "What he showed me was very similar to my own situation—sharecropper living," Norman recalled. "He encouraged me to finish high school and to go off to college."

In his junior year, one of his teachers recommended that Norman take an examination sponsored by the United Negro College Fund (UNCF) to gain early entrance into college. When his test results qualified him for admission into Tougaloo under an experimental program funded in part by the UNCF, Norman skipped his senior year and entered Tougaloo in the fall of 1960.

College was a different world. Norman was shy and younger than most of his classmates, although a dozen like himself had been admitted early. And he was from a background to which he felt his economically better-off classmates could not relate. He also found that his migratory schooling had not adequately prepared him for the rigorous study required. He became a loner, spending most of his time in the library or in his room, with few friends and little recreation or socializing.

Even affording to attend college was a challenge, but through a series of summer jobs at home and on-campus jobs at Tougaloo, he was able to scrape by. One area of college life that Norman was decidedly not interested in during his first few years at Tougaloo was civil rights. "It seemed that people who were the most active in the civil rights movement were somewhat radical. Different. Sort of wild-eyed, crazy people," he recalled. "There were only a handful of students that got actively involved in demonstrations. And many of them had poor academic records." Norman had decided upon a good education with the hopes of lifting himself out of poverty and perhaps helping his family as well. Despite his initial objections, however, Norman soon encountered a man who changed his views on the civil rights struggle.

In his junior year, he beat out a number of other students for the plum post of serving as assistant to Dr. Ernst Borinski, the German-Jewish émigré whose Social Science Lab was the heart of Tougaloo's liberal reputation. This paid position provided Norman with needed financial stability while also giving him the opportunity to join Borinski's inner circle.

Norman's duties in the lab were largely administrative—typing Borinski's extensive correspondence, checking books in and out of his large library, receiving the mail, and keeping track of daily newspapers from around the world. Through this two-year stint as Borinski's assistant, however, Norman received an eye-opening education about the most piercing social issues of the day. "Dr. Borinski had a very profound influence on my life in terms of race relations," Norman recalled reverentially.

Borinski also helped Norman plot a strategy for his future. He suggested that his young aide take a trip north to experience a racially integrated society. In February 1963, Norman spent two weeks at the University of Minnesota, staying in the home of a white student. It was a trip that he later characterized as the first step in "my journey north." There he met people who opened his mind to the world outside of Mississippi. There was no segregated seating and no separate facilities for blacks. He was welcomed with open arms and a good deal of curiosity; everyone wanted to know about his life as a black man in the South.

Back at Tougaloo in March, Norman began to pay more attention to the boycott of the Capitol Street stores and to take an interest in the politics of people like Annie Moody and Joan Trumpauer. In late May, Moody asked him if he would be willing to participate in a sit-in at Woolworth's. "As soon as she asked me, I felt fear," he said. "But my fear was reduced when I heard that we would be arrested immediately. With that assurance, I said, 'Why not?'"

So with that simple assent, Norman let go of a lifetime of inbred reticence and fear. His time had arrived to join the struggle.

Pearlena Lewis

When the photographer snapped the picture that captured the essence of the sit-in movement, Pearlena Lewis was behind him, sitting at that same lunch counter, enduring the same abuse as those he caught on film. She had been there from the beginning and would remain throughout, at one point raising herself from the floor and grasping her seat as if it were a life preserver, determined that this was a moment not to be lost, that this would be the beginning of change in Mississippi.[2]

A MINISTER'S DAUGHTER, PEARLENA LEWIS GREW UP IN THE SHADOW OF THE church. She was the first of seven children born to Margaret (Tucker) and Clarence E. Lewis II, and like many first children of large families, she helped raise her younger siblings. Lewis approached this task as she would all those that followed, in a serious, unfaltering fashion. Her mother entrusted her at a very young age with the responsibility of running errands for her, including taking the bus downtown or shopping at the neighborhood store. These ventures opened her eyes to the segregated society in which she lived and from which she had been heretofore protected, and she began to question the strange practices that made her ride in the back of the bus or kept her from drinking from water fountains and using bathrooms downtown.

"As a child, segregation made me feel that I was different, that I was not important, that something was wrong with me," Lewis recalled. Her thinking was exactly the kind that helped Thurgood Marshall and the NAACP lift the false veneer of equality from the "separate but equal" defenses that white society in the South had used to rationalize their treatment of blacks. Lewis credited her parents, particularly her father, with helping her understand their situation without internalizing feelings of inadequacy. She learned, instead, that the system they lived under was wrong and needed changing.

Clarence Lewis himself had found a way to maintain his self-esteem while living under segregation. In fulfilling his dream to become a minister, he displayed the same hard work and tenacity that he would pass on to his firstborn. Working the night shift at a local Jackson factory, he attended seminary during the day and did part-time ministry work on weekends. He started out, as did many black preachers in those days, preaching in small country churches. Eventually he moved up to a part-time ministry in Jackson. In many ways, Clarence Lewis lived out the dream that Judge Norman could never quite attain.

With the elder Lewis's elevation to the ministry, the Lewis family became part of Jackson's black middle class. They lived in a new segregated subdivision in north Jackson called the Virden Addition. It was a close-knit, stable community where everyone looked out for each other, and kids went through grade school, high school, and often even college together.

Despite the family's improved prospects, Pearlena Lewis continued to feel the sting of segregation. "On TV," she recalled, "all the commercials were white. In the magazines you saw white. All the models were white. Everything seemed to be saying 'white is right.'" In Jackson, there was only one public park for blacks, one library, and no swimming pool. During her adolescence, Lewis was constrained from finding a summer job because blacks were not hired as waitresses or store clerks. Her father forbade her and her sister from doing domestic work or even babysitting for white families because he didn't trust the white men to treat his daughters with respect. As a result of segregation's barriers and her father's protectiveness, Lewis had a lot of time on her hands; she found ways to put that time to good use.

Lewis found a refuge from segregation in the church. It was the one place where she was able to feel positive about her life. Through the church, her large family, the neighborhood, and the all-black schools she attended, Lewis also built up a large network of friends and acquaintances. Despite her protests to the contrary—"I never did consider myself a leader," she said—Lewis was hugely popular and held the unique distinction of having been elected twice to an honorary position at Brinkley school. The first time she was elected Miss Brinkley, the school was a junior high. She went on to attend Lanier High School, but two years later, thanks to attempts by whites to prove that separate but equal education was working, Brinkley was upgraded to a senior high school as well. So Lewis and her neighborhood friends spent their final high school year back at Brinkley, where she was again elected Miss Brinkley. Her main duty in that role was to serve as good will ambassador to the other black schools in Jackson; as a consequence, she developed strong ties with students from all over the city. Medgar Evers would later marvel at Lewis's social connections.

Lewis met Evers during her final year in high school at a church service, where he gently recruited her into the NAACP's North Jackson Youth Council. Always cautious and thoughtful, Lewis didn't jump right in. Instead, she studied the history of the organization and its legacy in Mississippi. She also talked to her friend Colia Liddell, who was considering joining as well. "I think as a team, we could really do some good," she told Liddell.

Lewis and Liddell thus became allies in their fledgling efforts to take on the segregationists. Liddell was elected president of the youth council and Lewis, vice president. They entered Tougaloo College together in 1961,[3] the same year that John Salter, Joan Trumpauer, and Annie Moody arrived. As a native Jacksonian, however, Lewis lived in town with her family and commuted to the college as a day student. As a result she never forged deep bonds with fellow students that those living on campus usually do. Instead, she became more active in the youth council and in Mississippi's NAACP infrastructure. She also formed an enduring friendship with Lillian Louie, who had become the secretary to Medgar Evers in 1960.

Louie was no stranger to Mississippi's racial codes and was a pioneer in her own right. A native of Hazlehurst, thirty miles south of Jackson, she found escape from a difficult economic and family life by signing up in 1956 for a three-year tour of duty with the U.S. Air Force, where she experienced life in an integrated setting. Having experienced firsthand how the races could peacefully coexist, Louie returned to her native state ready to do what she could to end segregation. Becoming Evers's secretary was the only job she considered after leaving the air force—a gutsy move for a young, single mother with a five-year-old daughter. She recognized early on that her work with Evers could have a significant impact not only on her own life, but on the lives of thousands of others. Her NAACP work also led her to friendship with Pearlena Lewis and the strong, enveloping fabric of the entire Lewis family. "Her parents were Mommy and Daddy to me," Louie said of the elder Lewises. As for Pearlena, "She was Miss Everything. Just cream of the crop."[4]

John Salter called Lewis "a quiet, courageous presence" in the Jackson Movement.[5] For her part, Lewis remembered that when Salter became youth council advisor in the fall of 1961 at Colia Liddell's request, many parents and friends questioned his involvement. "Eyebrows were raised," she said. But Medgar Evers apparently saw no problem with Salter's role as a nonblack advisor to a black youth group. "As long as he's legit," Evers told Lewis. After Evers had a chance to work more closely with Salter, he quietly reassured the parents of Salter's capability and sincerity.

Lewis began working more closely with Salter once her friend Colia decided in the summer of 1962 to get involved with SNCC voter registration in the Delta and Lewis reluctantly took over as youth council president. Although she would have preferred remaining behind the scenes, quietly influencing and contributing, other council members saw her potential, her connections, and her leadership ability and insisted that she take on the role. Even her parents encouraged her, as they did her siblings, to get more involved in the NAACP.

It was Medgar Evers who asked Lewis to participate in the Woolworth's sit-in. As president of the North Jackson Youth Council and a native of Jackson, she was an obvious choice. She recalled strategy sessions that began a full week beforehand where many of the details were worked out: how they would get there, what they would say to the press, who would speak at the mass meeting just after the demonstration.

For Lewis, the intervening week was also filled with increasing tension and excitement, for she knew she represented the hopes of the youth of Jackson, who were growing impatient with the adults' attempts to achieve change slowly, through negotiation. "We were just tired of sitting around listening to the adults say, 'Let's try this; let's try that,'" Lewis recalled. "I thought we had waited long enough."

When Lewis entered Woolworth's that day, she was certain of her mission and determined to see it through. Her questioning spirit had led her from Jackson's segregated buses and water fountains, past parks she could not walk through and libraries she could not enter. The same segregated society that kept her out of the white world had facilitated the development of her leadership abilities and her strong social network with her peers at church, in the schools, and in her neighborhood.

So with the quiet, confident style that had led her to the forefront of her generation's aspirations in her hometown, with apprehension along with a healthy dose of pride, and with an unshakable belief that God would see her through, Pearlena Lewis moved into her position at the lunch counter, ready for the siege ahead.

Lois Chaffee

She was so camera-shy that somehow her face never appears in any photographs of the sit-in. The only surviving sit-in image that shows her clearly is a short film clip. In it, she seems mesmerized, frozen—not looking at the camera, not looking at her neighbors on their stools. She simply stares, terror-stricken, trying to hold on and make it through this hell into which she has stumbled.

Born in Indiana and reared in northern Idaho, Lois Chaffee was a white, western outsider who found herself and her calling as a result of the brief but significant period she spent in the South on freedom's front lines.[6]

LOIS CHAFFEE IS THE ELDEST OF FOUR DAUGHTERS OF LOUISE AND SID Chaffee. Her mother was her "lantern," she says—the woman who introduced worlds of possibilities to her children. An itinerant nurse from a Pennsylvania coal mining family, Louise Schneider landed a job in the mid-1930s in Lafayette, Indiana, the home of Purdue University and Alcoa Aluminum. In that thriving town where scholarship, agriculture, and industry converged, she met her husband-to-be. Sid Chaffee had had a "kind of Tom Sawyer childhood," Chaffee said, growing up on a farm as the oldest of seven children.

When Schneider met him, Sid Chaffee worked as a shop foreman in an Alcoa plant. With his knowledge of production, he was exempted from the World War II draft so he could stay on at the plant to provide raw materials for the war effort.

Lois Chaffee was the first of four siblings, all girls. Born on July 16, 1939, Chaffee lived her early life in Lafayette until her father moved the family to Kellogg, Idaho, in the northern panhandle, just after the war ended. There he went into business with his brother, who had started a grocery business; the two brothers would develop a strong enterprise that eventually branched out into surrounding towns.

Idaho, in Chaffee's recollection, was a "small, mean place" with strongly conservative leanings and little tolerance for dissent or differences. No blacks lived there that she could recall, and those that did show up on occasion were run out of town. Native Americans were tolerated, but only because there were so few of them around. She remembered only one small racial incident while growing up—a joke one of her teachers told at the expense of a Native American classmate. Lois laughed along with everyone else until she realized her fellow student wasn't laughing. Then she was embarrassed at her own thoughtlessness.

Chaffee would later vividly recall the close-minded McCarthyism of the era. In junior high, for instance, her music teacher suggested that all public school students take a loyalty oath to the U.S. government. In a move completely out of character, the shy Chaffee raised her hand and said, "That's not a good idea!" Even in seventh grade, she intuitively sensed that a public education should not come at the price of freedom of expression. The teacher dropped the notion when it became clear that not even the conservative school administration would support such a plan.

By contrast, Chaffee's early life was shaped by her mother's openness to new ideas, including her membership in the Congregational/Methodist federated church—a consolidated approach taken by many small western congregations to gather together enough people to support a church. Chaffee believed her mother was primarily influenced by the liberal Congregationalists, but she was generally a woman who thought for herself, had strong opinions, and would stick up for what she believed was right. Louise also had a strong sense of service to the community and little interest in material wealth. She passed these attributes on to her daughters, as well as a love for reading and a thirst for knowledge.

The Chaffees expected their daughters to go to college and then find work—an ambition for women that was unusual in small-town Idaho in the mid-1950s. Chaffee herself was eager to get out of Kellogg, so in 1957, at her mother's suggestion, she enrolled in Pacific University, a small Congregational college in Forest Grove, Oregon. After two years her grades were good enough for her to transfer to Oberlin College in Ohio, a distinguished liberal arts college which her father's mother had attended. It was at Oberlin that Chaffee discovered just how poorly she had been prepared for higher learning. "I kind of blundered through," she said. It took her three more years to graduate and when she did, in the spring of 1962 with a bachelor's degree in English, she had no idea what she wanted to do. "I didn't have a sense of direction," she admitted. "I was really very confused."

Like many white youths outside the South, Chaffee had paid little attention to the civil rights struggles of the 1950s. She hadn't heard of Emmett Till and was only vaguely familiar with the Montgomery bus boycott; the Little Rock school integration crisis was just a blur. It wasn't until the student movement of the 1960s, and its images of young people being dragged from their stools at sit-ins and attacked on the Freedom Rides, that Chaffee became engaged. She began to feel she wanted to be close to activities that were forcing change and progress. Having found college almost as confining as her Idaho experience, she was looking for a way to contribute to positive, progressive social change in an open atmosphere.

The perfect opportunity seemed to have arrived when, in the spring of 1962 during her last semester at Oberlin, recruiters from Tougaloo visited campus to offer teaching positions to graduating seniors. Chaffee applied and was accepted. She moved to Mississippi with her Irish setter, Ivan (a parting gift from a dorm mother), and her few belongings in the late summer of 1962, just as Medgar Evers was helping James Meredith integrate the University of Mississippi and John Salter was planning the opening salvos of the Jackson Movement.

At Tougaloo, Chaffee's main task was to teach remedial reading and writing to freshmen who were inadequately prepared for the rigors of college study. She felt ill-equipped for the job, but later would come to see that even with her own educational deficiencies, she served as a bridge between poorly educated, mostly rural students and what they wanted to become: productive, contributing citizens. She enjoyed the students immensely and remembered their enthusiasm and vigor. "They were a lively bunch," she recalled, "very vivacious, very capable. These were comers. These were people who were going to make good lives."

One role she didn't expect to fill was that of house matron, which she was told was part of her job only after she arrived on campus. Watching over students and their personal lives was the last thing Chaffee wanted to do. If anything, she had seen her own college life as too confining, even repressive, and found Tougaloo even more so. Women were locked in their dorms at night, for instance. She was not interested in enforcing what she considered turn-of-the-century rules for student behavior, so she largely ignored this aspect of her job, to the dismay of the administration and the delight of her charges.

Chaffee finally found the type of open-minded, inquisitive, activist souls she was searching for when she made the acquaintance of the Salters and the line of visitors who regularly showed up at their door. "These were the kind of people I had longed to find," she said. "The kind I always knew were out there somewhere. They were educated, interested, involved, and really cared."

She remembered the Salter home as a drop-in center for campus activists, with John presiding especially over the conceptualization, strategy, and details of the Jackson Movement. In part, Chaffee spent more and more of her time at the Salters' because she found so little in common with the students under her care. Although she was not much older, they were preoccupied with their own world—a culture foreign and apart from hers. In addition, like it or not, she was faculty, part of the administration. So Chaffee spent her free time chatting with Eldri and helping with baby Maria, as well as stuffing envelopes and mimeographing leaflets for the Jackson Movement—the usual behind-the-scenes work that serves as the backbone of any community organizing effort.

Like Joan Trumpauer, Chaffee didn't expect to get involved in the sit-in on that late May morning in 1963, though she also had agreed to be a spotter. She was wearing a "church-type" dress that she'd made herself; people dressed up for demonstrations in those days to show they were upstanding members of the community and worthy of respect. She first went with Trumpauer to observe the street picketing and remembered the two of them heading to Woolworth's only after the pickets had been arrested.

When they entered the store, what struck Chaffee most was the noise: "It was a tremendous racket," she recalled. She could see Pearlena Lewis and Annie Moody hunched over the lunch counter, with the crowd shouting at them. A rope cordoned off the demonstrators from the mob. At some point, trying to chase the rowdies away, the manager threatened to close the store. As he was shooing people out the door, Chaffee found herself in a dilemma.

"It wasn't a planned thing," she said. "I didn't want to leave [the demonstrators] there. I thought I should stay." She thought she would be forced out of the store unless she joined the demonstration, so she "ducked under the rope" and sat down. It seemed Lois Chaffee had found her place at last.

George Raymond

He appears in only one photograph of the lunch counter scene that day. In it, the camera's flash and his deep black skin provide a double shadow against Pearlena Lewis's bright summer suit. He sits stone-faced, staring straight ahead while a pint bottle of silky white cream is poured down the back of his muscular neck and onto his white T-shirt and crisp bib overalls—clothing that would become his trademark in the Mississippi Movement.

The fact that he entered the store when the mob was at its wildest is testimony to his courage and commitment, but this was only one in a series of angry white mobs he would face in his quest for freedom. Sadly, however, George Raymond would stay at the front too long, ultimately sacrificing his health, his heart, and his life for a cause that captured his imagination while he was just a youth.[7]

"HE WAS A VISIONARY,"[8] SAID RAYMOND'S NEPHEW, ROBERT. "HE HAD A DIVINE calling,"[9] added Raymond's older sister, Lois Raymond Blakes. "He tried to free himself and his people,"[10] said Verna Raymond Polk, the baby of the family. "He was a sacrificial lamb,"[11] concluded Raymond's brother, John.

George Raymond, Jr., was born in New Orleans, Louisiana, on New Year's Day in 1943. His mother and father were backwoods people, born into sharecropping families. George, Sr., was from Woodville, Mississippi, Annie Moody's home area, while Elsie Smothers grew up in Laurel Hill, Louisiana, eighteen miles south of Woodville on Highway 61. Elsie and George, Sr., met in the late 1930s, fell in love, moved to New Orleans together, and eventually married.

In New Orleans, Elsie Raymond worked as a domestic, cleaning homes and caring for the children of whites, while her husband landed a job as a shipping clerk for a nationwide grocery store chain, the A&P Company. They raised their five children in a three-room shotgun house on Delachaise Street in a segregated section on the outskirts of the Big Easy's Garden District, seven blocks from ritzy St. Charles Avenue.

Just as in Jackson, the indignities of segregation were ever present. Blakes remembered the all-black schools, sitting in the back of the bus "behind those little screens," and the "humiliating"[12] experience of shopping on Canal Street. Just as on Jackson's Capitol Street, blacks shopping in New Orleans were not allowed to try on clothes or work as clerks. "All of us had the same slap in our face," remembered John Raymond. But whereas the rest of the family was more "laid back" about these things, "George was restless, extremely restless."[13]

Early on, young George Raymond began to exhibit the characteristics of a fighter. Courageous, action-oriented, and vocal, he was a striking contrast to his reserved, "church mice" siblings. Even Raymond's singing and church recitations were confrontational. "He would recite poems with all kinds of emphasis and force,"[14] remembered Blakes.

Despite his youthful bravado, George Raymond's school years passed without incident. He played football in junior and senior high, and grew into an attractive, muscular—although short—young man. But in the spring of 1960, while he was finishing the last semester of his senior year, Raymond began to stay out late and not come home for days at a time. His parents worried that he was getting into trouble, and his mother castigated him for missing school. Raymond, however, had begun following his own inner calling.

RAYMOND'S INTRODUCTION TO THE CIVIL RIGHTS MOVEMENT HAPPENED EN-
tirely by chance. In 1960, while still in high school, he had accompanied a
young woman he was dating to a community meeting she was interested in.
There he met Jerome Smith, a twenty-one-year-old former Southern University student who had become an active longshoreman unloading banana boats
on the docks of New Orleans. A committed pacifist with a deeply Gandhian
nonviolent yet assertive style, Smith was already a CORE volunteer and had
participated in several demonstrations in New Orleans and elsewhere.[15]

As a result of recent police brutality in the neighborhood, the community
was up in arms, and at the meeting Smith suggested the group put its anger to
positive use by marching to the police station and staging a sit-in. Raymond
was one of only two in the audience to join CORE regulars in the impromptu
demonstration. That very night, about twenty-five people sat-in inside the police station at Tulane and Broad streets; all were promptly arrested and thrown
into jail. Smith and Raymond shared a cell, and from that night until Raymond
began working for CORE full-time, the two were never far apart.[16]

Raymond once explained his motives simply: "I went to some of the CORE
meetings and decided that their cause was my cause also."[17] A day or so after
high school graduation in June 1960, Raymond left home to commit himself to the freedom struggle, not telling his parents what he was doing until
months later. He became part of the local CORE infrastructure and began
picketing New Orleans establishments, including shops on Canal Street and
in his own neighborhood, for fair and equal treatment of blacks. His brother
John benefited from one of Raymond's early protests. "I became one of the first
[black] cashiers at the Winn-Dixie across the street from the church thanks
to George,"[18] he recalled. For the most part, however, Raymond's family didn't
support his newfound mission, at least not at this stage.

Despite family opposition, Raymond continued to strengthen his CORE
involvement throughout the remainder of 1960 into the spring of 1961. In June,
Raymond, Smith, and other New Orelans CORE regulars decided to join the
CORE-sponsored Freedom Ride to Jackson, Mississippi.

With characteristic brevity, Raymond described his first foray into Mississippi: "I spent my time in jail; then I left."[19] But it wasn't long before he was back
in the Magnolia State with Smith, this time sitting-in at a Greyhound lunch
counter to test a recent federal court order halting the arrest of the Freedom
Riders. The two made a dramatic exit from the station after being harassed
and, in the case of Smith, brutally beaten as the police failed to protect them.[20]

Raymond's brush with violence only strengthened his resolve. Early in 1962,
he became a full-time CORE worker, going first to Greensboro, North Carolina, the site of the first sit-ins and where tensions still ran high, then moving
on to other hot spots in the area, including Raleigh and Durham, North Carolina, and Danville, Virginia.

On Easter Sunday in 1962, Raymond returned to Mississippi with a truck full of clothes and food for impoverished blacks who had been thrown off sharecropping farms for working on voter registration campaigns. One of the first people Raymond encountered was the legendary Fannie Lou Hamer, who had just begun her civil rights activism.

Raymond stayed in Ruleville with Mrs. Hamer for about a year, all the while forging deeper bonds with the community. In a letter home to his family— apparently the only written record in his own words of his early Mississippi experience—Raymond revealed his feelings about his new home. "Just a few line[s] to let you know that I am safe and still fighting for freedom," he wrote. "The Negro [has] it bad in Mississippi—some without food, some without clothes and some children are going to school without shoes because [their] parent[s] don't have any money or job and can't find one because they are trying to vote and become free." After indicating that he intended to write the family church to solicit additional help, Raymond ended the letter in spiritual terms: "Your darling son, with his hands in God['s] hand, and praying that God may throw his arm of protection around you always. Yours in freedom."[21]

While in Ruleville, Raymond deepened what would become a lifelong friendship with CORE's new Mississippi field secretary, Dave Dennis. Another Louisiana native, Dennis had been a student at Dillard University in New Orleans when the student movement emerged. Dennis quickly volunteered with CORE, joined the Freedom Rides, and, by the fall of 1961, interrupted his college education to go to work full time for the organization, first in his hometown area of Shreveport and later in Mississippi. Together, Dennis and Raymond would lean on each other as they struggled to change Mississippi's intractable racial codes.[22]

Dennis was starting a new CORE project in Canton, Mississippi, just twenty miles north of Jackson, and landed on Raymond as someone who could successfully spearhead the campaign because of his natural rapport with the local people. "George could relate," Dennis said, "and he was a hard worker."[23] By May 1963, Raymond was establishing a foothold in Canton while living with Dennis and his wife, Mattie, in Jackson. It was during this period that Raymond became familiar with the Jackson Movement.

On the day of the Jackson Woolworth's sit-in, Raymond was supposed to be only an observer—a decoy walking up and down the street to keep the police guessing about what would happen next. "George wasn't supposed to be part of the demonstration," said Dennis with a laugh. "But he got caught up in the action and went on in."[24]

So with the determination and courage he'd been building up for years, George Raymond pushed past the throng of hostile whites and police outside and entered the store. There he edged his way up to the lunch counter and fearlessly took his seat.

Tom Beard

He arrived too late to be included in the most-famous photograph, although had he been present, he would have appeared on the other side of Annie Moody, just in front of the lemonade machine. The youngest of the demonstrators that day, Tom Beard was an eighteen-year-old black high school senior working just up the street from Woolworth's at another five-and-dime. As word filtered up Capitol Street that violence had broken out at the sit-in, he abruptly left his job and hurried to the scene to see if he could help. Without thinking of the danger he might encounter, he rushed in and took his place at the counter.[25]

TOM BEARD WAS A MAN WHO WORKED MUCH TOO HARD AND FAR TOO LONG for the little bit of happiness he found in life. His involvement in the Jackson Movement would change his native city but would do little to significantly change his own social standing or economic opportunities.

Beard was born on May 11, 1945, just as World War II was winding down and Jackson was settling into a period of benign neglect regarding race relations. He grew up in an isolated section of the city known then as Baxter's Alley at the crossroads of Jefferson and Commerce streets, where the NBC-TV affiliate, WLBT, would later be housed. At that quiet spot, white and black kids played together with little if any attention to the color of their skins, so it wasn't until his first day of school that Beard had any inkling of the social apartheid practiced beyond the alley's borders.

On that day, he walked with his white friends to what he assumed was their common destination. "They went up in a school, and I went in behind," he said matter-of-factly. "Then my sister was comin' down the hall calling me. She said, 'We don't go to that school! We have to go to another school!'" When he got home that afternoon, his mother explained that because of segregation, he would attend a different school from that of his white friends. Beard had a hard time understanding why.

Beard's mother, Corrine Beard, had had her own challenges with segregation. She once worked for Westinghouse in Jackson, just around the corner from where they lived, as a maintenance clerk. Her northern boss liked her enthusiasm and work ethic and asked her to join the assembly line, putting together irons to satisfy the postwar appliance boom. The white women on the line objected, however, and rather than force her boss to make an uncomfortable choice, she decided to quit the well-paying job.

Corrine Beard commanded respect, and her example taught her son that he didn't have to feel like a second-class citizen, even though white society constantly treated him like one. She also said that, for him, fear would be a waste of energy. "You might as well not be afraid," she told him, "because if you're born a black male, anything can happen to you at any time." As a result, "I guess I didn't grow up with fear in me," Beard observed.

After his initial shock at the reality of segregation, Beard successfully matriculated at Martin Elementary in south Jackson and went on to Jim Hill High School, which then served as both a junior and senior high. When he was sixteen, just after entering his sophomore year, Beard came upon some civil rights workers on his way home from school.

The Freedom House that Freedom Riders Diane Nash and James Bevel had set up on Rose Street was directly on Beard's school route. Nash and Bevel would talk to the kids as they left school and try to get them interested in their SNCC nonviolence classes and voter registration activities. Beard immediately showed interest, became a regular at the house, and started trying to convince a wary adult black population that things would not improve unless they began to take some risks.

At first he felt that he was getting nowhere fast, but then he heard Medgar Evers speak. "I think that's when it really got started in me," Beard said. He realized that the discrimination against his mother laid the groundwork for his involvement, along with his own pent-up emotions over his station in life. "There was a lot of rage inside," he later acknowledged. "Medgar just happened to come along and push the button."

Evers was also something of an idol for the impressionable youth. His father's work required significant absences from home, so Beard may have been searching for a male role model. In Medgar Evers he found not only a strong black man but one willing to take on the racist system. "He was a person of action, not just talk," Beard said, not like some of "those people that was supposed to have been leaders at the time"—referring to the black ministers. Evers "was the only one that had the guts to stand out in front," Beard said. "A lot of things that was on my mind, he was willing to say. I think I just appreciated him having the guts to start something at that time."

As the NAACP began to take more of a leadership role with the black youth of Jackson, Beard naturally moved in that direction. He and his friends started the NAACP South Jackson Youth Council, which met in St. Peter's Missionary Baptist Church. Through that association, Beard got to know Pearlena Lewis and became a regular at the NAACP Lynch Street offices. During that time, he helped build support for the boycott by distributing leaflets in his part of town and by monitoring black shopping on Capitol Street on the weekends, reporting his findings back to Evers and John Salter.

Beard remembered hearing about the plans for the sit-in the night before, when he dropped by the NAACP offices and heard Salter, Evers, and others discussing how the events were expected to unfold. The next day, Beard was at his regular afternoon job up the street from Woolworth's at H. L. Green's, where he worked as a busboy.

He hadn't been on duty long when someone told him that all hell had broken loose at Woolworth's. When he heard about the brutal treatment that one of the students had received, Beard decided immediately that he would go to take his place at the counter. "I just dropped everything," he remembered, and walked out.

When he arrived at Woolworth's, later than all the other demonstrators, Beard found a mob in full frenzy, hysterical, out of control. He described a "crowded store" that was "stuffed full." Still, he was not deterred. He pushed his way forward, found the nearest stool, and sat down.

CHAPTER 4

OTHERS ON THE SCENE

BESIDES THE DEMONSTRATORS, THERE WERE SCORES OF OTHERS OUTSIDE OF the focal plane of the camera that shot the famous photograph of the Jackson sit-in. Some of these individuals played pivotal roles, either in what happened that day or in publicizing the event to the broader world. Their stories add to the pastiche of images assembled to tell the story of the Jackson Movement.

Detective Jim Black and the Police

He was no longer at the store when the famous photo was snapped. He had done what he was told by his superiors, broken up some of the trouble, arrested a couple of participants, and was back at police headquarters booking and fingerprinting the suspects. He would eventually rise to the highest ranks of police service in the city of Jackson, but some of his most famous arrests were made at Woolworth's on this day, just five years into his thirty-plus-year career.

JIM BLACK[1] WAS NOT THE STEREOTYPICAL SOUTHERN POLICE OFFICER WHO relished the role of race enforcer. "When I got on the police department, I had no thought in my mind of having to battle American citizens on the streets of Jackson, Mississippi," he said. Instead, he wanted to "fight criminals" and keep his native state safe. Born in 1927 and reared near Clarksdale, Mississippi, in Coahoma County in the heart of the Mississippi Delta, Black hailed from poor, white sharecropping stock. His family scratched out a living by growing cotton and corn on the plantations owned by others. His father eventually became a plantation manager, overseeing the activities of the other sharecroppers, mostly black, and ensuring that the plantation owners received their "share" of the crop. While Jim Black was young, therefore, all of his playmates, aside from his five siblings, were black. He knew the desperation of sharecropping and understood the economic deprivation that many rural families faced.

Black found his way out by joining the navy as a minor at the age of seventeen during World War II. After basic training, he was deployed into the Pacific theater and served onboard one of the battleships that bombarded Iwo Jima a few months before the invasion. After the war, Black stayed in the navy and was stationed in San Diego, California, where he met and married his wife; they would eventually have two boys together. Black was discharged from the navy just before he turned twenty-one and started working a series of jobs with the burgeoning aircraft industry. Later he became interested in police work and applied for a job with the city's police force. Then disaster struck.

The Black family had always been a bit unlucky. Their home burned down the day they drove Black to Jackson to join the navy. Now, fifteen years later, Black's wife developed ovarian cancer and died soon thereafter, leaving him a single parent of two young sons. Black realized that he'd have to move home and get help from his parents, who had since moved to Jackson, while he figured out his next steps. Soon after arriving back in Mississippi in February 1958, Black joined the Jackson Police Department. There, he was befriended by the man who would become not only his supervisor but also a beloved mentor—police captain John Lee Ray.[2]

Captain Ray himself was a native of Mississippi and had grown up in Jackson; he even graduated from Central High School in 1937. Ray joined the Jackson police force in 1941, then quickly joined the navy when the U.S. entered World War II. After serving three years, Ray was honorably discharged and was back on the beat, working in a squad car and eventually covering and getting to know every nook and cranny of the city of Jackson. Known for his hard work and dedication, Ray earned only about a hundred dollars a month and worked twelve-hour shifts, seven days a week. Until serious illness struck in 1965, Ray never missed a day of work. Thanks in large part to that kind of commitment to his job, Ray was put on the fast track to the upper echelon of the force, first making desk sergeant in 1950, then lieutenant two years later. In 1956 he was promoted to captain, a managerial position that oversaw the day-to-day duties of some of the uniformed policemen.

Ray came to national prominence during the Freedom Rides, and it was largely his strategy and leadership that kept the kinds of violent outbursts that occurred in Alabama from happening in Mississippi during this period. Ray's concept was simple: enforce the law. If Freedom Riders were breaking the law—even if that law was under dispute—arrest them. It was, thus, thanks to John Lee Ray that more than three hundred Freedom Riders, including Joan Trumpauer and George Raymond, ended up in Mississippi jails in 1961. In appreciation for his adept handling of the Freedom Ride situation, the city of Jackson promoted Ray to a newly created position of deputy chief of police. From this position of prominence, Ray would oversee all of the uniformed police on the Jackson force and would also be on hand for nearly every significant demonstration in Jackson during the next six years. Jim Black had indeed found a powerful ally and mentor.

Thanks in large part to Ray's tutelage, as well as Black's own natural curiosity and hard work, Black himself was promoted to the rank of detective in less than five years, an anomaly at the time. Black's advancement, also in late 1962, came just at the right time for his superior. Ray asked the newly minted detective to go undercover and begin spying on the activities of the city's civil rights organizations so that the police could have the inside information they would need to maintain order. By the time of the Woolworth's sit-in, Black had already begun to pose as a reporter and was accompanying other reporters, particularly W. C. Shoemaker[3] of the *Jackson Daily News,* to picketing and whatever public meetings the Jackson Movement was holding. Besides looking the part of a newsman, with stenographer's pad and pen in hand and a classic fedora on his head, Black was also wired for sound. The police department would, on occasion, outfit Black with undercover sound equipment so that the meetings he attended could be transmitted to a receiving station located in a police vehicle nearby. The "wire" had the added advantage of allowing Black the failsafe measure of calling for immediate backup should it be needed.

On the morning of May 28, 1963, Black was called by Ray—still police captain at this point—at about 11:00 a.m. and told to report to the downtown area in his undercover garb. Black was instructed to go into the store incognito and watch for any trouble that might occur. At about noon, Black made it onto Capitol Street and entered Woolworth's. Trouble found him soon enough.

Bill Minor and the Reporters

He wasn't there when the demonstrators first arrived; instead he was safely ensconced in the political reporters' lair—the press room in the state capitol building a few blocks away. A friend and fellow reporter tipped him off that something was happening down at Woolworth's, so Bill Minor, the Jackson-based veteran reporter for the New Orleans Times-Picayune, *grabbed his notepad and ever-present hat and headed over to Capitol Street.*

HE WAS CALLED "THE CONSCIENCE OF MISSISSIPPI"[4] MORE TIMES THAN HE cared to remember, but that's what happens when you've covered a beat longer than most people have been alive. A native of neighboring Louisiana, Bill Minor[5] started covering Mississippi politics in 1947 when the *Times-Picayune* assigned him to its Jackson bureau. By this time already a seasoned reporter, Minor had begun learning his craft at the *Bogalusa (LA) Enterprise* starting in 1939, the same year he entered Tulane University. He started working as a stringer for the *Times-Picayune* while pursuing a degree in journalism at Tulane. Graduating in 1943, Minor, too, joined the U.S. Navy to help America fight World War II. He saw extensive fighting in the central and south Pacific from the deck of a destroyer as an ensign.

Once back from the war, Minor picked up his pen again and began working for the New Orleans paper full time. His first assignment in Mississippi that fateful summer of 1947 was covering the funeral of the virulent segregationist Theodore Bilbo, who had ruled the state twice as governor and had been its U.S. senator for twelve years. It was one of Minor's many encounters with the racial politics of his adopted state. He also covered the Emmett Till trial in 1955, and was on the scene when the Freedom Riders rolled in six years later. His was an interesting conundrum; he was a white native southerner who, just like Joan Trumpauer, began to see that the values his culture espoused did not match what his now much-heralded conscience believed to be right and just. Yet, as a reporter, he was required to report as objectively as possible without allowing his opinion to color the facts. Eventually, he would solve this problem by becoming a syndicated political columnist and his "Eyes on Mississippi" would be widely read throughout the state. But that would be years in the future. Still a reporter as the civil rights struggle began to heat up, he could only use his blow-by-blow reporting to bludgeon home the fact that the South was out of step with the rest of the country and that something needed to change.

Minor was not alone in this dilemma. There were a handful of news reporters stationed in Jackson for various news outlets who had similar twinges of conscience, some of whom also arrived at Woolworth's just as the tension was starting to escalate.

Ken Toler,[6] the reporter who tipped Minor off about the Woolworth's demonstration, worked for the Memphis *Commercial Appeal*. Minor and Toler often showed up at the same events and stood together observing as the action unfolded. "[Ken] and I would work together a lot,"[7] said Minor.

By then, Toler was considered the "dean of Mississippi newsmen."[8] A native of Louisiana and a journalism graduate from Louisiana State University, Toler began covering and living in Mississippi in 1927 when the Associated Press stationed him in Jackson. Toler jumped to the *Commercial Appeal* in 1932 and became its bureau chief there. Known as "Mr. Mississippi"[9] to his colleagues, Toler covered the state's politics, its economy, and its way of life and was friend and advisor to many of its top politicians. Toler was considered a fair and balanced reporter, and didn't flinch in reporting about Mississippi's racial tensions. So it was no surprise that he and Minor hit it off.

Another local reporter, Cliff Sessions,[10] was no stranger to the race beat, as it was called, and would also be on hand at Woolworth's. A native of Mississippi, Sessions worked for United Press International (UPI), an international news service whose stories were picked up by newspapers across the globe. Like Minor, Sessions lived in Jackson and was a regular at all of the civil rights events that were occurring with more frequency within the state. Sessions also had the distinction of having established a personal relationship with Medgar Evers—one which served both men well over the years. Evers would provide tips to Sessions to help advance the NAACP agenda, and Sessions would write stories with an insider's view that would help advance his journalism career. In fact, in 1958, Sessions wrote a full-blown profile of Evers for UPI, the first of any major news organization to draw attention to the civil rights leader. Sessions and his wife had even socialized with the Everses, being so bold as to invite the two prominent blacks to their home for cocktails. (When Evers tried to reciprocate by inviting the white reporter to his home, Sessions begged off, recognizing the danger he could be inviting to both families.)

Like Minor, Sessions was raised in a southern household and was taught that segregation was part of the natural order. He began to question this assumption once he started reporting on the horrific race stories he encountered throughout the South. Sessions and Minor were part of a small vanguard of liberal reporters who would gain sustenance from each other while facing the incredibly harsh social stigma of being progressives in a society dominated by reactionaries.

A fourth reporter within Minor's orbit who would also appear at Woolworth's was W. C. (Dub) Shoemaker. Unlike the others, Shoemaker was firmly in the segregationist camp, as evidenced by his employer, the *Jackson Daily News*. The afternoon *News*, as well as the morning *Clarion-Ledger*, were owned by the socially prominent and politically conservative Hederman family, whose media empire of TV, radio, and newspapers launched them into the inner circles of political and commercial power within the state. Their newspapers reflected the family's reactionary beliefs. The *News* in particular used its editorial page and its news analysts to fan the flames of racial paranoia and suspicion. Shoemaker's beliefs fit comfortably within his organization's culture. Even so, his own code of journalistic ethics pushed him to "gather the news and pass it on fully and fairly."[11] As such—and somewhat surprisingly given the environment he worked in—Shoemaker's reporting from Woolworth's would be some of the most detailed and thorough of all the reporters on the scene that day.

When Bill Minor heard from Ken Toler that a demonstration was under way on Capitol Street, he casually made his way from his state capitol office, walking the two blocks to Woolworth's. Some of his fellow reporters were already there; others would arrive later. They would all get caught up in the "ugly"[12] scene that would ensue, and then use their training to get the word out to the broader world that something new and unusual was beginning to stir in Mississippi. But none of these four newsmen had any idea that the story they were about to cover would set in motion events that would dramatically impact Jackson's delicate racial balance.

Ed King

His still-intact face cannot be found in the most famous sit-in photograph, but he was in the store at that moment, doing what he could to keep the violence from escalating, urging the police to take action, lending support to the demonstrators under fire. He appears prominently in a later photo, taken just after the mob had dispersed. In it he dominates the scene—the Methodist minister in priestly garb, tending to his flock. He holds Joan Trumpauer's glasses in one hand and wipes John Salter's bloodied cheek with the other, while Annie Moody and Tom Beard look on, dazed and bewildered by what they had just been through.

This sit-in is the first of many Mississippi demonstrations that the Reverend Ralph Edwin (Ed) King, Jr., would join as he struggled to ease the racial animosity deepening in his home state. At first reluctantly—and then boldly—he would become the only native-born white clergyman to stand firmly against segregation. His radical choices would cost him his good looks, his friendships with Mississippi moderates, his lifelong dream of pastoring a church, and nearly his life. None of this is known to him as he steps forward to the Woolworth's counter, a model of Christian virtue, to give aid and comfort to the afflicted.[13]

HE BECAME A WALKING HISTORY OF THE CIVIL RIGHTS MOVEMENT IN MIS-sissippi, participating as he did in nearly every key event from the time he settled there in February 1963 until the movement imploded after James Meredith's 1966 March Against Fear. He was there for most of its great triumphs and tragedies, both a casualty of and an enduring testament to the upheaval. He was a born storyteller and would tell layer upon layer of stories—about himself and his family, his beloved South, and the movement to which he devoted his life. These rich, textured tales meander far and wide, like the Mississippi River itself, but eventually come around to the point, all the richer for the journey.

Ed King was born almost literally on that river, in a hospital high on a bluff in the city of Vicksburg. As a boy, the stories told to him by his elder relatives and neighbors made a deep impression on him: stories about the deprivation his family suffered during the Civil War, stories of the terrible "Yankee torture" the city endured as the people of Vicksburg starved while General U. S. Grant and the Union army laid siege to the place. King was a southerner through and through, which is all the more reason for surprise over the path he eventually chose.

His father, Ralph King, had moved from Louisiana to Vicksburg in the early 1930s for a job with the U.S. Army Corps of Engineers. He was introduced to Julia Tucker by mutual friends. They fell in love and married in 1935.

On September 20, 1936, Ed was the first of two boys born into this genteel southern family of modest means, not far, in fact, from where Myrlie Evers was growing up.

King's boyhood was spent near the Vicksburg battlefield. As a youth, he hiked areas where soldiers had fought and died. Such closeness to death caused him to think deeply about war and violence. In fact, one of his earliest heroes was Mohandas Gandhi. "My pacifism came earlier than my feelings about race," King explained.

As a youth, King had learned to accept the common segregationist wisdom of "separate but equal," and even participated in its contradictions. He accepted the chiding of his teachers when they urged their white charges to care for their already well-worn band uniforms and schoolbooks because the following year they would be passed on to the "colored" schoolchildren. "We thought this was just great Christian charity," he recalled.

Then, in his senior year of high school, during the 1953 Christmas season, a tornado swept through a substantial part of Vicksburg. The tornado killed blacks and whites indiscriminately, including one of King's classmates. But it was the aftermath that really caught King's attention. Black homes caught fire and burned to the ground because fire trucks could not maneuver the unpaved, narrow, muddy roads into the black neighborhoods. Rescue teams also had difficulty negotiating the hills and bluffs down to the black district. King witnessed the damage up close as he volunteered with his church group and the Red Cross to aid victims of the disaster. "I saw enormous poverty that had always been there," he would later recall, "but I hadn't seen it." The experience caused him to question why blacks bore a disproportionate share of the suffering. Like Joan Trumpauer, King began to realize that the "equal" half of the "separate but equal" equation wasn't holding up.

FROM AN EARLY AGE KING ATTENDED METHODIST YOUTH EDUCATION PROgrams, where he found a broader context for his questioning of social conditions. By the time he graduated from high school, he had decided upon a career in the ministry.

In the fall of 1954, he entered Millsaps College, a generously endowed Methodist liberal arts institution near downtown Jackson. At Millsaps, the race question often came up for discussion and, one by one, the defenses of segregation that King had always taken for granted were stripped away. At Millsaps, he met Tougaloo's Dr. Ernst Borinski, who in those days was holding joint classes with students from both colleges. Later, after one of his Social Science Forums at Tougaloo, Borinski introduced the undergrad to Medgar Evers, who courted King as a potential ally, careful never to expose him to ideas or literature that might seem too radical, but always trying to lead him one step at a time to a deeper understanding of the race issue. "He was very warm, very friendly,"

King said of Evers, "almost treating me like he was an older brother . . . to sort of pull me along."

By the end of his college years, King had determined that, like many white moderates, he would have to leave the South and never return. By then, the spring of 1958, the Citizens' Council had fully infiltrated polite white society and silenced any moderate views on race. King had experienced its tactics firsthand: his college room was ransacked and integration literature stolen, presumably by students paid to spy on him and other liberal classmates. He had also heard about calls made by Council members to parents of his class-mates who were considering going north for their college education. The par-ents were told that their children would never find work back in Mississippi if they decided to return.

King had already informed his Methodist bishop of his interest in the min-istry and had asked to receive theological training at Boston University, which was home to one of the most radical theology schools in the country. The Millsaps faculty members he most respected had graduated from there, and he was also keenly aware that this was the graduate school from which another hero, Martin Luther King, Jr., had received his doctorate and his training in the pacifist tradition. The idealistic aspiring minister had seen Dr. King's han-dling of the Montgomery bus boycott as a "sign of immense hope" in applying Gandhian principles to America's race problem. The thought of learning from the same teachers that Dr. King had studied under thrilled the younger King. Although he assumed that he would never be able to practice his ministry in the South, he fostered a wistful hope that somehow a window would open that would enable him to return.

At BU, King got caught up in its intellectual and activist spirit. He became involved in the Fellowship of Reconciliation's local chapter and worked with the Quakers and other progressive groups. During a trip home for Christmas in 1958, he rode in an integrated car through the South and visited Dr. King's church in Montgomery, where he and his traveling companions dined with the civil rights champion and his family.

In January 1959, the aspiring minister attended a week-long seminar on nonviolence at FOR's headquarters in Nyack, New York, where he was any-thing but a cooperative student. In the role-playing exercises, Ed King could not go along with the idea that southern policemen would stand by while seg-regationists verbally and physically assaulted nonviolent demonstrators—a situation he would witness firsthand at Jackson's Woolworth's four years later. King reacted even more strongly when asked to portray an abusive cop. "I insisted that policemen would not curse at anyone, much less be brutal," he admitted with a laugh years later. "They finally had to give up on me."

King's education continued the next year when FOR sent him back to Mont-gomery to help build bridges between the city's white and black communities, primarily between clergy and students. While in Montgomery, King attended a private luncheon in a black-owned restaurant with some black clergy and white Methodist college students visiting from Illinois. The police must have been tipped off to this violation of the state's Jim Crow laws because the group was arrested, tried, and convicted of disorderly conduct and breach of the peace. King later found out that police had been trailing him since his arrival.

The arrest had significant consequences for King's family back in Vicksburg when the story made national news. Although his parents did not share King's beliefs and remained segregationists themselves, they were attacked by the Citizens' Council and the John Birch Society. Neighbors and church members stopped speaking to them, and King's younger brother was taunted at school. By the fall, the family reluctantly moved to Memphis, Tennessee. Ralph King died not long afterwards—his demise hastened, King believed, by the stress of the circumstances. Julia King never moved back to her native state.

Eventually, King returned to Boston to continue his graduate studies in theology, but he came back regularly to Alabama on behalf of FOR and Dr. King's Southern Christian Leadership Conference. At one point he was arrested, again for attempting to have a meal with a black minister, but this time he was sentenced to thirty days' hard labor. For King, a "jail, not bail" Gandhian in theory, the experience of extreme physical labor in the hot Alabama sun caused him to pray to be bailed out after only a few days. Bail money was finally secured after about a week and he was released.

The arrest led to an intrusion into King's personal life. While he was being booked, police searched his luggage at his hotel and discovered he was engaged to a Mississippi social worker employed by the state welfare department. King had met Jeannette Sylvester, a Jackson resident, at Methodist youth gatherings during high school. Their friendship deepened while both attended Millsaps, and they kept in touch during King's travels to Boston and Alabama.

While in jail for the second time and unaware that police now had information about his fiancée, King granted an interview to a Montgomery reporter, hoping to clear up the inaccurate report that he was a northern agitator. His strategy backfired, however, when the reporter instead photographed him returning to his cell in black-and-white-striped prison garb. The story and photo became front-page news in the Jackson papers, along with information about his soon-to-be bride. As a result, the minister of the church where they were to be married canceled the ceremony, fearing a bomb attack. The couple settled for a quiet wedding on the Millsaps campus with a few friends and family. Then it was back to Boston for King's final year of graduate school.

Ed King graduated from Boston University in May 1961 with a master's degree in theology, then returned briefly to Jackson to discuss his future with his bishop and to be ordained into the Methodist ministry. Since the bishop was unwilling to assign King to a pulpit in Mississippi, he was pleased to hear that the young theology student had decided to continue his education in Boston—not realizing that King was still hoping for an appropriate opportunity to open up in his home state. Before administering holy orders, however, the bishop offered King a halfway measure for his future: ordination to the priesthood without admission into the Mississippi Methodist Conference. This unusual procedure, called ordination without "full connection," meant that King would not have full voting rights within the group, the right to speak at state Methodist assemblies, nor the ability to speak publicly on behalf of the Mississippi Methodist Church. Knowing he could have done much worse given his arrest record, King accepted the bargain, grateful that at least he would become a full-fledged minister, which at the time was his primary goal.

The Kings returned to Boston so that Ed could begin work on a second master's degree in social ethics, while waiting for an opening in Mississippi. They didn't have to wait long. The Tougaloo College chaplain hired the year before was not working out, so Dr. Beittel was in search of someone to be chaplain as well as dean of students. Ernst Borinski suggested King for the job; Medgar Evers added his support; and even his Methodist bishop agreed. "[He was] so relieved not to have to put me in a white church," King later would scoff.

When he visited Tougaloo for an interview in November and saw what the Salters were doing with the campus movement and the NAACP youth council, King realized that this was exactly the kind of break he had been praying for. He accepted the job, and after finishing the semester at BU, he and Jeannette moved home to Mississippi in February 1963.

King's appointment was not without controversy, as he was the first white chaplain for the Tougaloo students since the early days of the college. "I think because he was a white native Mississippian," Annie Moody wrote, "almost every student at Tougaloo doubted him at the time. I remember I used to look at [Jeannette] going in and out of the chapel after visiting [him] there and just hate the thought of a white southern minister and his wife taking over the most beautiful and cherished building on campus."[14]

Whatever initial reservations the students may have had, King soon quieted them by his full support of movement activities. He kept a low profile at first, not wanting to interfere in the dynamics of what seemed to him an impressively organized effort by John Salter. King, however, frequently visited the Salters' home, just a few steps away from his chaplain's quarters, to stay informed of activities of the youth council and the progress of the Capitol Street boycott. By late April, King was beginning to attend strategy committee meetings and trying to serve as a bridge between white and black ministers in Jackson, just as he had in Montgomery three years earlier.

When it became clear that negotiations between movement activists and the city leaders were going nowhere, he concurred with the decision for direct action and volunteered to serve as the spotter for the sit-in at Woolworth's.

On the morning of May 28, before the demonstrators arrived, King entered the store and took his place among the plastic placemats and other household displays. He would not be among those sitting-in, but he was surely there to take a stand.

CHAPTER 5

NORTH JACKSON ACTION

THE JACKSON MOVEMENT CAME INTO BEING THROUGH THE CONFLUENCE OF varied forces and personalities that by synchronistic convergence found themselves pushing in the same direction for social change. There was Medgar Evers, the NAACP man who had been on the ground in Mississippi for the better part of ten years and who, like Sisyphus, had been working for change each day only to see his efforts unravel with each new vengeful twist of Mississippi's social fabric. There was the NAACP organization itself, which sought a way to remain relevant in an era of increasingly dramatic advances by what it considered upstarts—competing organizations like CORE, SNCC, and Martin Luther King's SCLC. There were the CORE workers and SNCC volunteers themselves whose idealism was infectious and who believed change could happen quickly, even in Mississippi, if enough youthful enthusiasm and audacious tactics could be employed to shock the tired and inflexible system into a new social consciousness.

In addition, there was Tougaloo College, which by its very existence challenged the state's cultural mores by demonstrating that a more egalitarian society was, in fact, possible without significant social upheaval. There were the thousands of young blacks in Jackson, who, through the power of mass media, were witnessing change occurring elsewhere, and who wanted to be part of bringing that new wave of change to their home state and city. There were the black adults—some ministers, some NAACP volunteers—who were becoming more emboldened by seeing the changes occurring all around them and hoping such change would also one day be theirs.

There were a few sympathetic native white adults like Ed King who were also looking for a way to advance the cause of freedom by consciously deciding to return home and actively work for it. And, yes, there were several "outside agitators" like John Salter, who had been part of other social movements and wanted to help usher in a new openness through dramatic, targeted, persistent pressure.

All of these varied forces converged on Jackson at what appeared to be an opportunistic time and set in motion a flood of activity that would, in fact, jolt an intransigent system into a senseless, violent, and ultimately unsuccessful defense of the existing order.

There is no doubt that Medgar Evers, as his secretary Lillian Louie was quick to point out, served as "the overall director of everything"[1] that happened in the Jackson Movement. He couldn't have achieved the full-fledged "movement" status, however, without the help of a few key lieutenants. First among these was John Salter, whom historian John Dittmer has called "the chief strategist" of the Jackson Movement.[2] As an outsider, Salter didn't feel bound by the bureaucratic traditions of the NAACP, which required substantial approvals prior to any action, particularly for youth activities. So Salter forged ahead, crafting a strategy for the youth council that would gradually build to a crescendo and directly challenge the city's strict racial codes.

Salter collaborated closely with Evers as he worked his plan with the Jackson youth. "We'd keep him posted,"[3] Salter acknowledged. "He had good faith in us." Ed King believed that, in fact, Evers "was letting John and the Tougaloo students make the decisions" so that he could deny them, if necessary, to the NAACP national leadership. "But [those decisions] were never made without his [Evers's] knowledge," King said, "and never made over his objections."[4]

And so, while Evers went about his daily duties as statewide NAACP field secretary—a broad portfolio of work that left little time for much else—Salter focused his energies on crafting a movement out of little more than a few high school and college kids, a mimeograph machine and, of course, the auspices of the most-heralded civil rights organization in the country.

It can be said, then, that the story of the Jackson Movement began with John Salter on that hot, humid Mississippi afternoon in mid-September 1962 when he sat down at his old Underwood typewriter, sweat dripping from his face, to bang out the first issue of the youth council's newsletter, *North Jackson Action*. Salter could not have known at this point that, by the end of the school year, he and his small band of high school and college followers—with the initial tacit approval and eventual wholehearted embrace of Medgar Evers and the adult branch of the Jackson NAACP—would bring a firestorm to the city. All that was clear at the time was Salter's intent to apply every lesson learned from his hard-fought earlier battles to this new battleground.

Before Salter could really get things going, however, both the state of Mississippi and the nation were thrown into turmoil over the James Meredith case—with Medgar Evers right in the middle.[5] Meredith was a black Mississippian who had been seeking admission to the all-white University of Mississippi since January 1961 when, as a student at Jackson State College, he had contacted Evers to see if the NAACP would back his effort. At Evers's urging, the NAACP had taken up the Meredith case as a challenge to Mississippi's segregationist codes, with Constance Baker Motley of the NAACP's Legal Defense Fund as chief attorney. While the more public activities were handled by the

NAACP national office, Evers worked behind the scenes, including counseling Meredith on a regular basis and shuttling among Meredith's home in New Orleans, the university campus at Oxford, and Evers's own home in Jackson. After much legal maneuvering, a federal court ruled in early September 1962 that Meredith must be admitted.

As it became apparent that the federal government would back Meredith's admission with force if necessary, Governor Ross Barnett and the state legislature grew increasingly belligerent in their efforts to block the university's integration. For the entire month of September, local and national newspapers were filled with the unfolding drama. Three times, Meredith, accompanied by federal marshals and John Doar of the U.S. Justice Department, attempted to register—twice at Oxford and once in Jackson at the offices of the university's board of trustees. Three times, Meredith's efforts were rebuffed by Barnett, Lieutenant Governor Paul Johnson, the state legislature, and an outraged white populace. A fourth effort was aborted before Meredith reached the Ole Miss campus because of the armed white mob that had gathered there.

Finally, on the fifth try, on Sunday, September 30, after Barnett had been enjoined from blocking the doors under threat of arrest, a deal was struck with the Kennedy administration that Barnett hoped would help him save face with his constituents. Meredith would be surreptitiously brought onto the campus early Sunday evening and registered—without resistance from state or university officials—the following day. Instead of a peaceful scenario, however, a riot broke out on campus Sunday night once students and the white agitators gathered there learned that Meredith was in their midst.

It seems that everyone in Mississippi at the time can remember that month of turmoil and where they were when they heard news of Meredith's admission. In a letter to fellow white activist Anne Braden, Joan Trumpauer described the mood on Tougaloo's campus in late September after one of Meredith's failed registration attempts, this time in Jackson:

Today has been like Alice in Wonderland—totally unreal. Studying was impossible. We kept the radio low, listening for the frequent interruptions reporting the latest on the Meredith case. These came at least every 20 minutes. By 3:15—if not earlier—we just gave up on lessons. Between news flashes, we talked about our own experiences with life in the South and about Meredith.

From the time [Meredith] arrived to the time Gov. Barnett left by the back door there was live TV coverage. It was so unreal that sometimes it didn't seem possible.

The little scene when Meredith and his escort arrived at the door and were greeted by the Governor was such that you almost expected him to ask them to come in and stay for supper. But when Meredith stepped forward to hear Barnett read his proclamation and again deny him entry to Ole Miss, I just wanted to cry.

After the Governor left, we went to the dining hall and sang "We Shall Overcome." Then, at an integrated school just 3 miles from the city where the Governor had defied the Supreme Court to preserve school segregation in the state, students from Tougaloo and Millsaps sat down together and watched the news before holding a meeting of their intercollegiate, inter-racial Africa Study Group. Some of us couldn't help remembering the times Meredith had come to similar meetings in the same room—and now. . . . such a fuss and furor over something we know could be accomplished so easily: students studying together to gain a greater understanding of what it means to be a Man.[6]

Two people died in the riot that ensued when Meredith was brought onto the Old Miss campus the night before his successful registration. And although he endured severe ostracism, harassment, and threats on his life—and required the protection of federal marshals during his entire year on campus[7]—Meredith's entrance into the state's most hallowed educational institution signaled that the walls of the closed society were beginning to crack.

THE FIRST ISSUE OF *NORTH JACKSON ACTION*,[8] DATED SEPTEMBER 22, 1962, WAS published in the middle of the Meredith crisis. "Let's be Free by '63!" it proclaimed, echoing the NAACP's slogan marking the one-hundred-year anniversary of the Emancipation Proclamation. Many black youth throughout Mississippi interpreted Meredith's entrance into Ole Miss as a sign of hope for the future; John Salter wanted to build on that enthusiasm with a plan to break down segregation's hold on the state's capital city.

North Jackson Action was a mimeographed, typically two-paged announcement sheet that seems as harmless as a church newsletter. But from the start, this "official bulletin of the North Jackson Youth Council," as its masthead read, was nothing less than a call for revolution against the established order. In that first issue, Salter laid out a two-pronged approach to enhance participation in the youth council and to set the stage for a boycott. First, he proposed that the council initiate a "community educational program" that would attract additional young people into the group. The programs, announced in the bulletin, would focus on how other groups had organized for social change, while providing an enjoyable and liberating environment in which the youth could discuss their feelings about Mississippi's racist system. Second, through newsletter articles and discussion groups, Salter focused the youth council's attention on the inequities of the state's employment practices.

At the youth council's meeting in mid-September, Pearlena Lewis was elected president, and Cleveland Donald, then a Brinkley High School student, became vice president. Pearlena's younger brother, Alphonzo, also was involved from the outset. At the council's next meeting, on September 27, Salter began to put in place the pieces of a long-term strategy for a boycott by pushing through a resolution identifying Mississippi's "extreme prejudice and discrimination against Negro workers and consumers" and calling for "study and appropriate negotiations and direct action in the very near future."[9]

With Pearlena Lewis's many contacts, it wasn't hard to draw a crowd to the first community education program, held in early October at the Virden Grove Baptist Church in her family's north Jackson neighborhood. Salter had convinced Medgar Evers that, for the education program to be effective, the NAACP needed to purchase a movie projector so that the council could rent films for its members to view and discuss. Evers consented, with the proviso that the projector be bought on installment and that the youth council make payments out of the dues and donations the activities would generate. Salter and Lewis agreed and planned to show *Salt of the Earth*, the story of the Mine-Mill successful mining strike, at the first meeting.

Instead, Evers decided to attend and be the program's first speaker. Fresh from the Meredith victory, Evers discussed this precedent-setting case at length and considered its ramifications for the thirty or so young people in the room. He also praised the youth council for the community work upon which they were embarking. Then Salter turned the discussion to fair employment practices, and he, Evers, and Pearlena Lewis led a discussion about the need to push ahead with reforms. Lewis formed a committee to study the employment policies and service practices of the city's white stores toward black customers; the committee was to report its findings at the council's next meeting.[10]

Evers's decision to speak at the first of these community outreach programs suggests that he recognized the potential in what Salter and the youth council were starting. Doris Allison, a local NAACP volunteer and staunch Evers ally, wondered if Evers might also have wanted to keep an eye on what Salter was up to. "He [Medgar] would always say, 'I trust him this much [using her thumb and index finger to show a large measurement] but I hold this much in reserve' [indicating a smaller measurement]."[11] According to Allison, Evers maintained a small degree of skepticism about Salter's activities and intentions, at least at first.

The youth council decided to have community meetings every other week, but to have weekly membership meetings. *North Jackson Action* was also initially published weekly. As its circulation increased and as the youth council's officers encouraged their friends to join the community education programs, the youth council grew. Salter ordered such thought-provoking films from his union connections as *The Color of Man*, *You Can't Run Away* (a shortened version of *Intruder in the Dust*), *The New Girl*, and *People of the Cumberland*. Each film, dealing with either race relations or people organizing to improve their lives, sparked lively discussions among the teens and attracted additional members.[12]

The youth council also decided to support the second annual boycott of the segregated Mississippi State Fair, which Medgar Evers and the local NAACP, along with some SNCC and Tougaloo students, had initiated the previous year. Youth council members distributed leaflets and started a phone-calling tree. *North Jackson Action* carried notices entreating blacks to boycott the fair; in one article, Salter urged local blacks not to attend because of the upsurge in assaults on blacks across the state since the Meredith crisis. Evers issued an NAACP press release as well, calling on all black Mississippians to stay away.

With more publicity and a stronger explanation of why blacks should not attend, the boycott was more effective the second time around. And the North Jackson Youth Council, along with some other groups—including a contingent of activists from Tougaloo—could take credit for this increased success. With that, the students began to realize that their efforts could have an impact without much help from the grownups. They were beginning to learn important lessons about the power of involvement and group effort and standing their ground, and Salter was ready to take them to the next level.

His launching of the *North Jackson Action* newsletter had been a way to keep Evers, the adult branch of the Jackson NAACP, and even the NAACP's national office informed of the youth council's activities. The bulletin also provided news to the world outside of Mississippi's insular society and served as a fund-raising tool for council activities, beginning with a page-two story, "The Chips Are Down in Mississippi,"[13] in early October. It was the first time the council had solicited funds in the publication and the first time the newsletter was expanded to three pages. In the solicitation, the council listed its projects, including educational sessions, voter registration efforts, the state fair boycott, and the study of employment practices. Then came the plea for financial aid: "Our North Jackson Youth Council desperately needs financial help—and we ask you to help us."[14] Funds were to be sent to Pearlena Lewis's address, and Salter and Lewis planned to follow up with a letter to all newsletter recipients, including some of Salter's well-heeled union contacts and family members.[15]

It took a while, but by early November, funds began to trickle in from student groups, labor unions, and individuals from all over the country.[16] Although the donations were generally small—most under ten dollars except for a hundred- dollar donation from a Canadian labor group—they helped pay for newsletter production and postage and the monthly payments on the film projector. Perhaps more importantly, news of what was going on in Jackson was making its way to a widespread group of individuals and organizations. The letters of support that accompanied the contributions often appeared in the newsletter and boosted the morale of the students, helping them realize they were not alone in this struggle. Strangely, though, there was no letter of encouragement from the NAACP's national office, despite Salter's insistence that the New York office was on his regular mailing list.[17]

Also in early November, the NAACP held its annual statewide conference in Jackson. The North Jackson Youth Council played a prominent role in the concurrent statewide youth council conference, and Salter and the youth council officers found opportunities to be of service to the adult chapters, including showing off their new projector. As a result of their involvement, the North Jackson Youth Council received a commendation from the Mississippi adult branches, and *North Jackson Action* was singled out for praise as an exemplary youth council publication.[18]

At the conference, Salter led a workshop for the adults on discriminatory employment practices, setting the stage for them to support the Capitol Street boycott he and Evers were already planning. Salter also got his first glimpse of the regional and national staff. Ruby Hurley, the southeast regional coordinator and Evers's immediate supervisor, gave the keynote address at the Freedom Fund Dinner, and NAACP leader Roy Wilkins addressed a larger crowd the following day at the Masonic Temple. Both Gloster Current, national director of branches, and Laplois Ashford, national director of youth activities, were also on hand. Salter had the opportunity to meet all of these organizational leaders while demonstrating what he had done with only a small group of young people and limited resources. Ashford in particular seemed interested in building on the momentum. "Try to get something going around here," he told Salter.[19]

After the conference, however, Salter felt a sense of disappointment. "I had the feeling that we had possibly planted a few seeds," he wrote in his memoir of the period, "but it was also clear that no grassroots revolution was going to develop in Mississippi in the near future." In particular, he felt that although the young people seemed ready to take on whatever was to come, the adults had little "if any intention of challenging the system."[20] Salter was looking to throw the throttle into overdrive, while most were content to let it idle in neutral. Characteristically, he plugged away and hoped something would cause a spark.

LUCK PLAYED A HAND IN THE DEVELOPMENT OF THE JACKSON MOVEMENT, AS well, when William Kunstler, the noted New York civil liberties attorney, showed up at Tougaloo to visit his daughter, Karin, late in the fall of 1962. Karin had heard of Tougaloo through press coverage of the freedom rides and determined to spend her sophomore year "abroad" on the Mississippi college's campus. Kunstler later wrote that he was "intensely disturbed by her decision," both because he understood how deeply most white Mississippians detested integrationists and because her last name might stir additional resentment. Although he apparently made no effort to stop his daughter from attending Tougaloo, Kunstler visited the campus a number of times that fall to see how she was faring. During one of those visits, Karin took him to meet the Salters.

When John Salter told Kunstler about his plans for the boycott, the lawyer offered his assistance if legal help were needed. With Kunstler as an ally, Salter felt more assured about his plans to launch a full-scale boycott.[21]

Medgar Evers had a few tricks up his own sleeve as the new year approached. With the longtime president of the Jackson NAACP branch in poor health, Evers saw the opportunity to replace him with someone willing to take bolder steps than the local branch had done previously. He needed a leader with vision and guts, someone he could trust implicitly; he decided the person he wanted was Doris Allison.

A Jackson native ten years older than Evers, Allison had been an NAACP regular for years before Gloster Current came to town late in 1954 to announce the association's pick to head the new Mississippi office. "It was a big semi-circle on stage," she remembered, and from the start of the meeting, she had been wondering, "How did that little boy get up there with all of them old men?" When Current said that the "boy"—the twenty-nine-year- old Medgar Evers—would be the first field secretary for the state, she couldn't believe her ears. "I need to get out of here, Ben," she snapped at her husband. He made her stay until the meeting ended, but Allison was still furious at Current. "When we came on home, boy, I fussed and I raised sand," she said. "It's open season on the Negro, and that man from New York knows that. Why would he come down here and try to talk this little ole boy into going into something of this magnitude? What could that little boy do with this system?" She felt that Evers was being set up for failure and that his appointment was an insult; she aimed to tell him so—just after he got settled in.[22]

A few weeks later, Allison made an appointment to raise her objections with Evers directly, but she never had the chance. "He would start to talking," she recalled, "and every time I would see him, he would let me know right off for real what was on his mind. He was going to break these shackles here in Mississippi. And I said to myself, 'How in the world does he think he's going to do this?'"

Despite her reservations, Allison was won over by Evers's considerable charm and conviction. She began visiting him almost daily at his office to get information and see if she could help. But when she began to fear she was taking up too much of his time, Allison decided to stay away for a few days. To her surprise, Evers called to ask her why she hadn't been around. "Lord, I was thrilled!" she gushed. She felt needed and never again questioned her usefulness.

After working together for years, Evers must have felt confident that Allison would be a strong leader of the adult branch, but when he asked her to take the job, she immediately declined. "Mr. Evers, you know I don't know anything about the functioning of this organization," she protested. Although she was a stalwart NAACP member—and there weren't that many in Jackson at the time—Allison had never attended a board meeting or participated in the inner workings of the Jackson branch. To her mind, she and Evers were just friends, and she was a good volunteer.[23]

Evers thought differently and devised a plan to win her acceptance. He asked her to attend a meeting of the board in late November 1962, saying there was something he wanted to discuss that he thought would interest her. At first Allison said she didn't think she could make it, but after some friends on the board kept dropping hints, she decided to go with her husband to find out what was up.

Evers wasn't there when the meeting began, which Allison thought a bit strange. As the board took up its business, she just sat quietly and figured she'd talk to Evers when he arrived about why he wanted her there. Eventually the discussion turned to nominations for a new president. Since she wasn't on the board, Allison didn't pay much attention to that matter either. When the nominating committee suggested her name, she was stunned. Then the full board voted unanimously for her to become president. Evers came rushing in afterwards, feigning an excuse for not being there earlier and congratulating her on her election. "I was so weak I couldn't even walk down those stairs," she recalled. "I was in shock!" Despite Allison's initial reluctance, Evers had just put in place a firebrand who would seize the cause of the Jackson Movement and make it her own.

THE FIRST SERIOUS DISCUSSION OF A BOYCOTT IN *NORTH JACKSON ACTION* came in the November 16, 1962, issue, just after the NAACP convention had ended and the national office staff had departed.[24] Perhaps Salter felt he had received from Laplois Ashford the endorsement that he needed. Perhaps he was just trying to get something going. "Start Putting Your Money on Strike," his headline read. In the story, Salter and the youth council made the case for why blacks should not spend their money in stores where they weren't fully welcome, particularly as the Christmas season approached. The story reads like a trial balloon—a suggestion for consideration rather than a call to action. It clearly laid out the arguments for a boycott, but indicated that the youth council was still studying the situation. In fact, Salter and Evers both knew that the black citizens of Jackson would be unwilling to commit to anything more than a boycott. But this form of activism was not asking the justifiably fearful black community to do anything; it was asking them *not* to do something, which required far less risk.

In the next newsletter, the call was sounded: in a two-line, all-caps headline, Salter proclaimed:

THE BOYCOTT IS NOW OFFICIAL; IS AIMED AT CAPITOL STREET STORES AND OTHER BUSINESSES
IT WILL LAST UNTIL VICTORY; PICKET LINES AND MASS MEETINGS ARE DEFINITELY SET.[25]

Salter later said he had been talking at length with Medgar Evers about the group's plans, and in his memoir he wrote that Evers "was increasingly optimistic about the possibilities involved with a boycott campaign."[26] Obviously Salter felt comfortable enough with Evers's support to announce the boycott. How much the national office knew about it, however, is unclear.

After the announcement of the boycott, Salter recalled that the youth council meetings took on a decidedly spirited tone. The youth took the freedom song "We Shall Not Be Moved" and turned it into their own anthem:

> *We're going to have a boycott, we shall not be moved.*
> *We're going to have a boycott, we shall not be moved.*
> *Just like a tree that's planted by the water,*
> *We shall not be moved!*[27]

Although at this point the boycott had no specific demands other than "clearing up discrimination against Negro workers and Negro consumers," it did have a specific focus. "The basic target of the boycott is downtown Capitol Street—from State Street westward to Mill Street," the newsletter announced. It indicated that leaflets and mass meetings would be the means of spreading the word and offered a brief "Statement of Grievances" about discriminatory hiring practices and treatment of black customers. It also pointed out that many white businessmen whose stores were targeted were members of the "viciously anti-Negro White Citizens' Council—whose national office is in Jackson." Another article indicated that the boycott would last at least through the Christmas season "until the demands of the movement have been met."[28]

Eventually Salter, Evers, and the youth council settled on four basic demands, and Salter developed a leaflet spelling them out:

- equality in hiring and promoting employees;
- an end to segregated drinking fountains, restrooms, and seating;
- the use of courtesy titles—Mrs., Miss, and Mr.—when addressing black customers; and,
- service on a first-come, first-served basis for all customers—blacks as well as whites.[29]

While in retrospect these points seem less than revolutionary, they were absolutely radical at the time. Although Salter and the youth council were working independently of most other area civil rights groups, including the adult NAACP chapter, Salter included the names of several groups as boycott sponsors after receiving verbal approval from their local representatives. Besides the North Jackson Youth Council, Salter listed the Tougaloo College NAACP Branch (which he and his wife Eldri had reinvigorated), the struggling West

Jackson Youth Council, the Campbell College NAACP Branch, and the Jackson NAACP Adult Branch. Salter had also received clearance from Joan Trumpauer to list SNCC as a participant and had talked with Dave Dennis, who had only recently arrived to spearhead CORE's efforts in the state. This consortium came to be known as the Jackson Movement.[30]

Salter wanted to kick off the campaign with a bang, so he decided that a few members should picket the downtown stores—something never before done in Jackson. Woolworth's was chosen because it was in the heart of the downtown shopping district and situated right on Capitol Street. Since those picketing would most likely be arrested, he discussed the plan with Evers, who, Salter said, "indicated that since we had things moving so decisively, he thought there would be no difficulty in securing enough bail" from the NAACP's national office. The bail bond issue turned out to be not as easily resolved as Evers had thought, but eventually Salter secured enough funds to send out six pickets. Evers usually handled publicity for any local NAACP function, but just before the picketing was to begin he was on a speaking tour in the North. Salter asked for Bill Kunstler's help in contacting the media. Kunstler announced the impending demonstration the day before to UPI and AP in New York, which notified their Jackson affiliates. The local affiliates then notified other local media as well as the police, assuring a crowd for the boycott's big send-off.[31]

When the morning of December 12 arrived, Salter had a case of nerves. Even the seasoned activist could not predict how Mississippi would handle the situation. By midmorning, Salter, his wife, and four Tougaloo students with no in-state family connections were making the twenty-minute trip from Tougaloo to Jackson. Karin Kunstler had agreed to watch little Maria Salter in case she was needed after the regular babysitter went home. The pickets rode in "tense silence" to their drop-off point, Salter reported, where they were greeted by a cadre of police cars, paddy wagons, and motorcycles. The demonstrators hastily exited their car in front of Woolworth's and, careful not to block the entire sidewalk, arranged themselves in a line and began to exercise their constitutional right of free speech. Their hand-drawn signs read "Negro Customers—Stay Away from Capitol Street—Buy Elsewhere" and "We Want Equal Rights for Negro Workers—Boycott Capitol Street."[32]

They had just enough time for photographers to pop off a few pictures and for Salter to hand the newsmen copies of the November 30 edition of *North Jackson Action*—the issue announcing the boycott—along with a leaflet. Then the "wave of police—perhaps fifty or more" closed in, Salter recalled. "I felt as if it were all a dream."

The carefully planned boycott was, indeed, taking place, and the specifics were all too real—and a bit mundane. The pickets were all arrested without incident and charged with "obstructing the sidewalk."[33] Because all the bail money had not yet arrived from out of state, Salter and two students were kept in jail overnight, while Eldri Salter and the other two students were released after a few hours. Salter's jail stay seemed even less meaningful after he scanned the next morning's *Clarion-Ledger* and discovered that it hardly mentioned the picketing. He became concerned that the city's power structure had intentionally played down the event.

Once out of jail, though, Salter found much to be excited about. On the afternoon of the picketing, Joan Trumpauer, Pearlena Lewis, and student body president Eddie O'Neal had held a rally at Tougaloo's Woodworth Chapel to explain the boycott. More than half the student body of five hundred attended and many pledged their support. In addition, Lewis and the youth council had already begun distributing boycott leaflets, and the phone-tree calls informing blacks about the boycott were under way. Most significantly, Mayor Allen Thompson had denounced the "outside agitators" and the picketing on television—providing the boycott with exactly the kind of attention Salter had hoped for.

That afternoon, more good news arrived. Evers, just back from his speaking tour, dropped off the *Jackson Daily News*, the afternoon paper, whose lead story focused on the mayor's remarks to his city department heads that day. Not only had Thompson again denounced the pickets, but he had threatened the organizers and their sponsoring organizations with a million-dollar lawsuit. In addition, he pledged to put "one thousand police" on Capitol Street to prevent further disruptions to the city's commerce. "Good old Allen Thompson!" Salter exclaimed. "Good old *Jackson Daily News*!" The pickets had hit their mark: the boycott was off to a rousing start.

IT DOES NOT SEEM TO HAVE OCCURRED TO SALTER AT THE TIME THAT HE WAS, in the eyes of any casual onlooker, an outsider: a white man—at least in appearance[34]—involved in a black struggle. It was fine to be helping, to be in a back-office position like Joan Trumpauer or Lois Chaffee. But to be out front leading the charge was quite different. Salter claimed that his race "didn't make any difference"[35] in the internal struggle that followed, and perhaps he is right. His confrontational style, however, if not his race, was bound to cause trouble sooner or later, not only with the local authorities—that was a given—but also with the organization he represented, the NAACP.

In addition, it was becoming clear to Salter that something was not quite right. Although he had the enthusiastic support of the youth council, many Tougaloo students, and Evers, the bail bond money from the national NAACP office had been slow in coming. In fact, the first demonstration had been scheduled to occur ten days earlier, but when Salter found out that no bond money would be available, he scrapped the plan until other arrangements could be made.

Although Evers had assured him that the money would be there, somehow when push came to shove, it just wasn't. When Salter contacted Evers on his speaking tour to find out what had happened, Evers was vague. "Clearly he had people around him," Salter recalled. "He couldn't talk. Basically what he was saying was 'I can't get the bail bond.'"[36] Attempts to find local blacks to put up surety bonds against their property were similarly unsuccessful, so Salter had to go elsewhere to obtain the five hundred dollars for each picket to ensure that they could get out of jail quickly. Through Joan Trumpauer, Salter solicited funds from Anne Braden and the Southern Conference Educational Fund (SCEF), which put up one thousand dollars. He asked Karin Kunstler to call her father; Bill Kunstler then contacted radical leftist attorney Victor Rabinowitz, who put up fifteen hundred dollars from his own personal trust. The Gandhian Society for Human Rights—a legal defense group initiated by Dr. Martin Luther King, Jr., Kunstler, and others to support nonviolent resistance to segregation—put up the additional five hundred dollars.[37]

Yet why this reluctance from the NAACP, for which Salter was now working, albeit as a volunteer? Salter and Ed King suggest that the NAACP's Roy Wilkins had made a deal with the Eisenhower administration after the Little Rock school desegregation incident in 1957 that freedom in Mississippi would have to wait until it had come to the other southern states—the trickle-down approach to civil rights. Salter later would emphatically claim that Evers himself informed him of this deal, which Salter believed carried over into the Kennedy administration.[38]

Bob Moses, SNCC's lead field person in Mississippi at the time, said he never heard of such a deal, but suggested that the NAACP's standard policy would have dictated that Mississippi be the last place they would try to change. "The strategy [for the NAACP] was you work the softer areas and use your leverage there to tackle the hardest areas," Moses explained. "Change *around* Mississippi and tackle Mississippi last. So they had a holding operation in Mississippi."[39]

Pearlena Lewis believed that the organization was hesitant to fund the first demonstrations of the Jackson Movement because the group included other organizations; SNCC and CORE, for instance, were recognized on the boycott handbills and leaflets. "They felt they didn't have control over some of the groups," she said, "so they were reluctant."[40]

The NAACP's Laplois Ashford suggested that the reluctance was more institutionally driven. "Our organization was very conservative in its movements," he said. "An organization that had a lot of contributions from major corporate America . . . always tried to appear balanced and considerate of all sides. [They were looking for ways to accomplish things] that may not have been so controversial."[41]

Whatever the reasons for the delay, it seems clear that the national office of the NAACP was unprepared to respond quickly to any specific request for support. Like any long-established bureaucracy, the wheels of the organization's national office turned slowly: they were simply not ready to move as swiftly as Salter wanted. Also, direct action was completely counter to the culture of the NAACP, which preferred to take the legal route to social change. The leadership believed freedom would come eventually, once the white lawyers and judges and politicians understood the full impact of the Constitution and the Bill of Rights. That was, after all, how Roy Wilkins and Thurgood Marshall had won the *Brown* decision in 1954.

Wilkins in particular, the man whom the *New York Times* called "the chief planner of the legal battle that resulted in the 1954 Supreme Court decision outlawing 'separate but equal' public schools,"[42] was deeply conservative in his approach to gaining rights for American blacks. A grandson of Mississippi slaves, Wilkins was born in 1901 and came of age when presenting members of his race as upright, dedicated, and nonintimidating members of society was the way to gain a measure of acceptance from skeptical and powerful whites.

Not that Wilkins hadn't tried in his own way to challenge segregation. In his early years, he was a crusading journalist for the *Kansas City Call*, a black newspaper that under Wilkins's editorial guidance was able to steer blacks toward political activism, culminating in the defeat of a U.S. senator that Wilkins believed to be a "militant racist." From there, in 1931, Wilkins joined the NAACP and eventually took over the editorial duties of the association's call-to-arms magazine *The Crisis* from none other than the pioneering W. E. B. Du Bois.

Wilkins took over as executive secretary of the NAACP in 1955, just at the dawn of the modern civil rights movement, and almost immediately seemed out of step to some of the more aggressive and younger black leaders on their way up. Wilkins's philosophy was summarized in a telling synopsis of his approach: "The Negro has to be a superb diplomat and a great strategist. He has to parlay what actual power he has along with the good will of the white majority. He has to devise and pursue those philosophies and activities which will least alienate the white majority opinion."[43]

Such a philosophy—particularly after the *Brown* decision was rendered and southern states failed to adhere to its dictates—seemed too cautious and fawning. In Mississippi, especially in 1962, many blacks wondered—what good was the *Brown* decision without enforcement? Hadn't it been nearly a decade since the Supreme Court had decided the case? What impact had that decision had on the Mississippi educational system? James Meredith aside, the childhood experiences of Annie Moody and Memphis Norman suggested that it could have been 1902 rather than 1962.

When John Salter began his assault on Mississippi's racial caste system, a new day was beginning to dawn across the South, and black Mississippians were anxious to awaken to it at the same time as their southern contemporaries. They were tired of the go-along-to-get-along mentality of the earlier generation. They wanted action. So it did not seem to matter to them that a man with light skin was attempting to lead the charge, or at least share the lead with their own Medgar Evers. "I was glad to see someone standing up there with Medgar," Doris Allison admitted.[44]

Despite the lack of national support, almost from the start the boycott was a success. Leaflets were distributed quietly, since one could be arrested for simply handing out such literature in Mississippi. The phone chain was working; youth council members were speaking at black church services; and just to make certain that the boycott was observed, Salter posted young people posing as shoppers in the downtown area to talk to fellow blacks who approached the stores. Just as with the state fair boycott, the police were out in force, sending a subtle message to whites as well as blacks that shopping in the downtown area was dangerous. Once again, the crowds stayed away.

In his American government class back at Tougaloo, Salter noticed that his students were taking new interest in the subjects of due process and the rights of citizens, for they now had something specific to which to relate these concepts. And, more and more, the Salter residence was looking like a campaign headquarters. Eldri Salter would host regular get-togethers to boost the youth council's spirits, and every Saturday morning, Tougaloo and youth council kids would drop by Pope Cottage, get their marching orders, and head off to distribute leaflets.[45] Alphonzo Lewis recounted that many a door was slammed in his face, but he and the others persisted, largely because of the Salters' encouragement. Lewis recalled that the couple's involvement was "very motivational. If they could go out on a limb and risk their lives to do this," he remembered thinking, "certainly we could do something for ourselves."[46]

Just before Christmas, John Salter consulted with Medgar Evers and determined that another small picket would heighten awareness of the boycott and keep people out of the downtown area. Salter announced to the wire services that on Friday, December 21, a set of pickets would appear on Capitol Street. Again police descended on the shopping district, and when the two pickets arrived—Tougaloo students Dorie Ladner and Charles Bracey—news cameras captured the scene as the police immediately arrested them. The event received only a brief mention in the afternoon's *Jackson Daily News* and none in the next day's *Clarion-Ledger*, although Salter said radio and television coverage was more extensive. This time, Evers and Salter were able to make different arrangements for bail, as two local blacks agreed to post property bonds in the amount of five hundred dollars each to get the students out of jail that afternoon. It seemed the shackles of fear were slowly beginning to drop.[47]

But despite signs that Jackson's black population was starting to believe that real change could come, there were disturbing omens as well. On the night before the Christmas picketing, a sign appeared on the lawn in front of the Salter home asking Santa to "Boycott Tougaloo." The message was "signed" by the "National Advancement Association for Poor White Trash" and ended with the greeting, "Merry Christmas, White Folks."[48] Although the Salters had been receiving threats by phone since they picketed the downtown area more than a week earlier, this was their first alert that their home could be a target. Late on the night of December 21, as Eldri Salter and two female students were sitting up talking about the picketing that day, a bullet blasted through ten-month-old Maria Salter's bedroom window, shattering the glass and whizzing over her head as she lay sleeping in her crib. John Salter and some male students armed themselves and stood guard during the remainder of the Christmas holidays. They were not bothered again.[49]

Medgar and Myrlie Evers invited the Salters to their home for Christmas dinner that year; John Salter recalled that the foursome talked at length about the historic changes occurring in the South. Medgar speculated about the backlash that might follow. "The white man won't change easily," Salter remembered Evers saying. "Some of these people are going to fight hard. And more of our people are going to get killed." Salter looked at Myrlie as her husband uttered these words. She was staring back at him in stony silence, poker-faced, knowing full well whose life was on the line.[50]

THE BEGINNING OF 1963 SAW ACTION ON SEVERAL FRONTS. THE FIRST OFFICIAL mention of the boycott in any national NAACP materials appears in Medgar Evers's December activity report of January 4, 1963. In it, he provided details of the "selected buying campaign" which he said had been 60–65 percent effective. He noted the picketing and the arrests; mentioned that the attorneys for the pickets were Jack Young and Jess Brown, two NAACP attorneys from Jackson, as well as "William Kunstler of New York"; and briefly summarized some maneuvers the legal team was pursuing. Kunstler had devised a plan to challenge the arrests of the Salters and the other four in the first group of pickets who, if convicted, could be fined five hundred dollars and sentenced to six months in jail.[51]

On December 17, Kunstler had filed a petition in federal court requesting that the trial, which had been postponed at his request, be moved to federal jurisdiction because the Mississippi courts were segregationist and because the arrest of citizens exercising their free speech rights violated the First Amendment of the U.S. Constitution. In addition, Kunstler had asked that the federal judge scheduled to hear the petition—Harold Cox—voluntarily remove himself from ruling on the case because of his well-known segregationist beliefs. The strategy, if nothing else, would tie up the case for years in appeals. In early January, Judge Cox decided not to recuse himself, and Kunstler appealed the case to the Fifth Circuit Court in New Orleans.[52]

Medgar Evers's monthly report for December also summarized his extensive travel schedule in November and December. Just after the NAACP Annual Conference in November, Evers had gone on a ten-day speaking tour of the West, followed after Thanksgiving by a twelve-day tour of the North and Midwest. People across the country were eager to hear the specifics of the Meredith case, and the NAACP wanted to use its renewed prominence to raise funds. After reporting a number of instances of harassment and murder—incidents that regularly peppered his monthly reports—Evers wrote a brief sentence under the heading "The Future." "We anticipate 1963 being the most exciting and productive year for the NAACP in the State of Mississippi," it stated. His prediction now seems both prophetic and uncommonly tragic.[53]

The boycott continued into the new year. Although there were no signs that the politicians or the businessmen were willing to negotiate, it became apparent to Salter and others that the targeted businesses were suffering real losses. After-Christmas sales lasted well into February, and Mayor Thompson announced that the stores' proprietors would be granted a waiver if unable to pay their taxes.[54] In an attempt to show local blacks that they were respected, the mayor announced a Capitol Street parade for Willie Richardson, a black all-American football star from Jackson State College who had been signed to play for the Baltimore Colts. Seeing through the ruse, Salter and the youth council called for black citizens not to attend. "No one begrudged Willie Richardson his honors," Salter recalled, "but we were not going to see the boycott impaired in any way." By Salter's estimate, only about 350 of the city's more than 52,000 blacks attended the festivities—a report confirmed by television footage of the widely publicized event.[55]

Also during this time, Salter expanded the distribution of *North Jackson Action* to additional supporters outside the state—primarily student, labor, and civil rights organizations. He begged for financial support and suggested widening the boycott to all stores affiliated with those in downtown Jackson, including seventeen national chains like Woolworth's and Walgreen's. His additional request for help with publicity generated articles in the publications of many civil rights groups operating in the South—SCEF, SNCC, CORE, and even the National Student Association. Once again, however, the NAACP remained silent.[56]

At the end of January, Salter decided to take the offensive in his dealings with NAACP's national office. He sent letters to Gloster Current and Laplois Ashford, reminding them of their meeting the prior November and enclosing the letter he had sent to his other outside supporters calling for a boycott of the national chain stores. The enclosure also provided specifics about the Jackson Movement's activities, including the arrests.[57]

To his credit, Gloster Current immediately passed along Salter's letter to Roy Wilkins and other national office staffers, and indicated his belief that the matter should be put before the national board since it requested a nation-wide boycott.[58] Current was an interesting blend of activism and conservatism. Born in 1913 in Indianapolis, he grew up in the urban centers of Chicago and Detroit. It was in Detroit that he started participating in the NAACP's youth council and gained prominence in 1939 when he became chairman of the national college chapters. Current was hired by the NAACP in 1941 and in 1946 became its director of branches and field administration. As such, he had sway over the fund-raising and field operations, including hiring and firing field staff. It was a powerful position and Current wielded it with a strong hand. He was often the first to hear of developments in the field and would pass them along to Wilkins and other NAACP brass on the board.[59]

Current said he first heard of the boycott in December through an attorney for one of the Capitol Street businesses, not through Evers, who would have been the most likely channel. He stated, however, "I think the NAACP should take some action backing up our North Jackson Youth Council and give this matter nationwide publicity." On the same day, Current notified the organization's Committee on Branches and Youth Work about the boycott and asked that they take up the issue at their next meeting, scheduled for the first week of February.[60]

The first time the boycott made its way into the highest echelon of the NAACP bureaucracy, the Executive Committee, was during its February 11 meeting, only four days after the Committee on Branches and Youth Work met. As reported in fewer than four lines in the three pages of single-spaced typed minutes, the Executive Committee received the report of the Committee on Branches suggesting support for the boycott, then forwarded its findings to yet another board committee—the Committee on Program.[61] At this point, Roy Wilkins would have certainly been aware of the youth council's activities, although he may not have realized they were working in tandem with SNCC and CORE as "the Jackson Movement." Wilkins also, quite clearly, had no idea that Kunstler was involved. The March Executive Committee minutes indicate that yet another NAACP committee—the Committee on Administration—recommended that the board "approve a national boycott against certain chains discriminating against Negroes in Jackson." The Executive Committee voted to advise the North Jackson Youth Council that "we sympathize with their situation and will take action."[62] As with most bureaucracies, word of the top-level decision was a little slow in filtering down to the field staff and volunteers. In fact, the NAACP Executive Committee minutes during this period portray a large, bureaucratic organization handling an enormous variety of civil rights issues. Wilkins could not possibly have stayed on top of every one of the initiatives in fifteen hundred branches across the country. At this point, the North Jackson Youth Council was hardly a blip on his radar screen.

While news of the youth council's activities was winding its way through the maze of the NAACP committee structure, Salter, characteristically, was not waiting for permission to act. In early January, he had drafted a memorandum—"To The Jackson Businessman." With the immediate sting of lost profits during the Christmas holidays still fresh, he hoped to gain some ground in the negotiation process. Salter noted the effectiveness of the boycott, detailed the tactics used, restated the Jackson Movement's four essential demands, and indicated that the effort would continue "week after week and month after month" until the demands were met. "It is your decision," the memo concluded.[63]

Then, in February, Salter released a three-page educational bulletin to all students on the Tougaloo campus.[64] It provided background facts about boycotts in general, the specifics of the Jackson Movement, and information about how interested students could get involved. The bulletin stated that more than twenty-five thousand boycott leaflets had been distributed throughout Jackson's black neighborhoods and asked for volunteers to distribute more. The youth council's ranks began to swell, and Salter estimated that by March 1963 the council had more than one hundred members.[65] Even if the NAACP's national office was slow in recognizing the movement's efforts, local support was growing.

Doris Allison was the instigator of another key development.[66] In early December, just after Allison's election as president of the Jackson branch, her sister in St. Louis became seriously ill with cancer; by February, with doctors predicting the worst, Allison felt she had to go visit her. But before leaving, she hatched a plan that she had been thinking about for a while. "Mr. Evers, where are the ministers?" Allison would often ask her mentor, knowing that the black community would rally behind its religious leaders if they took a stand. Few, however, had stepped forward, fearing economic reprisals from the whites in power. Without telling Evers exactly what she was doing, Allison indicated she would take a stab at getting some ministers to his monthly board meeting before she left for St. Louis.

On the morning of February 26, the day she was scheduled to leave, Allison called thirty-seven ministers, introduced herself, and told them this: "I have recently been elected, unopposed, to preside for the next two years as the president of the Jackson branch of the NAACP. There's going to be a crucial meeting held tonight. A *crucial* meeting. If you aren't present at this meeting tonight, whatever happens from here on in, *hold your peace.*" She then left on the afternoon train.

The next day, Evers called her. "Mrs. Allison, I want to know *exactly* what you told those ministers," he insisted. She laughed and told him the whole story. Evers reported that the ministers showed up in force—something he had been trying to get them to do for the past three years. "They crammed this place out!" he told her. Evers advised the ministers of recent developments within the Jackson Movement and solicited their support. With the groundwork laid by Salter and the youth council, some ministers seemed more receptive to involvement.

DURING SPRING BREAK, EVERS TRAVELED WITH SALTER TO GREENWOOD IN the Delta to attend a mass meeting at which Dr. John Morsell, an aide to Roy Wilkins, was scheduled to speak. Seeing the enthusiasm that had been sparked among the local blacks by the SNCC voter registration drive there, Salter became depressed. "Matters [are] much too quiet in Jackson," he thought. Even though the boycott had been substantially effective, no flames were igniting, not even a brush fire. Jackson was on the slow burn compared to the enthusiasm and momentum on display in the Delta. He determined to do more.[67]

Bob Moses, the leader of the SNCC Greenwood Movement, believed that Evers was also inspired by the meeting. "He wanted to capture some of that spirit and bring it back to Jackson," Moses said.[68] Evers himself said as much when he was given a brief opportunity to speak at the Greenwood mass meeting. "You have given us inspiration in Jackson," Evers said, "and we're going to go back to Jackson and fight for freedom as you're doing here in Greenwood."[69]

Evers's subsequent actions indicate that he was as good as his word. His monthly report for March indicates that, immediately upon his return, Evers launched a three-month voter registration drive with the help of the NAACP adult branch and some youth council members, including Pearlena Lewis, who began conducting voter education classes in her parents' living room.[70] Salter says that he helped out with voter registration efforts too, but cites how "incredibly complex" the procedures were for blacks. Although he was impressed with the Greenwood Movement, Salter was essentially uninterested in what he considered a quixotic adventure with limited results. Despite all of SNCC's efforts, only small numbers of blacks were being registered by the white clerks; it would take years to effect significant change at the rate they were going. Salter was interested in more immediate returns on his investments of time and energy.[71]

With the Easter shopping season came another opportunity to show the strength of the boycott, so Salter suggested and Evers concurred that more picketing was needed.[72] Once again, the NAACP national office was offering no support, despite Salter's continued efforts to get them involved. Apparently he had not been informed about the national board's statement of support for the Jackson Movement, and since Salter had not heard directly from either Gloster Current or Laplois Ashford, he assumed nothing was being done at the national level to assist the local efforts.

Evers's February and March reports to the NAACP do not mention the boycott, although perhaps those efforts had simply been pushed aside for other compelling matters that absorbed his time: persuading James Meredith to return to Ole Miss after a first semester filled with threats and harassment; conducting Emancipation Day Centennial Anniversary celebrations throughout the state; overseeing the transfer of his dying friend, Clyde Kennard, from Parchman penitentiary to University Hospital in Jackson; and investigating the lynching and castration of a black Madison County resident.[73]

With Evers largely unavailable, Salter again turned to outsiders for help with bond money. He wrote a long letter to Bill Kunstler expressing his frustration and asking for more help. Kunstler again contacted Victor Rabinowitz, who came through with another thousand dollars, as did Anne Braden of SCEF, once again at the urging of Joan Trumpauer. These funds provided the support for four pickets to take to the streets.[74]

It is interesting to note that throughout the Jackson Movement, men and women shared the job of picketing. Eldri Salter and Bettye Anne Poole had joined John Salter and three other men in early December, and Dorie Ladner accompanied Charles Bracey onto the picket line in late December. For the Easter picket one female Tougaloo student, Arverna Adams, accompanied three Tougaloo men to the demonstration. In the early afternoon of April 4, 1963, the four stepped out onto Capitol Street and were promptly arrested by the waiting police.

Initially the pickets were charged, as before, with "obstructing the sidewalk" but in an effort to thwart Kunstler's earlier court challenge, the charge this time was changed to "breach of the peace." "Their presence could have led to violence," Chief Detective M. B. Pierce claimed. Later that afternoon, the four were released on bond. Both the *Jackson Daily News* and the *Clarion-Ledger* ran brief front-page stories on the protest, and Salter recalled that television and radio coverage again was substantial. The youth council mailed out more than one thousand leaflets to prominent members of the black community asking for continued support of the boycott. *North Jackson Action* also ran a story on the renewed effort, indicating that "there will definitely be more picketing in the near future—and matters, from this standpoint, will become increasingly interesting."[75]

Just prior to the April picketing, Salter had written another letter to the white businessmen of Jackson, reviewing the progress of the boycott and indicating the local NAACP's willingness to negotiate. A few days later, Evers heard from a white minister who had talked with some of the businessmen. He said that they wanted to "work something out," but when pressed, would only offer vague promises of change if the boycott were called off. Although Salter considered their response "unacceptable," it clearly indicated that the boycott was having an effect.[76]

Outside of Jackson, there was some progress as well. With various civil rights and student organizations now publicizing the Jackson Movement's actions, the flow of supportive letters increased. Many writers said they were initiating boycotts of the seventeen chain stores listed in Salter's January letter. Letters from James Farmer, national director of CORE, and Julian Bond, communications director for SNCC, also heartened the youth council.[77]

Encouraged by these responses, Salter composed a long letter to Jackson's black business community. Modeled on a similar letter he had composed and youth council members had delivered to black teachers from across the state attending their annual convention in Jackson in March, this letter exhorted the black business leaders to support the boycott, which he termed 80 percent effective. "Please do not buy at any of the boycotted stores," he entreated. "We shall win a free society."[78]

In addition, Salter made one last attempt to get a response from the NAACP national office. In late March, just prior to the Easter picketing, he wrote Laplois Ashford to update him on the boycott's progress and to ask again for help. This time, perhaps as a result of the Executive Committee's recommendation earlier that month, Ashford responded. He called Salter on April 9 to say the national office might be able to offer some financial and publicity help. Salter immediately sent Ashford all the relevant documents about the boycott, including a complete set of *North Jackson Action* bulletins.[79]

Finally, it appeared that the national office was interested. A week after sending the materials, Salter received a letter from Ashford urging him to "[k]eep up the good work." Attached was a check for five hundred dollars for use in future picketing along with a letter from Roy Wilkins saying that the national office "stand[s] ready to assist in any way until success has been achieved."[80]

The news was like manna from heaven for both Salter and Evers, who had been laboring tirelessly in the Mississippi wilderness, seemingly ignored by the very organization they represented. But why the sudden interest? What had changed to make Roy Wilkins himself pen a personal note to NAACP volunteer John Salter? There seem to be two reasons.

The first was that one of the youth council's fund-raising appeals had reached the board of a civil liberties group on which Roy Wilkins sat. When the matter came up at the group's April meeting, Wilkins was taken off guard and promised to follow up with the youth council directly. In his letter to Salter, Wilkins admitted to being "a little embarrassed to have a man connected with another organization present me with a general appeal from one of our youth chapters which has been broadcast to the country." Wilkins went on to congratulate the council on its successes thus far.[81]

The other reason for Wilkins's interest had to do with what was going on nationally on the civil rights front. Dr. Martin Luther King, Jr., and his Southern Christian Leadership Conference were in the headlines again with a direct action campaign to end segregation in Alabama's largest city, Birmingham.[82] King's group had strategized for months to ensure the success of the Birmingham initiative. Unlike in Albany, Georgia, where the SCLC had focused its attention the prior year with mixed results, Birmingham promised to be an easy target. The NAACP was outlawed in Alabama, and no other civil rights groups had much of a foothold there. Fred Shuttlesworth, an SCLC board member, had been holding mass meetings and preparing at the grass-roots level for seven years, attempting to create an environment where change could take hold.

Dr. King's decision to move on Birmingham proved apt. Within a month of the campaign's early April kickoff, the city had erupted, and the infamous Bull Connor, the city's police chief and aspiring mayor, turned out his men in full force. The Birmingham campaign was the first time the nation witnessed the dramatic sight of children marching through city streets for their freedom. It was also the first time that television cameras showed fire hoses and attack dogs being used to quell nonviolent demonstrators. The intensity of the Birmingham struggle sparked additional demonstrations throughout the region as America got its first complete and unavoidable view of the viciousness of the white South's defense of its way of life.

By mid-May, after sit-ins, mass marches, a boycott of the downtown shopping district, and hundreds of adults and children being sent to jail, including Dr. King himself (from whence came his famous "Letter from Birmingham Jail"), the SCLC reached a negotiated settlement with the city's power structure that included integrated facilities; an increased number of black store clerks; release of all jailed civil rights demonstrators; and the formation of a biracial committee to discuss black citizens' grievances. "It was all that we wanted," Salter later wrote. "And we wanted it in Jackson."[83]

Birmingham had also brought intense media attention to King and the SCLC, suggesting they were at the forefront of the civil rights struggle. A relative newcomer and his fledgling organization were overshadowing the NAACP, the traditional standard bearer in the fight for civil rights, and making the NAACP look out of step—old and stodgy. Something had to be done to counteract this perception.

It is clear that Roy Wilkins and his inner circle believed that the activities then taking shape in Jackson could become their ticket to a new, improved image for their organization. In his autobiography, Wilkins suggested as much: "Anyone who thinks the NAACP worked through the courts alone would do well to review that [Jackson] campaign."[84] Wilkins thus took a calculated risk to attempt to change his organization's fading image; he wanted in on the Jackson Movement at last.[85]

So in late April, after Salter received the Wilkins letter and the five-hundred-dollar check from Laplois Ashford, a few of the NAACP's national office staff paid a visit to Jackson. Ashford and his protégé, Willie Ludden, who had just signed on as the NAACP's southeast regional youth field secretary, were sent down to scope out the situation and report back to New York.[86] Both men were relative newcomers to the NAACP bureaucracy. Ashford had joined in September 1962 as the organization's national youth director at the invitation of Gloster Current, who had witnessed Ashford's expertise in working as a volunteer with the Rochester branch and the New York State youth councils. A native of McCool, Mississippi, Ashford was smart, well educated, and had a burning desire to achieve full citizenship rights for the country's blacks, having experienced firsthand the scourge of racial discrimination both at the University of Rochester (NY) and during a stint in the U.S. Army.[87]

Ludden was young, enthusiastic, and a natural leader. A graduate of Savannah (GA) State College and leader of the successful 1960 Savannah direct action campaign, Ludden embodied the spirit of the new black youth movement. He could be brash, calculating, and iconoclastic—just what Jackson needed, but the last person one would have expected to be employed by the stolid NAACP. Ludden had been hired in January 1963 to help organize youth councils in the Southeast; he had been handpicked by Roy Wilkins to help keep things moving in Jackson.[88] Ludden, in fact, confirms Wilkins's motives in Jackson. "He wanted me to organize the people of Jackson in order to supersede King's movement in Birmingham," Ludden wrote in his memoir.[89]

Ludden and Ashford, however, came away with differing impressions of the budding Jackson Movement. Ashford was favorably impressed with the organized youth councils and their willingness to stay involved with the boycott. Ludden, however, had reservations. He spoke not only with the youth, but also with leaders in the black community, and he came away with a sense that Jackson wasn't ready for a mass movement. "All of the people I talked to expressed doubt that a movement could ever take place in Jackson," he later wrote. Nevertheless, both pledged the support of the national office.[90]

In his discussions with them, Salter emphasized the need for direct action demonstrations, as in Birmingham, for the effort in Jackson to be successful. Ashford and Ludden carried that message back to New York. In early May, Ashford called Salter to say that the national office would support a demonstration in mid-May and that both Roy Wilkins and comedian/activist Dick Gregory—who recently had been active in both the Greenwood and Birmingham movements—would join them. On the strength of Ashford's phone call, Salter quickly recruited more than forty Tougaloo students and youth council members to participate in the demonstration.[91]

Later that week, however, Ashford called to renege, indicating that some of the national office staff feared that events in Birmingham would overshadow anything they might do in Jackson.[92] Bitterly disappointed and sensing that there was more to the decision than Ashford was letting on, Salter wrote a long letter to Ashford expressing his frustration, providing background on the Jackson Movement, explaining the urgency of the need for demonstrations, and begging for financial help from the national office. He copied the letter to Wilkins and Current, a number of state NAACP board members, and, of course, Medgar Evers.[93]

Ashford was in a tough spot at the time. Still viewed as a new recruit by the NAACP bureaucracy—"I was a peon," he later said—Ashford was chomping at the bit to have the NAACP's youth groups take on a more substantive role. But the first hot, then cold, national NAACP leadership was having none of it. According to Ashford, "The North Jackson kids . . . wanted to get involved and really start some action. The national office was saying, 'No! No! No!'"[94] Perhaps Wilkins was more inclined to listen to Ludden's advice that the time was not ripe for an all-out assault in Jackson. Even so, there was more to the story.

Salter unwittingly had provided the national office leaders with a striking reason to back away. The lawyer he had engaged to defend the December pickets had become a major sticking point. The appeal of the arrests of the December pickets had been lumbering along. In April, Bill Kunstler began working on another legal strategy to foil the segregationist Judge Cox. Late that month, Kunstler filed suit against Jackson's mayor, chief of police, and municipal court justice, calling for the appointment of a three-member federal judge panel to enjoin further arrests for picketing. Kunstler also requested damages of ten thousand dollars each for violations of each plaintiff's civil rights and asked that the cases be removed to the federal courts under a little-used 1868 Reconstruction statute. The timing of the petition coincided with the scheduled hearing of the appeal in Judge Cox's court.[95]

At about the time of Ashford and Ludden's visit, Salter had issued a press release summarizing these most recent developments,[96] and this time, news of the case and Kunstler's involvement reached Wilkins, most likely through Ashford, who wrote a detailed report of his visit to Jackson.[97] Wilkins was furious when he heard of Kunstler's participation. "I was greatly disturbed yesterday to learn in our conference that certain other groups and individuals have become a part of the operations of our youth group in Jackson, Mississippi," he vented in an internal memorandum to Gloster Current in early May. Without stating his name, Wilkins complained about Kunstler's involvement and mentioned the most recent gossip about his handling of the Birmingham cases for the SCLC. He went on to say that Kunstler had brought into the Birmingham case another lawyer, Bob Stein, whom Wilkins believed the FBI had under surveillance.

"Our youth group in Jackson seems to have gotten itself thoroughly mixed into the very kind of associations that we have avoided for so many years," Wilkins continued. Taking a swipe at Medgar Evers, he went on to say, "I cannot for the life of me understand how this was permitted to happen by our staff member in Jackson who must have known our policy." Wilkins requests in his memo that Current inquire into the situation and write a full report, including "the attitude of our Mississippi office during the whole development."[98]

Kunstler's presence in the case had touched a nerve in Wilkins's politically hypersensitive operation. For years Wilkins and his predecessors had struggled to create an image of an organization that was mainstream, an organization that had only the best interests of American democracy at heart. Having someone of Kunstler's radical reputation involved in an NAACP case, and in the very city where Wilkins now hoped to demonstrate his organization's renewed relevance, was an enormous blow that seems to have caught him completely off guard. Although he didn't state it plainly, he clearly was concerned about having his organization's reputation tainted by the "communist" label. It is obvious from his memo that Wilkins wanted somebody to pay for this unthinkable breach of protocol, and he was ready to point the finger at Evers unless someone else could be held responsible.

Back in Mississippi, when Salter received no immediate response to his urgent letter to Ashford, he reasoned that there must be an internal split among the national office staff over whether to support the Jackson Movement. Yet, knowing he must move ahead with or without the national office's blessing, Salter decided he at least needed the support of the state NAACP board, which was to meet on May 12. The night before the meeting, Salter drafted a resolution that he hoped would put the state board on record as supporting not only the boycott, but "massive and intensive direct action" including picketing, sit-ins, and mass marches.[99]

Clarence Mitchell, the long-time NAACP lobbyist and attorney and close friend and confidante of Medgar and Myrlie Evers, was at the state board meeting the next day when Salter proposed his resolution. Mitchell was to be the keynote speaker for a mass meeting of NAACP regulars the next day to commemorate the ninth anniversary of the Supreme Court's *Brown* decision. Events suggest that Mitchell had been forewarned about Salter's activities and asked to report back to Current and Wilkins in New York.

When Salter handed out his resolution just prior to the start of the meeting, Mitchell almost immediately began revising it, removing any reference to direct action. Mitchell said he didn't want the national office to be "put on the spot." Apparently unaware of Mitchell's national reputation or prominent role within the NAACP, Salter blew up at what he considered this intruder's audacity. "I'm a member of the board," Salter stormed. "You're not! What right do you have to modify my resolution?" He pushed the board to decide the merits of the resolution without Mitchell's interference. Evers and Aaron Henry, the board president, helped calm the tension and agreed to present the resolution as Salter had written it, although Henry suggested that the group might wish to moderate the tone for public consumption. The resolution passed unanimously, and Salter participated in making some cosmetic changes. The state branch of the NAACP would stand behind the Jackson Movement and support demonstrations if necessary. In the process of securing that support, however, Salter had made a powerful enemy within the NAACP's upper echelon.[100]

That evening, Salter and Evers drafted eight identical letters to the Jackson power structure, including Governor Barnett, Mayor Thompson, the chamber of commerce, and the Downtown Jackson Association. "The NAACP is determined to put an end to all forms of racial segregation in Jackson," the letter began.[101] It listed all of the boycott demands and stated: "We are determined to end all state and local government-sponsored segregation in the parks, playgrounds, schools, libraries and other public facilities." A variety of tactics would be used to secure these goals, the letter stated, including "picketing, marches, mass meetings, litigation and whatever other legal means we deem necessary." Lastly, the letter pleaded with city officials and community leaders to negotiate, and even called upon President Kennedy and other national leaders to help get negotiations started. The letter was signed by Evers, Salter, and Jackson Branch President Doris Allison. "We were now moving, headlong, into a new dimension," Salter later commented.[102]

The NAACP's national staff clearly had their eyes trained on Birmingham and its possible impact on Jackson. This concern is evident by the content and tone of a memorandum from Gloster Current the next day, May 13, to all regional and field secretaries. Current's memo focused on "the apparent success of the Birmingham protest" and his suspicions that "Jackson, Mississippi, will be the next scene of attack of the King forces."[103]

Neither had the lessons of Birmingham been lost on the Jackson business community, the Citizens' Council, or the mayor; all three became more firmly resolved not to allow any compromise and their rhetoric became increasingly shrill. The letter from the Jackson Movement leadership simply caused them to tighten their ranks. Mayor Thompson went on television the night he received it to denounce the NAACP and offer his own vision of what it was like to live in Jackson.[104] "Tonight I want to try to reassure each one of you that we are going to continue our way of doing things," Thompson declared, "and although we are going to have turbulent times, when all of the agitation is over, Jackson will still be prosperous, people will still be happy, and the races will still live side by side in peace and harmony. We have some of the best facilities you can find anywhere," he continued:

> Beautiful, wonderful schools, parks, playgrounds, libraries and so many, many other things. There are no slums. Have you ever thought about it? You can go into practically any other large city and you will find slums, but you won't find them here. You will not find anything that will breed discontent. Then we have the spirit of unity, with everyone trying to work together to work out our problems peaceably. Probably most important of all, we have good people. Good

white people, good colored people. We do not tolerate law violations of any kind, and we do not tolerate any intimidation by any person.

After asking whites to continue to work towards peaceful solutions to race problems ("be tolerant and sincere in all your dealings"), Thompson appealed directly to "our Nigra citizens":

> All of this is being said in a way so as not to worry anybody, to create any agitation, but to get over to you some of the things that are in my heart. You live in a city, a beautiful city. You have twenty-four hour protection by the police department. You live in a city where you can work, where you can make a comfortable living. You are treated, no matter what anybody else tells you, with dignity, courtesy, and respect. Ah, what a wonderful thing it is to live in this city!

Thompson then reminded black citizens of their responsibilities and asked them not to listen to "false rumors which will stir you, worry you, and upset you. Refuse to pay any attention to any of these outside agitators who are interested only in getting money out of you, using you for their own selfish purposes." The mayor firmly asserted that there would be no changes in the city's segregation codes—insisting, in fact, that they were voluntary—and that he and his staff would resist all pressure from both the federal government and "agitators." He said that in his assessment, other cities that had tried compromise typically ended up, thanks to the NAACP, "just about in worse shape than they were before." He concluded by asking all citizens for their support and prayers to help keep "our city the finest and greatest in the nation."

Thompson's claims about the city's harmonious race relations were scoffed at by the black community, but the speech opened up a window of opportunity. Since Thompson had singled out the NAACP specifically, Evers requested equal television time for rebuttal through the Federal Communications Commission. He also believed that, since the situation was beginning to appear more prominently in the news, the NAACP national office would have no choice but to back the Jackson branch's call for demonstrations. In addition, Evers suggested that a strategy committee be formed to help manage the escalating crisis and named Salter as the chair. Salter agreed to serve only if Pearlena Lewis, as representative of the local community, was named cochair. Lewis accepted on behalf of the youth council.[105]

The next day—now just two weeks before the Woolworth's sit-in—the NAACP national board came through at last with a public endorsement of the local group's activities. "We pledge the support of the national organization to the Mississippi state NAACP board of directors in its announced intensified program against racial discrimination and segregation in Mississippi," the national board resolved. They also authorized Roy Wilkins to raise whatever funds necessary to support the North Jackson Youth Council's "drive toward the objective of putting an end to all forms of racial discrimination and segregation in Jackson." At last, the Jackson Movement had the backing it needed to move its agenda forward.[106]

THE FRENZY OF ACTIVITY DURING THE NEXT TWO WEEKS READS LIKE A FAST-moving Hollywood script: mayor announces he wants to meet with "responsible 'Nigra' leaders"; primary black leader responds that any negotiations must be with true representatives of the black community; adult black business and clergy leaders begin to get involved; black leaders are invited to join the strategy committee; strategy committee begins to split; white ministers try to negotiate a settlement; police chief announces his forces are readying for riots. With Birmingham still in the news and on everyone's minds, Jackson seemed ripe for the next battle in America's escalating race war.

At the beginning of this frenzy, once the NAACP national office had endorsed the Jackson Movement, the strategy committee chaired by Salter and Lewis began to meet nightly. Tougaloo's Ed King and CORE's Dave Dennis increased their involvement, as did an independent group called the Citizens Committee for Human Rights in Jackson.[107] Comprising primarily affluent black ministers and businessmen—none of whom were directly dependent on the white community for their livelihoods—this committee wanted some say over the direction the demonstrations would take. Evers asked them to participate in the strategy committee sessions and invited representatives of other ministerial groups he had courted over the years as well. The NAACP also began sending some of its key lieutenants to Jackson. Gloster Current and Laplois Ashford arrived the day after the national board passed its resolution of support; others who soon followed included Willie Ludden, Georgia Youth Advisor Mercedes Wright, and Southeast Regional Secretary Ruby Hurley.[108]

Almost immediately, an internal split developed within the committee, with most of the newly involved adults wanting to take a slower, more cautious approach, while Salter and the youth council members urged immediate demonstrations. The Citizens Committee for Human Rights was the first to break ranks.[109] Earlier in the week the group had denounced the mayor's claims of racial harmony and demanded "an immediate end to segregation and discrimination" in Jackson. By Friday, May 17, however, the Citizens Committee had issued a statement—without advising the strategy committee—asking for a negotiating session with the mayor and indicating that its members would not participate in the threatened demonstrations. The Citizens Committee's statement was an obvious betrayal of Evers, Salter, and the youth council, but the movement leaders adopted a wait-and-see attitude, and the two groups decided to hold a joint mass meeting to elect representatives to meet with the mayor and other city officials. The election was set for the following Tuesday night, May 21. All agreed that if the mayor refused to meet with the elected group, then demonstrations would begin immediately.[110]

Nothing like this had ever happened before in Jackson. Never had such tensions been exposed nor hopes raised as high as with these new, very public developments. Every move by the mayor, by Evers, by the Citizens Committee became front-page news. Both the black and white communities hung on every new development. Despite all the back and forth, however, no real progress was being made.

The strategy committee telegrammed some of Jackson's more liberal white clergy asking them to consider meeting with the Capitol Street businesspeople to urge them to be more realistic in their response to the boycott.[111] When some of the white clergy offered to act as go-betweens, other whites in the city threatened to launch a boycott themselves if any of the businesses agreed to negotiate. The *Jackson Daily News* carried this warning: "Any ambitious pseudo-dictator who wishes to bypass the duly elected officials of Jackson and negotiate with hate groups might as well set up shop in Hong Kong or a more distant city."[112] Deputy Police Chief M. B. Pierce announced that the police department was prepared to handle whatever type of demonstrations would ensue.[113] On Sunday, May 19, the Hinds County sheriff met with his deputies and constables—a group that included D. C. Sullivan's father—and pledged his support to the Jackson city police.[114] Governor Ross Barnett also entered the fray, offering his "wholehearted cooperation" and "any and every facility at my command."[115]

To add to the drama, Evers won his appeal for equal air time from the FCC to take issue with the mayor's characterization of race relations in the city. The date for his rebuttal had been set for Monday, May 20, and Evers taped his seventeen-minute response that afternoon for broadcast later that night. He had worked on the draft of his remarks for days, and copies had been telegrammed to the national office for review and comment. Evers knew that this might be his only chance to reach a broad cross-section of Jackson's residents, black and white. He had crafted the most forceful argument ever put forth publicly by a native Mississippian as to why the state should desegregate. His on-camera delivery was slow and deliberate; his points were well-supported; his calm voice sounded steady and reassuring, without a hint of guile or resentment. It was a moment for which he had prepared most of his adult life.

After introducing himself and providing a brief history of the organization he represented, Evers defended the NAACP and its activities: "The NAACP is not subversive. It has never been on any official subversive list. In fact, FBI chief J. Edgar Hoover commended the NAACP for its stand against communism."[116]

Evers offered to negotiate with Mayor Thompson and the white businesspeople, and then moved to the heart of his presentation. In this very personal passage, Evers attempted to bridge the gap between the moderate whites in his target audience and the very people who had touched his own heart while traveling the dusty Delta roads more than a decade earlier.

> Tonight the Negro plantation worker in the Delta knows from his radio and television what happened today all over the world. He knows that Willie Mays, a Birmingham Negro, is the highest paid baseball player in the nation. He knows that Leontyne Price, a native of Laurel, Mississippi, is a star with the Metropolitan Opera in New York. He knows about the new, free nations in Africa and knows that a Congo native can be a locomotive engineer, but in Jackson he cannot even drive a garbage truck.
>
> He sees a city where Negro citizens are refused admittance to the City Auditorium and the Coliseum; his children refused a ticket to a good movie in a downtown theater; his wife and children refused service at a lunch counter in a downtown store where they trade; students refused the use of the main public libraries, parks, playgrounds and other tax-supported recreational facilities.

Evers then asked the rhetorical question, "What, then, does the Negro want?"

> The Negro citizen wants to get rid of racial segregation in Mississippi life because he knows it has not been good for him nor for the state. The Negro citizen wants to register and vote. The Negro Mississippian wants more jobs above the menial level in stores where he spends his money. He wants the public schools and colleges desegregated. He feels strongly about these and other items although he may not say so publicly.

Evers chided the mayor about the kind of peaceful integration he suspected Thompson had witnessed on visits to northern and even some southern cities, and then he made a direct request of his white listeners: "Let me appeal to the consciences of many silent, responsible citizens of the white community who know that a victory for democracy in Jackson will be a victory for democracy everywhere." Evers ended by quoting from a speech by President Kennedy two days earlier at Vanderbilt University: "This nation is now engaged in a continuing debate about the rights of a portion of its citizens. That [debate] will go on and those rights will expand until the standard first forged by the nation's founders has been reached—and all Americans enjoy equal opportunity and liberty under law." "To these words," Evers concluded, "one can only say, 'Amen.'"

It would be difficult to overestimate the importance of this television appearance—of this moment—on the racial balance in Jackson. For a black native Mississippian, one who still resided in the state, to address white and black citizens in a public forum about matters of race and conscience was simply unheard of. The speech emboldened local blacks and enabled them to begin to believe that change was possible, even in Mississippi.[117] For at least one white, however, the speech caused such furor that he would not be satisfied until its messenger had been permanently silenced.

AS EVERS MADE HIS TV DEBUT THAT EVENING, REPORTERS HAD THEIR EYES ON the television screen while their minds were attempting to assess the meaning of the U.S. Supreme Court ruling handed down that day on the legality of the sit-ins. Six months earlier, the Court had heard six separate cases appealing sit-in and other demonstration convictions that dated back to 1960—the first year of student protests. Sit-ins from four states were represented: one from Durham, *Avent* v. *North Carolina*[118] (which included Joan Trumpauer as a defendant); one from New Orleans, *Lombard* v. *Louisiana* (which included George Raymond's friends from CORE as defendants); two cases from Birmingham, *Shuttlesworth* v. *City of Birmingham* and *Gober* v. *City of Birmingham*, the former filed on behalf of Fred Shuttlesworth, the pioneer of the Birmingham Movement; and one from Greenville, South Carolina, *Peterson* v. *City of Greenville*. Another case, *Wright* v. *Georgia*, involving the integration of a city playground in Savannah (the movement that Willie Ludden and Mercedes Wright spearheaded) was also heard. NAACP attorneys were involved in five of the six cases; the U.S. Justice Department had filed briefs on behalf of the protesters in five of the six cases, as well.

In a surprise ruling—at least for the South—the court decided eight to one that the sit-ins were legal and should not have been interfered with by local police. In every case but one, the court reversed the convictions of the protesters; in the remaining case—the one in which Trumpauer had a stake—the court remanded the decision back to the state supreme court to reconsider in light of the high court's rulings on these other cases.

In a news story the following day, the Associated Press summarized the complicated legal questions:

> The court ruled Monday that a state or city may not interfere in any fashion with peaceful sit-in demonstrations in public places of business. However, the court did not draw a clear line of when a shopkeeper may on his own refuse to serve Negroes or call police to have them evicted from his property. The court declared it unconstitutional for a state to require segregation and use its powers to enforce it.[119]

The Court's murkiness on the issue of a merchant's right to discriminate, and how police might be used in such an instance, left an opening through which the Jackson Movement would slip, without a full appreciation for the danger it would invite.

MEANWHILE, ANOTHER ARM OF THE FEDERAL GOVERNMENT WAS ABOUT TO enter the fray in a more direct way. From documents obtained through the Freedom of Information Act, it is now clear that by this third week of May, the Justice Department was keeping a fitful watch on Jackson and by week's end would order some of its agents from the Federal Bureau of Investigation's New Orleans office to head to Mississippi's capital city. Tellingly, their orders were "to have agents available at demonstrations which may take place in Jackson to photograph any incidents involving police action."[120]

FBI agents would be on the scene throughout Jackson's entire three-week ordeal and would record in great detail every demonstration and mass meeting they attended. But they would be woefully ineffectual in influencing the course of those events—silent witnesses to the tragedy that would gradually engulf the city and its residents.

The FBI were not the only undercover sleuths on the scene. Agents from Mississippi's own spy agency—the Sovereignty Commission—were making regular reports to state authorities. These reports, long under seal, were opened to the public in 1998 and provide a running commentary on the events leading up to the Jackson standoff. Interestingly, at least one Commission agent, A. L. Hopkins, opined as late as May 16 that there wasn't enough local black support to pull off demonstrations in Jackson—a belief similar to the one expressed by the NAACP's Willie Ludden. Hopkins had several informants, both black and white, who were serving as his eyes and ears in the community. He posited that "after thoroughly investigating the probability of Negroes demonstrating in Jackson within the next few weeks, I am of the opinion that they will not demonstrate in the near future...."[121]

Of the many reasons he gave for this erroneous assessment, Hopkins stated that "Medgar Evers, field secretary of the NAACP in Mississippi, is a weak character and a coward"; "Doris Allison is seldom heard from as an agitator"; and "John Salter is getting very little cooperation from local Negroes [or] from both the Negroes and white students at Tougaloo College." Hopkins suggested that since the school year would be ending soon, most college students would return home, "which should lessen the likelihood of a demonstration in this area."

Hopkins concluded his report by asserting: "From all indications, Medgar Evers, Doris Allison and John R. Salters [sic] are bluffing when they threaten demonstrations in Jackson in the near future due to their weakness and lack of leadership." Hopkins went on to state that demonstrations would only happen if Negro leaders from outside the state finished in Birmingham and moved west to Jackson. His assessment of Evers, Allison, and Salter—and his predictions for what might happen next—could not have been more inept.

ON TUESDAY, MAY 21—THE SAME DAY THAT THE SUPREME COURT'S RULING ON the sit-ins appeared in the press and just one week before the demonstrations would begin—the black community turned out in force to elect representatives to negotiate with the mayor. Salter estimated that six hundred people attended the first real mass meeting of the Jackson Movement, though newspapers reported only about half that many.[122] To Salter, Evers, Pearlena Lewis, and others on the youth council, the substantial turnout was an encouraging sign indicating that people might not only be supportive of the boycott, but that they also might be willing to take a stronger stand when it became necessary to do so. The evening included freedom singing and speeches by community and boycott leaders, including Evers, Salter, and Tougaloo's Dr. Beittel. Gloster Current also publicly pledged the "full legal and financial resources" of the NAACP, and Mercedes Wright and Willie Ludden talked about the Savannah Movement's long, successful NAACP-led boycott.[123]

A list of eight demands—the number had doubled from the early days of the boycott—was presented and ratified. The Jackson Movement was now demanding that the city achieve the following:

- desegregate all public facilities, including parks, playgrounds, and libraries;
- eventually desegregate all public schools;
- remove segregation signs from all public places;
- desegregate lunchrooms and lunch counters in downtown stores;
- hire blacks on the city police force;
- upgrade the salaries of black municipal workers;
- employ black crossing guards for school zones; and,
- form a biracial committee to continue working to improve race relations.[124]

The group also approved the sending of telegrams to the mayor, to city businessmen, and to the national chain stores being boycotted strongly suggesting they negotiate or face demonstrations.[125]

At the end of the meeting, fourteen representatives were elected to negotiate with the mayor. The group included Evers and Salter, the only nonblack representative. Of the others, there were seven ministers, a doctor, and two businessmen, as well as the NAACP's Mississippi youth coordinator Johnnie Frazier, and Tougaloo activist Bettye Anne Poole.[126]

It was all for naught. The next day, the mayor rejected ten of the fourteen elected representatives (including Salter and Evers) and replaced them with his hand-picked delegates, one of whom was known to be a paid spy for the segregationists.[127] Technically, demonstrations should have started immediately, but again, most of the adults on the strategy committee urged caution and restraint, and the young people dutifully held back.

Mayor Thompson called for a meeting the following Monday, May 27, with his select committee. The four elected representatives not struck from the mayor's list issued a statement that they would not participate, but reconsidered once the mayor agreed to allow other ministers and representatives of the black community into the room, including some of those he had initially rejected.[128] The fact that the mayor was even considering talking to such a large group of black leaders was unique in the history of Jackson, so some felt encouraged that progress was being made.

Meanwhile, Ed King had also asked for a delay in the demonstrations. He had been working with some liberal white clergy as he had years earlier in Alabama and thought there might be a breakthrough over the weekend. In fact, a few white clergy thought they had made some headway with the Jackson Chamber of Commerce and also asked that demonstrations be postponed until after Monday's meeting with the mayor.[129]

The plan for Monday was that the black community representatives would meet with the mayor, but would walk out if it became obvious that he was not willing to make significant progress on the list of demands. All Jackson Movement participants agreed that such a walkout would trigger immediate demonstrations. Salter, Evers, and others, therefore, began considering what type of demonstrations they would call for should the negotiations reach a stalemate. The overall plan for the direct action phase was designed to bring Jackson officials to the bargaining table by the end of the summer.[130] The idea, Salter said, was to start small, with one or two simply executed demonstrations, followed by mass meetings to build community support. The small, attention-getting demonstrations would be repeated regularly, with the hope that support would grow and mass marches would ensue. No one expected the early protests to generate much in the way of results.[131]

For the first demonstrations, the strategy committee settled on a two-pronged attack: outside pickets of the Capitol Street stores and a lunch counter sit-in to test the Supreme Court's recent ruling. The sit-in, in fact, was an afterthought. Considering how the police immediately handled sidewalk protests, the committee was merely hoping that the sit-in would buy extra time—perhaps as much as twenty to thirty minutes—while the police struggled with the new legal question the Court had raised. The expectation was that, despite the ruling, the police eventually would decide to enter the store and arrest the demonstrators, but the added time would allow for more media coverage and thus, the strategists hoped, kickstart the direct action campaign.[132]

Years later, Salter would explain that Woolworth's was chosen as the logical location for the sit-in because it had been the site of the three earlier picketing protests.[133] The decision was not without controversy, however, even within the strategy committee. "In a sense, we were violating our own boycott by shopping at Woolworth's," Ed King observed.[134] In the end, the symbolic value of staging a sit-in there outweighed other considerations.

Evers and Salter began to line up demonstrators for the sit-in, should the talks with the mayor break down. Evers wanted Pearlena Lewis there because of her leadership ability, her standing in the youth community, and her strong alignment with the local NAACP. Salter asked Annie Moody from Tougaloo because she had been one of his most faithful workers during the buildup phase of the boycott. When he asked Moody to find another in-state participant, she thought of Memphis Norman. All three were residents of Mississippi. None could be accused of being an outside agitator.[135] By Friday, the plan was set. It then was just a waiting game until the meeting with the mayor on Monday.

That weekend, as he often did when he needed to think, Salter went for a drive in the country near the Tougaloo campus. While turning over in his mind the recent dramatic events—the national NAACP's new outlook on the Jackson Movement, the escalating tensions with the local power structure, and the overwhelming realization of what it would take to finally throw open the gates of Mississippi's closed society—Salter suddenly had an unshakeable premonition: the national NAACP is going to sell you down the river. "Perhaps it was just an intuition of a good radical agitator," he later speculated, "or maybe the spirit of an ancestor saying, 'Look, Sonny, be careful. These bastards aren't your friends.'" Whatever it was, wherever it came from, Salter became suspicious.

The next day, he shared his unease with Evers, and in the tension of the moment, Evers exploded. "You're too paranoid, John! Way too paranoid!" Evers shouted. "I know these people! They've given their word and they won't let us down." It was the only time the two men ever really had it out. Once they both calmed down, they agreed there was no choice but to move forward, despite Salter's nagging sense that something wasn't quite right.[136]

ON SUNDAY, MAY 26, TOUGALOO HELD ITS COMMENCEMENT EXERCISES. JOAN Trumpauer, Memphis Norman, and Annie Moody all attended and saw many of their friends graduate and move on. Ed King provided the opening benediction, and John Salter and Lois Chaffee were also in attendance, along with many of the students who had worked on the boycott since November. Salter found out who was going to be staying around until summer school and recruited them for various jobs in the likely event that negotiations the next day broke down. He also suggested that they go to the Masonic Temple on Monday and begin lobbying the strategy committee to start demonstrations. He wanted to create a sense of urgency so that the adults could not again call off the demonstrations for yet another failed attempt at negotiation.[137]

The gambit worked. Salter said that Evers in particular felt that the time was right to make a move. Perhaps he had been heartened by the day's international news. His Mau Mau hero, Jomo Kenyatta, had been democratically elected president of Kenya, and Evers seemed ready to try something new. When the national media began to sense a big story developing and called on Monday to find out if demonstrations would take place the next day, Evers told them, "In all likelihood, yes."[138]

While some white clergy met with white business leaders that day, eleven of the elected representatives of the Jackson Movement and six of the mayor's designees met with the mayor and two of his city administrators at city hall. Tougaloo's chaplain, Ed King, tried to join the negotiating team, but was turned away at the door and left peacefully, still hoping that some good could come from the meeting. To no one's real surprise, however, Mayor Thompson balked at nearly every demand. He did offer to hire some black police and crossing guards to serve the black portions of the city once the racial crisis settled down. But he also threatened that certain projects planned for blacks, like building a community swimming pool and upgrading the schools, would not move forward unless the threat of demonstrations was called off. He flatly denied the request for a biracial committee and refused to interfere with the practices of white-owned city businesses, including the segregation of lunch counters. Thompson disingenuously claimed he was "not in a position to bargain for Jackson businessmen." Still, he urged the group to work things out with him rather than following "outside agitators" into demonstrations.[139]

When he had heard enough, one of the ministers from the elected group announced: "I don't believe, from the speech that you gave, that there is anything in it that would coincide with the things that we have in mind." Most of the group started to leave, but perhaps as a way of delaying the inevitable, the mayor appealed to the clergyman to at least read to him the list of the Jackson Movement's demands. After doing so, the minister and twelve others—including two of the mayor's own handpicked representatives—got up and left the room.[140]

The signal was clear. It was time to hit the streets.

By this point, the FBI had descended on the city and were infiltrating the meetings with city officials. At least one FBI undercover agent attended the mayor's meeting with the black clergy and filed a full report to J. Edgar Hoover that evening.[141] Even the highest officials in Washington, D.C., were getting skittish about what might happen next.

That night, the strategy committee worked late putting the finishing touches on plans for the next day's demonstrations. Ed King clearly recollected that the picketing was expected to cause greater interest than the sit-in. "The Woolworth thing was secondary," he said.[142] In fact, no one expected much to come of either of the protests. They were only supposed to provide a slow, solid start to a long siege.

Salter advised everyone involved to arrive early the next morning at the Masonic Temple for a final briefing.[143] As the strategy committee meeting broke up, everyone went home to ponder what the next day might hold. No one knew quite what to expect when the long-awaited direct action phase finally began.

CHAPTER 6

"THE BEGINNING OF CHANGE IN MISSISSIPPI"

PEARLENA LEWIS DIDN'T SLEEP VERY WELL THE NIGHT BEFORE THE SIT-IN.[1] Her feelings were a jumble: somewhat anxious though also excited, Lewis felt honored that, despite her youth, Medgar Evers had chosen her for a key role in the demonstration. She awoke early and gave her family no warning of what she was about to do; she had told Evers she felt "of age to make [this] decision myself." She had gotten her hair done the day before and decided to wear a simple blue and white knit outfit: "nice, but not overly dressed," she recalled. (In the early 1960s, students still dressed up for civil rights demonstrations to show their respectability.) Lewis left the house early and joined Evers and Lillian Louie at the NAACP offices adjacent to the Masonic Temple.[2]

It was a warm, muggy Mississippi morning, with clouds rolling in from the west and a thunderstorm expected later in the day.[3] Lewis confided to Louie her mixed emotions. "I wasn't frightened," she would recollect years later. "It was just a matter of not knowing what would happen."[4]

The Tougaloo crowd arrived at the Masonic Temple about 9:30 that morning and reviewed the agreed-upon plan once more. Lewis, Memphis Norman, and Annie Moody would be driven to a spot convenient to Woolworth's Capitol Street entrance. They would enter the store at 11:00, browse separately for some small items to purchase, and then, at precisely 11:15, converge on the lunch counter. Lewis gave her watch to Norman so he would know when to give the signal for them to take their seats.[5]

Salter also went over plans for the second demonstration, scheduled for 11:30, just up the street from Woolworth's near one of the busiest downtown intersections. Though the picketing would be done by an integrated group, white and black picketers would be driven to the scene separately so as not to raise suspicion. Carrying their signs in paper bags, the groups would arrive at the agreed-upon spot from two different directions, then pull out the signs and begin walking up and down before another targeted store. Both the picketing and the sit-in strategies contained an element of surprise, a favorite Salter tactic. Additionally, to ensure the police didn't figure things out too quickly and arrest the protesters before the media arrived, more young people—including George Raymond—would leave the Masonic Temple at intervals to act as decoys, walking up and down Capitol Street, entering stores or window-shopping at will. The police would have to follow everyone leaving the temple and would not know which students were the demonstrators.[6]

It was Evers's job to handle the media. He called the local newspapers and TV stations around 10:30 to tell them to expect some action on Capitol Street within the hour. As on other occasions, the media contacted the police, who were thus on full alert when the groups left the Masonic Temple ten minutes later, split up, stepped into cars, and headed toward the downtown area.[7]

NAACP regular James Wells drove Lewis, Norman, and Moody in his green station wagon. If Lewis didn't admit to being frightened on the trip downtown, Norman surely did. "We were all three so afraid," he recalled. "This was the moment of truth."[8] They entered Woolworth's exactly at 11:00, then separated and wandered around the store. Norman remembered buying a fountain pen and some batteries. As with other sit-ins, the idea was to establish that black customers' money was accepted everywhere in the store except at the lunch counter. This discrepancy could theoretically provide a source of discussion with waitresses, store managers, newsmen, and hecklers and might even have some legal bearing for future court rulings.

At precisely 11:15, Moody, Norman, and Lewis took their seats in the middle of the fifty-two-seat lunch counter. Norman recalled choosing that spot because there were several empty seats together. Lewis and Norman sat side by side. Moody dropped her handbag and sweater on the seat to the right of Norman, which had a large lemonade maker right in front of it, and sat on the next stool over.[9]

Once in position, the students first attempted to place an order. When the waitresses pretended the new customers weren't there, the three began writing their own orders on the order forms lying on the counter in front of them. Norman wrote out a request for a hamburger and a cup of coffee. One of the others asked for a soda and a piece of pie. They even wrote down prices, figured the tax, and computed the totals.[10]

Film footage reveals a calm, eerily quiet demonstration at this point—as if the city were trying to ignore its significance, hoping it would just go away. The three joked among themselves, wondering aloud if they'd ever get served anything to eat that afternoon.[11]

Eventually, a waitress came over and explained, somewhat condescendingly, that if they wanted to be served, they would have to go to the end of the counter near the back of the store and order at the "Negro counter," which had about thirty seats. She "didn't act angry," Norman said. "It was just as if we had sat in the wrong place and we didn't know what we were doing." However, when Moody responded to her, "But we'd like to be served here," and it was clear that the three weren't moving, the waitress moved brusquely away and turned out the lights above the counter, signaling to all customers that the counter was now closed. At that point, all the waitresses moved to the back of the store.[12]

Most of the half dozen or so white customers, primarily women, including one with a toddler in tow, got up and quickly left the counter and exited the store. One young woman took her time finishing her banana split, sneering all the while at the demonstrators but not saying a word. To the students' surprise, a short, middle-aged white woman, dressed as if she were having tea at a church social, white gloves and all, walked over to them and apologized for having to leave. "I'd like to stay here with you, but my husband is waiting for me," she said. Dub Shoemaker, the *Jackson Daily News* reporter, had appeared in the meantime and asked the woman to identify herself, but she would only say she was a native of Vicksburg, had lived in California, and had only recently relocated to Jackson. "I am in sympathy with the Negro movement," she stated firmly. Lewis was stunned. "I didn't think any of them would talk to us," she said.[13]

Once the white customers had left, store manager Howard Braun[14] roped off the entire counter—except for the area where the demonstrators were seated—so no one else would sit down and expect service. By that time, other reporters had discovered what was going on. Newsmen—print, radio, and TV—and cameramen rushed to the scene and swarmed around the students, asking them who they were, where they were from, and why they were taking this action. All three responded that they were Tougaloo students and residents of Mississippi. "All we want is service," Moody explained. Lewis made a point of mentioning that she was a native Jacksonian, thereby challenging Mayor Thompson's myth of the city's satisfied black population.[15]

Norman, Moody, and Lewis began to get worried when their little demonstration lasted more than fifteen minutes. "I was just sure they would come in, say we didn't belong, and take us right on out," Lewis later said. Norman remembered their banter: "Where are the police?" "When are we going to get arrested?" "What do we do now?" Just then, a black busboy came out of the kitchen, apparently unaware of what was going on. As he began to replace a set of glasses under the counter, Moody tried to engage him in conversation, but he quickly left, likely worried he'd be fired if he spoke to her. The three continued to sit, somewhat skittishly, at the darkened counter, waiting to see what would happen next. Would they simply be ignored? Moody thought the newsmen were beginning to lose interest, although the three told the journalists that they were determined to stay until served or until the store closed that evening. It looked like, either way, it would be a long wait.[16]

Meanwhile, others were also getting suspicious about the lack of police involvement. After dropping off the demonstrators in front of Woolworth's, James Wells parked his car a few blocks away, walked back to the store, and from the phone booth in the back reported to Evers what was happening. In his first call, made about 11:30, he told Evers that nothing much was going on, that the students had not yet been arrested, and that police were not entering the store. "This was fatally ominous," observed Salter, who by that point had taken a carload of pickets to the downtown area and returned to the NAACP office. "It was a departure from the norm in Mississippi. That's when you start wondering."[17]

ED KING WAS DISTRACTED THAT MORNING. HE WAS SUPPOSED TO BE THE OF-ficial spotter for the sit-in and was inside Woolworth's when the demonstration began, but something was bothering him. He had seen news clippings of the Salters being arrested together the prior December and wanted a similar experience for himself and his wife. But Jeannette King was part of the picketing up the street, while he felt stuck at Woolworth's.[18]

King's six-foot, five-inch frame towered over the small group of onlookers near the counter and his clerical garb of white collar and black shirt—what the SNCC kids called his bulletproof vest—set him even further apart. He had seen the white woman speaking to the demonstrators and was surprised to hear she was from his hometown. "I was just so impressed that a southern white woman didn't faint," he joked. "Nor did she get up angrily in a huff and walk out or scream for help. She stayed. She made it all very normal and cool." King thanked her for her bravery and wanted to talk more, but he sensed anger from the dozen or so other whites who had begun to gather.[19]

At this quiet point in the demonstration, King recalled that many white and black customers were still shopping in other parts of the store. Any who glanced over toward the lunch counter quickly looked away, not wanting to believe what they saw, perhaps, and certainly not wanting to have any part of it. As the demonstration continued without incident, King became convinced that the students would be ignored until they decided to leave. Figuring they were safe, King tried to persuade one of the reporters—Ken Toler of the Memphis *Commercial Appeal*—to accompany him up the street for the picketing. However, Toler had better news instincts. "This isn't over yet," he told King. "We can't have a sit-in this quiet in Jackson. I'd better stay here."[20]

King decided to leave the store for a few moments anyway in hopes of catching a glimpse of his wife on the picket line. Instead, he saw her being hauled off in a paddy wagon. All five pickets—two white and three black—had been arrested less than a minute after revealing their signs and walking briskly before the Wilson Discount Store. "Jackson Needs a Bi-Racial Committee," some of their signs read. Accompanying Jeannette King were Tougaloo student body president Eddie O'Neal, Jackson State College student Doris Bracey, a black waitress named Eddie Jean Thomas, who lived near the NAACP offices, and Swiss-born Margrit Garner, wife of a Tougaloo professor.[21]

With one demonstration over, the police and bystanders shifted their attention to Woolworth's, so King walked the half block back down Capitol Street,
past the small gathering of police and bystanders forming outside, and reentered the store. All was still relatively calm at the counter when he returned,
and Norman, Lewis and Moody continued their experiment in civil disobedience and wondered why they weren't being arrested.

IN FACT, THOUGH NONE OF THE DEMONSTRATORS KNEW IT AT THE TIME, ONE
of the sit-in strategies was working more effectively than anyone could have
imagined. Based on the Supreme Court's recent ruling, the police had been
advised by legal counsel to remain outside the store and to follow the Court's
directions explicitly. Rather than overrule the federal court and declare state
jurisdiction as the Jackson Movement leaders had assumed they would, the
police followed the letter of the law. If they were confused, it was only over
what to do if trouble broke out. Some would come to believe the police inaction, particularly as the situation became more and more volatile, was an
intentional misinterpretation of the Court's ruling. Others on the scene that
day disagree.

Jackson police detective Jim Black was on call the morning of May 28
when Captain John Ray asked him to go down to Capitol Street in his civilian
clothes. Ray had a plan to accommodate the Supreme Court decision while
attempting to offer some protection to the demonstrators. "Captain Ray covered his bases real well," Black recalled admiringly, and he felt certain that Ray
would have advised the store manager about the Court's ruling and the fact
that the manager would have to invite the police into the store, in writing, if a
problem occurred. To hedge his bets, however, Ray sent in Black undercover
to be available should he be needed.[22]

When Black entered Woolworth's that day, store manager Braun and his
employees were trying to ignore the demonstrators and allow business to go
on as usual. The police force, however, was growing into a small army outside
the store entrance, while a group of hostile whites was forming inside.

Newsreel footage at this point of the sit-in shows Lewis, Moody, and Norman still quite calm. If they were scared, they weren't showing it. Norman
ducks his head down and around to look at the cameramen. Lewis and Moody
look straight ahead, hands clasped as if in prayer. A photograph of this quiet
scene, taken from a low, side angle, features a backlit sign above their heads
that reads "Roast Turkey Dinner, 70 cents." The light from the sign is the only
illumination on their faces since the lights above the counter had been turned
off and the students' backs are mostly turned toward the camera. The demonstrators appear at peace, even serene.[23]

Outside, however, word had been leaking out across the city that something was happening at Woolworth's, and more and more curiosity seekers

were trickling in. Just before noon, some kids from Central High School began to drop by to see what was going on. The high school students were joined by locals like Red Hydrick, an old bootlegger from the next county over who sold the kids liquor on Friday and Saturday nights. Hydrick was a virulent racist who had roughed up Medgar Evers and others outside the courthouse two years earlier during the trial of the Tougaloo Nine for their library sit-in. A number of Citizens' Council members from the business community also came by, as did some Sovereignty Commission spies. Several FBI agents also arrived, attempting to go unrecognized in their sunglasses, which they wore for the duration of the sit-in. And two certifiable thugs—one a former Jackson policeman named Bennie Oliver—happened along, as well. King estimated that at this point about fifty whites were gathered around the three black students.[24]

This growing crowd began to buzz with excitement as they realized that the police were not taking action: something new was happening on Mississippi's freedom front, and they were on the scene to witness it. The noise from the crowd began to take on a hostile tone; curses and threats started to be hurled at the demonstrators. "Go back to Russia, you black bastards!" someone shouted.[25]

Some teenagers made hanging nooses—evoking the specter of a lynching—from the rope cordoning off the counter, and they mockingly began trying to put the noose over the necks of the demonstrators. When the store manager came out and chased the rowdy teens away, he also announced that the counter was closed. No one moved.[26]

Lewis recalled that she, Norman, and Moody had decided by then not to turn around to allow their taunters to see any fear on their faces. They would instead remain peaceful, nonviolent, and still. Moody, however, said she glanced back every so often to get a feel for the crowd. When she spotted the drunk from her earlier bus station sit-in among the group and saw that this time he had a knife, she quickly told the others. Norman suggested they bow their heads and pray.[27]

ONCE INSIDE THE STORE, DETECTIVE BLACK NOTICED RED HYDRICK AND Bennie Oliver. He knew both to be what he later referred to as "hatemongers" and realized that either could cause serious trouble. Oliver was of particular concern: at age twenty-six, and with a sizable six-foot, two-inch, 210-pound frame, he was both young and fierce. A native Mississippian, Oliver had grown up on a riverboat in the swampy Glen Allan area, just off the Mississippi River near where the Louisiana, Arkansas, and Mississippi borders meet. "He was a raised-up river rat," Black said. "His people were all trappers and fishers, and he was one tough guy." Black had helped train Oliver for the police force during his patrolman days, but Oliver had been fired for his tendency to pick fights and cause trouble—mostly off duty—particularly after he had been drinking. "He was as tough as a lighter knot," Black said, referring to the dense pine knots found in the region, suitable for starting fires. Oliver "would always pick out the toughest guys to fight," recalled Black. "I used to think he ought to be a prize fighter because he hit *so* hard."[28]

At Woolworth's, when Oliver moved closer to the counter and spoke to Hydrick, Black had a feeling that something was about to happen. Then Oliver, spotting Black, went back to have a word with him. "If I knock that son of a bitch off that stool, what'll happen?" Oliver asked excitedly. "I'll put your ass in jail," Black snapped back, none too happy to hear the question. Forewarned, Oliver headed back toward the counter.[29]

At about 12:15, as the lunch crowd was making its way into the store, Oliver decided to spark the action to life. As he approached the counter, reporters heard him say, "I'm gonna go up there and push that black bastard off that stool." Oliver tapped Norman on the right shoulder—the side next to the seat Moody had left empty—and, as Norman turned, Oliver decked him with a powerful punch to the head. "He hit him right in the spot that would knock him out," Black said. The crowd squealed with delight and lunged forward to get a better look.[30]

Norman was certain he had been hit by a baseball bat, though Detective Black insisted that Oliver only used his fists. "I've never been hit that hard in my life," said Norman, who for the rest of his life would feel pain where he was hit that day. The blow didn't knock Norman out immediately, but he felt himself losing consciousness as he fell backwards onto the floor. Oliver and his friend then began laying into Norman with full-force body kicks. They first kicked him in the stomach, then moved up to his chest and head. Although he had never been trained in nonviolent resistance, Norman instinctively curled up in the fetal position and put his arms over his head. Oliver continued kicking and then started stomping on Norman's head until blood began spurting from his mouth, nose, and ear. Oliver's buddy and others in the crowd cheered.[31]

In the surviving film footage—and there is precious little of it despite the presence of cameramen from all three major networks—this crucial scene is hard to make out. Once the violence erupted, the cameramen scattered, running back toward the other end of the counter, trying to avoid getting hurt themselves. What remains is a blurred image of Oliver's white tennis shoe connecting with a dark mass on the floor. In slow motion, it becomes obvious that the mass is a human being.[32]

The still photographs are more revealing. Jack Thornell, senior photographer for the *Jackson Daily News*, took some of the photographs that would be flashed across America that afternoon and the next day. In one, a boy who could not be more than twelve years old is standing watching Oliver's foot moving toward Norman's head. The boy looks mesmerized, not frightened. In the same frame, Oliver's friend smiles and stands ready to kick again, while older crowd members gaze down at the scene with expressions of surprise mixed with curiosity. No one attempts to intervene.

The photographs show the brutality of Oliver's attack, as the entire force of his muscular body connects again and again with Norman's slack frame. In one photo Oliver kicks Norman in the head, as if he were kicking a football. In others, he pulls Norman up by his collar, preparing to punch him in the face.[33]

Oliver was still performing his "dance macabre," as Ed King would later allude to it,[34] when state senator Hugh Bailey, who had rushed to the scene from the state capitol building three blocks away, brought the ex-cop to his senses. "Bennie, stop now before you get into serious trouble!" Bailey yelled. Clearly the senator saw how the scene might play itself out if unchecked.[35]

When asked about the experience years later, all Norman could remember was the pain, along with his determination not to strike back. For him, what actually took only a matter of minutes seemed like much, much longer. He recalled focusing on the stainless steel footrest at the bottom of the counter as he was being beaten. He felt the blows to his body and knew there was no way he could get up. He vaguely remembered curling up to avoid serious injury. "My instincts told me to do that," he says. Semiconscious, he began moaning in pain as the crowd grew quiet.[36]

Blood was everywhere. Norman's lower lip had burst open from the force of one of the kicks to his head. He felt a warm sensation near his right ear and temple where he had been first hit. "All of these stories about brutality against blacks by whites, and suddenly I'm in this environment where I'm the object of violence," he recounted more than thirty years later, still visibly shaken by the experience.[37]

Some news stories reported that Detective Black watched the assault on Norman and headed toward the counter only after it was finished. Black insisted, however, that as soon as Bennie Oliver unloaded his first punch, he began to move in. Black was about forty yards away, he reckoned, and, without the benefit of a police uniform, had to push his way through an excited, dense crowd intent on seeing all the action. Oliver had already halted his attack and Norman was moaning on the floor when Black finally reached them. The detective helped Norman to his feet, told him he was under arrest, and then delivered the same news to Oliver. Next, Black grabbed Norman under one arm, snagged Oliver with the other, and, to a chorus of boos from the crowd, forcefully and swiftly escorted them both from the store.[38]

Norman recalled that "blood was dripping down" as he walked. "I could taste it in my mouth. And I was very afraid." Here he was, having just been brutalized by the mob behind him (he wasn't sure how many had been involved), and now he was being led through that same mob to an uncertain destination. "All those little bastards. They were really heckling," he recalled years later while viewing photos of the incident. "I remember all the screaming and yelling: 'Commie! Nigger!'" Norman was terrified of having to walk through that crowd. "It was the most frightening thing I've ever had to do in my life," he said, and this from a future veteran of Vietnam. "I could have been shot. I could have been knifed or hit with a brick. I looked at them and saw anger on their faces. They were out of control and they wanted to hurt somebody."[39]

Norman recalled that the crowd opened up—like in a movie scene—as Black whisked him and Oliver outside to the waiting police cars. When he got outside, Norman became disoriented. He said it was so hot that the asphalt on the street felt "squishy." Time had slowed for him since that first blow to the head, and everything seemed to be happening in slow motion, every sensation was magnified. The crowd outside erupted with jeers when they saw the bloodied freedom fighter and his attacker. Norman and Oliver were put into separate (but equal) police cars and driven to the station a few blocks away.[40]

Meanwhile, back inside, Pearlena Lewis and Annie Moody were having a rough time. When the violence erupted, it was as if a bomb had gone off at the center of the long counter. Cameramen rushed into one corner of the store as chaos broke out. At some point, Moody was slapped in the face, then pulled off her stool and thrown against an adjoining shelf of knickknacks. Some reports say she tried to run away; others say she was dragged down an aisle. She remembered being down on her knees watching Norman being beaten. She believed that she was pushed by a store employee; other reports say she was pushed by Oliver's friend. A photograph that ran a few weeks later in the African American newspaper the *Pittsburgh Courier*, however, clearly shows Oliver hurling Moody into the nearby shelves.[41]

Although most newspaper accounts tell of both women being knocked off their stools simultaneously, Pearlena Lewis remembered it differently. She recalled being alone at the counter. She could see Norman getting pummeled, but was powerless to help him; and she knew something had happened to Moody, but she wasn't sure what. All she knew for certain was that she was the last demonstrator at the counter, so she just held her ground, hoping for a miracle. "I had prayed that morning for direction, peace of mind, self-discipline, and self-control," she said. With her strong spiritual focus, Lewis believed that they were all being protected and that no serious harm would come to any of them.

Determined to stay until she was carried from the store, the twenty-two-year-old college student kept telling herself, "We're here for a purpose, and it *must* be accomplished." Lewis reminded herself of segregation's effects—"the feeling of helplessness all around, every day"—and she intuitively saw this moment, this stand as "the beginning of change in Mississippi." Alone, with no one else at her side, feeling deep concern for fellow demonstrators yet with an unyielding sense of mission, Lewis held her own against the angry mob.[42]

But suddenly, while Norman was moaning on the ground, just prior to being taken out, Lewis heard someone in the crowd yell, "OK, we got one, and the other one's gone. We still have one sitting." Instantly, she felt her hair being pulled, and then she too was knocked off her stool. She felt the air move as another blow headed her way, perhaps a more harmful one, but she was already on her way down. She hit the hard, linoleum-covered concrete floor with a thud. Although she wasn't knocked out, she was off her stool and wondering how the demonstration would continue.[43]

Her miracle came in the form of Detective Black. When he emerged from the crowd and grabbed both Norman and Oliver, his actions had a sobering effect on the crowd, at least momentarily. The break gave Lewis the opportunity she needed to pull herself back up on her stool—although not before being kicked in the head by someone as she got up. Her attacker then ducked into the crowd so as not to be arrested. The lull also gave Moody the chance she needed to take back her seat. A roar of disapproval went up from the crowd as they watched the two young black women return to the counter. Much to the crowd's chagrin, the nonviolent protesters had shown their staying power.[44]

JOAN TRUMPAUER AND LOIS CHAFFEE HAD LONG SINCE COMPLETED THEIR assignment as spotters for the picketing up the street, and Trumpauer had phoned back to Salter and Evers to say that everything had gone as planned: quick demonstration, quick arrest; nothing out of the ordinary. Their jobs accomplished and with nowhere else to go, the two women headed to Woolworth's to see how things were going there.

A veteran demonstrator, Trumpauer quickly purchased some small items to establish herself as a customer and proceeded toward the counter. She got there just in time to see Norman knocked from his stool: "I saw him on the floor, just being kicked and kicked and kicked," she said, "and the crowd was just cheering it on. I just got this really sick feeling."[45]

Once Norman was taken out, Trumpauer moved closer to the counter. She would have blended right in because, as Chaffee remembered it, the crowd was a mixture of men and women. "And they weren't all yelling and screaming," she said. "There were some people who were just bystanders."[46]

Pearlena Lewis distinctly remembered (although Joan Trumpauer did not) that Trumpauer called out to her: "Pearlena, be careful! The man behind you has a big knife!" Lewis looked around, saw the knife, and froze, imagining the knife going right through her. "There were those in that group who could have done anything to us and not felt any remorse about it," she said. The man put the knife back into his pocket, but there was a heightened sense of danger as the crowd, which had swelled by then to more than one hundred, began to get carried away. Their shouts and screams became louder, though less specific, like a home crowd's hoots and hollers at a football game when the visiting team is being routed. Individuals were walking up and down past the counter, crisscrossing past Lewis and Moody, and hurling epithets: "Nigger bitch! Black whore! Goddamned communists!"[47]

As the tension mounted, Lois Chaffee's most vivid memory was of the noise. "I don't think I've ever been in a situation of just din," she said. "It was like being at a heavyweight boxing match." Ed King likened the sound to some insane southern symphony: "The white ladies in the crowd sometimes joined the men in the cursing, sometimes just screamed out their hatred in high-pitched shrieks, usually nonverbal but occasionally—like an emphatic piccolo—came a long, drawn-out wailing, 'She-e-e-e-y-i-i-t, she-e-e-e-y-i-i-i-t!' While some older southern gentlemen provided a ground bass, solid chord of 'Gahd dayumn, Gahd dayumn, Gahd dayumn,' the teenage boys chanted a more rapid, 'mothuh-fuckuh, mothuh-fuckuh, mothuh-fuckuh, mothuh-fuckuh.'" Things were clearly out of control.[48]

Next, a one-sided food fight broke out. One young blonde woman in a print dress swooped out of the crowd, grabbed a bright yellow plastic bottle of mustard from the counter, pulled back the collar of one of the black women's dresses, and squirted the bottle's contents down her back. "Take my picture!" the blonde woman shouted to the photographers. As the crowd applauded her efforts, she turned to acknowledge their applause and then rejoined them.[49]

Some teenaged boys picked up where she left off, grabbing salt and pepper shakers and a sugar canister, opening them, and then—each with his own unique style—dramatically jumping, gyrating, and screaming as they doused the demonstrators with the contents. One newsman reported that a city detective—most probably Black, although he did not recall this—stood by while the condiments were hurled. When he suggested that the teens stop, he was ignored.[50]

Meanwhile, Trumpauer was beginning to feel more vulnerable in the crowd, thinking it was only a matter of time until the mob discovered she was not on their side. By calling out to Lewis at the counter, Trumpauer had already blown her cover. "The only thing worse than a 'nigger' is a 'nigger lover,'" she remembered thinking, describing the views of the mob, and she didn't want to be by herself when they realized which side she was on. She talked to King about joining Lewis and Moody at the counter. Although King's recollection is vague on this point, Trumpauer was emphatic. "It's not the kind of decision I would have just up and made myself," she said. "We worked a lot on a consensus basis. My feeling is that [King] told us we'd be safer sitting down with the other kids, and that they needed us there with them."[51]

So Trumpauer joined the demonstration—the first white to do so. Now there were three at the counter, all women, holding the line for freedom. The crowd began to buzz like hornets. Not only were blacks sitting in the whites-only section, but a white woman had joined them. This had to be stopped. They started taunting Trumpauer: "White nigger! Commie! Nigger lover!" An older man (probably Red Hydrick) called out to the young rowdies to pull the women off their stools. "Which one should I get first?" someone asked. "The white nigger," the old man responded.[52] A six-foot, one-inch, nineteen-year-old construction worker named James Glenn Sparkman[53] grabbed the diminutive Trumpauer by the waist, pulled her off her stool, and dragged her all the way out of the store. He then "shoved her into the street" and into a waiting throng of onlookers and police. The crowd, both inside and out, cheered his bravado, but the police demanded that Sparkman release his captive, and Black, who was still on the scene, arrested Sparkman for assault.[54]

While this was going on, two white rebels grabbed Moody by the hair, pulled her off her stool, and dragged her about halfway toward the store's nearest exit. Somewhere in the fracas, she lost her shoes.[55]

Although they reacted without violence, the two women were not about to let these young toughs get the better of them. Once free of Sparkman's grip, Trumpauer immediately reentered the store and fought her way back to where Annie Moody was standing. Moody had gotten another baptism with mustard and was just waiting there, wondering what to do. Together they stood for a while, trying to find a way back to their seats, where Lewis again was alone at the counter. But since all pathways to her were blocked by an ever-growing, ever-angrier crowd, they decided to straddle the rope blocking off the counter and grab a seat—any seat—to keep the demonstration alive and themselves safe.[56]

While Trumpauer and Moody were being dragged around the store, some-one—Lois Chaffee thought it was the police, but more likely it was the store management—made another attempt to clear the lunch counter area. Manager Howard Braun began asking everyone to leave and started turning off more lights, hoping they would just go home. Chaffee, who until that point had just been watching, finally came to life. She knew she didn't want to leave Pearlena Lewis there alone. And even though it seemed that the whole thing might be called off at any moment, she didn't want to be forced out of the store. "I may have been too hysterical to comprehend what was happening," she later said, "[but] I remember feeling like I would have to leave if I didn't do something." Though she had never intended to join the demonstration and had always played a backseat role in the movement, Chaffee marshaled her courage, crouched under the rope, and joined her Tougaloo compatriot at the counter.[57]

With the return of Moody and Trumpauer to the counter, now there were four. All women. Two pairs. A black and a white in each outpost. They just sat there, calmly and quietly, continuing to absorb the verbal and physical abuse the crowd was pouring on them. Catsup had been added to the list of condiments used by the mob to douse the demonstrators, making the women appear to be bleeding.[58]

WHILE THE FOUR WOMEN WERE HOLDING THEIR OWN, JAMES WELLS HAD BEEN waiting and watching from the back of the store with some friends. A native Mississippian, Wells was born and raised about thirty miles south of Jackson. Like Medgar Evers, he was a World War II veteran, though Wells had served in the Philippines and other South Pacific locations as pilot of an amphibious vehicle in the segregated U.S. Army. After the war, Wells joined the NAACP and when Evers became Mississippi's first field secretary in late 1954, James Wells and his brother, Houston, became two of Evers's most loyal supporters.

Aside from transportation and reporting duties, Wells characterizes his role at the sit-in as part of a small but determined force of mature black men providing "security" for the demonstrators. He and two others had decided on their own to carry weapons into Woolworth's in case something really treacherous happened. "We knew it wasn't going to be nonviolent," he said. Wells knew enough about Mississippi to realize that the violent possibilities were only a knife or a gunshot away. As a southern gentleman, he also felt particularly protective of the women and intended to ensure their safety, even at gunpoint.[59]

The lessons of nonviolence seem to have been lost on Wells, and when some of the surviving demonstrators heard—thirty years later—that some of their own contingent were carrying guns, they were horrified. "If they had used their weapons, there might have been a massacre," Memphis Norman commented.[60] Nonetheless, Wells and his friends were in the back of the store and, without the knowledge of Evers, Salter, or anyone else on the strategy committee, they were ready to start shooting if the lives of the women had been endangered.

Wells again phoned Evers back at the NAACP office just after noon to report that the store was filling up with hostile whites. Soon after Wells hung up, Ed King called to report on Norman's beating and arrest. Evers responded in his typical, understated fashion, King recalled. "There was never any panic. Very matter of fact. He would want to know the details, you know, 'Do you think he's seriously hurt? OK, I'll try to see what hospital he's in. OK, now what next?'"[61]

Salter had a decidedly different reaction. Upon hearing of the violence, he leapt into action. "I was the chairman of the strategy committee. I was the advisor to the youth council. I was the person who more than anyone else had gotten this thing going. If I belonged anywhere," he said, "I belonged right there." As Salter prepared to head downtown, Evers expressed interest in going along, but Salter, fearing for Evers's life, convinced him to remain at headquarters and report the violence to the media and federal authorities. Salter then left with NAACP staffer Mercedes Wright. Walter Williams, a student at Jackson State

College and a Jackson Movement regular, happened by just then and asked to go along. Needing all the reinforcements he could muster, Salter agreed. The three piled into Salter's Rambler and headed downtown.[62]

Back at Woolworth's, Ed King continued to place calls for help. He phoned Dr. Beittel at Tougaloo to advise him that his students and staff were under attack. King also tried calling some of his minister friends at Galloway Memorial United Methodist Church a few blocks away, but it was lunchtime and no one was available. He next went outside the store and begged the police to come in. They refused, citing the recent Supreme Court decision. "We're just doing what the Supreme Court wants. It's now Washington's responsibility for what happens at that lunch counter," they told him. King then went to the store manager and threatened to sue him and Woolworth's if something wasn't done. "That lunch counter was closed an hour ago," Braun groused. "There's no reason for anybody to be sitting there. That's all we're going to do." Finally, King tried to enlist the help of a prominent white minister in the crowd whom he knew to be a community leader. "You can help break this up," King told him. "Just tell these kids to go back to school and tell the men to go home. You don't have to agree with what's going on [at the counter] to do that." King's suggestion got shrugged off. After a pause, however, the minister retorted, "They're *your* demonstrators. Why don't *you* tell *them* to leave. They're the ones causing the trouble!"[63]

Meanwhile, people in the crowd couldn't figure out who King was and what role he was playing in the demonstration. "You're with them niggers, ain't you?" someone asked. "I'll bet you're one of 'em." King wouldn't confirm or deny the allegations, but only repeated, "I'm a Christian minister and a native Mississippian."

In desperation, King began asking people at the edge of the crowd to disperse. "Those colored girls aren't hurting anyone," he'd say. "Why don't you just leave them alone?" But the hostility and ridicule he received convinced him that his efforts were pointless.[64]

During King's now-frequent calls back to the NAACP office, Evers expressed interest in coming down and joining the demonstration. "The NAACP would have fired him if he had," King believed. But the white chaplain admired Evers for the sentiment. "[He felt] that maybe his place should be at that counter, going through the hell other people were going through." Lillian Louie recalled that Evers, in fact, did leave the office for a while during the demonstration, although she couldn't say for how long. Evers did not tell her where he was going, and it is tempting to imagine him surreptitiously driving down Capitol Street to witness for himself the beginning of the first real uprising in what *Newsweek* would dub "The Battle of Jackson."[65]

King, too, wondered whether or not he should join the demonstration, but he had his own reasons for keeping a low profile. Aside from needing to carry out his assigned task as a spotter during the demonstration, King had finally won an opportunity to address the Mississippi Methodist Congress which, in a stroke of mind-boggling coincidence, happened to be holding its annual conference at Galloway Memorial that same week. Still hoping to be fully accepted into the Mississippi ministry, King was looking ahead to a vote on his status scheduled for Friday—just three days away. Maybe, just maybe, he could keep his name out of the papers until then. While he did what he could to support the demonstrators, even updating them occasionally on what was developing outside the store, he purposely minimized his presence in the demonstration in hopes that his life's mission, as he then conceived it, could still be salvaged.

BOB BULLOCK WAS ON CALL WHEN THE WOOLWORTH'S DEMONSTRATION OC-curred. As the news cameraman for WJLA-TV, he generally found his way into whatever significant story was breaking each day. Originally from Texas, Bullock had transferred to Jackson two years earlier from an affiliated station in Louisiana. Since the Jackson station wanted to beef up its live coverage of local news, "Radar Bob," as he would later be called, became its roving camera-man, capturing footage for the morning and evening news with a borrowed 16 millimeter handheld camera. That morning, when the short and stocky cameraman received word that the sit-in was under way, he hurried down to capture the action on film.

Soon, Bullock himself became part of the story. Just after Memphis Norman had been beaten, someone from the crowd took a swing at the cameraman. "All of a sudden this person—an older guy—appears and tries to grab the camera," Bullock recalled. "I wouldn't release it, so he hit me and knocked me down. Then he disappears back into the crowd." Bullock said this was only the first of many times he would be taken down in the line of duty. "People think that if they do damage to the camera, then [the news] will never get out."[66]

Other media representatives had less cause for worry about their own safety. Bill Minor, legendary Mississippi correspondent for the New Orleans *Times-Picayune*, was on hand, as were Dub Shoemaker from the *Jackson Daily News*, Ken Toler of the Memphis *Commercial Appeal*, Karl Fleming of *Newsweek*, and Jack Langguth of the *New York Times*. "They would always go after the cameramen and leave us writing stiffs alone," Minor later joked.[67]

After Memphis Norman was arrested and Bob Bullock accosted, most of the press huddled down at one end of the counter to get away from the mob. A few, however, like Freddie Blackwell, rookie photographer for the *Jackson Daily News*, and Cliff Sessions, reporter for United Press International, ventured closer to get better pictures of the demonstration and to interview some of the participants. There is a photograph and some film footage of Sessions interviewing Pearlena Lewis from behind the counter, while Lois Chaffee characteristically manages to evade both cameras—a near-invisible presence in the middle of a mob.[68]

PEARLENA LEWIS'S MOTHER HAD BEEN WORKING HER USUAL HOURS AT A local appliance outlet where a bank of TVs was turned on to attract customers into the store. At some point, the regular programming was interrupted with a news bulletin about developments on Capitol Street. Film footage of the early segment of the Woolworth's demonstration flashed across the screen as the commentator reported on the violence and mayhem under way. Margaret Lewis caught a glimpse of her daughter at the counter and let out a scream. Her boss and some white salesmen came running. Although Mrs. Lewis was unsure how they would react to her daughter's involvement in the sit-in, the salesmen seemed to be more concerned about how Lewis was handling the shock. Once sufficiently recovered, she called her husband, who had also just heard the news.[69]

Eldri Salter was at home with little Maria when news about the sit-in came over the radio. The station the Salters listened to was, in John's words, a "cracker, redneck station" which he liked "because they played Woody Guthrie's 'This Land Is Your Land' each morning." On this particular afternoon, however, the station was sending strong signals to its target market. The rebel anthem "Dixie," along with "Roll With Ross" (Governor Barnett's campaign ditty) and "Go Mississippi," boomed over the airwaves, while the station occasionally cut away to Woolworth's where a reporter provided live coverage of the chaos. Eldri remembered hearing the announcer say with increasing excitement, "A Negro from Tougaloo College has been assaulted and arrested!" and then a while later, "Professor Salter has just joined the demonstration!" Her fears heightened as she heard, "And now they're beating up on Professor Salter!" Then the station cut back to "Dixie," and there were no more live reports. To help remain calm, Eldri began baking a cake and pacing the floor. Things certainly were not going according to plan.[70]

John Salter speculated that he, Mercedes Wright, and Walter Williams arrived at Woolworth's at about 12:45 p.m., perhaps even earlier. At least one reporter, however, put their entrance closer to 1:15, and an FBI report suggests they entered about 1:30. Salter had sped down Lynch Street, cut over towards Capitol Street, and then driven around a bit in the downtown area to get a sense of the crowd and figure out a strategy for entering the store. He parked a few blocks away on a street where access to Capitol Street and the front entrances to Woolworth's were unencumbered. Then he had Mercedes Wright walk on the other side of the street from him, with Walter Williams about a hundred yards behind. This way it wouldn't look as if they were together, and if one were stopped, the others could keep going into the store. Wright was so light-skinned that Salter knew she could "pass" for white and thus move through the crowd without suspicion. For Williams, however, who had a much darker complexion, it was another matter. "Don't ask me how he did it, but he did," Salter said of Williams's entry into the raging white mob. "That kid had a lot of guts."[71]

Salter was also concerned that he might be recognized, since many of the police knew him and had been following him around town for months. As they approached Woolworth's, the professor slipped on his sunglasses, making him less likely to be immediately recognized. That, along with his youthful appearance, tricked the police, and Salter slipped right in. So did Wright and Williams. In fact, the police weren't stopping anybody; to Salter it looked like they were ushering people in, as if this were some sort of must-see civic event.

Once inside, Salter came upon a scene that he later characterized as "surreal, really wild! You had a hundred people outside, three hundred people inside, most of them ranging in age from fifteen to eighteen. Then you had these thug adult types—call them redneck agitators—then some well-dressed agitators, who I'm convinced were Citizens' Council types. And then there were FBI agents, who were always wearing sunglasses." One of the Jackson papers confirmed the FBI presence and reported that one agent was filming the scene.[72] Salter quickly sized up the situation and told King that he was there to join the demonstration. Salter and Williams then conferred briefly and decided to split up, each joining one of the sets of women. Wright was to stay in the crowd and, like King, report back to Evers and try to get word to the Justice Department.[73]

When Salter approached the women at the counter, the crowd at first thought he was on their side and was perhaps moving in to hurt the demonstrators. Once the rowdies realized that, instead, the Tougaloo professor was there to reinforce the protesters' lines, all hell broke loose. "Who's that son of a bitch?" someone screamed incredulously as Salter took the empty seat next to Joan Trumpauer. Then, once his name was circulated, Salter could hear the shock of the crowd. "Oh, him? HIM!" Most were familiar with Salter since his photo had been in the local paper the prior December for his role in the first round of picketing on Capitol Street. Now, he became the focus of the mob's furor.[74]

Just after Salter got settled on his stool, someone hit him on the side of his head with brass knuckles. His forehead and cheek immediately began to bleed. Someone else broke a glass sugar container and began cutting the back of his neck with the broken glass. Others started punching him from behind. *Time* magazine reported that Salter was beaten "until his face was raw." After getting hit again on the head, he had to steady himself from passing out by holding on to the counter. Half a dozen jeering youth swarmed around him and began to rub salt, pepper, and other condiments into his bleeding wounds, causing searing pain.[75]

Salter stoically sat there, determined to make it through. "I was committed to not letting these people have the satisfaction of seeing any of this hurt me," he said pointedly. Salter also felt that, just then, "some weird inner resources shifted." At moments of great danger in his life, an internal force would take over: "Something within me feathers out and pervades all of my heart and mind. My judgment is never better, my nerves never steadier. I'm at my very best." At such times, Salter could remain extremely focused and effective. "I can handle these things, so I was a perfect person to be in this deal." To demonstrate his inner calm, Salter tried to light a cigarette. "I was trying to smoke my Pall Mall, but I didn't have a chance," he said, "because slop was being thrown all over."[76]

Professor Salter saw that Walter Williams had made it through the crowd to the other women, but Salter was unable to help or communicate with him once Williams sat down. Even though only about half a dozen seats separated them, the noise and the crowding-in of the mob made it impossible for the two groups to have any contact. "They might as well have been on the other side of the Grand Canyon," Salter said of the other demonstrators. "It was another world away."[77]

Pearlena Lewis was grateful for the reinforcements and thanked Williams for joining them. She was encouraged by the new developments. "By the others coming in and joining us, it meant that this wouldn't go away," she said. "It was just starting." Lois Chaffee continued to be terror-stricken. "I was frozen," she said, "just focusing on the immediate. All I was able to do was hang in there— just me and that stool!" Joan Trumpauer vividly recalled the tension and the noise. Although it would rise and fall in stages, overall it just kept escalating. "It was like the tide coming in," she said. "The waves go in and out, but the tide keeps getting higher."[78]

At this point, some of the "duck-tailed white teenagers," as Newsweek's Karl Fleming described them, were standing on top of the counter, trying to get a better look at both groups, not wanting to miss a second of what they must have felt was the most historic event they had ever witnessed.[79]

Young D. C. Sullivan and his Central High friends had entered the store just after Salter and Williams arrived, and they quickly maneuvered their way to the front of the action. What Sullivan saw shocked his well-honed southern sensibilities. He had expected to see blacks being terrorized by the crowd; he hadn't conceived that whites would be with them. "It was just remarkable seeing whites and blacks sitting together," he recalled, referring to his ringside view of Salter, Trumpauer, and Moody. "Down here, that just wasn't done." In fact, Sullivan felt more hostile toward the white demonstrators. "I just knew it wasn't right," he said. "I felt the whites were the ones making the mistake and downgrading their selves." His feelings are confirmed by his vivid memory of Salter and Trumpauer; more than thirty years later, he could still remember the color and cut of their hair, the clothes they wore, their features. He could hardly remember anything about Moody at all, other than the fact that she was black.[80]

At this point, all the players are in place. Freddie Blackwell is straddling the lunch and service counters, determined to get the perfect photograph to show his Jackson Daily News audience exactly what they are missing. He points his camera, checks his flash, frames the action, and shoots. What we see in the result is a barrage of stories—individual stories, group stories—woven together to make a unique tapestry about race and resolve in a southern town.

D. C. Sullivan's friends, for instance, were encouraging him to do something about Salter. Sullivan is not, in fact, looking at the camera; rather, he is staring at Salter with a mixture of rage and incomprehension. Dragging on his Winston cigarette, Sullivan is trying to take it all in—and wondering what he should do about it.

Sullivan's best friend, Joe Johnston, with a shock of hair hanging down his forehead, stands on tiptoe trying to look over the crowd at the other demonstrators on the other side of the counter. Jimmy Madden stands next to Sullivan, just looking at him, perhaps suggesting that he and Sullivan go take Salter out. An unidentified classmate next to Madden tries to cop a hit from Sullivan's cigarette. Roger Scott, another Central High student, sits only a few stools away from Annie Moody and watches as another kid from Central High pours more sugar down the back of Joan Trumpauer's neck. Two FBI agents in dark glasses stand behind Scott, watching carefully so that later they can write reports on the incident; but in line with federal policy, they take no action to stop the riot.

Across the room, in the upper left of the photo, Red Hydrick looks over the melee, seeming a bit pleased at the scene before him. He is the patriarch in the picture: his generation will not go quietly, will allow no change to the established order, will gladly inflame youthful hysteria to try to ensure that life will continue as they all have known it.

Just in front of Hydrick stands a young man who looks bewildered. Hands by his side, he seems quizzical, wondering perhaps how he got there. His name is Smitty, and he happened on the scene quite by accident while delivering frozen french fries on Capitol Street for his new business venture, Smitty's Spuds. Woolworth's was one of his scheduled stops, but he had no idea what he was walking into. After arriving, he stayed around because he couldn't believe what he was seeing. Although he took no part in the riot, his sympathies ran strongly with the crowd, not the demonstrators. "I was mad as hell at what they were doing," he said, "sitting there and all. They had no right!" In the photograph, he looks hypnotized by what he is witnessing.

At the end of the counter to the right slumps a lone, middle-aged man. He is a cameraman taking a break from filming the action. Behind him stand several more Central High students, elevated on some Woolworth's display to get a better view of

the entire scene. At the forefront, holding their own, sit three combat-weary veterans
of so many past and future battles, wondering if they will get out of this one alive.
Whether they believed in nonviolence as a way of life, as did Trumpauer; or only as a
tactic, as did Salter; or whether they knew to fight back was pointless, as did Moody,
all three used the only weapon left to them, their vulnerable humanity, to tell the
world that this insanity had to stop.

The moment passed and the riot continued.[81]

"THEY WERE LOOKING FOR THIS KIND OF ACTION, AND THEY GOT IT," D. C. SUL-
livan later said of the demonstrators. Sullivan was part of that action and looking back more than thirty years later, he coyly admitted that he "might" have
hit Salter. He probably remembered more than he let on.[82] It might have helped
him to know, however, that Salter eventually came to forgive what the young
Jackson men and women did to him that day. "I'd love to be able to work up a
good hate," Salter would say decades later, "but even at the time I couldn't. I did
and I didn't. Because the fact of the matter is, I kept remembering when I was
that age. I can still make allowances for them, then and now." He can even be
seen in one Blackwell photo laughing along with a joke that apparently someone from the crowd shouted out. Salter instead reserved his wrath for "the
haters" in the crowd, men like Red Hydrick, and the middle-aged businessmen:
"The ones who should have known better. The Citizens' Council types who
could have stopped this if they had wanted to." By that point, however, stopping it was out of the question.[83]

Someone in the crowd discovered the spray paint aisle and began distributing cans to those closest to the counter. Suddenly, the demonstrators became
human billboards, carrying the crowd's messages in shades of pink, blue, and
green. Salter had the word "nigger" sprayed on his tan jacket. On Lewis, someone wrote, "Won't work." "Hell," "Shit," and "Red" were other crowd favorites for
what Trumpauer later ruefully referred to as "body graffiti." The spray-painting
of the demonstrators just added to the carnival atmosphere and elevated both
the hysteria and the horror.[84]

The surviving film footage of this point in the demonstration is shocking, the noise level deafening. The cameraman stands on top of the counter
and shoots down as Annie Moody moves her head and an avalanche of sugar
slowly descends from her sinking bouffant. Another shot pans the faces of
Salter, Trumpauer, and Moody. Trumpauer looks particularly dazed. Freddie
Blackwell, having just taken his most famous photograph, can be seen, dressed
entirely in black, legs still straddling the food and service counters. The blonde
woman who started the food fight reemerges from the crowd to go after Salter with some sugar. *Look* magazine published this frame of the footage as a

two-page spread to show just how venomous the scene had become. Although fuzzy, the image is a cacophony of motion and madness. Taken from atop the far corner of the counter, the shot shows a much larger, more mixed, and more raucous crowd than any captured by the still photographs. There are men and women laughing uproariously—as if they were watching a comedy act. Others are just waiting for what will come next. Bill Peart, a tall, lanky *Jackson Daily News* reporter, stands in the middle of the mob, poised to jot down the next bit of news. Moody, Trumpauer, and Salter have their backs to the camera, but the mess on their heads and backs tells as much of the story as their faces might have.[85]

On film, after the blonde woman retreats back into the crowd, a spirited young man throws yet another concoction at the back of Salter's neck. Then a scream goes up from the other side where Lewis, Chaffee, and Williams are sitting; the crowd instantly shifts to catch the new development, with kids jumping up on the counter to get to a better vantage point. The footage is a quick study in mob psychology: everyone forgets for a moment the three demonstrators they were just tormenting and shifts attention to the other tortured trio.

The scream that got everyone's attention occurred because Walter Williams had just succumbed to the crowd's blows. He had already been beaten on the back by several people in the mob, but at this point Williams had been knocked senseless by a flying object—some say it was a heavy glass, an ashtray, or a metal container; others say it was a milk pitcher, a salt shaker, or a sugar container. Whatever it was proved heavy enough to knock Williams out, and he slipped slowly from his stool onto the floor, face down, his white pullover shirt decorated with condiments and paint. Williams lay moaning on the floor while the mob surrounded him. Most were reluctant to do any further damage, knowing that Bennie Oliver had been arrested for such actions earlier. They just howled and dared him to get up. One enterprising youth was taking notes, perhaps for the school newspaper.[86]

Newsweek relates that, just then, "a thick-necked man jumped full-weight on [Williams's] back, whooped a Tarzan yell, and ran off into the cheering crowd." The perpetrator—probably Bennie Oliver's friend—fled to avoid capture by any remaining undercover police. There were none, however. Jim Black had gone to the police station to file reports on his three arrests, and the remaining police force was still outside holding to their noninterference directive, ignoring the crimes being committed inside the store.[87]

Film footage shows Williams slowly returning to consciousness, then carefully standing up and getting back on his seat next to Pearlena Lewis. Just as he does, milk is thrown against the side of his face, which registers a look of surprise mixed with resignation. At that point, he put his head down on the counter, covering himself with his arms in an attempt to prevent further abuse.

Lewis, who had just missed getting hit by both the ashtray and the milk, speaks comfortingly to Williams. Chaffee, in her only moment recorded on-camera all day, stares vacantly into space.[88]

At this point, Mercedes Wright, the NAACP official who had entered with Williams and Salter, decided to stop being a silent bystander. Although she did not sit down at the counter, she fended off would-be attackers, particularly those approaching Pearlena Lewis, whom she knew personally.

As one white woman approached Lewis with a vase, ready to hit her on the head, the short, fiery Wright intervened, screaming, "Bitch, you can hit her if you want to, but if you do, your ass is grass. *She* may be nonviolent," Wright yelled, "but *I'm* not! And if you hit her, I'm going to kick your ass!" The woman put the vase down and disappeared back into the crowd.[89]

Back down at the other end of the counter, Salter was enduring yet another ordeal. His young tormentors dabbed their lit cigarettes on his skin, creating burn marks all over the back of his neck and his cheeks. Someone smashed a glass right in front of him and it shattered, sending little bits of glass flying in every direction. "God, they were fiendish!" Salter commented years later. But in the moment he simply sat there and took it, at times putting his head on the counter and covering the back of his head with his arms. One creative youth reached around Salter's head and threw the pepper and water concoction mixture right into his eyes. This attack was not so easily ignored; Salter had the sensation of his eyes catching fire. "My eyes felt as if they were being eaten out," he later wrote. Moody passed her handkerchief to Salter to wipe his eyes. Although they continued to burn, at least he could see again. A little later, after Salter received another dose of pepper and water in his eyes, UPI reporter Cliff Sessions couldn't resist setting aside his journalistic objectivity long enough to bring over some dry napkins to him. The young reporter was shaken, calling the scene "the worst thing I've ever seen."[90]

During this time, Salter, Trumpauer, and Moody tried to make small talk to distract themselves. Trumpauer remembered the banter, but also recalled having part of her mind trained on the crowd, making mental notes in case she was questioned by police or interviewed by a reporter afterward. She had kidded around with Moody even before Salter arrived, just to keep their spirits up. "Nice hair you have," Trumpauer remarked. "That yellow goes so well with your dress," Moody responded, referring to the mustard they both wore. Trumpauer also provided encouragement to Moody, whose confidence and endurance were flagging. They recited the Lord's Prayer aloud several times.[91]

Salter also worried about Moody. "Annie was shaking," he said.[92] No doubt she was remembering how blacks back in her hometown had been treated at the hands of white mobs, how members of her race had been burned alive or lynched. Perhaps she was thinking of her mother's entreaties not to participate in such demonstrations for fear the family would suffer retaliation. Nervous though she may have been, Moody found the inner resolve to fight on.

Trumpauer also seemed to be holding her own. "Joan could be cool right in the middle of World War III," Salter later observed. Perhaps her source of strength came from so many other protest experiences. She later recounted that at about this time, she went into what might be described as an out-of-body experience. She had the sense that she was looking down on the crowd from above, taking it all in, while at the same time trying to console Moody and keep herself safe. "My main feeling that carries over from sitting at the counter," she recalled, "is of my mind being disembodied from me, which I think is a survival technique. When you're disengaged from it, you can sort of view what's going on, but not feel the terror or the emotional involvement. [I felt like] I wasn't there," she insisted. "My body was there, but I was above it—literally, just floating somewhere overhead, looking down on it." Such a feeling of separation is typical of people under severe stress, she observed, "like on the front lines of war zones."[93]

Trumpauer had the feeling that death was near, as did other demonstrators. "We could have been killed," she calmly noted years later. But that wasn't particularly upsetting to her at the time. What she carried away from the experience was a sense of commitment to those she was with—the sense that they were willing to die for each other and for their beliefs.[94]

AT SOME POINT (SALTER ESTIMATED IT AT ABOUT 1:40 P.M.), GEORGE RAYMOND joined the demonstration. As far as anyone can tell, he had been walking up and down Capitol Street for two hours, acting as a decoy, probably being followed by one or two policemen. When the crowd on the street began to get hostile, he decided to go in to see what was up. "He told us later that he felt safer inside the store," CORE's Dave Dennis recalled.[95]

Approaching the counter, Raymond must have quickly assessed the scene and decided that the Williams, Lewis, Chaffee contingent needed the most help, so he squeezed in between Williams and Lewis, making it a foursome at their end. In the only extant photograph of him at the counter, Raymond—outfitted in his trademark bib overalls and white T-shirt—looks straight ahead and projects a strong, calming presence.

Shortly after Raymond arrived, eighteen-year-old Tom Beard heard about the melee at Woolworth's and left his job up the street at H. L. Green's and rushed to the scene. He joined Salter, Trumpauer, and Moody at the other end of the counter. He was jostled a bit as he made his way through the crowd, but he hardly noticed. "I was so hyped," he said. "The only thing on my mind was getting to the counter." Beard took a seat to the left of Moody, who cautioned him not to be nervous, but Beard said he felt more anger than nerves. "There was no fear," Beard remembered. "I was just focused on protecting myself and trying hard not to strike back." After being punched in the back a few times and having whatever food remained thrown on him, Beard had to really work at remaining nonviolent. "In the neighborhood I was raised in, you didn't just sit and take stuff," he would later say. "That was as hard as keeping my feet on the floor."[96]

Beard wouldn't repeat everything the crowd said to him, but he did say someone called out that the demonstrators should be lynched. Then Beard, too, shut down his mind, just as he had learned from the nonviolence workshops he had attended. Like the other demonstrators, he succeeded at keeping his anger in check.

WHEN ED KING HAD CALLED DR. BEITTEL AT TOUGALOO EARLIER IN THE demonstration, he had asked for help, but he certainly didn't expect the college president, then in his sixties, to come down to the riot scene himself. King suggested that Beittel call Woolworth's national office in New York and ask them to close the store. And King believed that Beittel did just that. King also opined that phone calls were exchanged between the manager of the Jackson Woolworth's and his New York superiors, but they could not come to an agreement as to what should be done. King's view was that the store manager wanted to put the onus of deciding to close the store on the national office, while the New York staff felt the local manager should make the call. From King's perspective, it was only when Beittel saw that his intervention by phone was having no effect that he decided to go downtown to seek a solution.[97]

Dr. Beittel provided a somewhat different chronology of how he got involved. In an interview given shortly before his death, Beittel said that he heard about the sit-in when he turned on his television during lunch that afternoon. Once he realized that his students and professors were involved—and in serious danger—Beittel said he headed immediately downtown. When he arrived at Capitol Street, Beittel described what he saw as something akin to "a military encampment: There were policemen on horses, policemen on foot, policemen in cars—policemen everywhere up and down the street."[98]

Tougaloo's president then entered Woolworth's and sought out the store manager. Beittel described how he was directed upstairs and found Harold Braun in his office, apparently hiding out and hoping the whole thing would blow over. "He was afraid to go down to the store, even though he was the manager!" Beittel recalled in disbelief. "You'd better do something about this!" he told the manager. "They brought it on themselves," Braun replied. "There's nothing I can do about it."

Next, Beittel went outside to talk to the police. "Do something or someone's going to get killed!" he admonished. Captain Ray repeated his Supreme Court rationale. "I can't do anything until a manager asks me to do something," Ray told him. "You mean to tell me that if you looked in and saw somebody robbing a safe, you couldn't do anything because you haven't been asked to come in?" an astonished Beittel asked. Ray repeated his directive. Incredulous, Beittel next went to the counter to check on the demonstrators. He then began moving back and forth between the manager's office and the police trying to get someone to act. Eventually, Beittel recounted, a regional Woolworth's representative arrived on the scene and went upstairs to talk to Braun.[99]

IN A STRANGE AND STARTLING COINCIDENCE, AN EXECUTIVE OF THE F. W. Woolworth's Company was composing, perhaps at this very hour, a response to a request that Roy Wilkins had sent the prior week asking that the national chain store integrate its lunch counters nationwide. "If racial turbulence is to be averted in Jackson and elsewhere in the South it is imperative that steps be taken immediately to renounce the pattern of racial discrimination in service and employment," the NAACP's telegram read.[100]

E. F. Harrigan, a Woolworth's vice president, replied in a two-page letter dated May 28, 1963, with a polite but firm "no thank you, it's not our job" type of response. "Since the 'sit-in' demonstrations in the South began . . . it has been our policy to desegregate, under local leadership and without violence, our lunch counters there, along with those of other local and department variety stores. We believe this record of successful desegregation of lunch counters in department and variety stores is unmatched by any other business or group, including churches."

Harrigan goes on to claim how difficult Woolworth's position is: "It would be impossible for any manager of a national variety store in the South to assume the leadership in any desegregation program, because if he did so he would be regarded as being under the supervision and influence of 'outsiders.'"

The letter ends up promising cooperation while doing little to advance the more tolerant social policy. "The desegregation of eating facilities in some communities in the South is still, as you know, a highly emotional issue," Harrigan states without irony. "I want to assure you . . . that we are continuing to do our very best to solve this exceedingly difficult and volatile problem."[101]

Clearly the Woolworth's VP was unaware of the events occurring on that very day that would continue to tarnish his organization's reputation, particularly since his corporate offices did little if anything to clarify what a local manager should do when faced with a challenge that threatened the very viability of the store's continued operation.

MEANWHILE, THE RIOT CONTINUED AT THE JACKSON WOOLWORTH'S. INSIDE the five-and-dime, those in the mob searched for more and more objects to hurl at the demonstrators. They ransacked shelves filled with "the plastic junk of America,"[102] as Ed King put it, and threw it at the demonstrators. Placemats, knick-knacks, and other paraphernalia went flying through the air, sometimes hitting, sometimes missing the human targets. When the crowd headed for the picture frame counter, the regional manager took decisive action by turning off the remaining store lights and announcing forcefully and repeatedly over the loudspeaker that "Woolworth's is now closed!" At last, at about 2:00 p.m., after a nearly three-hour marathon of wills and tempers, the crowd finally began to disperse.[103]

Once he knew that no more harm would come to his students and teachers, Dr. Beittel headed once again toward the lunch counter. He first checked that everyone was all right; then he moved toward a seat at the far end of the counter to talk with the reporters. When a huge white man stopped Beittel and asked who he was, the college president glared at him sternly and kept moving. He took a seat at the counter, symbolically linking himself with the demonstrators even as their protest was drawing to a close. Ed King acknowledged that Beittel's action that day took great courage. He was perhaps the first college president to take part in a demonstration staged by his students against the established order.[104]

As the demonstration ended, King also rushed to the counter to offer what assistance he could to Salter, Trumpauer, and Moody. Mercedes Wright followed to reassure Lewis and others at the other outpost. King began cleaning Trumpauer's glasses and helping Salter wipe away the food and debris on his head, shoulders, and neck. A still-working Freddie Blackwell captured this scene in a photo that would have serious consequences for both King and Beittel when it ran not only locally, but nationwide. The photo shows King holding Trumpauer's glasses and talking with Salter. Trumpauer's head is crowned with what looks like the contents of an entire bottle of ketchup; Annie Moody is covered with at least as much mustard. Tom Beard stares somberly into space, and Beittel, a few stools away, talks to Memphis *Commercial Appeal* reporter Kenneth Toler. (In many places, including Jackson, this photo would run with Toler cropped out, making it appear that Beittel had been there as a demonstrator.) Kosciusko Pete, a mentally handicapped man who liked to "keep an eye on things" for the mayor and the police, can be seen in the background of the photograph chewing on a toothpick and wondering what all this could mean for his beloved city.[105]

ONCE MOST OF THE CROWD HAD GONE, THE FOCUS SHIFTED TO FIGURING OUT how to provide the exhausted, filthy demonstrators with safe passage from the scene. Dr. Beittel tried to help clean up Salter until the activist snarled that he wanted the cameras to see exactly what the mob had done to him. So Beittel went out to talk with the police, determined to get the demonstrators away safely. Captain Ray offered a ride in one of the many paddy wagons lined up on Capitol Street. When Beittel proposed this to the group, however, Salter again balked. He wasn't about to give the police or the crowd the satisfaction of see-ing them ride in a police vehicle, particularly since they hadn't been arrested.[106]

Beittel went back out and, according to Moody, told the police they'd better protect the demonstrators once they were outside. Captain Ray agreed to cor-don off part of the sidewalk as a safe area to await their transportation. Beittel then brought out the shell-shocked demonstrators to a chorus of boos from the lingering crowd. Even though the police were now offering protection, the crowd continued to hurl items they had looted from the store.[107]

Ed King went to get his car—a green Rambler station wagon—as did James Wells. Mercedes Wright got Salter's keys and brought his white Ram-bler around to the Capitol Street entrance. While waiting for the cars, Salter took the opportunity to drive home a point to Captain Ray, who had been outside for the entire demonstration. "Fine brand of Christianity you people practice here in Jackson," Salter said. Then something interesting happened as Ray couldn't face up to Salter's biting remark. "He was shaken very badly in his own way," Salter recalled. "I could tell it. I mean, these were human beings." Finally Ray said, "If you're going to do this sort of thing, John, you're going to have to expect this." Salter realized that even the toughest hearts were being moved by the power of nonviolence.[108]

Then Salter had another unforgettable experience. In a chauffeur-driven black limousine headed up Capitol Street, he saw an older woman who re-minded him of one of his aunts back home. As she passed by, gazing out the window from the back seat, she had a look on her face that Salter first inter-preted as hate; but as the limousine got closer, he realized the look was one of shock and horror. Then she covered her face with her hands and slumped down into her seat. Apparently not everyone was in a festive mood, nor were all Jacksonians proud of what had just transpired.[109]

While the demonstrators waited for their rides, Freddie Blackwell shot his last roll of film. In his final photo of the day, the faces of all the demonstrators cannot be clearly seen, but each individual can be identified, standing under the Woolworth's sign. It is the only picture that shows most of them together in one spot. Captain Ray is also pictured, finally providing protection to the beleaguered crew.

After a brief wait, the eight colorful, curiously attired sit-in participants were driven back to where they had started the day—the Masonic Temple on Lynch Street. Medgar Evers had anxiously awaited their arrival and was over-joyed that they had survived their ordeal. Then, after a congratulatory huddle, the eight went their separate ways. John Salter and Walter Williams were taken to Dr. Adrian Britton, a noted black doctor who served on the Mississippi Council on Human Relations with Dr. Beittel. The two freedom fighters were examined and treated, then taken to James Wells's shop to clean up before heading home. Joan Trumpauer and Annie Moody were taken to a nearby hair salon where Trumpauer remembered having a "beauty parlor experience" while Moody had both her hair and her condiment-covered legs washed. Ed King and Lois Chaffee made their way back to Tougaloo, and Pearlena Lewis was driven home. It's not certain what George Raymond did; most likely he found Dave Dennis and told him all about what had happened. Tom Beard stayed at the NAACP office to talk to Evers, who took on a fatherly tone, asking Beard—the youngest of the demonstrators—why he had risked his life in such a situation. "Somebody had to do it," the quiet teen replied.[110]

Evers had not sat idle once he returned to the office during the demonstration. He had been on the phone with anyone who would take his call, including the NAACP's lobbying staff in Washington, D.C. As a result, the association's Washington bureau counsel, J. Francis Pohlhaus, registered a protest directly to Attorney General Robert Kennedy, demanding an immediate FBI investigation for the "unjustified arrests and refusal of police protection" for the demonstrators.

In an uncharacteristic show of bravado, Evers also asserted to Bill Minor that he had "a hundred persons a day lined up for the next thirty days to participate in demonstrations."[111]

Once Salter got a clean bill of health from Dr. Britton, he headed home to Tougaloo. After a tender reunion with Eldri, he took a number of long-distance phone calls from friends all over the country who had seen the sit-in on the national nightly news. For Salter, this was the first indication that the incident had reached beyond Mississippi's borders. In fact, it had become international news. The photographs and film footage were so gripping that people from all over the world later wrote to express their admiration for the demonstrators and their outrage at the behavior of the mob.

When Pearlena finally made it home, she was only looking for a place to drop her soiled clothes and get cleaned up. In a hurry to head back to Lynch Street to prepare for the mass meeting that night, she was rushed, but also happy to find that her parents weren't too upset with her. Alphonzo and the other Lewis brothers, however, were furious about how their sister had been treated. "She had a brand new suit—an outfit that was new!" recalled Alphonzo. "And to see her with ketchup and mustard and spray paint in her hair, all over her clothes—it had an effect." The brothers vowed to seek revenge, but Pearlena persuaded them that she had anticipated the treatment she received and that it was an effective way to publicize the conditions brought about by segregation. The Lewis brothers agreed to channel their anger by getting more involved in the additional demonstrations that would surely follow.[112]

Meanwhile, Dr. Beittel went off to check on Memphis Norman, who had suffered through his own ordeal after being taken away from Woolworth's. Although Beittel did not recall this during an interview years later, when he left Tougaloo earlier that afternoon to go downtown, the college president must have first stopped by the Hinds County Jail to see Norman before heading to Woolworth's. The time sequence bears this out, and Norman clearly remembered being "so awfully glad" to see a familiar face just as he was being booked for his first and only criminal offense.[113]

But what had happened to Norman once he was escorted from the scene of the demonstration? At about 12:30 p.m., when Detective Black had ushered him out of the store, Norman had stepped into a waiting squad car and was met by a wall of stony silence from two policemen. It remained that way for the entire ride to the police station just a few blocks away. Norman said he felt the police were "really pissed off" at him for participating in the demonstration and they looked at him "as if I was the worst thing that ever came to town." They made him wait around for a while, then fingerprinted and booked him for "breach of the peace." Once that process was completed, two deputy sheriffs took Norman to University Hospital on North State Street so the medical staff could attend to his wounds.

Norman recounted what now sounds like a comedic Richard Pryor spoof of his hospital visit, though at the time it was anything but funny. Because he had sustained such severe blows, he was taken first to the X-ray department to determine if any bones had been broken. As was customary, he disrobed, put on a skimpy tie-in-the-back hospital gown, and was wheeled on a stretcher to the X-ray room. He felt completely vulnerable. Not only was he bruised and still disoriented; now he was nearly naked, and in what he perceived to be a hostile white environment.

The white nurse, who had apparently been advised of her patient's notoriety, entered and, perhaps out of nervousness, began chattering away. Norman recalled her "trying to make a little too much conversation and trying to be too friendly." In his eyes, it was a setup: a white woman alone with a nearly naked black man who had just openly challenged segregation. Two deputy sheriffs were standing right outside the room, guns at the ready. "All she would have had to do was scream and I'm a dead duck," Norman remembered thinking. "I was so happy to get out of that room with that nurse!" he exclaimed. "I guess that's what made me become fully conscious and get well!" When Beittel returned to the hospital after the sit-in was over, he caught up with Norman just after his X-ray experience. Again, the young student was relieved to see a friendly face.

Although his head still ached, Norman was relieved to hear that none of his bones had been broken and that he didn't have a concussion. Miraculously, he had survived the beating without suffering any significant bodily harm. He was bruised and cut, but was told that he would be all right. Norman wasn't sure who put up the bond money to get him out of jail, but looking back thought it had to have been either Dr. Beittel during his earlier visit or A. A. Branch, Tougaloo's dean of students, who picked him up and drove him back to the college once he was released. Still in shock after his ordeal, Norman went back to his dorm, got cleaned up, rested a bit, then got ready for the mass meeting that night.[114]

BY ALL ACCOUNTS, THE MASS MEETING AT THE PEARL STREET AME CHURCH overwhelmed any previous effort to bring out Jackson's black population to support the freedom movement. "Pearl Street was jam-packed," Lillian Louie recalled. "Wall-to-wall people." News reports estimated between five hundred and a thousand in attendance, but any way he counted, Medgar Evers couldn't help but beam at the outpouring of support from the local community. For someone who had labored so long, counting it a success when ten or twelve people showed up for a voter registration drive or twenty people constituted the "mass" of a mass meeting, the turnout must have seemed like a vindication, finally, of all of his efforts.[115]

John Salter even sensed begrudging respect from the police who showed up in force that night. He also received a quiet but significant accolade from one of the reporters who had endured the sit-in along with him. "Professor, that was a very impressive performance you put on," Memphis *Commercial Appeal* reporter Ken Toler told him as he shook Salter's hand. "All of us put on," Salter retorted. "All of you," Toler agreed.[116]

All of the demonstrators—both the sit-ins and the picketers, who had already been bailed out of jail—were given seats of honor at the front of the church. The aisles were crowded with long-time supporters as well as with people who had never attended an NAACP meeting in their lives. According to the meeting program,[117] Ed King delivered the invocation, and then a number of black ministers spoke. Although an order of service had been prepared and distributed,[118] the leadership agreed to allow Reverend G. R. Haughton, pastor of the church, to speak out of turn. Haughton was, by most accounts, the most outspoken of the Jackson Movement's ministers; he had some incredible news.

Haughton reported that he and five other black representatives, mostly ministers, had called the mayor while the sit-in was going on and asked for another meeting with him. The mayor agreed, and an hour after the sit-in concluded, the six were in the mayor's office at city hall. Haughton told the mass meeting that Mayor Thompson had agreed to six of the Jackson Movement's eight demands. He said that the only things the mayor had balked on were the issue of school integration, which was in the hands of the courts, and the formation of a biracial committee, but the mayor had implied that this, too, might be forthcoming. The ministers from the original negotiating group were elated when they heard the news, as were Evers, Salter, and the entire audience. It seemed almost too good to be true. The ministers had hedged their bets with Thompson, however, informing him that while they would call off demonstrations during the next several days, they would also test his agreement to open

up the parks, hire black policemen and crossing guards, desegregate public accommodations, and take down the signs that enforced segregation. If the mayor
was true to his word, demonstrations would be suspended indefinitely. If he
was not, they would begin again immediately. "The doors are being opened to
us," said Haughton hopefully. "Let us walk through them with dignity."[119]

Next, Reverend Charles A. Jones, another leader of the ministers and dean
of nearby Campbell College (another historically black college in Jackson)
revved up the crowd with an impassioned address, suggesting that "Jackson
is like a chicken with its head cut off—gasping a last breath before dying!"[120]
A redacted FBI file indicates that someone, likely Jones, thought the mayor's
promises were a bit too much. "I think you had better go find out. I want you
to be satisfied he means what he says." Jones went on to warn the mayor and
his advisors: "If they are not honorable to their words, we shall make them feel
the regret of their dishonor."[121]

Then Evers was brought on. He first introduced the demonstrators to wild
applause and cheers. He also provided some enthusiastic remarks of his own,
ending with the statement, "This is only the beginning!"[122]

Next, Dave Dennis of CORE announced that at Evers's request he would
start holding nonviolence workshops at the Masonic Temple daily for the
youth to begin preparing for future demonstrations, should they be needed.
The audience was ecstatic and sang with fervor many freedom songs, including
"We Shall Not Be Moved":

We shall not, we shall not be moved.
We shall not, we shall not be moved.
Just like a tree planted by the water,
We shall not be moved.

We're fighting for our freedom, we shall not be moved.
We're fighting for our freedom, we shall not be moved.
Just like a tree planted by the water,
We shall not be moved.

We're black and white together, we shall not be moved.
We're black and white together, we shall not be moved.
Just like a tree planted by the water,
We shall not be moved.

We'll stand and fight together, we shall not be moved.
We'll stand and fight together, we shall not be moved.
Just like a tree planted by the water,
We shall not be moved.

As cochairs of the strategy committee, Pearlena Lewis and John Salter were asked to say a few words. Perhaps a bit prematurely, Lewis stated, "We have accomplished our goals," and emphasized that no one could say that she was an outside agitator. She then challenged the young people to stay involved. "Ain't nobody gonna turn us around now!" she promised.[123]

"It was a little rough out there today," Salter told the crowd, with classic understatement. "But I'd do it a hundred times over." He went on to say, "We aren't asking for anything. We're going to take our rights!"[124] The audience cheered exuberantly.

Mercedes Wright, who had been put in charge of the boycott, told the audience of Savannah's successful "selective buying campaign" and described how Jackson's could be just as powerful.

The two-hour meeting ended with a rousing rendition of "We Shall Overcome," and it appeared for once that the masses really believed it possible. Pearlena Lewis remembered Medgar Evers being "very excited" during the meeting. "He now saw the beginning of something he had dreamed about for a long time," she said. "His face was lit up."[125] Indeed, there had never been an evening quite like this one in Jackson. The sit-in had finally sparked the grassroots into action. Every faction was represented, and all seemed united in their approach to the future. It was a joyous, inspirational evening.

Sadly, however, the resolve would not hold, and even the elation would not last the night. When Salter drove home and parked his car, Eldri came out to meet him. "Did you hear what the mayor did this afternoon?" he asked excitedly. "Have you heard what he just did?" she asked sardonically. All the wind began to go out of Salter's sails.[126]

It seems that when the reporters who were covering the mass meeting heard Haughton's description of the mayor's capitulation, they were skeptical. Some left immediately to find a phone and confirm with the mayor the concessions he had reportedly made. Instead of verifying Haughton's assertions, however, the mayor denied that he had made any agreements, suggesting that the black negotiating team had either set him up or badly misinterpreted what he had said. He did admit to suggesting that segregation restrictions might be relaxed for a few days but that he expected things to return to normal after a short reprieve. To one reporter, he admitted to agreeing to hire black policemen and black women crossing guards, "but since I've been so badly misrepresented," he exclaimed, "I don't think I will consider that now." Thompson went on the radio that very night to disavow Haughton's claims.[127]

Disappointed but not exactly surprised, Salter characteristically took charge. He called around town to boycott supporters and got word to Tougaloo students to meet at the Masonic Temple the next morning to plot out their next move. He was not about to let the mayor's reversal, and the ministers' promise to delay further demonstrations, stop what he knew was a need for continued pressure, forcefully applied.[128]

THAT VERY EVENING, JUST AS THE MASS MEETING WAS GETTING UNDER WAY, the Kennedy administration's assistant chief of staff of intelligence contacted the FBI to let them know that he had received a UPI report about the sit-in and that the U.S. Army was following the situation. From this point forward, all FBI reports from Jackson were provided to the army office at Fort McPherson, Georgia. All eyes were trained on Jackson.[129]

THE LAST NOTABLE EVENT OF THE DAY HAPPENED VERY LATE IN THE EVENING, near midnight, and reinforced the point that the established order was not about to give up without a fight. A firebomb was thrown from a passing car into the carport of the Evers family's home. When the makeshift explosive landed close to Myrlie Evers's car, flames flared dangerously close to the gas tank. Medgar had not yet arrived home, and Myrlie watched in horror from the front window of their house, wondering if it was safe to go outside. She called a neighbor across the street, but no one answered. She realized she had to do something or risk an explosion. Dressed only in her slip, she quickly went out the front door, which faced the carport. She scurried past the car and the flickering flames and turned on the water spigot, only to find that the fire had burned through the hose. With remarkable presence of mind, she found the place in the hose where the water was escaping and, swiftly pulling the hose toward the fire, doused the flames.

Shaken, she called Medgar, but his line was busy. When the fire flamed up again, she again put it out. This time, two neighbors saw her and hurried over. One had gotten in touch with Evers and after alerting the police and the media, he rushed home.

Once the police made their inspection—judging the bomb to be "just a prank"—and the reporters had gone, Myrlie and Medgar settled onto their couch to piece together the day's events. It was then that Myrlie realized the enormity of what had just happened. She began to shake, she later wrote, as "the whole experience hit home. Someone had tried to kill us."[130]

CHAPTER 7

MORE DEMONSTRATIONS, LESS UNITY

IN THE WEEK AFTER THE SIT-IN, THE GRASSROOTS PHASE OF THE JACKSON Movement sparked to life, a direct response in large part to what had happened at Woolworth's. The impact of the sit-in began to be realized the next day, when every major newspaper in America carried front-page coverage, many with pictures of Memphis Norman being attacked by Bennie Oliver. Even Jackson's conservative *Clarion-Ledger*—which had published limited stories on the Jackson Movement's prior picketing efforts—put a photo of Oliver grabbing the back of Norman's neck on page one.[1]

In the *Wall Street Journal*'s front-page analysis, James Tanner noted, "It seems practically assured that Jackson is in for a siege similar to Birmingham's." Interestingly, he also wrote that Medgar Evers believed, even at this early stage, that Dr. Martin Luther King, Jr., would eventually take part in the Jackson demonstrations. Tanner knowingly suggested, however, that it would be a tougher place to crack. Noting that the Citizens' Council's almost six thousand members nearly ruled the city, Tanner quoted Evers saying, "They have infiltrated government here from the governor's chair down to the policeman on the beat." Tanner described the white power structure as puzzled about black citizens' demands: "They have their own playgrounds and parks," an anonymous civic leader was quoted saying. "A group of white businessmen cleaned up their slums. We built them a golf course. I don't know what more they could ask for." "But," Tanner concluded, "the Negroes are asking for more."[2]

Jackson NAACP president Doris Allison had heard about the sit-in on her way back from St. Louis, where she had buried her sister the Friday before and stayed over the weekend to console her father. On Monday afternoon he had called her to the television screen for the news about the ministers walking out of the mayor's meeting. That night, Medgar Evers called. "Mrs. Allison, I need you."[3] She was on the next afternoon's train. As the train entered Tennessee, some white teenagers listening to a transistor radio let out a scream. "Some Negroes are getting stomped in Woolworth's in Jackson, Mississippi!" they cried. Allison rushed over and asked them to turn up the volume. Once she heard the report for herself, she let out a holler. "Keep those stompin' shoes on, sweetheart," she exclaimed, "because you're gonna have to do some more stompin'!"[4]

The next morning, Allison arrived at the NAACP office just as the day's plans were being made for limited picketing and sit-ins up and down Capitol Street. "I got my stompin' shoes," she told Evers. "I'm ready." Evers tried to dissuade her, saying, "Let the group from Tougaloo go." But Allison would have none of it, so Evers asked her to hand over her valuables for safekeeping and cleared her to participate. She became the first of the NAACP elders to join in the direct action phase of the Jackson Movement.[5]

That same morning, CORE's Dave Dennis and George Raymond began conducting workshops on nonviolence to help the cadre of young people now eager to get involved. Evers had also told the media to expect demonstrations that day, but he didn't reveal their times or locations. As was the case the day before, he and Salter hoped that stealth would help them gain a few precious extra minutes for reporters to snap photos and get the story from the demonstrators' perspective before they were arrested.[6]

By this point, however, the police were intently watching the comings and goings at the NAACP office. Despite the surveillance, Doris Allison was determined to outfox them. Instead of heading east toward Capitol Street, she headed west toward Jackson State College, walking slowly toward a restaurant up the street. There, she met others who had brought handmade posters to hang over their shoulders like sandwich boards to carry their messages to the TV audience. "No Fear, No Doubt, No Retreat," one read. "Jackson Needs a Bi-Racial Committee," stated a second. "Don't Buy on Capitol Street," demanded a third. Rather than carrying their signs in paper bags as the picketers had done the day before, Allison's group rolled up the posters in newspapers held under their arms. From the restaurant, two separate groups were driven toward Capitol Street, half an hour apart. Allison led the first group of six, which included white Tougaloo student and Jackson Movement regular Steve Rutledge, Woolworth's sit-in participant Tom Beard, and NAACP staff member Willie Ludden.[7]

Police officers, news reporters, and Jackson's white citizens were all in a state of high alert when the picketers arrived on Capitol Street just after noon. All morning, rumors had been spreading like a block fire, jumping from one building to another with alarming speed. Everyone knew something would happen, and in the wake of the Woolworth's demonstration, no one wanted to miss it.[8]

Overnight, Woolworth's and most other five-and-dimes on the street had closed their lunch counters, removed the tops of the stools, and transformed the areas into merchandise display space. At Woolworth's, the scene of the previous day's brutality had become a showcase for luggage and artificial flowers, while the fifty-two stool bases were covered with white paper bags tied at the bottom like little paper goblins on Halloween.[9]

It was rumored that the next target for a demonstration would be H. L. Green's, another five-and-dime just up the street from Woolworth's, and the only store that had kept its lunch counter open. But when groups of white youths began to congregate there—many of them recognized by reporters as the rabble-rousers from Woolworth's the day before—the manager closed the entire store. Green's employees then went to the second-floor windows and looked out to see what would develop. They didn't have to wait long.[10]

First, George Raymond arrived, dressed again in his overalls and white T-shirt. Just as he had done the day before, he began walking up and down Capitol Street, taunting the police by his mere presence. Initially they followed him, but after a while they concluded he had no intention of demonstrating.[11]

Then, just after noon, Doris Allison and her group walked briskly down Capitol Street. With their newspapers under their arms and spaced apart so as not to attract attention, they slipped under the gaze of the police and headed right for their target. Allison halted just as she reached Woolworth's, and at the precise moment when Memphis Norman had been attacked the day before, she called out to Steve Rutledge behind her, "Steve! Ready!" With that, she slipped her sign from her newspaper and quickly slid the cord holding it over her head. Rutledge, Beard, Ludden, and two others immediately followed.

The crowd squealed in delight. "Those Negroes are making fools out of y'all!" someone shouted to the police. Captain Ray, who was on the scene almost immediately, fired a question at Allison. "Where'd you come from?!" he blustered. "That's for you to find out!" she responded curtly.[12] Then Ray attempted to remove her sign, but the cord got caught on her hair, which she had curled into a bun much like Joan Trumpauer's the day before. The delay gave photographer Freddie Blackwell just the opportunity he was hoping for. Once again, the Jackson Movement would be on the front page of the local papers.[13]

Half an hour later, after Allison's group had been arrested, another set of demonstrators made their way up Capitol Street toward the same point. Dave Dennis's wife, Mattie, led this second force of five. All were swiftly arrested when they reached Woolworth's.[14]

Ed King, once again dressed in his ministerial collar, was spotting both demonstrations and told reporters to expect more. "It looks like a busy afternoon," he said. As he was leaving the downtown area after the second set of arrests, King was knocked to the ground by a young thug who apparently didn't appreciate King's brand of Christian ministry, but King simply got up and moved on.[15]

Two additional planned demonstrations happened just after 3:00 that afternoon. At 3:15, four Tougaloo men staged a sit-in on the curb in front of J. C. Penney, just across and up the street from Woolworth's. They were quickly arrested.

Then, four Tougaloo women attempted to sit-in at Primos Restaurant, a down-town watering hole for politicians, but were stopped at the door by Kenneth Primos, a prominent Citizens' Council member. Primos called the police, who quickly arrested the demonstrators. Both the men and the women were carried to waiting paddy wagons by black trusties from the city jail. Chief of Detectives M. B. Pierce said the use of trusties was necessary to avoid charges of police brutality, though the practice seems more to reflect the reluctance of white po-licemen to deal with the black demonstrators. The Associated Press reported that FBI agents observed the arrests but, once again, did nothing to intervene.[16]

The most astonishing demonstrations that day, however, happened not on Capitol Street, but at black high schools across town. At Lanier High, a seemingly spontaneous demonstration erupted when students, inspired by the Woolworth's sit-in, announced a boycott of a nearby white store owned by a notorious Citizens' Council supporter. When the youths tried to enforce the boycott, someone called the police. The police arrived with attack dogs and called out to the students to disperse. But when they held their ground, the police, alarmed by their boldness, left without making any arrests.[17]

Later that day, students from Brinkley High decided to test the mayor's re-tracted promise to integrate parks and libraries. Four Brinkley students visited the municipal library on State Street, the scene of the 1961 Tougaloo Nine sit-in. Surprisingly, they were not disturbed, even though they stayed for three hours. It seemed that the Woolworth's sit-in had prompted local officials to take a gentler approach, at least temporarily.

That night at the mass meeting, Reverend Haughton would tell the crowd, "The old way of handling the Negroes doesn't work anymore."[18] Perhaps the police were beginning to wonder just what would work in this new environ-ment—although they were not completely without a strategy.

Captain Ray asked Detective Jim Black, the arresting officer at Woolworth's, to go undercover once again to spy on plans discussed at the mass meetings. For the next two weeks, Black sat with the press, taking notes and trying to fit in. All the while, he was wired for sound. All he had to say was "Come get me," and a squadron of motorcycle cops would have come crashing through the doors.[19]

The police might have made better use of their time had they chosen to protect the demonstrators and their families. Pearlena Lewis's family began to receive threatening phone calls after their address was printed in local papers. "You'll never see your daughter alive again," one anonymous caller told her parents. Her brother Alphonzo remembered getting bomb and arson threats, as well.[20] In Wiggins, Memphis Norman's family considered him a local hero once they heard of his role. The only serious repercussion was that his mother's white doctor—one for whom Memphis had worked for several years—refused to treat her from that point on.[21] Annie Moody worried incessantly about her family's well-being, especially after the publicity she received from the sit-in coverage. "I waited to hear in the news that someone in Centreville had been murdered," she wrote. "If so, I knew it would be a member of my family."[22]

Both the *Jackson Daily News* and the *Clarion-Ledger* reported that Tom Beard had a prior police record for shoplifting and burglary. Beard nevertheless continued to demonstrate fearlessly as one of the youngest protesters and the only one to participate in both Tuesday's sit-in and Wednesday's picketing. Joan Trumpauer's parents weren't aware of her role until they saw her photograph the following week in *Newsweek*. By then she was back home in Falls Church, Virginia. It would be a few more weeks before Lois Chaffee's involvement would surprise her family in Idaho; for the time being, she retreated to her behind-the-scenes role.[23]

As for John Salter, the Arizona papers ran the story on the sit-in and some highlighted Salter's Arizona ties. The Flagstaff paper even interviewed Salter's mother, who said, "We're behind him all the way!" For his part, Salter finally agreed that in order to protect his family he would take Evers up on an offer the NAACP leader had made a while back: Salter borrowed one of Evers's rifles, just in case.[24]

EVEN IN THE WAKE OF ITS INITIAL UNEXPECTED SUCCESS, THE JACKSON MOVEment and its leadership were in disarray. Almost immediately, the same old rifts began to appear in the strategy committee. The black ministers and businessmen, who were becoming more vocal, urged conservative tactics; many didn't feel comfortable with teenagers demonstrating and going to jail. Salter and others encouraged the youths' actions, hoping they would inspire the adults to join in. The ministers and members of the NAACP national staff also didn't buy into the Gandhian principle of filling the jails to overflowing in order to put pressure on the power structure to recognize its inhumane behavior and negotiate a settlement. If young people were arrested, the conservatives felt they should be bonded out immediately so as not to be put in danger of police brutality.[25]

At the national level, NAACP leaders wasted no time in taking credit for the sit-in, but they also attempted to use it to direct attention to the Jackson Movement. The public relations staff hastily prepared a press release and distributed it, with Jack Thornell's photo of Memphis Norman being attacked, to all fifteen hundred branches nationwide. In it, they mistakenly identified Norman as an "officer of the North Jackson Youth Council," but accurately described what happened. The release asked each branch to send a committee to its local Woolworth's to protest the attack and to back up the protests with picket lines. The release ended with a plea to "Back up the Mississippi Frontline Fighters for Freedom!"[26]

In the other camp, Mayor Thompson went on the offensive on Wednesday morning, taking the unprecedented step of inviting the national media in as he tried to explain what happened during his meeting with the black ministers the day before. Thompson asserted that the six ministers and businessmen had requested the meeting and that they had apologized to him for walking out the day before. He then launched into a two-and-a-half-minute disingenuous explanation of why he, as mayor, could not order most of the changes the Jackson Movement was insisting on—mostly because they were either federal matters or because he could not interfere with business practices of local merchants. He did hold out the possibility of hiring black police and crossing guards, but only if "pressure groups" (in other words, the NAACP) had no influence on who was hired.[27]

The mayor's entire statement was carried in the afternoon paper. The *Jackson Daily News* also reported that in the wake of the sit-in riot, Congressman Charles Diggs of Michigan had requested that President Kennedy send in troops to Mississippi to quell the violence. "Act now," Diggs demanded. "It may already be too late." Referring to the prior day's violence, Diggs said, "This puts Negroes and whites on a collision course in Mississippi, the snake pit of America. In the absence of federal protection . . . I shudder to think what might be anticipated."[28]

Having been put on the defensive, Mayor Thompson clarified that in the future, police would handle demonstrations differently—not waiting to be invited into stores while demonstrations occurred. "We are trying to operate under the new Supreme Court decision," he said. "[But] we are not going to sit back and wait where there looks like there is going to be real trouble."[29]

That night at the mass meeting, Medgar Evers exhorted the crowd of newly energized supporters to stay away from Capitol Street. "Let's let the merchants feel the economic pinch," he said. He also told about a phone call he received earlier that day. "I had one merchant to call me today, and they want me to tell you: 'We don't need nigger business.' These are stores that help to support the white Citizens' Council—the Council that is dedicated to keeping you and I second-class citizens." Evers also had critical words for the mayor: "Mayor Thompson let everyone know what kind of a man he is by talking out of two sides of his mouth and duping people with his pronouncements." He concluded with a call to continue the protests: "Now finally, ladies and gentlemen, we'll be demonstrating . . . until freedom comes to Negroes here in Jackson, Mississippi!"[30]

In her memoir, Myrlie Evers suggests that Medgar wavered about the benefits of demonstrations and direct action, but on this night he does not sound like a man with reservations. In the film footage of the mass meeting, with young people excitedly applauding his every gesture and statement, he seems like a man at the forefront of a revolution. His Mau-Mau moment—nonviolent but nonetheless dramatic—had finally arrived.

THURSDAY STARTED OUT MUCH LIKE THE PREVIOUS DAY, WITH LOTS OF EARLY morning activity around the Masonic Temple and NAACP offices. Kids dropped by to find out what was being planned; Medgar Evers, John Salter, Willie Ludden, Ed King, and others were upstairs plotting the day's strategy; Dave Dennis and George Raymond, this time with Joan Trumpauer and Annie Moody, were ushering teens into their workshop on nonviolence.

By 11:15 a.m., small demonstrations were taking place on Capitol Street. Eight black pickets met in front of J. C. Penney and sat down on the sidewalk, refusing to move. They were promptly arrested. Ten minutes later, three students, including one young white woman, Jan Hillegas, entered Primos Restaurant just across the street from Woolworth's and requested service. Police arrested them when they refused to leave.[31]

Willie Ludden had also used his influence with the youth to stir up some interest in the teens staging another "spontaneous" demonstration while still at school. At noon, as many as five hundred students emerged from Lanier High School, some carrying American flags, others with handmade signs, all chanting, "We want freedom!" and marching around the outside of the building. They sang freedom songs as well as "God Bless America" and "When the Saints Go Marching In." Some girls danced the twist, while others chanted, "Two, four, six, eight. We don't want to segregate." When the students refused to return to class after lunch period was over, the white-appointed black principal called the police, who arrived swiftly. But before acting against the students, they cordoned off the area, forcing reporters and adult onlookers back about a block from the school. Then the police began to move on the students, who by that time were heckling and taunting them, especially the ones who had arrived with police dogs in their squad cars.[32]

What happened next is not clear. Annie Moody, who was not there, based her description on accounts from students who were present. She said that the police let the dogs loose on the crowd of demonstrators and that students were clubbed. Reporters on the scene, though a block away, said dogs were not used and little force was employed. Rather, they said the police chased the students back into the school once some young people began throwing rocks. Some black observers at the scene told the *New York Times*, however, that police began to push and beat students who tried to hold their ground in the schoolyard.[33]

Two arrests occurred. A black female student was arrested for using abusive language and resisting arrest, and an adult black woman was arrested when she tried to get between the girl and the police. A black observer reported that the woman was dragged to a police car and beaten on the legs and stomach.

After that, the students were not allowed to leave the school until their parents arrived. Mothers and fathers who emerged said that some parents were being beaten as they came for their children. Brinkley High students also staged a demonstration, but police there remained calm and no violence occurred.[34]

John Salter and Ed King, who had rushed to Lanier High once they heard about the flare-up, decided it was time to counter police brutality with a demonstration of their own. King had been attempting to bridge the gap between moderate white ministers and the black clergy, and he, Salter, and Mercedes Wright wanted the black ministers to stage a protest. They spread the word among clergy and others to meet at 4:00 p.m. at the U.S. Post Office on Capitol Street. Since the site was federal property—the building also housed the federal court and regional offices for federal agencies—the strategists believed the police might not have jurisdiction to arrest demonstrators there.[35]

This strategy is one Joan Trumpauer recalled researching through the Justice Department when she was in Washington, D.C., during spring break. She talked to a federal attorney by phone, laying out the scenario without giving a specific locale. "If you're being arrested real fast for picketing on the sidewalks, where would you be able to demonstrate?" Trumpauer had asked. She was told that local police would have a harder time claiming jurisdiction on federal ground.[36]

Although the post office demonstration had been planned primarily for the black clergy—the ostensible leaders of the black community—it ended up being dominated by Tougaloo activists. In fact, six of the fourteen demonstrators had been at the Woolworth's sit-in two days earlier: John Salter, Joan Trumpauer, George Raymond, Annie Moody, Ed King, and Mercedes Wright. Only two prominent black ministers participated, along with Eddie O'Neal (who had picketed up the street the day of the sit-in), Mattie Dennis, Steve Rutledge, a white Tougaloo professor, and two additional young people. From 4:00 to 4:30 p.m., the group assembled inside the post office. Trumpauer purchased stamps to establish that she had legitimate business there. Salter stood around and talked to the others as they gathered. King was the last to arrive, fresh from a meeting with some white moderate clergy he was hoping would take a stand on the developing crisis. By then, hundreds of downtown workers had gathered at the end of the work day, having heard that yet another demonstration was about to occur.[37]

At about 4:40, the group moved outside onto the front steps. The plan was for Eddie O'Neal, president of the Tougaloo student body and an ordained minister, to lead a short prayer. Then another minister was to make a statement about police brutality at Lanier High, calling on all moderate-leaning whites to pressure the mayor to negotiate.

But the plans fell apart quickly. A group of whites who had also gathered inside the post office moved with the demonstrators as they took their places on the steps and bowed their heads. When Eddie O'Neal began a prayer for "love and leadership," the white group stirred restlessly. This time Captain Ray wasn't taking any chances. Rather than risk another Woolworth's-like riot, he decided to ignore the jurisdictional fine point and announced to the demonstrators, "You are participating in a breach of the peace. You are breaking the law." Later, Ray's boss, M. B. Pierce, told the press that arrests occurred because "the crowd was beginning to get nasty."[38]

As the demonstrators were guided to the waiting paddy wagons by police officers, Ed King, who had abandoned his lay-low strategy after the sit-in, decided to make his first Jackson arrest memorable. When the police came for him, King—wearing his clerical garb, including a small stole of purple (the liturgical color for penitence)—knelt down on the steps and began to pray aloud. He refused to move or even acknowledge the police. Finally, two black trusties lifted him by the legs and shoulders and took him to the paddy wagon. Carried aloft, King extended his lanky arms, clutching his New Testament in one hand, and intoning "God is on our side," a verse of the civil rights anthem "We Shall Overcome."[39]

At the police station, King said that he and the other ministers escaped any harassment "because these were some very important black ministers that had never been arrested. The police had sense enough not to let their brutality out toward these people." The ministers also got bonded out quickly, while the others had to stay in jail. Salter explained their early release by suggesting that the ministers were still hoping to negotiate a settlement. King believed if the arrested ministers could meet with the moderate white clergy he had lined up, perhaps some breakthrough could occur and escalation of the demonstrations would not be necessary.[40]

It was a dream that fizzled in the humid Mississippi evening air. No white moderates stepped up to urge the mayor to negotiate. If anything, the mayor strengthened his resolve that no compromise was possible and announced that temporary facilities were being readied at the fairgrounds, just behind the old capitol building, that could "accommodate" about twenty-five hundred demonstrators. In addition, he had secured from Governor Barnett access to the state penitentiary at Parchman should it be needed. The mayor did ask whites to refrain from violence against demonstrators so as not to encourage federal intervention. He also blamed the entire racial crisis on Tougaloo and Campbell colleges—"the cancer of this racial mess. They are filled with race agitators."[41]

Medgar Evers had his own frenzy of activity that evening. He telegraphed U.S. Attorney General Robert Kennedy, protesting "the unwarranted arrests on federal property of 14 persons on a charge of breach of peace while they were peacefully and orderly exercising their constitutional right of assembly and free speech by praying on the steps of the post office." He had earlier called the Justice Department to complain about the police brutality at Lanier High.[42]

Evers also talked to reporters that afternoon, saying that he wanted "to avoid another Birmingham"—by which he meant "a riot." Then he acknowledged that "things could get out of hand very quickly. Our young people are ready to march en masse right now. We're trying to keep some control over them." It had been a strain, Ed King admitted, and a credit to Evers's and Salter's leadership that they had been able to hold off the young students' enthusiasm for marching until the next day, when school would be dismissed for the summer.[43]

At Thursday night's mass meeting, Dave Dennis informed the young people what lay ahead for them and anyone brave enough to follow their example. "Bring your toothbrushes," he told them, "because tomorrow you're going right to jail." For those parents who might think it fine for the college students to protest but not their own children, Cleveland Donald, a high school junior and vice president of the North Jackson Youth Council, set them straight: "To our parents, we say: 'We wish you'd come along with us, but if you won't, at least don't try to stop us.'"[44]

FRIDAY, MAY 31, SAW THE FULL FLOWERING OF THE JACKSON MOVEMENT. THE day started quietly. No demonstrations were planned before afternoon, although police and reporters were ready on Capitol Street for any hint of trouble.

Medgar Evers spent the morning calmly composing perhaps his most forceful, succinct rebuttal to Mississippi's racist structure. Buoyed by the success of his burgeoning movement, Evers took on the Jackson power structure by writing identical letters to the editors of both of Jackson's daily newspapers. Both papers were still toeing the party line and not giving much credence to the building tensions evidenced daily through street demonstrations and picketing. The *Jackson Daily News* in particular seemed to scoff at the new turn of events and went so far as to publish an "Agitation Box Score"—as if the Jackson Movement were some sort of sporting event—that listed the number of "Sign Toters," "Stool Sitters," "Curb Squatters," and, most interestingly, "Sluggers."[45]

Evers's two-page letter boldly and clearly states the Jackson Movement's goals: "What Negroes seek is the full measure of their citizenship rights equal to those enjoyed by white citizens and on the same basis. This is no demand for special privileges for Negroes. Rather, it is a demand for removal of the unconstitutional, inhuman, unchristian and anti-democratic restrictions imposed upon Negroes in Jackson and throughout the state of Mississippi."[46]

"The first step toward our goal," Evers goes on to state, "must be the eradication of all aspects of segregation and other forms of racial discrimination." This does not sound like a man who is wavering in his conviction about which path he should take toward securing these rights. These are the words of a man on fire with conviction. "Time is running out for the South," Evers continues. "One hundred years after the Emancipation Proclamation, it is futile and inane to ask Negroes to be 'patient,' to wait a little longer, to prepare themselves for freedom."

After citing the uncomfortable truth that Mississippi ranks "at the bottom of the economic and cultural ladder," Evers concludes with a battle cry. "Freedom is our goal. We are on our way and nothing can stop us. We will arrive sooner than many people now think."

The morning's drama was focused primarily on the Hinds County Courthouse, just across the street from city hall, where Memphis Norman was being tried for disturbing the peace and Bennie Oliver—the most notorious of the "sluggers"—for assault at the Woolworth's sit-in. Those arrested for civil disobedience activities in the days after the sit-in were also on trial.

For Norman, the day brought sweet justice. Even though he later claimed never to have seen the face of his attacker during the assault, he could identify Oliver when asked on the stand because of newspaper photographs. Norman described how he had been brutalized and then sat down. With the national publicity surrounding the attack, the judge had no choice but to find Oliver guilty of assault, although the former policeman said he was acting in self-defense, falsely claiming that Norman had hit him on the elbow. Oliver was fined one hundred dollars and sentenced to thirty days in jail, which his attorney, state senator Hugh Bailey, immediately appealed.[47]

Once Oliver's conviction was handed down, the prosecutor convinced the judge to drop the charges against Norman. As a result, the young protester left the courtroom with a clean record and a sense that justice could find its way even to the state that had freed the murderers of Emmett Till only eight years earlier. The *New York Times* noted the irony of Oliver's sentence compared to that of the other demonstrators; the women who had attempted to integrate Primos Restaurant, for instance, were found guilty of trespassing, fined five hundred dollars, and sentenced to six months in jail. Nevertheless, when a black man won a measure of justice from a white judge in Mississippi, it was an occasion worth celebrating.

Also that day, most of the post office demonstrators were released at noon, although Joan Trumpauer's prior Freedom Ride conviction and subsequent parole held up her release until additional papers could be filed. Annie Moody and another demonstrator, Doris Erskine, were kept in jail a few extra days as well.[48]

When Salter was released at lunchtime, he headed immediately to the Masonic Temple to find out what had happened in his absence and to help plan the afternoon's mass march. Earlier in the day, Evers had feigned ignorance when he advised an FBI agent that "plans for demonstrations . . . had not yet been formulated." He did let on that "the young people planned to 'march.'" In fact, plans were well under way for the youth to march from all over the city to a designated gathering place. Later that morning, the same FBI agent was able to wheedle out of a concerned parent that her three children were going to march from Lanier High where they were enrolled and "join forces" with kids from other black schools, with plans to eventually "converge on Capitol Street."[49]

The parent was on to something. Pearlena Lewis, Cleveland Donald, and other youth leaders on the strategy committee had already asked their contacts at the three black high schools, as well as at Holy Ghost Catholic School and Campbell College, to organize marches from their locations to the Farish Street Baptist Church as soon as school was let out. Just after 3:00, a total of nearly five hundred students began to walk slowly and peacefully from all five points toward the church. Lewis directed the march from the NAACP offices: "The coordinators . . . called me to make sure what time all of them were to walk out. We had informed them to walk in twos from the school. Do not block traffic. Do not swear or use profanity. And don't be violent, whatever happens. I think it threw [the police] off guard."[50]

As they walked, four of the contingents were not interrupted. The Brinkley students, however, shouting slogans and proudly singing the anthem "We Shall Not Be Moved" were stopped and arrested after marching only two of the six miles. The group's leaders, including Alphonzo Lewis, Cleveland Donald, and Alex Span, were put into a police car. Lewis recalled hearing over the car's radio the increasing alarm of the police as they discovered various marches going on around the city: "You could hear, 'There's a group in Georgetown! . . . There's a group in west Jackson! . . . There's a group on Meals Street! . . . There's a group coming down Farish Street!'"[51]

In the car, the policemen began to interrogate the teens: "Who told you to do this? Why are you doing it?" When Donald started pleading his Fifth Amendment rights, the policemen told him to shut up. "You're not in a courtroom!" one shouted.[52]

These three student leaders, transported by squad car, were the first to arrive at the place the Jackson activists would later call the "fairgrounds concentration camp"; the *Jackson Daily News* dubbed it the "fairgrounds motel." The fairgrounds, used annually for the Mississippi State Fair, were close to downtown, just behind the old state capitol building, and were perfectly suited—or at least the police thought so—for holding the growing student demonstrators. The area was fenced in and was equipped with large metal Quonset hut–style facilities for housing livestock. The police had added barbed wire and police dogs for the demonstrators. The rest of the Brinkley students—seventy-five in all—were arrested just after their student leaders and were taken to the fairgrounds in foul-smelling garbage trucks, a mode of transport soon to be commonly used for the marchers.[53]

The rest of the students, more than four hundred strong, arrived successfully at Farish Street Baptist Church where they were further instructed by Evers, Salter, and the NAACP's Willie Ludden and Gloster Current. After everything that could be considered dangerous was taken from the students, they were each given an American flag (with the points at the end of the sticks removed so police could not misconstrue them as weapons) and lined up at the door. Some brandished prepainted signs, furnished by the NAACP, which read "No Fears, No Doubts, No Retreat," "The Movement is our Leader," and "Discrimination Must End." When Evers gave the command, "Let's march!" the kids filed slowly, two by two, out of the church entrance.[54]

What they saw as they exited should have been enough to scare them back in. Just two blocks away, hundreds of blue-helmeted policemen, highway patrolmen, and police auxiliary forces stood lined up—guns drawn, billy clubs held high, tear gas and dogs at the ready. It was clear the marchers would never reach Capitol Street, their intended destination. FBI agents estimated that there were at least 175 Hinds County police, 100 highway patrolmen, and 25 Hinds County deputy sheriffs. A special operations team of thirty highway patrolmen were armed with shotguns and pistols in sidearms holsters.[55]

Ludden led the group out of the church and into the late afternoon heat. Ludden had his own "out of body" experience, much like those experienced by the Woolworth's demonstrators, while leading the youth into the police barricade. "As I scanned the obstacles ahead of us, I don't know what came over me," he later wrote. "I suddenly felt alone and yet out of myself, as if I had been shot dead and [had] left my body. My feet seemed to lose contact with the street. . . . My mind was totally focused on the challenge ahead. . . . Our mission had never been so clear."[56]

When he reached the barricade, Ludden was stopped by none other than Captain Ray. "Where are you going, young man?" Ray asked. "Sir, I'm headed to the federal building," Ludden replied. "We're going to register a protest for those ministers who were jailed while praying on federal property."

"Do you have a permit to parade?" Ray persisted.

"I'm not parading," Ludden replied.

"Where are all those people going?" Ray asked, pointing to the hundreds of youth still emerging from the church.

"You'll have to ask them," Ludden responded.

After a few more rounds of back and forth volleying, Ray shouted, "You and your people had better turn back or go to jail!"[57]

Ludden decided to push forward and for a time was successful in confusing the opposition, making some slight additional forward progress. But when a young police lieutenant called out, "Nigger, where the hell do you think you're going?" it was all over. The policeman brought his night stick across Ludden's head, and he fell to the ground. He was then kicked in the ribs and hips. Surrounded by police, Ludden tried to get up but another nightstick came down right on his genitals, causing him to pass out.[58]

The police then began methodically arresting the marchers and leading them to the paddy wagons, canvas-covered vehicles, and garbage trucks. Tom

Beard, who had led the march from Jim Hill High School, was struck by the speed with which the police arrested his group.[59]

All of the four hundred–plus young marchers were arrested and all for the same crime: parading without a permit. The *New York Times* reported that children as young as "grade school age" marched from the doors of the church straight into police lines. Teenaged couples laughed and held hands as they were seized by police. Nearly all of the demonstrators waved small American flags as they joyously marched, two by two, shouting "We want freedom!" or singing "We Shall Not Be Moved" as they were led away.[60]

As some of the youth approached the police barricade, the cops tried to scare them, yelling, "Run! Run!" and wielding billy clubs and guns. When a small group took the bait and began running down a side street, a policeman fired two shots overhead to stop them. But even though this group broke ranks, they did not break the discipline of nonviolent resistance as they were arrested and taken away.[61]

Ed King believed that the nonviolent example set by the Woolworth's demonstrators had a profound effect on the young marchers: "After Woolworth's, everybody's [asking], 'Could you sit and not hit back, hour after hour?' [They] got the message that something good can be done with nonviolence."[62] Even the police could not quarrel with the young people's discipline and lack of antagonism. Once loaded into the trucks, the youth sang all the way to their new temporary home.

Willie Ludden was carried to one of those trucks and described his experience this way:

> I was tossed into the truck like a piece of trash and [I] crashed against the floor of the container. It was a filthy, stinking pit. The garbage truck had not been cleaned after the day's haul. . . . Other students were thrown in next to me. . . . It was a sunny, hot day and there was no ventilation. Some of the students started coughing or gasping for air. Two were overcome by noxious odors and vomited. We felt like Jews about to be transported to the death camps.[63]

Ludden was taken to the fairgrounds with the rest of the youth. He was greeted as a hero by the Brinkley High kids who had been picked up earlier, which caused the police to remove him from the scene and deposit him at the Hinds County jail, where he was arrested and put behind bars.

Back at Farish Street, Evers and Salter watched as pair after pair of youth were arrested. "Just like Nazi Germany," Evers observed, first to Salter and then later to the press. "Look at those storm troopers," he pointed out as a squadron of helmeted police marched by in formation, forcing spectators along the sidewalks back into their homes and businesses. Though angered by the police action, which he describes as "cold-blooded," Salter was also elated at the young people's disciplined behavior. His vision of mass marches was coming to life and on a more expedited schedule than even he could have imagined just a few days earlier.[64]

WHILE THE YOUTH WERE HAVING THEIR DAY, ED KING WAS ENDURING HIS OWN trial, literally, before the Mississippi Methodist Conference at Galloway Memorial United Methodist Church just a few blocks off Capitol Street. It was a grueling session. The ministerial training and qualifications board, which evaluated all candidates for the ministry, had recommended that King be "continued" as a potential candidate, rather than admitted into full participation. But King would not accept this halfway measure again and demanded a vote. He had decided he wasn't going to do the polite thing and just go away to some other state as many southerners with pangs of conscience over segregation had done before him. He would stand and fight and make every one of the conference participants vote on his fitness to serve and, by proxy, on their willingness to support Mississippi's racist system. "They didn't question whether I could be a minister for somebody, somewhere," King said. "But could I be a Mississippi minister? That was the question."[65]

The hour-long debate was fierce. Although the meeting was closed to the public and even King was not allowed to be present, details leaked out and were reported in a front-page *Clarion-Ledger* story the next day. Those in favor of him pointed to King's exceptional education and worried that a rebuke of him by the state conference would reflect badly on them at the national level. Other supporters argued that he should be allowed to act following his own Christian conscience. Opponents focused on his recent activities and argued that he had exceeded his duties as Tougaloo's chaplain by getting involved in demonstrations and being arrested. King and his wife, Jeannette, waited outside the closed doors as the debate raged. When it was over, many ministers emerged visibly shaken. Some were openly weeping.[66]

It was a close vote. While about a dozen ministers abstained, eighty-five voted to continue King's association with the conference, and eighty-nine voted to sever the connection. "It hurt enormously," he said, "but it certainly wasn't unexpected."[67]

King wasn't about to give up without a fight. After the conference had reconvened and the bishop had ordained new deacons and elders, King stood up in the church unannounced and addressed his superior. "Bishop Franklin," he said loudly. "I would like to speak. I believe you informed me this morning I would be given the opportunity to speak before the conference."

"No, sir," the bishop replied from his seat in the sanctuary. "I don't believe I did that."

"I would like to know how the decision was reached that I was not fit to be a minister in the Methodist Church in Mississippi. I would like to know why I am not fit."

The bishop tried to halt him, but King continued. He said he felt he had lived up to the faith placed in him by his home church in Vicksburg, his teachers at Millsaps (a Methodist college), and his fellow ministers. "My ministry was apparently satisfactory until last week," King continued. "I am a home product of the Mississippi Methodist Church."

Franklin remained composed throughout the challenge, offering platitudes to attempt to soften the blow. "We mean no reflection on your character," he said. "We will pray for you and assist you, help you in your ministerial calling in any way we can." When King began to accuse specific individuals of engineering the vote against him, the bishop interrupted and asked him to be seated. After staring at the bishop, King acquiesced. This battle was over. With more important concerns awaiting, it was time to move on.[68]

FROM THE MOMENT NAACP PRESIDENT ROY WILKINS SET FOOT IN JACKSON early that Friday evening, the Jackson Movement downshifted into a slower gear. Wilkins brought with him a group of attorneys and public relations staff from the New York office determined to turn the Jackson uprising into an NAACP triumph to rival Dr. Martin Luther King's success in Birmingham. There was only one problem: the national staff was woefully inexperienced at handling this sort of grassroots initiative.

The NAACP was noted primarily for its middle-class, middle-of-the-road, go-slow attitude toward racial progress, and its successes had come from years of painstaking legal action, not community organizing. For the New York staff, local activity meant fund-raising—recruiting individuals to become dues-paying members so that the national organization could expand their rights, one court brief at a time. The NAACP's idea of direct action was small, controlled demonstrations, since it only took two or three arrests for a legal challenge to be filed. The organization had the best civil rights attorneys in the country and a public relations machine to rival that of any large corporation, so it was a corporate mindset that Wilkins brought to Jackson. He was the national executive: the man who could calm a troubled situation, negotiate a deal, and move quickly to the next issue on the agenda. Neither Wilkins nor his executive staff were suited for daily strategizing, quick maneuvering, or rigorous attention to ideas bubbling up from the community.[69] Yet when they arrived in Jackson, they assumed control and swept everyone else aside, including their own Mississippi field secretary. Myrlie Evers shrewdly noted that "with his immediate superiors on the scene, Medgar was relieved of both the necessity and the opportunity of making policy decisions."[70]

Just before traveling to Jackson, Wilkins had issued a memo to the presidents of all NAACP branches taking credit for everything happening in Jackson. "The planning of the Jackson operation, the discussions, the organizing of the community, the communication with the Mayor, the picketing, the demonstrating have ALL been carried out by the NAACP—through its local units . . . and through its national staff." Wilkins clearly wanted all the glory.[71]

When he arrived just after the young people's march, Wilkins was briefed by Evers and Current and then immediately held a press conference to denounce the mass arrests. "In Birmingham," he said, "the authorities turned the dogs and fire hoses loose on peaceable demonstrators. Jackson has added another touch to this expression of the Nazi spirit with the setting up of hog-wired concentration camps. This vindicates the NAACP contention that Mississippi officials regard the Negro citizens of this state as animals, not human beings and fellow citizens. . . . There remains," he continued, "the establishment of the ovens to complete the picture of Nazi terror."[72]

It was a strong statement. Even Salter acknowledged that.[73] But he was hoping for Wilkins to call for additional demonstrations to protest police brutality and inhumane lock-up procedures and even for federal troops to be sent in. That call never came. Not at the press conference. Not at the mass meeting that night. Not the next day, after Wilkins himself had been arrested. The national leader was clearly uncomfortable with children being held in jail overnight and made every effort to get them out, even though he had been told that leaving them there would increase pressure on the mayor to negotiate. According to Ed King, Wilkins even dressed Evers down in King's presence just after the press conference for not preventing the children from marching and for not seeking the blessing of the national office before authorizing such a Birmingham-style tactic. "Who do you think you are," Wilkins demanded, "another Martin Luther King?"[74] Wilkins not only wanted his moment in the sun, but he wanted it *his* way—not in a way that would seem to mimic the tactics of his rival.

Wilkins's initial attempt to control the situation was foiled by the youths themselves when a majority of them refused to leave the fairgrounds, even after their parents arrived to take them home. The youths also objected to the police insisting that their parents sign a pledge to forbid their children to participate in further demonstrations. Although the police had agreed to release all children under the age of eighteen into the custody of their parents, many of the youths insisted on staying, even over the objections of the incredulous adults.[75]

Through all of this, Salter was increasingly baffled by what he saw as Wilkins's lack of leadership in the situation, and he became even more alarmed when Willie Ludden and some other students arrived at the mass meeting that night. Those released from jail were greeted with thunderous applause by the record fifteen hundred in attendance, and Ludden spoke about the need to continue demonstrations. Salter had thought all those arrested would remain in jail, and he felt duped when it became clear that NAACP lawyers had bailed some of them out. When he questioned Evers about the change of plans, Evers simply responded, "There were other opinions, I guess." Evers was caught between the local organizers and his national bosses; it was a dilemma he would never completely resolve.[76]

Memphis Norman remembered the mass meeting that last day of May for another reason. He was sitting in the audience when Evers spotted him from the podium and asked him to come up and say a few words about his experience at Woolworth's. Unprepared for such an invitation, Norman slowly approached the stage and talked briefly about what had happened to him. Still bandaged and bruised, he spoke with conviction, but later wished he had had more time to prepare. When he finished, Norman joined Evers and Wilkins on stage for the remainder of the meeting. A photo shows the youthful Norman sitting between the two civil rights giants looking like a young Joe Lewis after a prize fight—only this time the prize was freedom.[77]

Pearlena Lewis was busy that evening too. She had overseen the coordination of the young people's march but had not participated, so that night she went down to the fairgrounds and asked the police to let her in to lead the youth in prayer. She was allowed in, but when she began leading the singing of rousing movement anthems, the police arrested her. She thus became the sixth of her seven siblings (the exception was her youngest brother) being held at the fairgrounds. The next day, Lewis and other student leaders, including Tom Beard, Cleveland Donald, and Pearlena's brother Alphonzo, were taken to the Hinds County jail. She said her week-long jail stay was not horrifying: "The [black] trusties were very nice and would bring me food. And they'd say, 'We're proud of you.'" But her decision to stay in jail became problematic, particularly since she was one of the local student leaders. Eventually, the NAACP's Ruby Hurley convinced Lewis that she would be more valuable to the movement out of jail than in, and Lewis allowed Hurley to bail her out.[78]

Other Jackson Movement leaders were having more contentious problems with the NAACP national staff. On Thursday morning—the day before the youth march—while Evers and other strategy committee members had been discussing their next move, reporters wandered out of the NAACP office and over to the Masonic Temple where the Dave Dennis and George Raymond CORE workshop on nonviolence was in full swing. Jack Langguth's story on the workshop was the New York Times's page-one story on Friday. When the NAACP national staff arrived in Jackson that same day, they took Dennis to task for promoting his organization over the NAACP. Dennis laughed it off at the time but later saw their reaction as somewhat paranoid and indicative of the "who's in charge here?" concerns that would heighten as time went on.[79]

Tensions were also mounting outside the cocoon of the strategy sessions. FBI reports tell of a chilling arrest made at about the time Wilkins was getting up to speak on Friday night. At 9:25, police stopped a car for a minor traffic violation. While inspecting the car, they found two mayonnaise jars filled with gasoline, with rag wicks emerging from holes in the tops of the jar lids. When asked about the homemade bombs, the driver, who was white, said he was planning to use them as "torches to illuminate an automobile he planned to repair that night." Clearly he was planning to use the explosives to inflict harm. Perhaps this was the same individual who had firebombed the Evers carport earlier in the week. The police arrested the driver and charged him with unlawful possession of a gas bomb.[80]

ON SATURDAY, JUNE 1, THE DAY AFTER HE ARRIVED IN JACKSON, ROY WILKINS decided to join the picketing on Capitol Street. Thelton Henderson, the only black Justice Department lawyer working in the South at the time, said Medgar Evers had convinced Wilkins to come there to take part in a demonstration. Lois Chaffee believed that Evers was "very proud" that Wilkins had chosen Jackson as the place to take his stand.[81]

Still, the question must be asked: what was it that caused Wilkins to risk arrest and jail time at such a critical time for the NAACP? Willie Ludden claimed that there were no plans for Wilkins to participate in a demonstration when he arrived, but that Ludden engaged a precocious eight-year-old to approach the NAACP leader on stage during the Friday night mass meeting and ask him if he was "willing to go to jail for freedom." In front of a standing-room-only crowd, Wilkins had no choice but to agree. "I'm with you all the way!" he exclaimed. The deal was sealed.[82]

Even so, Ludden asserted that many of Wilkins's entourage, including Gloster Current, tried to talk him out of going to jail, being concerned for his safety. Nonetheless, Wilkins was good for his word, and so early Saturday afternoon, John Salter drove Wilkins, Evers, and Helen Wilcher, a prominent NAACP Jackson branch member, downtown to the picketing site. Woolworth's was chosen as the obvious target, since the NAACP had urged all of its branches to picket the national chain store after the sit-in violence. The three demonstrators emerged from Salter's Rambler with signs in paper bags, quickly walked the half block to Woolworth's, and pulled the sandwich-board signs over their heads. Wilkins's sign was directed at the boycott: "Don't Buy on Capitol Street," it read. Evers's focused more on the police actions the previous day: "End Brutality in Jackson," it stated. Wilcher's echoed a statement already popular in the press and movement circles: "No Fears, No Doubts, No Retreat."[83]

Since the police had been expecting a mass march rather than limited picketing, it took them a few moments to recalibrate their response. This provided the crucial time for photographers to capture the high-profile protesters on film—photos that would run in national newspapers the next day. In one of the photos, Wilkins, in a narrow-brimmed straw hat and sunglasses, looks like a vacationer out for a stroll. He is being lectured by the omnipresent Captain Ray, while Evers looks at another arresting officer. A third policeman points an electric cattle prod in the direction of the two black leaders, while other lawmen linger in the background.[84]

The police arrested all three demonstrators and took them to the station for booking. Because Wilkins's sign addressed the boycott, they were charged with restraint of trade, a felony that carried a one-thousand-dollar bail. Wilkins was angered by the trumped-up charge and the additional bond required. At a press conference after his release, he fumed that demonstrations in Jackson "have just started" and could continue for two years. Despite his bravado, however, after a brief stop at the local headquarters on Lynch Street, Wilkins was on the evening plane back to New York.[85]

The Justice Department's Thelton Henderson almost made headlines himself that day. He had been given a Jackson Movement flier while observing the picketing, and police approached him, assuming he was a demonstrator. "Open up that notebook," they demanded, wanting to see what kind of literature he was carrying. "Let me show you my identification," he responded. "Did you hear what I said?" retorted one policeman sharply, but then looked at Henderson's credentials. "It didn't register," Henderson told reporters later. The police couldn't quite comprehend the presence of a black government official in Mississippi. Four policemen marched Henderson up to Captain Ray, who asked him whether he was distributing leaflets. When Henderson said no, he was released.[86]

After witnessing the newsmaking arrests, Salter returned to the NAACP office and began organizing a march with the young people who had been waiting around for the next move. About an hour later he had collected a group of two hundred or so to march from the Masonic Temple down Lynch Street toward Capitol Street.

What Salter was unaware of, but what Wilkins surely knew, was that at that very moment, twelve black ministers and business leaders were holding a clandestine negotiating session with the mayor. He offered nothing new: some black police officers, some black crossing guards, and an upgrade for some black city employees. Reverend Haughton expressed reservations. "I doubt we will be able to sell our people on what was discussed," he said. "Until they are satisfied, there will be demonstrations." But despite Haughton's hesitancy, the mayor announced that a deal had been struck, and Haughton announced a community meeting for Tuesday night to vote on the mayor's offer.[87] At about the same time, Salter and a phalanx of young activists were preparing to hit the streets. Then Wilkins and Evers arrived after being bailed out of jail.

Wilkins looked at the group and said quietly, "No more marches. Not for today anyway."[88]

Salter was stunned. "These people are ready to go!" he responded heatedly. "We've got to keep this thing going!" With the youth wondering what was going on, Evers suggested the leaders continue their discussion in the NAACP offices.

Upstairs, Wilkins reiterated his position. Salter got some help from Ed King, but Evers remained silent, probably not wishing to disagree publicly with his superior. Finally, exasperated, Salter let loose. "It took us a long time to get support from the national office. . . . It's taken a long time to build this movement. If we don't have this march, and many more mass marches, we're never going to crack Jackson open—or Mississippi." Wilkins finally gave his assent for the march to proceed. "Well, go ahead and have it," he said halfheartedly. Undoubtedly, Wilkins was startled by the brazenness of Salter's aggressive tone, but he also likely didn't want to lose face in front of Evers or the large number of youth gathered.[89]

Still unaware of the negotiations with the mayor, Salter returned downstairs to the Masonic Temple to find that half the demonstrators had left, assuming the march had been called off. Salter quickly sent some scouts to retrieve as many as they could, and about 150 marched down Lynch Street toward the downtown area. Reporter Bill Minor called it "an abortive march" in the next day's New Orleans *Times-Picayune*, but the impromptu demonstration caught the police off guard because of the mayor's announcement. Thinking there would be no more marches, the police scrambled to get a force in place before the marchers got too far.

Salter and King watched the demonstration as it proceeded down Lynch Street and then saw the students take a sharp turn into a side street to avoid the growing number of police. Once the police saw that the marchers were trying to dodge them, they pulled out their weapons and quickly blocked off paths of escape. When the kids were finally stopped, many fled to avoid arrest. Eighty-eight were arrested, loaded into garbage trucks, and taken to the fairgrounds.[90] Annie Moody suggested that marching was becoming a badge of honor for the young people. "Those who did not go to jail were considered cowards by those who did," she later wrote.[91]

Hundreds of adults also watched the march from their porches and lawns, and once the young demonstrators were out of the way, the police began going after spectators as they had the day before. One man who had chided the police while they were arresting the young people was beaten to the ground and arrested for disturbing the peace. King and Salter reported the brutality to a nearby Justice Department attorney, who not only denied seeing it, but claimed that the beaten man must have "just sat down."[92]

When the two leaders returned to the NAACP office, they were treated with casual disregard by the national office staff who had all but taken over the Jackson operation. Salter noticed a multipage document that purported to tell the history of the Jackson Movement. As he read it, he grew more and more angry. If the report were to be believed, the movement had started with the announcement in mid-May that the national office would support a boycott. Nowhere was there any mention of the painstaking work that Salter and the North Jackson Youth Council had done for the past nine months. He complained to Jesse DeVore, the national press secretary. "I don't know anything about it," DeVore replied. Still seething, Salter left, determined to get the movement back on track.[93]

In his memoir, Salter noted that earlier in the day he had overheard talk about "entrenching the boycott" and "voter registration drives" but nothing about more direct action demonstrations. He was beginning to see where the national office was planning to take the movement he had labored so hard to create. Someone said that Dick Gregory, the black comedian who had taken part in both the Greenwood and Birmingham movements, would be arriving on Monday. This was supposed to be big news, but for Salter as well as King, it sounded like a distraction. They were looking for mass marches and the NAACP was providing an evening's entertainment.[94]

Evers was also trying to keep up the momentum, despite his superiors' reluctance to engage in direct confrontation with the authorities. That afternoon he had called Dr. Martin Luther King's office to discuss the Jackson campaign. According to Myrlie Evers, Medgar had earlier recommended that Dr. King be brought in to help, but Wilkins and Gloster Current dismissed the idea without so much as a polite discussion.[95] Apparently, though, Evers had been pondering the idea for some time. Evers's friend James Wells said that Evers had once asked him and others in their local circle what they thought of the idea. "Would you go get a carpenter to build a chain link fence?" Wells shot back. It was a pointed analogy. Although Wells was in the chain link fence business, Evers had once hired a carpenter to put up a chain link fence around his backyard. Evers probably didn't want to impose on his friend, Wells speculated, but problems developed and Wells eventually had to fix the fence. By bringing up the point at this time, Wells was suggesting that, unlike Dr. King, Wilkins and the NAACP didn't have the kind of experience needed to lead mass marches and large nonviolent campaigns. Why not ask the expert? Wells said he and others would back Evers should he decide to approach King's camp.[96]

Taylor Branch, whose *Parting the Waters* provides an overview of the entire civil rights movement through the March on Washington later that summer, confirms that Evers had begun covertly contacting Dr. King to ask advice and discuss strategy. That very Saturday night, Branch reports, King told his closest aides that Evers had called him again with an update on the day's events but refused to give him any specifics about future plans because Evers feared his phone was tapped. Dr. King responded gleefully to the news about the arrest of the head of the NAACP: "We've baptized brother Wilkins!" he told his confidantes.[97]

Particularly after his arrest with Wilkins, many close to Evers began to fear for his personal safety. His photograph was in the local paper and he was a prominent fixture at every mass meeting, now held nearly every night. Lillian Louie, Dave Dennis, and James Wells blame the national NAACP staff for pushing Evers up front and making him a target. Dennis in particular emphasized the NAACP's competitive stance against other civil rights groups, trying to take exclusive credit for the Jackson situation by insisting that Evers participate in every mass meeting, thus heightening his visibility. Doris Allison was also concerned and asked her mentor to accept a round-the-clock security force, headed by the Wells brothers and her husband, Ben. Evers refused.[98]

He did, however, begin teaching his family how to protect themselves if there were another attack on their house. That Sunday, June 2, he spent time with Darrell, eleven, Reena, ten, and Van, three, teaching them to pay attention to the sound of their dog Heidi's bark, to fall on the floor if they heard unusual noises, and to wait until the potential danger had passed. All agreed the bathtub would be the safest place in the house to seek shelter in a shoot-out. Myrlie Evers listened in horror. The discussion reminded her of the duck-and-cover drills that schoolchildren of the time were taught to follow in the event of a nuclear attack. Now her husband was teaching their children similar techniques to defend themselves, as she put it, against "white American citizens."[99]

Evers was supposed to be in Washington, D.C., that Sunday accepting an award rather than teaching his children the finer points of self-defense from homegrown terrorists. The American Veterans Committee, in which Evers had been active, had designated his work for their meritorious achievement award and had planned to present it to him at their twentieth annual convention that week. When Evers begged off attending because of the Jackson crisis, the group instead elected him to their national board and took up a collection totaling nearly five hundred dollars "to be used to help provide whatever aid is necessary to keep Jackson's courageous children safe and well."[100]

The Wilkins arrest was all over the papers on Sunday, although it was what Salter called a "token arrest" because Wilkins, Evers, and Wilcher were simply fingerprinted and let go. Evers's reputation was growing nationally all the same. Saturday's New York Times had published a "Man in the News" profile of him, summarizing his life and citing his commitment to Mississippi. "I may be going to heaven or hell," Evers was quoted as saying, "but I'll be going from Jackson."[101]

As for any movement activities in Jackson on Sunday, everything seemed to be at a standstill. The only official activities planned were a press conference and a mass meeting featuring James Meredith, who was announcing the creation of a scholarship fund for "deserving [Negro] youngsters."[102] Neither Salter nor King attended the evening meeting, but, hoping to catch up with Evers afterwards, they drove from Tougaloo to the Masonic Temple at about 9:30 p.m. When they arrived, they discovered that a surprise strategy committee meeting had been called. Salter in particular was caught off guard, since he was technically cochair with Pearlena Lewis, who was still under arrest at the "fairgrounds motel." When Salter and King arrived just as the meeting was about to begin, Gloster Current hurried up to Salter and said, "I've got a few things I want to say." Salter assumed there were some new developments that the national NAACP staff member wanted to discuss and gave him the floor.[103]

Current's ploy, however, was a trap. Now that matters had reached a crucial point, he announced, the NAACP had decided that the membership of the strategy committee needed to be expanded to include more of the ministers and the black community leadership, which tended to be more conservative. He also suggested that the committee chairmanship be rotated, and someone quickly nominated one of the ministers. Salter was dumbstruck. Current himself had invited the other ministers to the meeting, and hardly any of the youth council members were present since many were either still in jail or had not heard about the unscheduled meeting. Still, how could Salter—not least because he was not black—object to the rotation? He recognized what was happening but was defenseless to stop it. Current then presented the NAACP's new strategy for Jackson, which, not surprisingly, consisted primarily of legal action and a voter registration drive. The boycott would be strengthened, but there would be little if any direct action demonstrations—certainly no more mass marches. Salter was angry but remained uncharacteristically silent. Ed King was flabbergasted, not only at Current's audacity but also at Salter's acquiescence, though King himself apparently raised no objection either. It was a turning point from which the direct action advocates would never recover.[104]

Pearlena Lewis, on the other hand, though still in jail, was delighted with the change. She felt that the responsibility of cochairing the strategy committee was too great and welcomed the opportunity to share the burden with others.[105]

It now seems clear that the national leadership blamed Salter for Evers's embrace of direct action activism. Certainly Wilkins had correctly settled on Salter as the one responsible for bringing radical lawyer Bill Kunstler into the Jackson Movement's orbit; Evers had probably been required to tell Wilkins that much. And when Clarence Mitchell had checked around with his contacts at the FBI, they had told him that Salter was a dangerous person, perhaps a communist. Although Doris Allison only heard this assessment of Salter—which was not correct—from Mitchell weeks later,[106] it seems likely that Mitchell had already quietly alerted Wilkins and Current of his findings. During the short time Wilkins was in Jackson, it is likely that he arranged for Salter's removal as head of the strategy committee, as well as for the local black religious and business leaders' renewed negotiations with the mayor. Wilkins was trying to defuse the situation, negotiate a settlement, declare victory, and move on. A protracted grassroots challenge to the existing order was clearly not part of his game plan.

It seems evident, too, that Salter and King were out of the loop for many crucial developments from the time the NAACP nationals touched down. Ludden claimed that he was asked personally by Wilkins to lead the youth of Jackson—something even Evers apparently objected to when Ludden first arrived and something that Salter never seems to have been made aware of.[107]

For Salter and King, their base of operation was clearly Tougaloo College and the students there. That's where the majority of the Woolworth's demonstrators had originated from. But for Pearlena and other Jackson youth, the NAACP office was their base. From the time the national office staff began to arrive, Salter and King had slowly started to lose their standing as the balance of power gradually shifted to the Lynch Street offices and the national players who had set up shop there.

It is instructive that both Salter and King viewed the high school demonstrations as "spontaneous," whereas Ludden stated that they were planned out of the NAACP's Jackson headquarters. Ludden and Laplois Ashford were busy ingratiating themselves with the youths while Salter and King were attending to their duties at Tougaloo.[108] It seems also obvious that for most of Jackson's black populace, the NAACP national staff held a leadership cachet that Salter and King could hardly match.

It was Evers who somehow got stuck in the middle—trying to balance the demands of those wanting to put on the brakes to slow things down with those insisting on more direct and immediate action. It wasn't just Salter, King, and the Tougaloo crowd pushing for more demonstrations. The NAACP's Willie Ludden, Mercedes Wright, and Laplois Ashford all wanted to keep the pressure on through more demonstrations but they were too new within the NAACP organization to carry much clout.

No, it was Gloster Current, Clarence Mitchell, Jesse DeVore, and the stalwarts of "Wilkins's army" who held the balance of power. They trumped even Evers's strong voice for change. This movement was going to be handled the "NAACP way," which meant top down, not grassroots. The people would take their orders from the national staff, not the other way around.[109]

And perhaps it should be asked, what was so wrong with turning the attention of the Jackson Movement toward voter registration? Wasn't political power the ultimate prize? Certainly SNCC was already pushing for the vote in the Delta and elsewhere in the state, and a year later would launch the Freedom Vote project to call attention to Mississippi's unfair voter registration practices. So why shouldn't the nation's most revered civil rights organization try to cool things down and direct the sizeable energies of the local populace into what might ultimately benefit them more, and with perhaps less potential for violence.

The activist segment likely would rebut this assertion with the fact that it was at this very point that the entire nation's attention was fixed on Jackson. Now was not the time to slow down, but to press their advantage. Only by doing so could a clear victory be won, as had been done in Birmingham. The momentum from such a victory could add fuel for further change, not only in Jackson but also in other parts of the South. In addition, from the activist mentality, freedom meant so much more than being able to cast a ballot. It meant freedom to shop, to eat, to read, to work, to live, to learn, and to play wherever and whenever one wanted. It meant a totally integrated society on an equal footing. That's what Salter and his troops were fighting for. They wanted that openness and they wanted it immediately.

At this point, however, the tide seems to have turned and began to move at a slower pace, just the way the national office had hoped it would. Thus, it seemed that the Jackson Movement—at least at the grassroots level—was slowly dying. As if to emphasize the point, comedian and activist Dick Gregory arrived in Jackson on Monday, June 3, only to be told by Medgar Evers that he had to return to home. The comedian's two-month-old infant had developed a high fever shortly after Gregory left his Chicago home to fly to Jackson. Evers had to break the news to Gregory that his baby boy had died.[110]

The next five days saw a smattering of small demonstrations that Salter and others insisted on conducting, but no mass marches. Indicative of the shift was Annie Moody's experience. She got out of jail on Sunday and was arrested again on Monday with a group of six demonstrators who picketed the J. C. Penney store across the street from Woolworth's. This was the smallest number arrested since the Woolworth's sit-in nearly a week before. Moody had hoped to be taken to the fairgrounds so that she could see what was happening to the young people, who had complained of mistreatment by the police. Instead, she was taken to the Hinds County jail; the police were still separating the lead activists from the other youth to avoid what the police saw as radical influence.[111]

Evers and Salter were also continuing their efforts to move things forward, albeit on a smaller scale. Ed King claimed that, despite the national NAACP's decision to go slowly, Evers never quite gave up hope of restarting demonstrations. "Monday, Tuesday, Wednesday—the people are always ready," King remembered. "Every night Medgar says, 'We will march.' He closes every meeting with the threat." Evers also expanded the demands of the movement, calling for a moratorium on arrests for "peaceful picketing and parading" and suggesting that charges be dropped against those already arrested. For his part, Salter—despite his ouster as cochair of the strategy committee—continued to lobby hard for mass marches to put pressure on the Jackson power structure. He won some concessions, but the small demonstrations the NAACP would support were scoffed at by the mayor, who said he believed the crisis had "practically ended." And when the NAACP's Ruby Hurley took Dick Gregory's place at the mass meeting Monday night, she exhorted the adult men in the audience to rise up and not let their children go to jail in their place. Like Wilkins's, her rhetoric was strong, but she did not call for marches.[112]

Not all of the NAACP staff were so complacent. Willie Ludden advocated for another mass march but was told that he'd be fired if he led a march without the national office's authorization. His supervisors (including Hurley) indicated that they would not put up bond for anyone arrested in an unauthorized march. Ludden observed that Evers was "very disturbed and bewildered" by the stance of the NAACP leadership. He also rightly realized that "the engine of the movement was running out of gas. We were losing our people."[113]

On Tuesday, June 4, the *Clarion-Ledger* trumpeted as one of its lead stories "Agitation Is Over—Mayor." The article noted that Mayor Thompson had declared that "Jackson's racial disturbances are over . . . because right-thinking people have declared that it is over." The mayor went on to observe that "Jackson has about 50,000 Negroes, and agitators have gotten only a few hundred children to take part in mass demonstrations." Other press outlets were coming to the same conclusion.[114]

To counteract the perception of a dying movement, Salter, Evers, Ludden, and Mercedes Wright decided that, if only small demonstrations were allowed, then small demonstrations they'd have. In what Evers dubbed the "Allen Thompson Blitzkrieg," small demonstrations were staged all over Capitol Street, to further pressure the mayor. Thirty-two individuals were arrested that Tuesday, twenty-four of whom were under the age of eighteen, a point emphasized in the Jackson press to indicate that the adults still were not very involved. The FBI was quick to point out in their now daily reports that "none of the police were observed to push, shove, or strike the Negroes arrested." The police were just doing their job—keeping a lid on things, just as they had with the Freedom Rides two years earlier.[115]

The picketing and attempted sit-ins now took on a choreographed look, with the NAACP even issuing a timetable for where and when they could be expected—no more surprises. The most dramatic event that Tuesday was saved for last: a group of four demonstrators staged a prayer vigil on the steps of city hall. Three black women, along with one white woman from Concord, Massachusetts, knelt in prayer and called loudly for freedom in Jackson. The white woman held a sign saying, "When Children Suffer, All Americans Suffer."

Another sign read, "Do Unto Our Children as You Would Do Unto Your Own Children," while a third sign read, "The Truth Shall Not be Jailed," a clear swipe at the police policy of instant arrest.[116]

Captain Ray, who by that point had been promoted to deputy police chief for his adept handling of the demonstrations, first asked the women if they wanted to take their grievances directly to the mayor. When they refused, he told black trusties to carry them to the paddy wagon. Then Mayor Thompson himself came onto the steps and instructed Ray to ask again if the demonstrators would bring their grievances directly to him. Again they refused and were arrested and driven to police headquarters.[117]

Instead of a direct action campaign, the Battle of Jackson was becoming a public relations war, as the New York Times suggested: "Press releases and news conferences replaced mass marches in Jackson today as the Negro and white communities settled into what one Negro called 'the second phase of our campaign.'" NAACP lawyers pouring into Jackson from New York, Chicago, and Washington, D.C., began litigating the arrests, including those of Medgar Evers and Roy Wilkins.[118]

The mayor switched his strategy accordingly, announcing he might seek an injunction against further demonstrations. He also called for applicants for the black police and crossing guard positions—a minor concession to the ministers but one which drew sharp criticism from the Citizens' Council. Evers issued an NAACP-approved statement saying the mayor's move was "a ray of hope," but then demanded that at least twelve policemen and twelve crossing guards be hired during the next thirty days. He also called for another one of the movement's requirements: a biracial committee. On this point the mayor adamantly refused to budge.[119]

In essence, the NAACP was relying heavily on public image to fight its battle. The national press, sensing the change in strategy and the slowing of the movement, began to leave the city—over Evers's objections—for what they saw as more pressing news elsewhere. Even some of the stalwarts of the Jackson Movement could read the signs of the times. When she finally was released from jail for her post office transgression, Joan Trumpauer headed home to Washington, D.C., to get a job to help pay for her final year at Tougaloo. George Raymond moved on to Canton, Mississippi, to begin in earnest his new community organizing and voter registration project for CORE.[120] No new developments were expected in Jackson, so few were prepared for what was to come.

CHAPTER 8

THE DEATH OF MEDGAR EVERS

IT IS DIFFICULT NOW TO COMPREHEND JUST HOW HARSH AND BRUTAL MISSIS-sippi's racial war had become in the early 1960s. State-sponsored terrorism, as some have called it, was a way of life, and no one felt the jagged edge of that terror more acutely than did Medgar Evers and his family. Evers would get regular threats by phone at his office. "It just became a routine thing," remembered his office assistant Lillian Louie. "[Being] physically threatened was just a daily thing."[1]

Myrlie Evers intercepted similar calls at home and came in for a fair share of contempt herself. "Black bitch," one anonymous caller venomously spat. "You got another one of them niggers in your belly?" The Everses regularly received threats to blow up the house or the office, or to kill Medgar straight out. "We lived in terror," Myrlie said, particularly after the James Meredith victory at Ole Miss, for which Evers and the NAACP had played such pivotal and visible roles.[2]

Medgar and Myrlie openly talked of death. Evers knew he was a hunted man. "We knew his life was in danger," Myrlie later bitterly noted.[3]

But no one other than perhaps Evers's closest Mississippi friends seemed to completely comprehend the extreme danger he was in: not his New York NAACP bosses; not his younger charges in the youth council; not his activist partners from Tougaloo.

As the Jackson Movement heated up, Evers's friends offered to put up their own funds to pay for a security force for him if the NAACP would match their offer. Both Myrlie Evers and Laplois Ashford claim that Roy Wilkins and Gloster Current refused to hear of such a prospect. "The NAACP has more important things to do with its money," Current said. Ashford went so far as to suggest that the national office executives were concerned that Evers was becoming a bigger star than they were. "We need to keep him in his place," Ashford claimed to have heard Wilkins and Current say. "We need to put a lid on this."[4]

Their refusal to recognize the extreme danger Evers was facing and their dithering over how to conduct a large-scale grassroots movement put the emerging civil rights star at even greater risk. Evers alone among the NAACP staff regularly and publicly called for further demonstrations. He alone had

Hard at work. Medgar Evers (c. 1955), pictured in his cramped office that overlooked Lynch Street, just steps away from the campus of Jackson State College. "Every day he went forth," said Roy Wilkins at Evers's graveside ceremony. "He was offering his life for the things he believed in." Credit: AP Images

Welcome to Tougaloo. The historic gates of Tougaloo College welcome all who approach the campus, located about ten miles north of downtown Jackson. Six of the nine Jackson Woolworth's demonstrators were either students or teachers from Tougaloo. Credit: M. J. O'Brien

White students at Tougaloo. Tougaloo College's social sciences professor Dr. Ernst Borinski welcomes two white female students in the fall of 1961. Charlotte Phillips (left) was visiting for the fall semester from Swarthmore College (Pennsylvania), while Joan Trumpauer (right)—already an experienced demonstrator and freedom rider—transferred, after a year's hiatus, from Duke University (North Carolina). She would stay until she graduated in 1964. Credit: AP Images/Jim Bourdier

Capitol Street—1963. Capitol Street was the hub of commerce not only for the city of Jackson but for much of the state of Mississippi. Crowned by the old state capitol building, the eight-block boulevard was crowded with shops, restaurants, and theatres. Note the partial Woolworth's sign in the upper left corner of the photo. Credit: AP Images/Jim Bourdier

Central High. Central High School, looking very much like a fortress, looms over downtown Jackson. Just two blocks from Capitol Street, the school furnished many of the youths who tormented the demonstrators at the Woolworth's sit-in. Credit: M. J. O'Brien

Jackson Movement's first foray. On December 12, 1962, the Jackson Movement staged its first picketing of Woolworth's on Capitol Street. Eldri Salter (center) along with her husband, John (partially obscured), and several Tougaloo students were immediately arrested by Jackson police captain Cecil Hataway. Credit: AP Images

More picketing. On April 4, at the height of the Easter shopping season, the Jackson Movement put more picketers on Capitol Street. Pictured here are Tougaloo students Austin C. Moore III (left) and Frank Dickey, advising Negro shoppers to stay away from Capitol Street. Credit: AP Images

Eerily quiet. At the start of the Woolworth's demonstration, there was little commotion. Pearlena Lewis (left), Memphis Norman (center), and Annie Moody (right) wait to be served. Credit: Fred Blackwell

The press descends. Early on in the Woolworth's demonstration, only the press surrounded the demonstrators: (foreground, with back to camera) Annie Moody, (center) Memphis Norman, and (partially obscured) Pearlena Lewis. Credit: Fred Blackwell

Under attack. Former Jackson police officer Bennie Oliver "stomps" Memphis Norman after pulling him from his stool at Woolworth's. When it was over, Norman would be bleeding from his mouth, his nose, and his forehead. Credit: Corbis

The iconic photograph that captured an era. At the counter, John Salter (left), Joan Trumpauer (center), and Annie Moody (right) endure the torment of the mob as Red Hydrick (upper left, wearing hat) and D. C. Sullivan (center, with cigarette) look on. Credit: Fred Blackwell

Another demonstrator down. Walter Williams lies on the floor of Woolworth's after being struck by a glass object that was hurled through the air. Pearlena Lewis stays put at the counter and talks with UPI reporter Cliff Sessions. Lois Chaffee is directly behind Lewis. Credit: Fred Blackwell

More mayhem. Demonstrators further down the counter were not spared: (from left) Walter Williams, George Raymond, Pearlena Lewis, and Lois Chaffee (partly obscured). Credit: Fred Blackwell

Demonstration over. Reverend Ed King comes to the aid of his friends once the crowd begins to disburse. At counter: (from left) John Salter, Joan Trumpauer, Annie Moody, and Tom Beard (partially obscured). Note Dan Beittel, president of Tougaloo College, at the end of the counter talking to reporter Ken Toler (far right). Credit: Fred Blackwell

After the siege at Woolworth's: (from left) Tougaloo president Dan Beittel, George Raymond, Annie Moody, Lois Chaffee (obscured except for top of head), Pearlena Lewis, John Salter, Tom Beard, Joan Trumpauer (obscured except for her dress) and the ever-present Jackson deputy police chief, John L. Ray. Credit: Corbis

Teaching the basics of nonviolent resistance. The day after the Woolworth's sit-in, CORE leaders Dave Dennis (foreground) and George Raymond (center), along with the NAACP North Jackson Youth Council's Johnny Frazier, show students how to protect themselves during planned demonstrations. Note the presence of John Salter in the back at the door. Credit: AP Images/Jim Bourdier

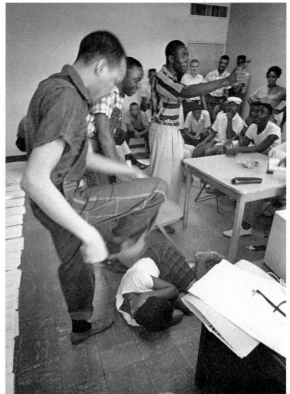

More demonstrations at Woolworth's. On May 29, 1963, NAACP Jackson branch president Doris Allison (center) and Steve Rutledge demonstrate in front of Woolworth's at lunchtime in downtown Jackson. Officer Ray removes the sign from Rutledge. Tom Beard (in straw hat, obscured by policeman), who had been at the Woolworth's counter the day before, also marches. Credit: AP Images/Jim Bourdier

"We Shall Overcome." The youth of Jackson enthusiastically took up the challenge after the Woolworth's sit-in. Pictured here are middle school and high school students protesting at one of the local high schools during recess just days after the Woolworth's sit-in. Their makeshift banner reads "We Shall Overcome." Credit: Fred Blackwell

King is removed. Reverend Ed King, in full clerical garb, makes a dramatic exit from the "kneel-in" demonstration at the U.S. Post Office on Capitol Street two days after the Woolworth's sit-in. The next day, in a painfully close vote, King would be denied full admission as a minister into the Mississippi Methodist Conference. Credit: AP Images/Bill Hudson

Ludden dragged away. On May 31, 1963, the NAACP's Willie Ludden led the "Children's March" of more than four hundred youths from the Farish Street Baptist Church toward Capitol Street. The march was stopped two blocks from the church when Ludden attempted to move through a phalanx of police. He was beaten and dragged off to jail. All of the marchers were arrested and transported— some in garbage trucks—to the state fairgrounds. Credit: AP Images

"You're under arrest." NAACP Executive Secretary Roy Wilkins (in hat and sunglasses) and Mississippi Field Secretary Medgar Evers are arrested on Capitol Street in front of Woolworth's on Saturday, June 1, 1963. A reporter (right foreground) holds a "shotgun" microphone to record Wilkins's comments. Evers's sign reads "End Brutality in Jackson—NAACP." Credit: Corbis

Current arrives. Medgar Evers and NAACP Director of Branches Gloster Current (right) in an undated photo. Current would engineer the takeover of the Jackson Movement's strategy committee and move it away from direct action. In her memoir, Myrlie Evers wryly notes, "with his immediate superiors on the scene, Medgar was relieved of both the necessity and the opportunity of making policy decisions." Credit: Medgar and Myrlie Evers Collection, Mississippi Department of Archives and History. Used by permission.

Waiting for their ride to jail. A youth march is interrupted by police on the streets of Jackson. Note the youth standing waist-high to the policeman with the extended baton near the front/center of the photo. It was Willie Ludden's idea to have the marchers carry American flags. Credit: AP Images/Bill Hudson

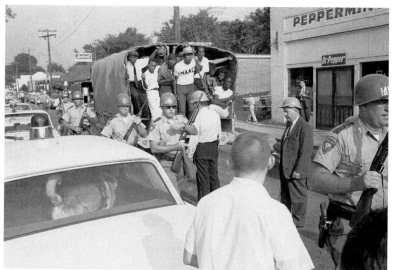

One more mass march. Police break up a march near the NAACP offices. Eighty-eight youths were arrested after Salter quarreled with the NAACP's Roy Wilkins, who wanted to call a halt to the demonstrations and mass arrests. "If we don't have this march, and many more mass marches, we're never going to crack Jackson open!" Salter argued vigorously. Credit: AP Images/Bill Hudson

Fairgrounds motel. Hundreds of young black men are housed where cattle and animals are usually displayed during the annual Mississippi State Fair. To keep up their spirits, the youths sang freedom songs. Note the young man sitting near the center of the photo looking into the camera. The *New York Times* reported that "grade school age" children were arrested for participating in the Jackson demonstrations. Credit: Corbis

Livestock holding area. The young women were segregated from the young men at the fairgrounds motel. Both were held in areas designated for prized sheep, cattle, and pigs that were shown off during the Mississippi State Fair each autumn. The fairgrounds are directly behind the old state capitol and just blocks away from the Capitol Street shopping district. Credit: AP Images

The ministers' march. "Medgar's blood loosened up every church door in Mississippi," said NAACP Jackson board president Doris Allison. Thirteen ministers were arrested in Jackson on June 12, 1963, the day news of Evers's murder was announced to the world. Credit: Fred Blackwell

Grieving widow. Myrlie Evers addressing the mass meeting at Pearl Street AME Church less than twenty-four hours after Medgar Evers was gunned down. "No one knows like I know how my husband gave his life for this cause," she said. "I hope by his death that all of you here . . . will be able to draw some of his strength, some of his courage, and some of his determination to finish this fight." Credit: AP Images/Jim Bourdier

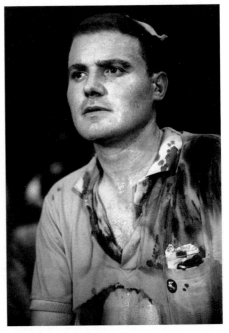

"We Shall Not Be Moved." John Salter as he appeared at a Jackson Movement mass meeting on the evening of June 13, 1963. Earlier that day he had been brutally beaten on Rose Street while peacefully standing on the porch of a Negro home. Note the bandage on his head. "A cop hit him so hard," reporter Bill Minor said, "it sounded like Joe DiMaggio knocking a home run out of the ballpark." "We can't meet violence with violence," Salter told the crowd. Credit: Corbis

"Freedom is our goal." On June 14, 1963, Flag Day, the NAACP allowed small demonstrations on Capitol Street. Thirty-seven youths, including the two pictured here, were arrested for "parading without a permit," despite their separating into small groups of two and three. Their T-shirts were meant to substitute for demonstration signs. Credit: AP Images

Last respects. Myrlie Evers and her two older children, Reena (left) and Darrell (right), visit the Collins Funeral Home the night before Medgar's funeral service in Jackson. Credit: Corbis

Evers memorial service. The Masonic Temple on Lynch Street, filled to overflowing at the memorial service for slain civil rights leader Medgar Evers. Note the significant media presence (foreground). "Nothing can stop the drive for freedom," declared the NAACP's Roy Wilkins, keynote speaker at the service. Credit: Corbis

The Evers "silent, mournful funeral procession." An estimated five thousand people marched in the 102 degree heat more than a mile from the Masonic Temple on Lynch Street to the Collins Funeral Home on North Farish Street. At the front of the procession are local ministers (from left) Reverend Allen Johnson, Reverend G. R. Haughton, and Reverend R. L. T. Smith. Reverend Martin Luther King, Jr., and Roy Wilkins march side by side in the second row. John Salter (still with head bandage) can be seen on the left in the eighth row; Ed King is three rows behind Salter in clerical garb. Credit: AP Images

"This Little Light of Mine." Jackson Movement regular Dorie Ladner (right, in light print blouse) and others make their way through the first police barricade in their attempt to head back to Capitol Street after the Evers funeral march. Credit: Corbis

Tense standoff. As the mourners attempted to return to Capitol Street, singing freedom songs in defiance of Mayor Allen Thompson's "silent march" permit, armed police are determined to block their way. Credit: Getty Images

"*The Negro Mississippian wants more jobs above the menial level in stores where he spends his money. He believes industries that have come to Mississippi should employ him above the laboring category.*"

— Medgar Evers, speech televised May 20, 1963, three weeks before he was murdered.

NEGRO CITIZENS
Please Do Not Buy
On Capitol Street
UNTIL WE ARE TREATED
With DECENCY and RESPECT
REMEMBER!

Jackson now. Today there are many memorials to the life and legacy of Medgar Evers, including this museum-quality display, one of many at the Jackson-Evers International Airport. Note the sit-in photo (tilted) and the Jackson Movement boycott flier that feature prominently in this display. Credit: M. J. O'Brien

Reconciliation. A sculpture at the Medgar Wiley Evers Pavilion at the Jackson-Evers International Airport aptly characterizes the state of race relations today in Mississippi's capitol city: "Reconciliation: A Work in Progress." Credit: M. J. O'Brien

to suffer the anxiety of the escalating threats to himself and to his family. The Salters had experienced some of this firsthand, but nothing like the daily taunts that Evers endured. Maybe the young folks at Tougaloo and the youth council had some vague notion of the danger—particularly after the scene at Woolworth's—but they weren't in a position to do much about it. Perhaps Ed King, a fellow native Mississippian, had the keenest sense of the danger to which Evers was daily exposing himself and his family. But he had long resigned himself to whatever might happen.

Evers, though hurt by the NAACP's refusal to provide protection, seemed impervious to his fate. "I don't want anyone to get hurt trying to save me," he told his wife. Besides, "when my time comes, I'm going to go, regardless of the protection I have." So he soldiered on. Facing the daily possibility of death, he kept pushing for change.[5]

One week after the Woolworth's sit-in, the Jackson Movement was facing ever-greater internal strains. Strategy committee sessions became more and more contentious. Pearlena Lewis remembered the nasty tone committee meetings had taken, with John Salter in particular heatedly calling for additional mass demonstrations. Evers, however, remained strangely quiet during the impassioned debates, seeming to just go through the motions. Ed King believed Evers was in a "blue funk." Lewis said his interactions with national office staff took on a formal tone. Louie attributed her boss's demeanor to frustration with the national office and the extreme stress he was under. Salter believed that Evers was torn between the NAACP friends who had supported him during the many lean years and his growing conviction that direct action could work if given a chance.[6]

All of those close to him began to see that there was more going on just below the surface. "He was haunted by premonitions of death," Salter recalled. Lewis agreed, recounting a dinner conversation with Evers after a full day of activity. "He said he wanted to live and he wanted to see his children live," she said. "But he had gotten that strange feeling that something [might] happen to him. He said that if it [did], 'I want you to carry on. One man doesn't stop the movement.'" Lewis was so shaken by the conversation that she shared it with her parents when she got home that night. Doris Allison, too, had heard Evers predict his own death. "I know that I'll pay for [this agitation] with my life," she remembered him telling her. "I don't know how, and I don't know when, and I don't know where. But I do know I will fall."[7]

AT THE MASS MEETING ON TUESDAY NIGHT, JUNE 4, THOSE ATTENDING RE-sponded negatively to the ministers' most recent negotiations with the mayor, and the assembly voted not to end the protests, just as Reverend Haughton had predicted. It was not enough for them that the mayor was offering to hire some black policemen and crossing guards and to promote a few black municipal workers. The crowd insisted on a biracial committee and the other demands outlined at the beginning of the siege; they weren't about to settle for anything less.

The actual pages from which Evers delivered his remarks to the meeting that night are in the NAACP archives. This haunting document is typed so cleanly—most likely by Lillian Louie—that it could have come from a modern-day computer. All around the edges are notes Evers made to himself— last-minute announcements, exhortations to continue the boycott, even some cryptic messages for which the meaning is now lost.[8]

In his prepared remarks, Evers suggested, perhaps a bit defensively, that the mayor might not be as good as his word because "in many cities where Negroes first apply for police, firemen and other positions, there is a tendency to disqualify colored applicants on flimsy reasons of health and other technicalities, including participation in civil rights demonstrations." Since the mayor had set out no specific eligibility requirements for the hiring, Evers itemized general qualifications gathered from police forces around the country. He did the same for crossing guards, adding that participation in peaceful demonstrations should not disqualify applicants for either position.

It is unclear when Evers began to ad-lib from his handwritten additions to the text, but words in the margins like "Golf" and "Library" suggest that he talked about the mayor's statements regarding integrating the city's public facilities. The scrawled and underlined words "Barq, Hart, Capitol St." refer to the boycott. Barq's root beer and Hart's bread had become the first products added to the boycott, which up until that point had been directed only at stores. Alphonzo Lewis explained that those two companies had provided food for policemen holding the black youth at the fairgrounds, and Myrlie Evers said both companies had made substantial contributions to the Citizens' Council. Those at the meeting that night report an addition not in Medgar's notes. They report that he stepped up his rhetoric on the boycott, threatening to show films at the next mass meeting of any black resident who ignored the boycott and shopped on Capitol Street.[9]

The crisply typed notes also indicate that Evers spoke about the prior week's "pray-in" on the post office steps, the day's "pickets," and the actions to be taken by the NAACP's "Lawyers." When he announced, finally, that Lena Horne would be coming to town for a benefit concert that Friday night, a wave of excitement rippled through the crowd.

The next day, the *New York Times* reported the most ironic fallout of the Woolworth's sit-in. Bennie Oliver, fresh from his conviction for assaulting Memphis Norman, was named political aide to David L. Perkins, who was running for lieutenant governor. In announcing the appointment, Perkins said that Oliver "knows how to handle the racial problem."[10]

The demonstrations that Wednesday were small but tactically significant. The NAACP had been searching for ways to get its message of protest across without having demonstrators arrested and then putting up large amounts of cash to bail them out. Someone—most likely Willie Ludden or Mercedes Wright—had hit upon the idea of having T-shirts printed with the NAACP logo on the front and individual messages on the back. This was a tactic that had been used successfully in the Savannah campaign years earlier.[11] That afternoon, carrying American flags and wearing the T-shirts, nine young people marched up and down Capitol Street. Despite their efforts to stay out of jail, the nine were arrested and taken to the fairgrounds. Also in the courts that day, the fourteen post office demonstrators were convicted of breaching the peace, fined two hundred dollars, and sentenced to four-month prison terms. The convictions were immediately appealed.[12]

The strategy committee meeting that day was the most contentious ever, with Salter and the young people demanding mass demonstrations, and the national NAACP forces, led by Current, and many of the local black ministers and businessmen opposing direct action. Current explained that finances were the primary reason that demonstrations could not continue. He even said that the NAACP had invested more funds in Mississippi during the prior week than all of the state's members had paid during the organization's forty-five-year presence there. It seemed a gratuitous slap in the face for the people who had labored diligently to keep any sort of NAACP presence in the state. Tellingly, it was also the first public acknowledgment that money was driving the national office's decisions. Although Salter and King continued to point out that the objective was to fill the jails, not to bail out demonstrators, the NAACP with its middle-class values was simply unwilling to go along with that approach. There would be no more mass demonstrations in Jackson, not while the national NAACP was calling the shots.[13]

On other fronts in Mississippi's race wars, Wednesday proved eventful as well. Annie Moody got out of jail again that day, this time to find a letter from her mother waiting for her. Toosweet had written the day after the Woolworth's demonstration but had sent the letter by way of Moody's sister, Adline, in New Orleans to avoid raising the suspicions of local officials. Toosweet's letter said that the sheriff had come to her house after hearing of her daughter's involvement in the sit-in and asked "all kinds of questions." He told Toosweet that Moody "must never come back" home since he couldn't be responsible for what would happen to her. Toosweet also asked her daughter not to write to her until things had settled down. In her own postscript to the letter, Adline added that their brother, Junior, was suffering severe harassment and that white men had beaten their elderly uncle in retaliation for Moody's Woolworth's participation. Then Adline took her sister to task, suggesting that she was "trying to get every Negro in Centreville murdered."[14]

On a more positive note, Cleve McDowell, an honors graduate of Jackson State College, successfully and without incident enrolled as the second black student at the University of Mississippi—the first in its law school, which Evers had tried to enter years earlier. Although Governor Barnett and his advisors considered trying to halt McDowell's admission, as they had with Meredith nine months previously, somehow cooler heads prevailed. It appeared that at least some parts of Mississippi were slowly adapting to the new political landscape.[15]

SUMMER SCHOOL BEGAN AT TOUGALOO ON THURSDAY, JUNE 6. SALTER AND King were on campus, as was Dr. Beittel. By midmorning, all three had been served with an injunction instigated by the mayor and issued by the chancellor of the Hinds County Chancery Court, enjoining them and others from participating in further demonstrations of any sort. Titled "City of Jackson Municipal Corporation vs. John R. Salter, Jr., et al.," the injunction cited thirteen individuals, as well as the NAACP, CORE, and the trustees of Tougaloo College. "I was honored with being the prime target," Salter proudly asserted. The injunction restrained those named from "engaging in, sponsoring, inciting, or encouraging mass street parades or mass processions or like demonstrations without a permit, unlawful blocking of the public streets or sidewalks, trespassing on complainants' private property, congregating on the streets or public places as mobs and unlawfully picketing . . . business establishments." The injunction also enjoined them from "doing any acts designed to consummate conspiracies to engage in said unlawful acts." In other words, they couldn't demonstrate nor could they help others demonstrate. Salter believed that this was "the most sweeping injunction handed down against any movement of any kind in the 1960s." Although the injunction technically was "temporary," no hearing was set to discuss its merits until September, long after the Jackson crisis would likely have ended.[16]

It was immediately clear to Salter that such a blatant denial of basic constitutional rights was illegal and had to be defied. When he told this to the strategy committee meeting that was hastily called at the NAACP offices just before noon, to his surprise many agreed. Gloster Current, Mercedes Wright, and Medgar Evers were all cited individually in the injunction, as were Dave Dennis and Dick Gregory, who had decided to return to Jackson to appear onstage with Lena Horne on Friday night.

King observed that the injunction cited none of the black business leaders or ministers by name. Evers suggested that the move was meant to further divide the factions within the strategy committee. It had the opposite effect, however. Although the committee wasn't ready to employ Salter's "get the masses into the streets" strategy, the group did agree that something dramatic had to be done to test and, they hoped, invalidate the injunction. Perhaps the

NAACP's eagerness to challenge the injunction isn't that surprising since it played to the organization's strengths. Consequently, while Salter, Evers, King, and others were planning demonstrations for the next day, NAACP attorneys began plotting strategies to unlock the legal handcuffs.[17]

In New York, to the surprise of the Jackson activists, Roy Wilkins issued a news bulletin to all NAACP branches, interpreting the injunction as a sign that the city was running scared: "The city never would have bothered to go to court for an injunction if it were true, as Mayor Thompson announced to the press, that the NAACP action was 'petering out,'" he wrote. "We are now in a stronger position than before. We are on our way to winning what the Jackson Negro community asked for." Wilkins went on to ask for money while asserting that the NAACP was at the forefront of the civil rights battle. "Mississippi is our territory," he explained. "The Jackson fight is an NAACP fight. If it is a good fight, we get the credit; if not, we get raspberries." He then discussed the costs: "Already we have sent $64,000 in bail bond money to Jackson out of our treasury here. If the cases are not dropped we will have to put up another $150,000 in appeal bonds." He asked the branches to "rush money from your treasury. . . . Join the Jackson fighting club," he concluded, "by laying your Branch's money on the line."[18]

That same day, Evers issued a statement to the Jackson press echoing Wilkins's remarks about the organization's tacit victory: "Jackson officials once more documented their unique capacity for speaking from two sides of their mouths today by seeking to enjoin NAACP-sparked demonstrations and selective buying activities. . . . Why spank a tottering infant?" he questioned. "Why enjoin a 'faltering' movement, as they describe it? White leaders in Jackson gave the world the answer today. Their injunction proceedings have proven that our movement is sharp, vital and inclusive. They are hurting inside. This is their outcry." Evers ended by saying that the NAACP attorneys were reviewing the injunction and would advise the movement what its next actions should be.[19]

Thursday was also a memorable day for the other contingent of the Woolworth's crowd as 180 seniors from Central High School graduated that afternoon. In a speech that couldn't have been more ironic, class president Dennis Jackson called on his classmates to preserve "individual freedom, the basic philosophy of our nation." "The basic tenet of our democracy," he said, "is respect for the moral worth of all human beings and the equal freedom of all men to shape their lives as they see fit." D.C. Sullivan heard those words, as did many of the other Central graduates who had done much of the damage at Woolworth's. When asked years later, however, Sullivan said he could hardly remember the demonstrations and racial strife that were tearing his hometown apart. He felt they weren't really his concern for they never threatened his neighborhood in south Jackson.[20]

On Friday, June 7, the NAACP legal machinery shifted into high gear, filing three lawsuits and stating that one more was in the works. Attorney Robert Carter announced that his motion to dissolve the injunction had been denied by the judge who issued it, but that attorneys were preparing a similar motion to present to the Mississippi Supreme Court that afternoon. Carter also announced that the NAACP had filed for a writ of habeas corpus in federal court to test the validity of the arrests of the youth who had picketed peacefully two days earlier in their NAACP T-shirts.

In addition, Carter filed a counterinjunction on behalf of Roy Wilkins, Medgar Evers, and others, including Willie Ludden, Ed King, and Doris Allison. Curiously, John Salter was not named in this legal action, confirming that he was persona non grata with the NAACP hierarchy. The brief asked the federal government to restrain fourteen state and city officials, including Mayor Thompson, Deputy Police Chief Ray, and Governor Barnett, from interfering with the exercise of constitutionally guaranteed rights of free speech, peaceful assembly, and picketing. Finally, Carter announced that within forty-eight hours he intended to file a suit—the first of its kind—challenging discrimination and segregation in places of public accommodation. It was a stunning statement that indicated the NAACP's capacity for legal maneuvering and its wizardry at public relations. While it did nothing to advance the immediate situation in Jackson, the announcement made headlines locally and nationally.[21]

To read the briefs, complaints, and affidavits filed by the NAACP at this time is to be educated on how expert and thorough were its national office attorneys. They clearly had the long arc of justice in mind and challenged the state of Mississippi on every conceivable charge. Primarily, they argued in their motion to dissolve the injunction that "the Law is clear that no state may use its authority, whether executive, legislative, or judicial, to prevent the exercise of freedom of speech and association." And in an accompanying complaint: "The Constitution of the United States, the Congress of the United States and the President of the United States by executive order, have unanimously condemned the exercise of governmental power to effectuate, maintain and achieve racial segregation and discrimination."[22]

The court filings are meticulously prepared, adroitly argued, and voluminous. They are strong evidence of the NAACP's total commitment to the Jackson Movement from a legal perspective.

On the other side of the law that day, forty-seven young people were arrested in both planned and spontaneous demonstrations. The day before, four black youths, on their own, had decided to test the city's whites-only golf course. Although two were turned away because they didn't have the proper shoes, the two wearing golf cleats were allowed to play. The pair had visited NAACP offices afterwards to recount their coup. Having heard about this success, on Friday morning about forty kids entered a whites-only park in south Jackson and played a game of softball. The police arrived and chased some of them away, but twenty-one of the youth then gathered in the street and refused to disperse when police instructed them to. They were arrested and taken to the fairgrounds.[23]

In addition, Salter and King helped orchestrate a number of "pinprick demonstrations" in direct defiance of the injunction. Pickets or attempted sit-ins occurred at Primos Restaurant, H. L. Green's, and Walgreen's. Twenty-six demonstrators were arrested in these actions. By defying the injunction, Salter, King, Evers, and Dennis all wondered whether they would be arrested. Techni-cally, the police could have taken them in, but for the time being, they went about their business without police interference.[24]

That afternoon, Eldri Salter and little Maria boarded a plane for Minnesota for an extended visit to Eldri's parents. The Salters had decided that the situa-tion was too unsafe for the baby, and Eldri had even used her birth name when purchasing the tickets. "I didn't want to leave," she would later say. "I didn't want to be that far away from [John] when there was danger and there was the possibility that we might not see each other again." Her premonitions were not entirely unfounded, as subsequent events would show.[25]

BY EARLY EVENING, IT APPEARED AS THOUGH JACKSON'S ENTIRE BLACK COM-munity was anticipating the Lena Horne concert that night. Doris Allison remembered coming upon Medgar Evers about 6:30, standing alone at the back of the Masonic Temple and fretting that no one had yet arrived. Allison reassured him that there would be an overflow crowd. Sure enough, just after 7:00 people began to come in, and the place was packed by 7:30.[26]

Three suspicious white men, unknown to the event's organizers, showed up and sat near the back of the auditorium. One lit a cigarette, in violation of the fire code. Allison, who was in the lobby selling NAACP memberships, spotted the smoker and sent a message up to Evers to make an announcement about the smoking restrictions. Evers handed the note to Ruby Hurley, who was on the stage, and she pointed to the man and told him no smoking was allowed. As he and his companions got up to leave, Allison's husband, Ben, who was selling programs, was headed back to get some change from his wife at the membership desk. The cigarette-smoking man exited his seat just as Ben Al-lison was passing, causing the two men to collide and Ben to accidentally push the stranger almost on top of Doris. It was an awkward moment, but they all recovered and the man and his friends left. Outside the auditorium, however, the three went upstairs to the NAACP office where Pearlena Lewis and Lillian Louie asked them pointedly if they needed any help. The men responded by quickly heading down the stairs and out the doors into the street. The two women followed to make sure the men had left the premises.[27]

None of the NAACP members realized at the time who it was they had encountered, but two weeks later, the man who nearly fell into Doris Allison's arms was arrested for the murder of Medgar Evers. That evening, Byron De La Beckwith had been stalking his prey, looking for the best place to hide out and shoot him. "I wished I'd have kissed him right then and there—right on the lips!" Allison later cried with regret. Considering Beckwith's legendary hatred of blacks, Allison wistfully imagined that such intimate contact might have caused him to have a heart attack and die on the spot.[28]

While Beckwith and company were leaving, another small drama was playing out inside the auditorium. Detective Jim Black—the undercover police officer from Woolworth's—was attending the event incognito as a reporter. He had been identified by Tougaloo activist Jan Hillegas, who had been arrested at an attempted sit-in at Primos Restaurant the week before. Hillegas knew that Black worked for the police department, so when she saw him sitting in the section cordoned off for the press, she rushed over and told Evers. Black's composure nearly faltered as Evers announced from the podium, glancing toward him, "My information tells me that we have a police officer in the house." After a brief pause, while the audience absorbed the news, Evers looked away and went on. "But that's all right," he said. "He's welcome. We have nothing to hide." Black relaxed and the moment passed. A little later, though, one of Black's African American acquaintances, who had also spotted him in the crowd, went over to needle him: "Make your hole pucker a little bit, honky?" "Yeah, it did," said Black. "From that day forward," the detective later said with admiration, "I never did fail to respect Medgar Evers."[29]

When the program finally began that night, it was clear that Lena Horne had reached a new level of commitment. She had been stung by the violence in Birmingham, and Ed King believed that Horne had come to Jackson ready to march. Just the week before, she had participated in an incendiary meeting with Attorney General Robert Kennedy that writer James Baldwin had hastily called together in New York City. Jerome Smith, George Raymond's mentor from New Orleans, happened to be in the city at the time and was also invited to participate. At the meeting, Smith told Kennedy in no uncertain terms that the situation in the South was getting worse, despite what the administration had done to try to ameliorate the problems. The attorney general also heard from the dozen or so mostly African Americans gathered that conditions in the North were only marginally better than in the South and that expectations for racial equality were rising to such a degree that the North was about to explode as well. When Kennedy asked the others if what Smith said was also their experience, every black person at the meeting, including Horne, said Smith was telling the unvarnished truth. The stormy meeting at first angered Kennedy but eventually opened his eyes to the scope of the issue and caused him to reexamine his assumptions about the depth of America's racial divide.[30]

In the aftermath of that meeting, Horne was raging with a desire to demonstrate her solidarity with the cause of freedom. At the Jackson concert, her first public involvement in the civil rights struggle, she spoke briefly about her southern upbringing—"I'm no carpetbagger," she emphasized—then told the audience why she had risked coming south. "I am an American," she said, "and the battle that is being fought here in Jackson, as elsewhere in the South, is our nation's primary crisis. . . . The courage and grim determination of the Negro people in these cities of the South have challenged the moral integrity of the entire nation." Horne applauded the NAACP for its legacy and paid a special tribute to Walter White—the previous executive secretary with whom she had once worked in the 1940s—for helping to eliminate lynching. Then she said, "I am not only honored but proud to be here tonight under the auspices of the NAACP to do what I can as a performer and a citizen for the cause of justice. . . . Let us here tonight pledge ourselves to continue this struggle until the finish." She followed this ringing declaration by singing some freedom songs and inspirational ballads, including "This Little Light of Mine," "I've Got a Home in That Rock," and "I'm Beginning to See the Light."[31]

Comedian Dick Gregory, who was next on the program, helped ease the crowd's fears of attending such a gathering by telling jokes. He even picked up on Evers's announcement about the policeman in the audience. "I know you policemen are down there at the press tables taking notes and pretending to be reporters," he taunted, to Jim Black's consternation. "Well, write this! Go downtown and tell your white daddy to get the barbed wire ready, 'cause we're coming tomorrow!"[32]

The crowd was in an upbeat mood when Gregory left the stage and Evers got up to send them off. "Freedom has never been free," Evers reminded them. "I love my children and I love my wife with all my heart, and I would die, die gladly, if that would make a better life for them."[33]

In the audience, Myrlie Evers couldn't believe what she heard coming from her husband's mouth. Sit-in participants Lois Chaffee and Memphis Norman were also there, and Chaffee later vividly recalled his speech: "It seems to me he had so much conviction, exhorting people to keep going forward, despite the fact that there were others within the NAACP trying to keep things under control." Ed King assessed the event even more harshly: "Lena Horne came down, like Gregory, prepared to go to prison. And they [the NAACP] turn it into a fund-raising event, with public relations. 'Look how powerful we are!' While we're getting weaker and weaker."[34]

Saturday, June 8, was a big day for Memphis Norman because Dr. Beittel and Ed King had asked him to accompany them to New York City to speak at the Broadway Congregational Church the next day. Excited by the prospect of addressing a large northern crowd, Norman was doubly nervous because he had never been in an airplane before. His case of nerves heightened considerably, although pleasantly so, when he was seated next to Lena Horne, who was returning to New York after the prior evening's concert.[35]

In Jackson, however, Saturday brought absolutely no activity in the way of protests, and it seemed to Salter that the remnants of the grassroots movement were slowly fizzling out. He described another "acrimonious" strategy session that afternoon. Thelton Henderson, the black Justice Department attorney in Jackson at the time, relayed in a memo to his supervisor that both Dave Dennis and Jerome Smith—on loan from New Orleans CORE—left "very disgusted and bitter."[36]

It was almost like rubbing salt in the wound when an angry Dick Gregory also left Jackson, saying heatedly, "The NAACP decided to go into the courts—and I'm no attorney. I came down here to be with that little man in the street, and I was willing to go to jail for ten years, if necessary, to set this problem straight." Henderson confirmed Gregory's falling-out with the NAACP national office in another memorandum to his superiors at the Justice Department—John Doar and Burke Marshall—saying that Gregory told him "it would be a long time before anyone tricks him into coming to town again." In his memoir, Gregory reported feeling that something bad was going to happen in Jackson. He also noted that Medgar Evers cried as they said good-bye.[37]

Evers had good reason to cry. Not only were things falling apart in the freedom struggle, but death threats against him were increasing in number and viciousness. He had heard from a reliable source about a Klan plot to kill him. He kept this information from Myrlie and the children but shared it with his physician and other local confidantes. In fact, Evers had been harassed that very morning as he got out of the car he was driving. Dave Dennis later told with gallows humor how he and Evers had traded cars the day before because Dennis had to make the twenty-mile trip north to Canton to assess George Raymond's project, and he didn't want to drive his car out of fear it would be recognized. The story shows how much stress the two men were under that they agreed it was a good plan for Dennis to swap cars with the most recognized civil rights activist in Mississippi in hopes that he wouldn't be noticed. As it happened, Dennis was stopped by a gang of whites while on his way back from Canton and was forced from his car. Fortunately, some trucks full of farm workers barreling down the same road interrupted the group before the situation turned violent. Evers didn't fare much better. When he had parked Dennis's car across from the NAACP office and started to cross the street, a car driven by whites tried to run him down. As he hurried out of the way, a group of whites watching the scene laughed at him. "This is what you must face to get free in Mississippi," Evers said to a reporter who witnessed the incident. When they compared notes that evening, Dennis joked to Evers, "Somebody could get killed driving your car!"[38]

In her first memoir of the period, Myrlie Evers described the painful conversation she had with her husband late that night. Medgar had always wanted four children, but when she brought up the subject that night, he hesitated. "Myrlie, this seems such a hopeless situation," he said. "Even though we're making strides, it's going to take a long, long time. I guess I really don't want to be responsible for bringing another child into this world."[39]

ON SUNDAY, JUNE 9, EVERS AND SALTER AGAIN DEFIED THE INJUNCTION AND drove an integrated group of students to downtown churches to stage what would become known as "kneel-ins" or "church visits." Five churches were targeted: one Catholic, two Methodist, and two Baptist. Evers drove a group to the First Baptist Church located directly between the old and new state capitol buildings. First Baptist represented the real power structure of Jackson—indeed of all Mississippi; Governor Barnett himself, for instance, worshiped and taught Sunday school there, and prominent legislators and businesspeople were members. Evers timed it so that the demonstrators would emerge from his car when Barnett exited his. There was no confrontation with the governor, but church ushers barred the visitors from entering, and the group left peacefully. Evers later commented, "It was good to see them walking up those steps to the church door, even if they didn't get in."[40]

In the end, only St. Peter's Catholic Church, whose services had years before been opened up to all worshipers, allowed five students through its doors. And only one of the other churches' clerics had public pangs of conscience over the incident. Following the service, Yale Divinity School graduate Reverend W. B. Selah, long-time pastor of Galloway Memorial United Methodist Church (Mayor Thompson's place of worship) offered a statement. "I understand the ushers turned several Negroes away," he said. "I didn't invite the Negroes to come, [but] I cannot judge the motives of people who come to worship in this church. Only God can.... I love all of you, but I know in good conscience there can be no color bar in a Christian church. So I will ask the bishop for another appointment." Dr. Selah's younger associate, Reverend Jerry Furr, also resigned.[41]

In New York that Sunday, Memphis Norman's speech at Broadway Congregational went well. He described his treatment at the Woolworth's sit-in and talked generally about the need for civil rights enforcement in Mississippi. His speech was filmed and broadcast over New York TV stations. In media coverage closer to home, the Jackson Sunday newspapers announced that the NAACP court strategy had stalled. On Saturday, federal judge Harold Cox had delayed until Monday a decision on the NAACP motion to overturn the city's injunction against further demonstrations.[42]

Meanwhile, at NAACP headquarters in Jackson, heated discussions continued about the future focus of the Jackson Movement. The New York contingent attempted to push the discussion in the direction of voter registration, with a continued emphasis on the Capitol Street boycott but with no direct action component. Salter and an ever-decreasing number of students—many had given up on the NAACP and gone to work for CORE and SNCC in other parts of the state—continued to demand demonstrations. Pearlena Lewis felt that Salter and the direct-action advocates were out of line, suggesting that voter registration had always been one aspect of the NAACP's and Medgar Evers's long-term strategy. Doris Allison agreed. "Get the ballot," she remembered him saying. "The ballot is our battle cry." Lewis in particular was becoming increasingly annoyed by Salter's militancy and shrill rhetoric. She tended to side with the more moderate elements and believed Evers did as well. "Sometimes John wanted to do it one way and Medgar thought it should be done a different way," she would later recount. Her sentiments about Salter, however, were not characteristic of the younger crowd not privy to the strategy committee discussions. Lewis's own brother Alphonzo, for example, cited Salter's presence as "very motivational."[43]

Both Salter and King describe Evers as increasingly distant at this point. Ludden, too, picked up on Evers's mood: "Worried about the stalemate in the movement, Medgar looked tired. . . . He was so frustrated." Caught in the middle, Evers rarely spoke up at the strategy sessions. Salter's frustration was leading him to consider calling Dr. Martin Luther King himself to see if he would be willing to come in, if only in an advisory capacity, to offset the conservatives who had taken over the strategy committee.[44]

Then, on Monday, June 10, a blow to the movement's legal strategy was dealt when the Mississippi Supreme Court refused to act on a motion to dissolve the injunction, delay its effective date, or hasten a court hearing about its legitimacy. NAACP attorneys, including Derek Bell, determined to take the case before the U.S. Supreme Court before it recessed for the summer.[45]

To add insult to injury, that same day, Clarence Mitchell sent a letter to Gloster Current advising him that the Jackson Movement's boycott was having limited impact. According to the Federal Reserve's "Monthly Department Store Sales" report, Jackson store sales for the months of March and April were up compared with prior year's sales, as compared to Birmingham's sales, which were down for the same period. Though these numbers do not reflect the results of the ramped-up boycott in May, the news could not have been welcomed by any of the Jackson Movement activists.[46]

At the strategy session that afternoon, Salter announced that he was going to call Dr. King and invite him in. "The lines drew tight and sharp," he later wrote. The national staff and most of the ministers took a dim view of Salter's plan, while those in favor of further direct action supported it. Discussion continued for hours and went nowhere; it seemed there was no way the two factions could find common ground. Salter reported that Evers continued to remain silent throughout, though FBI records show that Evers was himself in regular contact with Dr. King.[47]

NEARLY EVERYONE CLAIMED TO HAVE HAD A CONVERSATION WITH MEDGAR Evers on the last full day of his life, Tuesday, June 11. Myrlie and the children saw him whole for the last time that morning, just before he left for work. He spoke of how tired he was. Myrlie described how he had been up late the prior two nights just lying in bed staring at the ceiling, wondering what might happen, where the attack might come from. After getting into the car that morning, Evers uncharacteristically got out and went back into the house to say good-bye one more time to his family.[48]

Apparently, from home he drove straight to Doris Allison's house to pick her up and take her downtown. There was a court hearing that morning about the NAACP's counterinjunction against the city, and both of them needed to be there. Allison said they spoke of many things. Evers told her he'd be "kind of glad when things subside. I'm going to get some rest." "I think we all could sleep about a month before we ever started to get up," she replied. Then he told her something that surprised her. "I might be looking for a new job," Evers said. It's not clear if Evers had talked to Dr. King about becoming part of his staff, or if, as Ed King has suggested, the NAACP was on the verge of letting him go because of his ambivalence over the direct action issue. In her memoir, Myrlie Evers indicated that her husband had been considering taking an NAACP job in Los Angeles—far from Mississippi's race wars. Allison didn't have a chance to ask what Evers meant by his comment, for he suddenly realized he had left some papers at the Lynch Street office and had to turn back to get them. When they arrived there, he asked someone else to drive Allison to the courthouse so she wouldn't be late.[49]

Evers arrived at the courthouse just after the hearing had concluded. It was "just a lot of harassment," Allison said; the judge had postponed the hearing for another date. But as Evers and Allison were walking through the corridors, a swarm of sympathetic blacks crowded around them. "Mother," they called to Allison, "where's the meeting tonight?" And again, "Mother, we got a mass meeting?" Evers asked her what they were saying. She explained that they were wondering when the next meeting would be. "We don't have a church," Evers answered. Just then, Allison heard a deep, bass voice call out, "What's wrong with my church?" A young, new, black minister whom neither of them knew offered his church, New Jerusalem Baptist, for a meeting that night. Allison had grown up near the church and knew exactly where it was, so once Evers approved the idea, she headed home to get on the phone and spread the word about the newly scheduled meeting.[50]

Other legal business was supposed to have taken place that Tuesday, as Judge Cox was scheduled to rule on the NAACP's suit to dissolve the Chancery

Court's injunction. Nevertheless, Cox decided to leave town that day for his vacation, commenting only that he would make a decision "at the proper time."[51]

Back at the NAACP's Lynch Street offices, Salter continued his attempt to convince the NAACP national staff that demonstrations were still necessary. Finally, he was allowed to take a group of six young people to march up and down Capitol Street. Their only signs would be NAACP T-shirts with the logo on the front and the phrase "Jim Crow Must Go" on the back. This time, they would not carry flags, and they would walk far apart from each other so they could not be accused of parading. Alphonzo Lewis, who was one of the six, recalled that the marchers separated into two groups of three and walked up opposite sides of the street, their pace slow and meandering so that people could read their shirts as the youths pretended to window-shop.[52]

As with the earlier Capitol Street demonstrations, crowds began to gather as soon as they saw the black youths walking up and down the sidewalks. Stores emptied, and everyone wondered what the police would do. For the first time since the Woolworth's sit-in two weeks previously, though, they did nothing. Lewis could hear policemen exchanging messages on their walkie-talkies. "What are they doing?" asked one. "They're only walking!" said another. "They couldn't come up with a reason to arrest us," said Lewis, so the six ended their demonstration and headed triumphantly to Steven's Kitchen in the black shopping district, where they were treated to a victory meal.[53]

After Salter had dropped off the six young demonstrators, he and Tougaloo student Steve Rutledge drove around, trying to lose two detectives who were trailing them. Frustrated, Salter pulled over as he had during a similar occasion the week before, got out of his car, and walked back to confront his pursuers. As Salter approached this time, however, the driver of the police car quietly unlatched the car door and forcefully swung it open. The heavy door nearly knocked Salter off his feet, and the other detective swiftly emerged from the car with his revolver drawn. Thinking quickly, Salter asked for their names and police rank. They cursed him vehemently, but provided the information. Salter got back into his car and later reported the assault to a locally based advisor to the U.S. Commission on Civil Rights.[54]

After driving Rutledge back to Tougaloo, Salter returned to Lynch Street and came upon Medgar Evers standing alone in the Masonic Temple. "He was just standing there—tired, dejected," Salter recalled. Salter recounted for Evers his run-in with the law a few minutes earlier, and Evers told Salter about nearly being run over a few days before. Salter did not point out to Evers that his premonition before the sit-in that the national office would sell them out had come true. "He knew," Salter said. "The pressures were intense. I sensed we were past that point." They just stood there, two weary freedom fighters, making small talk about their families, neither one willing to admit defeat.[55]

After Salter headed back to Tougaloo, Evers called home for the third time that day. Myrlie teased him about not having enough to do. She begged off attending the mass meeting that night, but offered to fix him a nice dinner when he came home. Then someone came into the office.

"I've got to go, honey," Medgar said. "See you tonight. I love you."

"All right," Myrlie answered. "Take care."[56]

Later in the day, Evers told a friend what he couldn't tell his wife. "I got a telephone call," he told the Reverend D. L. Tucker of Greenwood, "and the man at the other end tapped a gun against the phone and said it was the gun that was going to kill me."[57]

THAT EVENING, AT 7:00 P.M. JACKSON TIME, PRESIDENT KENNEDY MADE A speech on national television about the civil rights crisis facing America. Earlier that day, Alabama Governor George Wallace, who previously had threatened a Ross Barnett–like stand at the University of Alabama to bar two black students from registering, had instead stood aside and let the students and federal marshals pass. The president had decided to express his gratitude that responsible heads had prevailed this time, but he wanted to do more. Events in Birmingham, Jackson, and other places around the country had convinced him that he needed to appeal to the conscience of Americans over the single most divisive issue of his presidency. Although it was a quickly cobbled-together speech, it turned out to be his best statement on civil rights and one that the New York Times later suggested "matched his magnificent Inaugural Address in idealism and fervor."[58]

President Kennedy began his speech with a summation of the day's events in Alabama, but he then broadened the context: "This nation was founded by men of many nations and backgrounds. It was founded on the principle that all men are created equal, and that the rights of every man are diminished when the rights of one man are threatened."[59]

The president pointed out that there is no discrimination when Americans are asked to defend their country abroad. In these situations, "we do not ask for whites only." By comparison, he stated, "It ought to be possible for American consumers of any color to receive equal service in places of public accommodation such as hotels and restaurants and theaters and retail stores without being forced to resort to demonstrations in the street." "In short," he said, "every American ought to have the right to be treated as he would wish to be treated, as one would wish his children to be treated."

Kennedy was appealing to the hearts of white citizens. He pointed out that black Americans had limited chances in life compared with their white counterparts. He emphasized that this was not just a regional problem, but that inequities existed all over the country. "The fires of frustration and discord are burning in every city, North and South," the president continued. "Where legal remedies are not at hand, redress is sought in the streets and in demonstrations, parades and protests, which create tension and threaten violence—and threaten lives." He called for congressional action to address the legal aspects of discrimination but also acknowledged that laws were not enough: "Legislation . . . cannot solve this problem alone. It must be solved in the homes of every American in every community across the country."

In concluding, the president unexpectedly praised those who had been struggling on freedom's front lines:

> I want to pay tribute to those citizens, North and South, who've been working in their communities to make life better for all. They are acting not out of a sense of legal duty, but out of a sense of human decency. Like our soldiers and sailors in all parts of the world, they are meeting freedom's challenge on the firing line and I salute them for their honor—their courage.

Jackson Movement leaders might have been heartened by Kennedy's speech, but none of them heard it because they were getting ready for the mass meeting that night.

NEW JERUSALEM BAPTIST CHURCH, LOCATED ON WHITFIELD STREET IN A black section of town not a mile north of Capitol Street, is a small community church sandwiched between single-story frame houses just blocks from Millsaps College. The church is so small that only about 150 people can be seated comfortably inside.

Everyone would later have their own version of what happened at the mass meeting at New Jerusalem that night. Some, like John Salter and Ed King, said it was a poorly attended affair. "Only thirty-five to fifty people—that would be max," Salter said. Their assessment is corroborated by some others attending, like Detective Jim Black and Dub Shoemaker, the only Jackson reporter still covering the movement. "It was a lackluster, nothing-came-of-it night," Shoemaker recalled. Black agreed: "That little bitty church . . . it wasn't half full." However, Doris Allison and Alphonzo Lewis remembered it quite differently. "I remember a large crowd," said Lewis. He recalled not having any place to sit until Evers called him and the other demonstrators up to show off their T-shirts from the demonstration earlier in the day. Lewis also remembered Evers's elation that no one had been arrested: "I remember him saying [this was] the first successful picket without arrest."[60]

Allison arrived late and had to wait outside because, as she remembered it, an overflow crowd had filtered out onto the front steps. Since she couldn't get into the church, she walked back across Whitfield Street to lean on her car and smoke a cigarette. Just after she lit up, a white car with a long antenna drove slowly by. She had to press up close to her car and bend backwards over the hood to avoid being run over. She could not get a good look at the driver's face—in fact, could only see him in silhouette—because the sun was setting behind him as he drove toward her. But she was later certain, after hearing a description of Byron De La Beckwith's vehicle, that it was he who drove by, once again tracking his target.[61]

The primary focus of the meeting was voter registration and the day's successful picket of the downtown stores. After spotlighting the six young picketers, Evers attempted to sell some NAACP T-shirts to other brave souls in the crowd to wear around town. There weren't many takers.

Detective Jim Black says that Evers wasn't his usual buoyant self that night; Ed King described him as "extremely depressed and thinking things had failed"; and Salter just remembered that he seemed "very tired." King described a private conversation he had with Evers at the back of the church in a little room off the portico. "He was basically telling me that SNCC and CORE and SCLC were right and the national NAACP was not," King said. "He had finally made up his mind that this side of the movement that had so inspired him—this really was what was needed. He was leaning toward the people."[62]

Pearlena Lewis, who was also at New Jerusalem that night, believed that Evers was tired but not deflated. "I don't think he felt that we were not making progress," she reminisced. "I think he was trying to see the direction we all were going." Although Lillian Louie didn't remember being at the meeting, both Alphonzo and Pearlena Lewis remember that Evers drove both Pearlena and Lillian to Louie's apartment afterward; Pearlena had decided to stay over since Evers had asked them to be at the office early the next day. (Louie, in fact, had a little get-together that night at her place that was attended by several of the movement regulars, including Willie Ludden, who was staying in a rooming house just a few doors down the street.) Evers also offered Alphonzo Lewis a ride, but the young man decided to wait on the steps for his father to return from driving others home. Lewis said he didn't see any police around that night, perhaps not so unusual since the movement was slowing down. Still, Evers had been followed for the past week and had called the FBI that afternoon to complain about the constant harassment. In retrospect, it does seem a bit strange that no one other than Black was keeping tabs on him that evening.[63]

Evers had spoken briefly with Allison at the meeting, also asking her to get to the office early the next day, as well. They said their good-byes, and then Allison and her husband, Ben, drove some students back to Campbell College before heading home.

King and Salter left the church together and both sensed danger so they drove their separate cars "almost bumper to bumper," back to the perceived safety of Tougaloo. After being so careful in their driving arrangements, the two then sat carelessly on King's porch talking over whether to invite Martin Luther King into the Jackson fray. When King finally realized the danger they might be in, he suggested they go inside where they talked a bit more before Salter decided to make the short trek across the dirt road to his house. Ed and his wife, Jeannette, urged him to stay the night rather than spend it alone. Salter resisted the temptation to give in to fear, but he did take precautions when he got home. He thinks it was a little after midnight when he put the shotgun Evers had loaned him down by his bed and fell into a restless sleep.[64]

After dropping off Pearlena Lewis and Lillian Louie, Evers made the rounds to other homes where some of the NAACP's national office staff were being lodged. He then stopped at an attorney's office on North Farish Street and finally headed home.[65]

Myrlie Evers had pulled the television into her bedroom toward the back of the house that night so that she and the children could watch the president's speech and then she could rest while the kids watched TV and waited for their father to come home.

About fifteen minutes after midnight, Myrlie was dozing on the bed and the kids were arguing over what TV show to watch when they heard Medgar's car drive up. Then they heard the blast of a gun. Their reaction was immediate. The kids hit the ground as their father had taught them, while Myrlie jumped off the bed and ran to the front door.

She turned on the outside light—she and Medgar had agreed it should be left off in case a sniper tried to ambush him—and then gasped in horror. There on the concrete driveway lay her husband, crawling slowly toward her, blood spurting from his chest and back. A pile of the NAACP T-shirts he had been selling were on the ground where he had been shot, just next to the car.

Myrlie screamed wildly, and the children came running. "Daddy, get up! Daddy, please get up!" they cried over and over.[66]

Next door, Houston Wells had heard the shot and Myrlie's scream. He scrambled out of bed, checked on his daughter, grabbed his gun, and sneaked out his front door into the bushes. He fired a shot into the air in hopes of scaring away the gunman and then shouted for help. His wife called the police. Other neighbors came running.[67]

Evers had made it about forty feet from where he had been shot, as far as the concrete steps leading into the house. The neighbors quickly realized that calling an ambulance would be futile; Evers needed immediate help if he was to survive. They rushed into young Reena's bedroom and grabbed her mattress, got it under her father, loaded him into Houston Wells's station wagon, and headed to University Hospital. Myrlie wanted to jump in the back with her husband but was held back by the growing crowd.

Medgar Evers died about forty minutes later. His physician, Dr. Britton, was on site but was unable to attend to Evers because he was not authorized to practice in a white hospital. He made it clear to the white doctors exactly who it was that they were treating, however, and he later told Myrlie that the doctors had done everything they could.[68]

James Wells questions Dr. Britton's assessment, however, arguing, based on what his brother told him, that the doctors really weren't that interested in reviving a dying black man until Dr. Britton made them aware of his prominence. But James Wells didn't arrive at the hospital until after Evers was already dead. He had gotten a call from his sister-in-law, Houston's wife, just minutes after Evers had been shot. Wells jumped into his truck, where he kept a loaded shotgun behind the seat, and drove quickly to the scene, making the sharp turn onto Guynes Street at the end of the block near the Everses' home. As he passed the vacant lot adjacent to the Everses' driveway, Wells ran over some aluminum cans that he believed were placed there by the assassin to alert him of any movement toward his hiding place. When Wells heard the noise from the cans, he stopped his truck, got out, and shot a few rounds toward the vacant lot just in case the gunman was still within range. Then he drove the few yards to the Evers home. He never got to say good-bye to his friend since he arrived after the fallen leader had been taken away.[69]

Pearlena Lewis and Willie Ludden heard about the murder when Johnnie Frazier, the NAACP's state youth advisor, knocked on Lillian Louie's door just after 2:00 a.m. Tom Beard said that someone from the FBI woke him up and told him the news. John Salter was awakened by George Owens, Tougaloo's business manager. Salter stirred King, then they both went over to Dr. Beittel's house to tell him.[70]

Annie Moody was spending the night with Dave and Mattie Dennis, but their stories differ about how and when they heard the news. Moody said they were all watching TV when a news bulletin announced just after 12:30 a.m. that Evers had been shot. "It was unbelievable," she later wrote. "Just an hour or so earlier we had all been with him." Then another announcement came on that he was dead. "It still didn't seem real," she said. Dave Dennis remembered already being in bed at the time, however, and that someone phoned to tell him about the shooting. When he was told that Evers was dead, "I was paralyzed. I just didn't move," Dennis said.[71]

Doris Allison had just fallen asleep when Ben picked up the ringing phone, heard the news, then handed it to her. "What is it, Ben?" she asked. He couldn't speak. "It was like a bolt from hell," she later said of the news. Doris and Ben jumped out of bed and rushed to the Evers home to express their sympathy to Myrlie and to see if there was anything they could do. Allison ran up the driveway and almost stepped into a pool of Medgar's blood. When she saw Myrlie, "we just fell into each other's arms." They had both lost the love of their lives.[72]

Allison also recalled seeing the bullet that felled her mentor and friend. It was sitting next to a watermelon on the avocado-colored kitchen counter. After ripping through its intended target, the bullet had traveled through the side window, pierced a four-inch wall dividing the dining room from the kitchen, ricocheted off the refrigerator, and shattered the coffee pot before landing on the counter. It was fortunate that Myrlie and the children had been in the back bedroom and out of the line of fire.[73]

Detective Jim Black was on duty that night. Dub Shoemaker had driven him home after the mass meeting since they lived near each other on the west side of town; then Black got ready to go to work at midnight. It was a fluke that he didn't get assigned to investigate the case. There were two teams of detectives working the midnight to 8 a.m. shift, but Black and his partner were immediately put on another case when they arrived at work that night and so were not available when the call about Evers came in. Black was stunned by the news. "It was devastating," he later said. "I wanted to cry."[74]

Another police detective advised the local FBI agents in Jackson at 1:30 a.m. of the shooting. Fifteen minutes later he called back to report that Evers was dead.[75]

Bob Bullock, the TV cameraman who had been knocked down at the Woolworth's sit-in, learned of the assassination in perhaps the most dramatic of ways. He had just finished covering a statewide youth function at Belhaven College, not far from University Hospital, and was grabbing a late dinner at an all-night diner nearby. A pair of policemen spotted him there and asked him to come with them. They wouldn't explain why until they had arrived at the hospital, and even then they only said that someone had been killed. It wasn't until Bullock found himself the only outsider in a roomful of doctors and nurses that he realized he was viewing the body of Medgar Evers. The coroner was explaining that the bullet had traveled through the civil rights leader's back, passed near his spine, and then tore a huge hole in his chest as it exited. Stunned, Bullock signed the coroner's report and left. The police made clear to him that, with such a high profile killing, they wanted someone beyond the hospital staff to witness the coroner's proceedings. They asked Bullock not to talk about what he had seen until they had finished their investigation.[76]

Roy Wilkins, in New York, heard of the assassination when his wife took the call from an NAACP staff attorney in the middle of the night. She relayed the news of Evers's murder to her husband. "Oh my God," he thought. "Don't let it be true." Then he began to cry—something he hadn't done since the death of his brother twenty-two years earlier. Later that day, Wilkins telegramed Attorney General Robert Kennedy requesting federal protection for all NAACP officials working in Jackson because "police have demonstrated that such persons may be murdered with impunity."[77]

Lena Horne, who was also in New York, had gone to bed early that night because she was scheduled to appear on the *Today* show the next morning and wanted to get a good night's sleep. She was having her second cup of coffee at the NBC studio, preparing for the live interview, when the floor manager told her the news. "I was so shocked and incoherent that I did not think I could go on the show," she later wrote. After composing herself, she appeared along with Roy Wilkins, talking about what they had witnessed firsthand in Jackson during the previous two weeks.[78]

D. C. Sullivan's reaction may have typified that of a certain segment of white Jackson. "It didn't bother me," he said, describing his feelings when he heard of the murder the next morning. "It didn't bother me at all. To me he was just another black. To me he was just a troublemaker."[79]

Back home in northern Virginia, Joan Trumpauer heard of the killing that morning on the news. She remembered feeling sick about it, then the thought flashed in her mind: "It could have been any of us." Lois Chaffee couldn't remember how she heard the news, although she thought it wasn't until late morning when someone at Tougaloo told her. She said that she and the other young people didn't realized the extreme danger they were in—or the danger that leaders like Evers were in—as a result of their stepped-up demands for change. "He was a man who very knowingly and consciously made a commitment and understood that he could die," she tearfully recounted years later. "I don't think we respected that sufficiently at the time."[80]

DORIS ALLISON—THIS TIME ACCOMPANIED BY LILLIAN LOUIE—RETURNED TO the Evers home after daylight dawned. There the women hesitated on the driveway a moment and then, in silence, reverentially bent to pick up the stray pieces of their slain leader's flesh that had been scattered by the high-powered bullet's exit from his body.[81]

As the news of Medgar's death sank in, the effects spread. In fact, the Evers assassination resurrected the Jackson Movement for a time. John Salter knew that he had to just pick up and keep going. "We were fighting a war," he recollected. "Nothing surprised me." Pearlena Lewis remembered feeling like a member of her own family had been killed. "It hurt so deep," she said, "but it just made me more determined."[82]

Doris Allison made the point that "when Medgar fell, his blood loosened up every hinge on every church door in Jackson." Until then, only a handful of ministers had been willing to hold movement meetings in their churches, and up to that point only two ministers had been arrested. That morning, when Ed King met with the black ministers to discuss their next move, he found that even some who had been reluctant to host mass meetings felt a new compulsion to demonstrate against the violence. Many, however, were still cautious and wondered whether a demonstration was a fitting tribute to the slain leader. About 11:30 a.m., one contingent decided to move from discussion to action, and thirteen of the ministers marched out the front doors of the Pearl Street AME Church toward the downtown area. They were arrested after being warned repeatedly by Deputy Chief Ray not to continue.[83]

Statements of sympathy and shock were coming into the NAACP offices from across the nation. Willie Ludden remembered taking calls from all over the world and also reported that many local whites dropped by the NAACP offices to express their sympathy—a fact that stunned him. "I hated how it had taken this disaster to bring people together, but they came," he reported. President Kennedy issued a statement saying that he was "appalled by the barbarity of this act." Martin Luther King described the murder as "an inexpressible tragedy and an unspeakable outrage" and hailed Evers as "one of those pure patriots whose paramount desire was to be an American and to live as an American." At a press conference at the NAACP headquarters in New York, Roy Wilkins condemned Mississippi as "the most savage of any state in the Union" and said that Medgar Evers was neither "abrasive nor provocative" but that he stood up for what he regarded as right. Wilkins also called for federal protection for the fifty or so Mississippi defendants in NAACP desegregation lawsuits.[84]

It is unfortunate that, behind the scenes, the Wilkins and King rivalry was heightening just when their organizations should have been coming together over this tragedy. At the one-year anniversary celebration of the establishment of his Gandhi Society for Human Rights that day, King—apparently at the suggestion of some representatives of the Jackson Movement—announced a Medgar Evers Memorial Fund to help raise bail money for those arrested while fighting against segregation. Wilkins was infuriated by what he saw as an attempt to steal the NAACP's hero and appropriate his sacrifice—and the funds that would surely flow from it—for the broader goals of nonviolent change. When Wilkins voiced his objections, King suggested that the two organizations sponsor a day of mourning for Evers. Wilkins told King to mind his own business.[85]

Prominent white southerners were somewhat less forthcoming in their condemnation of the murder. Governor Ross Barnett qualified his characterization of the murder: "Apparently it was a dastardly act." Even more striking were statements released by Mississippi's U.S. congressional delegation blaming the demonstrators for the violence. "This is the usual result of mass demonstrations of the kind in Jackson," said Representative John Bell Williams, who would later become governor. "The professional agitators of the NAACP, CORE and the SCLC must share some of the guilt," he proclaimed. Representatives Arthur Winstead and William Colmer, whose districts included parts of Jackson, made similar statements. Mayor Thompson's public statement was a bit more even-handed. Although Thompson—feeling confident that the Jackson crisis had subsided—was spending the weekend at his vacation home in

Destin, Florida, he returned immediately on hearing of the killing. When he arrived at the airport, he spoke to the press and called the murder a "cowardly act." He also urged all citizens to preserve the peace.[86]

Amid all the public hand-wringing, Salter knew some additional action was needed to give the community an opportunity to express their outrage and grief in a nonviolent way. He didn't ask the strategy committee for permission this time. Based on the ministers' march, Salter, Dave Dennis, Ed King, and Willie Ludden organized a group of about two hundred students who were willing to get arrested and stay in jail to protest the murder. Just before the students left the Masonic Temple at 4:00 p.m., "Ed King prayed a prayer for Mississippi," Salter later recounted, "a prayer that the death of Medgar Evers would never be in vain."[87]

The marchers headed onto Lynch Street, moving slowly toward the downtown area. The police, waiting only two blocks away with paddy wagons and garbage trucks, arrested 160 of the marchers and took them to the fairgrounds, which had been vacant during the few days that the demonstrations had subsided. Although news reports indicate that the arrests took place "without violence or friction," Salter said the march was "cruelly repressed," and King pointed out that, once the marchers were arrested, police began rounding up spectators as well. "The police started marching in squadron, hut, two, three, four," King said. "[They were] clearing out Lynch Street, aiming some rifles at us." An FBI report on the march states that more than fifty Jackson police were on the scene, along with twenty Mississippi highway safety patrolmen, "each carrying a shotgun. . . . The highway patrolmen spread out in a riot control formation" and moved the spectators off the streets. The report further states, however, that "no incidents of violence in any form were observed."[88]

King and Salter quietly slipped off the church porch where they were standing and quickly made their way back to the NAACP offices to plan for another march that evening. They were told, however, that any further marches were under wraps for the rest of the day. The thirteen ministers arrested earlier in the day had been released on their own recognizance "so they could work to promote harmony," an FBI report states. This meant that the ministers would try to prevent further demonstration for the time being. One of those ministers told an FBI agent, "We cannot afford another march at this time," suggesting that, with tensions now at fever pitch, the danger to the activist community was too great.[89]

ANY ADDITIONAL TALK OF DIRECT ACTION WAS HALTED WHEN IT WAS LEARNED that Myrlie Evers had decided to speak to that evening's mass meeting at Reverend Haughton's Pearl Street AME Church. Before she arrived, a despondent Dave Dennis addressed the crowd of seven hundred, saying ruefully, "We pulled that trigger, too. We let him stand alone. We said we were behind him, but we were too far behind him." One of the recently released ministers urged those in attendance to keep their protests of the shooting nonviolent. Reverend Haughton called for a thirty-day mourning period, suggested that everyone wear a black armband, and pushed for enforcement of the boycott. There were no calls for mass marches.[90]

Myrlie Evers slipped in after the meeting had started and the crowd quieted as she stepped into the pulpit. "I come to you tonight with a broken heart," she began.

> I came because it is my duty. No one knows like I know how my husband gave his life for this cause. He lived with this 24 hours a day. It was his wish that this movement would be one of the most successful that this nation has ever known.
>
> Sunday . . . he talked of death. He said he was ready to go. He said if he had to go, he'd rather go this way than to sleep away. He dedicated his entire adult life to this cause.
>
> He said he was fighting not only for his family, not only for the Negroes of Jackson, not only for those in Mississippi and in the United States, and not only for the colored people of the world, but for his white brethren as well. He felt it would help all.
>
> I am left without the comfort of a husband. I am left with three children to rear. But I am also left with a strong determination to take up where he left off. I have his strength.
>
> I hope by his death that all of you here—and those that are not here—will be able to draw some of his strength, some of his courage, and some of his determination to finish this fight. Nothing can bring Medgar back, but the cause can live on.
>
> My purpose here is to ask a favor of you. I do not want his death to be in vain. That would be as big a blow to me as his death itself. I ask you for united action in this effort in memory of my husband.[91]

A *Washington Post* reporter captured the mood of this solemn event. "There have been many Negro rallies and hundreds of speeches in the long civil rights effort," he wrote, "but seldom [have] the words stabbed the human emotions as they did here [tonight]."[92]

That evening, Salter recalled, even the visiting newsmen sang "We Shall Overcome."[93]

CHAPTER 9

"THE LORD'S SPONTANEOUS DEMONSTRATION"

ON THURSDAY, JUNE 13—THE DAY AFTER MEDGAR EVERS WAS ASSASSINATED—
the remaining Jackson activists got back to work in earnest. John Salter, Dave
Dennis, and Ed King ran a two-hour training session on nonviolence that
morning at the Pearl Street AME Church in anticipation of a march they were
planning for later in the day. Annie Moody and Dorie Ladner visited Jackson
State College to try to recruit more students for the march. No one at the college seemed interested, however, and the white-appointed black president tried
to chase them away until Ladner dropped to her knees in frustration while
pleading with him. Students looking on thought the president had knocked
her to the ground (a reaction apparently not out of character for him) and the
misperception convinced many to go with the two women. When they arrived
at the church shortly before the march was to begin, Moody was called up to
the pulpit to lead some freedom songs, and Ed King led the group in prayer.
Then, the doors opened, and the students filed out.[1]

The police were waiting for the marchers about a block down Pearl Street.
Salter, hoping to avoid the police, had directed the demonstrators to turn left
instead of right out of the church and then to cut through small residential
Rose Street toward the downtown area. But the police, led again by the ever-
present Deputy Chief Ray, moved immediately to cut off the march before it
reached a white neighborhood. After only a few blocks, the marchers were
stopped and led into the waiting garbage trucks and paddy wagons without
much difficulty on the part of the police.[2]

In fact, the real drama that day was not with the marchers, but with the
observers. Since the Evers killing, more and more black adults had become
open supporters of the movement, and onlookers at this event—mostly local
residents and the press corps—had followed the marchers down Rose Street.
At the point where the police halted the march, Salter estimated that about
three hundred were watching, many shouting, "Freedom! Freedom! We want
freedom!" as they milled around. After police had arrested most of the marchers—about eighty in all, including Annie Moody—Deputy Chief Ray instructed his men to clear the street, and the police began pushing the onlookers
onto the sidewalks. FBI agents and a Justice Department observer reported
that Ray used his bullhorn to announce that bystanders were to quiet down

or they would be arrested. Three times he repeated his demand for quiet as the crowd grew more boisterous, even making obscene remarks to the police. "If you don't cut out that noise, you will be arrested for disturbing the peace!" Ray shouted.[3]

By that time, Salter, King, Ladner, and Lois Chaffee were crowded onto the porch of a nearby house along with about forty others. Seventeen-year-old Tommy Miles, one of the young people on the porch, yelled out to Ray, "You can't keep me off this porch. My momma lives here!" Others in the crowd, who had quieted down a bit after Ray's demands, began again to loudly challenge the police. Ray shouted back, "You're disturbing the peace! You're under arrest!"[4]

With that, blue-helmeted policemen charged the porch, pushing people aside as they moved in on Miles, struck his head with a nightstick, locked him in a neck hold with a billy club, and dragged him away to a paddy wagon. Miles's sister Carolyn screamed, "They've got my brother!" When a policeman turned and began hitting her, her mother pulled her into the house. One report said the policeman also beat the mother. Many others on the porch rushed into the house to avoid arrest. Lois Chaffee recalled being pulled along, saying, "It was like the house sucked us in." Ed King said he was swept in as well and tried to see if he could help the mother and daughter. At that point, a policeman jumped in front of the doorway to stop the rest of the crowd from escaping through the house. Many ran the other way instead, jumping off the side of the porch and running down an alley.[5]

There are various accounts of what happened next. One FBI report says that Salter began to scuffle with the policeman blocking the door, forcing him off the porch and into the front yard. A news report states that when the officer tried to arrest Salter, the activist grabbed the policeman's nightstick and said he wasn't going anywhere. They then wrestled each other off the porch. Salter's own telling of the incident is that he was simply yelling freedom slogans with the rest of the crowd when the police charged the porch. He said that when the police saw him, they became hostile. "Here he is! Here he is!" one cried. "You're the one we want!" shouted another. With that, they pulled him off the porch and into the yard.[6]

What happened after that is indisputable. Film footage, though blurry, shows that some of the police went berserk. The discipline for which Ray and the others had prided themselves snapped in the extreme summer heat and extraordinary public tension. One policeman struck Salter on the crown of his head with his billy club. Newspaper accounts say that other police clubbed him on the arms and shoulders in an attempt to make him comply with the arresting officer.[7]

When Salter collapsed, blood oozing from his head, everyone was stunned into silence. Ed King emerged from the house and saw Salter lying there, a policeman astride him, billy club held high. As Salter came to in a pool of his own blood, he was pulled to his feet by policemen and led to a paddy wagon. The film shows blood dripping down the front of Salter's white shirt and the side of his face, his sunglasses hanging crookedly. He is unsteady on his feet at first; then a defiant look emerges as he is taken away. The *Chicago Daily News* reported that "a small pool of blood could be seen in the grass as officers picked him up and carried him away." When King went down into the yard, he was astonished by the amount of blood: "This was the yard of a poor black home. The kind where people sweep the yard. [It] was this hard baked dry dirt . . . as if it were concrete. . . . when I got down there it was muddy with blood."[8]

Lois Chaffee had returned to the porch and watched in horror as the police beat her fellow Tougaloo professor. She couldn't remember now what she did to attract their attention; perhaps it was simply that she was white. "I must have been totally hysterical," she said. "I had the impression that everybody was being beaten." The police pulled Chaffee off the porch and marched her to the same paddy wagon that Salter was in. Steve Rutledge, another white activist, was also arrested. As the police were getting ready to move on, Ed King called out, "You've beaten a woman in her own home! I know you're white and I know what you think of her, but won't you please call an ambulance for her?" "You call 'em yourself, motherfucker!" the officer yelled back. When another cop started after King, he ran off the porch to avoid arrest.[9]

The Justice Department's Thelton Henderson was present but didn't see the Salter beating. In support of his proposal to have the FBI investigate the beatings, however, Henderson told his superiors that reporters Karl Flemming of *Newsweek* and Claude Sitton of the *New York Times* stated that "these were some of the worst incidents they had seen" in all their years of covering civil rights protests. New Orleans *Times-Picayune* reporter Bill Minor, who was also on the scene, described the blow to Salter's head: "A cop hit him so hard, it sounded like Joe DiMaggio knocking a home run out of the ballpark." Minor also admitted to being so shaken by what he witnessed that, before returning to the press office to write his story, he stopped by St. Peter's Catholic Church downtown and sat there for an hour, considering all that had happened in Jackson during the past two days. "It just tore at my soul so much," he said. "That was the only thing I could think of to do."[10]

What the reporters didn't see were the horrific conditions to which Salter and the others were subjected once they arrived at the improvised jail at the fairgrounds. The trucks were parked, the heaters turned on, and the arrested left to bake in the blazing sun for what Annie Moody estimated was more than two hours. With Mississippi experiencing its worst heat wave since 1902, Jackson temperatures that day topped one hundred degrees.[11]

Alphonzo Lewis, who had been among the arrested marchers, witnessed Salter's beating and arrest and then saw him again at the fairgrounds. Lewis sat in a garbage truck for about an hour before being let out into the fairgrounds for his second stay. "It was like we had showered with our clothes on," he said. "You could just wring the water out." He was shocked to see Salter all bloodied and unsteady. "It was kind of a frightening thing," Lewis recounted, "to see a person like that . . . one of the ones instrumental in leading . . . and here he's been arrested and beaten. And knowing all the time, too, that Medgar Evers has already been killed. It was very hard not to allow hate to develop."[12]

Salter believed he was kept in the truck for only about half an hour but was close to passing out when the police let him out. His presence sparked an enthusiastic response from the young protesters in other trucks and paddy wagons. When they began chanting freedom slogans and waving at him, he waved and called back. The police quickly whisked him away to University Hospital, where Memphis Norman had been taken after his Woolworth's beating and where Medgar Evers had died less than forty-eight hours earlier. There, Salter's head wound required eight stitches, but he wouldn't allow the medical staff to give him anything for pain, wanting to show his police escort just how tough he really was. Afterward, Salter was taken to the Hinds County jail, where Steve Rutledge and Lois Chaffee were also being held. At one point, some police officers opened the door of Salter's cell and started to enter. Not knowing what to expect, Salter jumped up like a wildcat ready to strike. The police backed out. A few hours later, NAACP attorneys bailed Salter and the other white demonstrators out, but the black demonstrators, including Annie Moody and Alphonzo Lewis, were kept at the fairgrounds for another day.[13]

Just after the Rose Street incident, twelve black ministers and business leaders met with the mayor to complain about police brutality at the recent demonstration and to repeat the original eight demands of the Jackson Movement. Mayor Thompson discounted the charges against the police but said he'd look into the matter. As for the demands, he flatly stated that his position had not changed on any of them. The ministers responded angrily that police brutality might trigger black violence in response. "People are buying guns," Reverend Haughton told him. "They are mad. They want to shoot. We're trying to hold it down." Some of the ministers began to wonder aloud whether nonviolence was still a viable strategy given the brutality that had just occurred on Rose Street.[14]

Meanwhile, NAACP attorneys were trying to find a way to prevent the police from interfering with the peaceful protests. They pressed their counterinjunction against the city and its police force in the U.S. Court of Appeals in New Orleans, while requesting the U.S. Supreme Court to overturn the city's injunction against demonstrations. Disputes within the movement were also continuing. Although John Salter and Dave Dennis had planned another march for late that same afternoon, the NAACP's Gloster Current "temporarily suspended" any further marches and described Salter as "a special target" of the police. When Reverend Haughton emerged from the discussion with the mayor, he knew nothing of Current's move and denied that marches had been stopped. But without Salter present to push for another demonstration, nothing happened.[15]

Salter was released on bond later that afternoon and at the mass meeting that night, he made what he called "my most dramatic entrance ever." Still wearing the torn and bloodied shirt from his Rose Street confrontation and with a large bandage on his head, Salter walked through the doors of Blair Street AME Church to a thunderous roar and a standing ovation from the five hundred or so present. Savoring the moment, Salter took the opportunity to press for his activist agenda. "We must continue to intensify our mass marches until the evil system of racism falls," he shouted. "But we must do it nonviolently. That doesn't mean we must love the Jackson cops. I know how you feel about club-toting, gun-toting goons. I would sooner love a desert sidewinder rattlesnake! But we can't meet violence with violence."[16]

Salter then introduced activist attorney Bill Kunstler, who had flown in that afternoon after talking to Salter the night before about a possible SCLC takeover of the Jackson Movement. Kunstler told the audience who he was and whom he represented. "Dr. King wanted me to pass along the word that he is ready to do what he can to help the people of Jackson," he said. The audience responded enthusiastically, Salter claimed. But Kunstler experienced a different reaction: "As I spoke, I realized the will to resist had died with Medgar. In the audience there was fear, hatred, and bitterness—but no spirit to continue the fight." Salter and Ed King, however, were encouraged by Kuntsler's presence and by the possibility that Dr. King might soon join them.[17]

Also at the meeting, the ministers reported on their session with the mayor. Reverend R. L. T. Smith, Medgar Evers's early mentor, told the crowd, "All we got from the mayor was double-talk and smiles." The rest of the meeting involved the Evers funeral arrangements. The funeral would be held on Saturday, starting at 11:00 a.m. at the Masonic Temple, and the NAACP was trying to get the city to allow a two-mile march from the temple to Collins Funeral Home on North Farish Street. Salter and some of the youth council students asked people to spread the word that a demonstration would take place on Friday and probably after the funeral on Saturday as well.[18]

After that meeting, Salter finally decided to step out on a limb and call Dr. King himself. He and a relatively new, young black minister engineered the call to discuss the possibility of the SCLC leader coming in to lead the Jackson Movement. Dr. King was noncommittal on the phone but agreed to talk more when he arrived Saturday for the funeral. The conversation lifted Salter's spirits and made him think there might be a way to get the movement back on track.[19]

On Friday, June 14, the *New York Times* ran two front-page photographs, above the fold, of Salter being beaten and led away by the police. The headline, however, was strangely incomplete: "Jackson Negroes Clubbed as Police Quell

Marchers." The same story ran on the front page of newspapers across the country.[20]

Also on Friday, Salter and Dave Dennis held a workshop for about a hundred youths at the Pearl Street AME Church, hoping to generate interest for another large march. But to their surprise, the NAACP spread the word that marchers would not be bailed out in time to attend the Evers funeral the next day, and with that news, only thirty-seven agreed to take part. With too few for a mass march, Salter and Dennis decided to stage small picketing demonstrations on Capitol Street. The kids were sent out in twos and threes to have maximum impact and make it harder for the police to arrest them. Nevertheless, each group was arrested almost immediately and taken to the fairgrounds. These demonstrations had the distinction of pushing the total number of arrests in the two and a half weeks since the Woolworth's sit-in past the one thousand mark.[21]

Friday proved a significant day on the legal battlefront as well. The U.S. Supreme Court issued a unanimous statement saying that the petition for a stay and dissolution of the injunction against the Jackson Movement's demonstrations, "after due consideration, is denied." The court offered no explanation, but NAACP attorneys reasoned that it was a jurisdictional issue since the petitioners hadn't yet exhausted their remedies through lower courts. Whatever the reason, the high court made it clear that the injunction would remain in place until either Judge Cox or the Chancery Court lifted it.[22]

Meanwhile, Myrlie Evers was struggling with plans for her husband's burial. Although Medgar had wanted a simple funeral and Myrlie wanted him buried locally so that she and the children could visit his grave, Ruby Hurley had convinced the grieving twenty-nine-year-old widow that Medgar was a national figure who deserved a large funeral and a veteran's burial at Arlington National Cemetery. Because Myrlie had also asked that the casket be closed for the funeral, she took her two older children, Darrell and Reena, to Collins Funeral Home on Friday for one last good-bye and then sent the children out of the room. The night before, at the first public viewing, Myrlie had nearly collapsed when she saw Medgar's body for the first time. She then threw herself across the coffin, kissed his face, whispered in his ear, and stroked his hair. "He always loved me to rub his hair," she had cried. "He said it gave him strength and courage." At this final, private moment, with the children in tow, Myrlie wanted to stroke his head again, but she sensed she was not alone. And she was right. *Life* photographer Flip Schulke, who had been tracking her every move since the shooting, was in the room with her—but out of his audacious intrusion would emerge a moment of grace.

Since the assassination, Myrlie had felt an overwhelming hatred of white people, so strong the night of Medgar's death that she imagined herself with a machine gun, mowing down the police sent to work on the case. "I felt a hatred so deep and malignant," she later wrote, "I could have killed every one of them." But on this day, at this most private of moments, she looked around and saw the photographer who had just seen two children say good-bye to their father, who was now witnessing the final farewell of his grieving widow—and Schulke, who was white, had tears in his eyes. "For the first time since Medgar's death," Myrlie wrote, "the hatred I felt for all whites was gone. It never returned."[23]

After the family's private good-byes, the public was invited to an open viewing of the body. About one thousand people, most of them black, filed past the casket, the lower half of which was covered with a folded American flag.[24]

Additional statements of grief and support continued to be publicized throughout the day. James Meredith arrived in Jackson and concurred with the NAACP's decision to suspend marches. "My greatest fear is the eruption of major racial violence," he said. However, Meredith called for blacks nationwide to participate in a general work strike: "One hour should be observed for the purpose of solitude and prayer . . . to commence simultaneously with the memorial service." Gloster Current quickly dismissed the suggestion of this "amateur" and responded, defensively, that the NAACP knew what it was doing. In another statement, released exclusively to the *New York Times*, the Catholic bishop of Jackson—a white native Mississippian—decried the Evers assassination, offered sympathy to his family, and said that "the guilt for the murder and the other instances of violence in our community tragically must be shared by all of us." At last, the conscience of the moderate white clergy had been pricked. It was the first public statement of its kind by a prominent local white leader.[25]

Finally, late on Friday afternoon, it was announced that a march would be allowed the next day following the Evers funeral. An event the night before may have played some role in the shift of plans. Although there had been random black violence after some of the earlier mass meetings, most of it had been no more than the rock-throwing kind until, just after midnight on Thursday night, a young white man was shot as he drove through a black section of town. He was listed in good condition by Friday afternoon, but the *Jackson Daily News* gave the story almost as much play as the Evers assassination. Perhaps this incident, along with additional pressure by the black ministers, helped convince the mayor to allow a mass march to give Evers's friends and supporters a peaceful way to vent their anger, frustration, and grief. His stipulation in granting the parade permit, however, was that the march must be in silence—no singing of freedom songs, no chanting of freedom slogans. The march would be respectful, quiet and dignified, a restriction that suited the NAACP just fine.[26]

When John Salter, Ed King, and the students heard about the deal for the silent march, however, they were appalled. Salter suggested in the strategy committee meeting Friday evening that a contingent of students break away from the march and stage a demonstration as it crossed Capitol Street. His idea was quickly nixed by the ministers, since they didn't want to be seen as unable to carry through on their part of the bargain. Salter ultimately agreed that any kind of sanctioned march in Jackson was progress, so he committed himself to honor the agreement, as did Ed King and the others present.[27]

At a press conference just before the mass meeting that night, Roy Wilkins had kept open the possibility of a march on Saturday without revealing what had already been agreed to. The *New York Times* reported that Wilkins was under pressure from other civil rights groups to stage a massive demonstration after the funeral. Privately, Wilkins was livid over Kunstler's remark the previous evening that Dr. King might be invited in to help with strategizing the Jackson Movement's next steps.[28]

Wilkins kept his ire under wraps that night, however, as many national figures were in attendance at the mass meeting at the Pearl Street AME Church. Ralph Bunche, the black Nobel Peace Prize winner and then-undersecretary of the United Nations, was present, as were U.S. Congressman Charles Diggs, national CORE director James Farmer, and several high-profile labor officials.[29]

Behind the scenes, though, when John Salter stepped outside during the mass meeting, he saw lots of people he'd never seen before, all of whom wanted to participate in a loud and vocal mass march the next day. In particular, the SNCC leadership, many of whom had arrived from various parts of the South, thought that the Evers cortege should be brought past the state capitol as a sign of respect for all he had endured for the state. They began plotting to figure out how this could be accomplished. It seemed that the more militant activists might get their demonstration after all.[30]

ON SATURDAY MORNING, MORE THAN TEN THOUSAND PEOPLE, INCLUDING some whites, lined the streets to watch the funeral motorcade of more than one hundred cars wind its way through the black sections of town on the three-mile ride from the Evers home in north Jackson to the Masonic Temple, where the service was to be held. Another thousand people filed past the open coffin as it lay in state for two hours.[31]

The service began at 11:00 a.m. and lasted an hour and a half. The auditorium was packed with more than five thousand people. Another thousand or so were milling around outside in the still record-breaking hundred-degree heat.[32]

Myrlie Evers recalled that the overcrowded auditorium was stiflingly hot and she was annoyed that the funeral was so different from what Medgar had once told her he wanted—simple, short, and soon after he died. Instead the event would be long and complicated, and he wouldn't be in the ground for days to come. The plan was that his body would be driven to Meridian,

Mississippi, the next day and then taken by train to Washington, D.C., to lie in state for another day and a half. He would finally be buried on Wednesday at Arlington National Cemetery, a full week after he had been shot. Most of all, Medgar had always said that he wanted his funeral to be inexpensive. "When I'm gone, I'm gone," he had told Myrlie. "I won't know anything about it." The NAACP, however, was determined to stage a hero's burial. They tried to take Myrlie's wishes into consideration, but they ended up dictating—and paying for—every detail, including the clothes she and the children wore.[33]

They also decided who would take part in the service and sit on the stage. Just how much Wilkins had been irked by the turf war was made clear when Martin Luther King, the most prominent civil rights leader in the country, was met at the airport that morning not by a contingent of NAACP officials, but by John Salter, Ed King, and Bill Kunstler. Salter, who was hoping to talk with Dr. King after the funeral about joining the Jackson struggle, drove him to the Masonic Temple. Dr. King was then further rebuffed when the NAACP did not invite him to sit on stage with Wilkins, Bunche, and other dignitaries. Tougaloo's Dr. Beittel, who was invited to sit on stage, later said that he felt uncomfortable about his presence there, given Dr. King's exclusion, and would have gladly given up his seat. King was placed in a reserved section of the auditorium but was constantly reminded that this was the NAACP's show.[34]

Nearly everyone from the sit-in attended the Evers funeral. Pearlena Lewis was there with Lillian Louie; Annie Moody, Lois Chaffee, Memphis Norman, and George Raymond were all in attendance, as were Ed King, Mercedes Wright, and, of course, John Salter. Joan Trumpauer, who was by then in Washington, and Tom Beard missed this turning point in the Jackson Movement's story. Beard said he was too angry to attend, feeling that he didn't want to associate with those who hadn't helped Evers enough while he was alive. Doris Allison was there with her husband, as was Dave Dennis, though he tried to stay behind the scenes. Alphonzo Lewis was still jailed at the fairgrounds for demonstrating the day before. Detective Jim Black had the day off, having stopped posing as a reporter since the assassination because his superiors felt the situation was too volatile. Ironically, Black's sudden absence from the scene led some movement people to initially suspect him of the murder. Reporter Bill Minor was on hand, as was Bob Bullock, the cameraman, but photographer Freddie Blackwell was also taking the day off.[35]

President and Mrs. Kennedy sent a poignant personal letter to Myrlie Evers, which was released just prior to the funeral service. It read, in part: "Although comforting thoughts are difficult at a time like this, surely there may be some solace in the realization of the justice of the cause for which your husband gave his life. Achievement of the goals he did so much to promote will enable his children and the generations to follow to share fully and equally in the benefits and advantages our nation has to offer."[36]

Lois Chaffee recalled that it was at the funeral that the reality of the situation hit home for her. "I remember Myrlie," she said regretfully. "And I remember thinking that I had not really taken this as seriously.... I had been thinking big social causes and about changing lives—about marshaling our efforts to do something important ... sort of abstract. Medgar's killing was not abstract."[37]

Dave Dennis was bitterly angry over the NAACP's use of the event as an opportunity to enhance its image. "I felt that some individuals were exploiting Medgar's death," he later said. "At least if he's dead, you use that death to mobilize people to do something. But they just wanted to get the PR out of it. They wanted to get mileage out of it for the NAACP."[38]

For the funeral, the NAACP had selected as speakers local ministers affiliated with the Jackson Movement, while also including remarks by Roy Wilkins and others instrumental in Evers's life. Two ministers who had already taken strong stands and would emerge as key leaders in the days to follow, Reverend Charles Jones and Reverend G. R. Haughton, served as presider and invocator, respectively. Then Medgar's first employer after college, T. R. M. Howard, praised Evers and the NAACP while pointedly putting down Dr. King and his efforts. "Lest we forget," Howard stated, "and it does appear that some people have forgotten ... it was right here in Mississippi back in 1952 that the first statewide nonviolent protest was carried out. We put out some forty thousand fluorescent bumper signs on cars, saying 'Don't Buy Gas Where You Can't Use the Restroom.' Our martyred hero, Medgar Evers, was one of the individuals who participated in this first campaign, four years before Dr. King marched at Montgomery."[39]

After more prayers and remarks by local ministers, Roy Wilkins delivered the eulogy, eloquently summarizing the spirit of the slain leader's winning approach. "If Medgar Evers could live in Mississippi and not hate, so shall we," Wilkins stated. He blamed the "southern system" with "its outposts in the Congress of the United States" for helping to "put the man behind the deadly rifle this week." But he said that Evers was "a symbol of our victory and their defeat. The bullet that tore away his life [also] tore away at the system and helped to signal its end. The opposition has been reduced to clubs, guns, hoses, dogs, garbage trucks, and hog wire compounds.... Obviously nothing can stop the drive for freedom. It will not close here or elsewhere. After a hundred years of waiting and suffering, we are determined, in the language of James Baldwin, 'not upon a bigger cage, but upon no cage at all.'" Wilkins also announced that Evers's salary would continue to be paid to his family and that an education fund for his children had been set up. Then, borrowing Dr. King's idea, Wilkins also discussed a fund in Evers's honor to provide cash "for freedom workers, particularly in the South and primarily in Mississippi."[40]

After Wilkins finished, the crowd sang "We Shall Overcome," and Evers's own pastor, Reverend G. C. Hunter, delivered some final words of sympathy.

Just before the throng was dismissed, Reverend Jones solemnly read the entire text of the mayor's permit for the march. All were thus instructed that the event was to be "a silent mournful funeral procession" and that Jackson's police force would be on hand "for the purpose of handling traffic and the doing of whatever is necessary to cause the procession to move in an orderly and respectful manner." With that, the mourners were dismissed.[41]

Myrlie Evers and NAACP state president Aaron Henry, along with Medgar's brother, Charles, were among the small group who made the trip to the funeral home by car. Most, including Dr. King and Roy Wilkins, chose to walk the little more than two miles in the 102-degree heat and stifling humidity. All told, an estimated five thousand people marched in the blistering Mississippi sun that day to honor the memory of Medgar Evers.[42]

They started out three abreast in what the *New York Times* called "the demonstration of sorrow." A gripping photograph captures the scene as marchers moved slowly toward the downtown area. Despite their disagreements, Wilkins and Dr. King were the picture of harmony, striding side by side in the second row, just behind some local ministers. John Salter, with his sunglasses and bandaged head, can be spotted in the eighth row, and Ed King, wearing clerical garb, is three rows behind Salter—two of the fifty or so whites in the crowd. Doris Allison started out walking, but between the heat and her grief, broke down after a few blocks and couldn't go on. Dick Gregory, who had flown back from San Francisco, later wrote that "the line stretched so far back it looked like ants in a parade—ole folks, young folks, black and light and white folks. . . . They walked and they walked. It looked like we had enough folks to march on God that day."[43]

At the suggestion of Aaron Henry, Myrlie Evers looked back from the limousine and saw block after block of marchers jamming the streets. The size of the group encouraged her, but she also wondered why this couldn't have happened while her husband was still alive. Then she saw something that surprised her. As the hearse with Medgar's flag-draped coffin passed, many policemen took off their helmets—perhaps out of respect for the flag, but perhaps also for the fallen hero.[44]

As Salter marched, his thoughts turned metaphorical: "It came to me that here was Mississippi . . . the people around me . . . the man to whom they had come to pay homage . . . [and] that which had been dealt him . . . the police . . . the intense Mississippi sun. A great many things, all symbolizing the forces of Mississippi, were gathered together."[45]

The march took nearly two hours, as the nine-block stream of people slowly made its way from Lynch Street, down the Pascagoula Street cutoff, and then north onto Farish Street, where the route crossed over Capitol Street before reaching the funeral home. It was at Capitol Street—just half a block from Woolworth's—where the trouble began, and only after most of the marchers had passed without incident. Here, hundreds of policemen had amassed, fearing an attempted demonstration where so many others had occurred. Many of the young people affiliated with SNCC and CORE, as well as some from NAACP youth groups, were marching at the rear of the silent demonstration. As they crossed over Capitol Street, they began singing "We Shall Overcome." But as the young marchers continued up Farish Street to the funeral home, they fell into silence again.[46]

While most of the crowd dispersed as they reached the march's destination, many just stood around, not knowing what to do with their grief now that the funeral had ended. When the young people arrived, a woman in the crowd—most agree it was Tougaloo's Dorie Ladner, a SNCC activist—intoned in a hushed, mournful voice, the song "O Freedom."

"*O freedom,*" she sang slowly, sadly. "*O freedom. O freedom over me. / And before I'd be a slave, I'll be buried in my grave. / And go home to my Lord and be free.*" Some of the marchers joined in, thus violating the terms of the march permit. Once that song was through, Ladner broke into an up-tempo version of "This Little Light of Mine." Many more then joined in, adding clapping and hand gestures to the familiar but now rebellious sounds.[47]

Ed King, who had been standing with John Salter watching the crowd pass, said what happened next was completely misperceived by the police and led to the chaos that ensued. As the crowd was winding up its chorus of "This Little Light of Mine," someone threw in the verse "All over Capitol Street, I'm gonna let it shine." As this line was being repeated three times, following the structure of the song, some of the singers pointed toward Capitol Street a few blocks away. King said the jumpy white police force, unfamiliar with the song, mistook the gesture and thought the crowd was about to come after them or, at the very least, charge over to Capitol Street. In their confusion, the police began to back away from the crowd and head toward Capitol Street to defend it. Their retreat opened up a space on Farish Street that had been tightly controlled. Into the empty space flowed the crowd, led by Ladner, and they then, in fact, did begin to march toward Capitol Street. Suddenly and spontaneously, the marchers made their way through one intersection as the retreating police broke into a run and the demonstrators, as well as a sizable number of bystanders not trained in nonviolence, followed.[48]

Salter and King stood by and watched all this happen from the sidewalk near the funeral home—feeling shock and concern, yet pride at the same time. "It was the Lord's spontaneous demonstration," Salter later said. Both claim to have had nothing to do with the crowd moving toward Capitol Street, although they did follow it for a short time, along with King's wife, Jeannette, and Tougaloo student body president Eddie O'Neal. Primarily, however, as they witnessed the developments, King and Salter simultaneously thought of Dr. King as the only person who could direct this kind of uprising.[49]

Since he had been at the head of the march, Dr. King had waited for a while for it to finish. But his aides expressed concern for his safety and decided that the more quickly he got out of Jackson, the better off he and perhaps everyone else would be. So Bill Kunstler had taken Salter's car and, with Steve Rutledge driving, had whisked Dr. King and his group back to the airport, even before the young people had begun to sing.[50]

Now, after the flare-up around Capitol Street began, Salter, Ed and Jeannette King, and Eddie O'Neal hoped to catch Dr. King before his flight left and ask him to return. They rushed into a nearby office building in search of a phone to call the airport. Although it was Saturday, most businesses in the black shopping district had closed out of respect for Evers; the four were able to enter the building, but the offices were all locked. They ran upstairs to the second floor and found nothing open there either. When they looked out the window to see what was happening with the crowd, the police saw them and charged swiftly into the building and up the stairs.[51]

Neither Salter nor King knew then—and Salter never really acknowledged it later—that the police were only after Ed King. They felt he had eluded arrest after the Rose Street demonstration and were determined to bring him in, as they had Salter, Chaffee, and the other whites. When the police reached the top of the stairs, they went after King and left Salter alone. King fell to his knees as he had at the post office demonstration and would not cooperate, so the police dragged him down the stairs, feet first, and lifted him into a paddy wagon. Press reports agree that Salter was not a target and that he had done nothing to warrant arrest until he began harassing the police about arresting King. Chief of Detectives M. B. Pierce told reporters afterwards that Salter insisted on being arrested with his friend. "Officers at first refused to take him into custody," Pierce said. "But he followed them downstairs and onto the street, pestering them and they finally arrested him."[52]

As a consequence, both King and Salter were stuck in a paddy wagon when the final showdown of the Jackson Movement occurred. The singing, clapping young demonstrators had made their way only about a block and a half toward Capitol Street, at times charging through small groups of policemen. Finally, they reached a barricade of hundreds of police, walking shoulder to shoulder up the street with their clubs held in front of them. The two groups met less than a block from Capitol Street, thus halting the momentum of the impromptu demonstration. A tense silence ensued.

Deputy Chief Ray got on his bullhorn and admonished the break-away demonstrators. "Your leaders said you wanted to have a silent, mournful march," he shouted. "We agreed under those circumstances." The marchers, now numbering nearly a hundred, began yelling back, "We want the killer!" Toward the back of the group, people began chanting, "Freedom, freedom, freedom," while stomping their feet. Film footage shows young women and men, many dressed in their Sunday finest, shouting and crying, angry and sad, unable to hold back their rage at the system that had treated them so unfairly and led to the death of their leader. They yelled louder and louder at the police, not more than ten feet in front of them.[53]

At this point, policemen with leashed German shepherds moved in and chased a small part of the crowd, as well as about sixty newsmen, down the block back towards the funeral home. Once the cameras and reporters were out of the way, the police began to forcefully clear the area. A cameraman, seeking safety by standing in a doorway, saw police hit a black man in the head with the butt of an automatic rifle. Another officer cut a TV sound engineer's microphone cable. When a woman being clubbed by a policeman tried to escape into a waiting car, she was pulled out and beaten again.[54]

The brutal tactics were working, and the demonstrators were being cornered into a one-block area near the funeral home. But then someone in the crowd threw a brick at the police. Others joined in, including some from the roofs of the Farish Street office buildings and businesses. They continued to hurl whatever they could find at the police across a distance that had widened to about a hundred feet. Most of the debris fell short of its mark, but fourteen policemen were injured.[55]

Ray got on the bullhorn again, this time in a more heated voice. "You came here to honor a dead man," he shouted, "and you have brought dishonor! You have brought dishonor!" He shouted louder, "You have brought dishonor!"

As the crowd, now numbering about five hundred, screamed back, Ray spotted John Doar from the Justice Department and turned the focus on him. "Let the Justice Department see this," Ray yelled. He even instructed a TV news cameraman to turn his camera on the crowd. "Get pictures of how they're acting," he said.[56]

Some of the policemen had drawn their weapons in anticipation of increased violence. Seeing this, the crowd began to taunt them with "Shoot! Shoot! Shoot!" Bill Minor, who somehow had gotten behind the police line, overheard "some redneck county patrolman" saying to another, "We may as well open fire. If we don't do it today, we'll have to do it tomorrow."[57]

The situation had escalated to crisis proportions when John Doar stepped between the police and the crowd. With arms outstretched, he walked toward what had now become a mob, dodging flying objects as he begged the demonstrators to stop. "You won't win anything with bottles and bricks," he called out. Ray suggested that Doar introduce himself. "I'm John Doar. D-O-A-R. I'm from the Justice Department in Washington, and anybody around here knows that I stand for what's right. This is not the way!" Many of the SNCC and CORE representatives tried to lend their support to Doar, but they were drowned out by the now-furious black Jacksonians who had had enough of heavy-handed police tactics.[58]

Dave Dennis was one of those walking among the crowd trying to calm them down. Dennis spotted a youth with a gun pointed right at Doar. He quickly moved on the young man and got him to lower the gun. When another young man started to throw a brick toward Doar, Dennis held him back as well. Finally Doar spotted Dennis and called to him, "C'mon, Dave, let's get this stopped!"[59]

Dennis was continuing to try to calm the crowd when another young black man—perhaps the NAACP's Willie Ludden—stepped forward and called out, "This man is right!" Then he began dressing down those who were creating a violent scene. He grabbed Ray's bullhorn and spoke to the crowd: "Go home! That's the best thing you can do now."[60]

With much encouragement from others urging nonviolence, the crowd finally began to disperse. Some of the angrier participants broke windows and smashed bottles as they left, but it was clear that a major catastrophe had been averted.

While this confrontation had been occurring, John Salter and Ed King were still being held in the paddy wagon. Salter said that he heard some shots fired (although there are no press reports to back this up), and that he and King feared that a massacre was under way. "I could think only of Sharpeville," Salter later wrote, referring to the South African police slaughter of peaceful protesters only a few years earlier. Meanwhile, a number of bloodied demonstrators were arrested and stuffed into the paddy wagon with the two activists.[61]

Bill Kunstler, who had returned from taking Dr. King to the airport, was making his way down Farish Street to get a closer look at the scene when Salter spied him from the paddy wagon window. "Bill! Hey, Bill!" Salter called out. Unsure at first of where the sound was coming from, Kunstler eventually figured it out and began to make his way toward the police vehicle. He was suddenly stopped by an auxiliary policeman who jabbed the barrel of a shotgun in Kunstler's gut. "If you don't want to get in there with them, you'd better get the hell out of here!" the security officer warned. Kunstler moved along; it would take two weeks for the bruises on his stomach to disappear, he reported years later.[62]

Only twenty-seven people were arrested that day. Once the demonstration was over, all twenty-seven were taken to the fairgrounds and made to stand, leaning far forward, with their arms against a wall in the blistering sun until it was their turn to be booked. Salter and King were the last ones to be called. The police taunted the two as they stood in that difficult position and threatened them with death. Finally they were booked: King for a charge stemming from the Rose Street incident and Salter for "interfering with an officer's arrest." Dorie Ladner, the leader of the unauthorized march, was also arrested and charged with disturbing the peace.[63]

CHARLIE NEWELL, D. C. SULLIVAN'S FRIEND FROM CENTRAL HIGH, REMEM-
bered precisely where he was when the violence after the Evers funeral broke
out. Newell had been an ROTC officer during high school and was scheduled
to go into full-time Army National Guard duty starting in July. He and a friend
were driving along the Natchez Trace highway when they heard the radio announcer say that all members of the 113th and 114th Military Police companies
should report to their armories. At the request of Mayor Thompson, Governor
Barnett called out the National Guard in case additional protection was needed. Newell immediately turned around and headed into town. D. C. Sullivan
didn't have any recollection of the day at all.[64]

IT IS UNCLEAR WHO FIRST STARTED POINTING THE FINGER AT SALTER AND
King as the instigators of the Farish Street events: the police, the press, or the
NAACP. But death threats quickly flooded the phone lines of Tougaloo as the
erroneous word spread through white Jackson that these two were responsible for the demonstration and the violence. On campus, armed students
approached the two leaders and assured them that they would stand guard
for protection. When Salter was interviewed that evening by two FBI agents
investigating the Rose Street beating, one took him aside afterwards and urged
him to "Be careful, John. Be very careful."[65]

The *Jackson Daily News* headline the next day read "Funeral March Finishes
in White-Led Agitation." A photo caption said the "violent outburst [was] led
by Tougaloo staffers." The Memphis newspaper also blamed the incident on
Salter and King. Bill Minor, however, meticulously described the arrest of the
two white men and never drew the conclusion that they were in any way connected with the outburst. His headline also more accurately described what
had happened: "Near Riot Averted After Evers Funeral Services." While the
New York Times remained neutral on the role of Salter and King, focusing
more on the police brutality that had sparked the crowd's actions, that paper did use the word "riot" in its headline ("27 Arrested in Jackson Rioting
After Rites for Negro Leader"), insinuating that the crowd had instigated the
violence.[66]

At a strategy committee meeting following the funeral demonstration on
Saturday, Gloster Current lambasted Salter and King in their absence, wrongly
reporting that the police had charged them with inciting a riot and suggesting
that they be ousted immediately from the committee. Many of the ministers
were ready to blame whoever was handy, but Bill Kunstler and Eddie O'Neal
came to Salter's and King's defense, as did a few of the more activist ministers
and NAACP attorneys. Kunstler also took issue with Current's characterization
of the event as a riot and emphasized that the police had initiated the violence.
When Current, desperate for a scapegoat to take the pressure off the NAACP,
called again for Salter's and King's expulsion, some of the ministers—perhaps

still smarting from Current's earlier comments about money—pointed out that the Jackson police probably were not the best authority on the matter and refused to support Current's motion. The two activists would stay on the committee.[67]

A local attorney who did some work for the NAACP bailed Salter and King out of jail later that evening, just in time for King and his wife, Jeannette, to organize a group of visits by black students to four white churches the following morning. On Sunday, Annie Moody and a companion were taken downtown to the First Christian Church. "This is a Church of Christ, not a place of publicity," the usher told them without allowing them to enter, though he did offer them cab fare to the black church across town. As they were telling the usher, "No, thank you," a pair of white women came up and offered to sit with the two black students. "God is the judge of us all," one of the women said to the usher. "Who else can judge where we worship?" When the usher threatened to call the police, Moody thanked the women and left.

Then she suggested that Jeannette King drive them to St. Andrew's Episcopal Church on Capitol Street, where another pair of demonstrators had gone. Given the location of the church—directly across from the governor's mansion and down the street from the prior day's turmoil—the situation could hardly have been more dramatic. Moody was stunned to learn that the first two women had been admitted. She was further shaken when she and her friend were invited to enter, saying she "stood there for a good five minutes before I was able to compose myself. . . . I had never prayed with white people in a white church before. I [thought] any moment God would strike the life out of me." It seemed that even those most vocal about change weren't quite ready for it when it came.[68]

An Associated Press photographer caught the scene as the four women emerged after the service, and the picture ran in the *New York Times* the next day. The *Times* also reported that SNCC, CORE, and the SCLC were ready to aid the Jackson struggle. James Forman of SNCC said he was sending ten field secretaries to Jackson to "muster support for the protests," and James Farmer was sending additional CORE personnel as well. Dr. King suggested he was ready to help if asked by the local leadership.[69]

As the outside forces of change were gathering to help, however, the national NAACP leaders held fast to their belief that they knew best and continued to shun external assistance, at least in a leadership capacity. The NAACP's Willie Ludden told the press that nothing could be gained by Dr. King's coming to Jackson, although he did allow that SNCC and CORE representatives could be helpful with the planned voter registration campaign. In fact, Roy Wilkins was still annoyed by what he saw as Dr. King's attempt, in the wake of the Evers murder, to siphon off sympathy funds from the NAACP. At a meeting near Washington, D.C., where he had gone after the funeral, Wilkins denounced the other civil rights organizations—specifically, CORE, SNCC, and the SCLC— for taking "the publicity while the NAACP furnishes the manpower and pays the bills." "The NAACP is the only organization that can handle a long, sustained fight," he said. "We are not here today and gone tomorrow." He pressed his audience of eight hundred not to "go giving them your money when it should be given to us."[70]

Also on this day, the NAACP announced that Medgar's brother, Charles, would replace the slain civil rights leader in Jackson. Charles Evers had shared his brother's Mau Mau dreams and later displayed entrepreneurial skills, having created his own funeral and insurance businesses. But he had been run out of Mississippi by racist whites and was reduced to running numbers and operating a few bars in Chicago at the time of his brother's murder. He had no previous civil rights organizing experience. It was said that Myrlie Evers was not pleased with the choice; truth be told, neither were Roy Wilkins or Gloster Current. But Charles had insisted that he be allowed to step in for his brother, speaking of a pact they had made years earlier. After the funeral, the NAACP couldn't risk a public relations disaster by denying a grieving sibling his brother's supposed wish. In the announcement, at least, the NAACP said the choice was "temporary."[71]

Despite Salter's hopes for Dr. King to join the Jackson Movement, one of Salter's allies, Bill Kunstler, had discouraged Dr. King from returning to the city, telling him, "The Movement is dead here. Only Salter and his youth groups are prepared to keep going." Kunstler, however, only told Salter that he didn't expect Dr. King to be joining them in Jackson anytime soon. Salter's last hope of a massive grassroots uprising was being suffocated by others who thought they knew better.[72]

Salter felt a sense of gloom descending that evening as a light rain began to fall for the first time in weeks. The death threats against himself and Ed King had become constant. The Jackson papers' indictment of them opened up the floodgates of hatred within the white community. Now *they* were the clear enemies, just as Evers had been previously. They were getting calls from people who would laugh and hang up or who would say nothing, just hoping they would snap. One caller said to King, "You won't go to that funeral [Medgar's in Washington]. You won't get to that burial." Although neither Salter nor King had planned to go, the comment made them feel even more like marked men. Earlier that day both men had been visited by *New York Times* reporter Jack Langguth, who had been in and out of Jackson since the sit-in. Langguth was now nosing around, looking for information on the two leaders "in case something happens," he said. "Sounds to me like you're trying to get my obituary," Salter said glumly. "I guess that's it," Langguth replied.[73]

Salter's despondency also resulted from his knowledge that, as he put it, "a third party was getting ready to come into this whole thing, but not a friend."

The "party" he referred to was the Kennedy administration, which had been closely monitoring the situation since the Woolworth's sit-in.[74]

The phone logs of Burke Marshall, the top official for civil rights in the Justice Department, suggest a significant focus on Jackson beginning on the evening of the sit-in, when Marshall took a rare call from J. Edgar Hoover, who probably told him what his FBI men had observed at Woolworth's. Marshall then called Mayor Thompson and, when he got no answer, tried Jackson's chief of police, who apparently took the call. The Justice Department's John Doar arrived in Jackson the next day and there were regular, though not daily, calls between Marshall and the Justice Department staffers in Jackson, including Doar and Thelton Henderson. The calls intensified significantly after the Evers assassination. By the Monday after the funeral, Marshall was getting called up to Attorney General Robert Kennedy's office. By Tuesday, even President Kennedy was calling him. By Wednesday, Marshall was calling Roy Wilkins and Clarence Mitchell and working with Doar in Jackson to finalize a deal. Salter's perspective was that a Kennedy administration negotiated settlement would get people off the streets, but would do little to get them closer to their freedom.[75]

When Salter and King entered the NAACP office late Monday morning, the two were greeted amicably enough, but when they raised the issue of further demonstrations, it was clear that the NAACP had the committee votes to redirect the movement's efforts into voter registration and boycotts. However, the two activists were not the only ones upset. The SNCC and CORE representatives sent in to assist with the new voter registration campaign were shut out of the planning. Enraged, the SNCC people pulled out completely; the CORE contingent decided to stay for the time being. The NAACP then announced a "cooling-off period" following the funeral disturbance and called for a temporary suspension of demonstrations. It was clear to the press that the moderate forces within the organization had achieved victory. Salter talked to some SNCC people about restarting something on the side, but most were ready to move on.[76]

Salter sensed from the tone of that strategy session that some kind of deal had already been worked out or was in the process of being finalized. He was right. Attorney General Robert Kennedy had already been on the phone to Mayor Thompson to press for a solution to the Jackson crisis, and later that afternoon, during a ten-minute conversation, President Kennedy himself tested the waters to see what kind of settlement the mayor would accept.[77] Thompson first tried to ingratiate himself to the president. "The Associated Press was in this morning and I told him what a wonderful fellow you were," Thompson declared. "Of course, any other things you hear, don't pay any attention, because I really think the world of you." As the two men got down to business, the mayor attempted to persuade Kennedy that he had everything under control.

Knowing the southern court system was stacked against the freedom fighters, Thompson wondered if Kennedy couldn't just try to work through the courts to get what he and the demonstrators wanted. President Kennedy finally interrupted, indicating that he had talked at the White House with some of the ministers who were in town for the Evers burial. "When I talked to them there seem to be two or three things that didn't seem to me to be too unreasonable," the president asserted. He mentioned the demands for black policemen, crossing guards, and promotions for municipal workers. Thompson responded that he had all three concessions "ready to go. We have answered every other thing like I told 'em, except the biracial committee, and I just can't do that right now."

Kennedy fumbled around, not wanting to press too hard, then shifted to find out which of the ministers was really in charge. "I understand Reverend Smith . . . is he . . . is he the stud duck down there?" Kennedy asked. "He's not the power," Thompson replied. "Haughton is the one that causes problems, and he's real smart and they look to him a lot." Then the president asked for specifics on the deal: "If these people all stop demonstrating and went home for a period, when do you think you could take the policemen and how many?" Thompson indicated that he had a few lined up, but that they seemed to have backed out. "God, there must be some bright young fellow down there that you can get, a couple of those," Kennedy parried. Thompson threw in a qualifier. "The only thing, Mr. President," he said, "when I put a policeman on, I want him to be responsible to me and not the NAACP." "Well, I agree," Kennedy responded.[78]

It is apparent that the president and his advisors had decided they needed to cool the situation down, so they were putting a full-court press on Thompson, Wilkins, and the local ministers to negotiate a solution. The president and his brother believed that voter registration drives ultimately would be more fruitful for black citizens—and certainly more beneficial to the administration's own political goals—than would more demonstrations in the street and, possibly, more deaths. They were therefore determined to find a negotiated settlement to what had now become the nation's most contentious civil rights battle.

A DOZEN OR SO BLOCKS FROM THE WHITE HOUSE, MEDGAR EVERS'S BODY LAY in state. It had arrived by train Monday morning and, accompanied by nearly a thousand marchers, had been taken from Union Station to McGuire Funeral Home half a mile away, where a group of two thousand waited outside. There it was prepared for lying in state that evening and the entire next day at the John Wesley AME Zion Church at 14th and Corcoran streets, NW, where, a year before, Evers had spoken to a small group of NAACP supporters. More than ten thousand people filed past the body that evening. Medgar Evers, formerly little known outside of Mississippi, was now, in death, becoming a national hero.[79]

Joan Trumpauer was one of the handful of whites who came to pay her respects that night. She felt sick to her stomach and "very sad" when she saw the man she had worked with lying in a flag-draped, steel gray casket. Unaware of the turmoil within the Jackson Movement, she was still hoping for "some sort of victory in Jackson" so that the NAACP leader's death would not be for naught.[80]

Myrlie Evers, having left three-year-old son, Van, with family friends, flew in with Reena and Darrell the next day, accompanied by her brother-in-law, Charles. In Washington, Evers began to realize just how much the nation had been following the events in Jackson and how her husband had become a symbol for the freedom movement. "Medgar didn't belong just to Jackson and Mississippi, but to the whole nation," she said at a brief press conference at Washington, D.C.'s National Airport. Throughout the day, another fifteen thousand mourners passed by his body lying in state. One young boy said to an interviewer, "I'm here to see the colored man who died for all the colored people. He was proud of us."[81]

ON TUESDAY MORNING, JUNE 18, ED KING GOT A CALL FROM JACK YOUNG, A local Jackson attorney who handled much of the NAACP's legal work in Mississippi. Young asked King to find Salter and come to his office on North Farish Street to discuss legal matters related to their activities after the funeral. He didn't want to say more over the phone, but indicated that the matter was urgent. When the two left Tougaloo in Salter's white Rambler, they were followed by police all the way to their destination. Salter stared the cops down as he exited his car and made his way across Farish Street and up to the attorney's office. There, Young advised them that it was probable that both men would be indicted for inciting a riot. Salter said he explained to Young that he and King were not guilty and then suggested that they fight this indictment as they had all the other arrests—through a series of legal maneuvers in the courts. He said that he and King then left the office to return to campus.[82]

King, however, was much more specific about what went on during the meeting. He said Young told them that they had until sunset to leave Mississippi or face arrest. The attorney also said, according to King, that the NAACP had no plans of bailing them out and the bond would be set at the incredibly high sum of fifty thousand dollars. Young never did tell the two men who specifically had contacted him with this information—King speculated that it was a "white city attorney"—but said he had to know their decision right away so he could report it to "the authorities."

King remembered that both he and Salter "were appalled and frightened," but decided not to exile themselves from the local movement. Instead, they told Young that once they returned to campus, they would immediately call the national media, Dr. King's office, and other activist groups to fight what

King described as a "virtual lynching." Young called his contact while King and Salter considered their next move.[83]

When the pair left Young's office, they walked to a local store to pick up some newspapers, then returned to Salter's car and headed back to Tougaloo. The police continued to track their every move. There were only a few ways to drive back to campus, and Salter chose the western route, through a black neighborhood and onto North West Street. When Salter turned there, he and King both noticed that the police cars had stopped following them. A misty rain was falling. Then, as Salter made his way toward a major intersection at Northside Drive, he saw out of the corner of his eye a car darting out from a side street on his left. It appeared to both men that the car was deliberately headed right for them. The car was driven by an eighteen-year-old white Ole Miss student named Prat Pyle, who steered his car into an oncoming vehicle. When that car swerved to avoid hitting Pyle's car, it headed straight into Salter's Rambler. The two cars collided head on, while Pyle managed to maneuver his car away and avoid any damage to himself or his vehicle.[84]

The others were not so lucky. Salter's car was totaled, and both he and King were critically injured. In that time before seatbelts were commonplace, King's head was thrust through the windshield on impact, then came back through again as the car came to an abrupt halt. The right side of his face was sheared off upon reentry. Salter took a near-fatal blow to the ribs and the head, and his right eyelid was almost completely sliced off. Both men were knocked unconscious and were covered in blood. Salter awoke first, and after looking at himself in the mirror to wipe the blood from his face, he turned and called to his friend—but there was no answer. "I thought Ed was dead," Salter later said.

Then he noticed that a number of whites had gathered on the opposite sidewalk and were smiling and waving at him. No one came over to help. "I wished that I had had a gun right there with me," he said, "so that I could just shoot those sons of bitches, I hated them so badly." It was just about noon, exactly three weeks to the hour since the Woolworth's sit-in had begun.[85]

When the police arrived, they first talked to the crowd, then to Pyle and the black woman driving the other car, neither of whom was hurt badly. As an ambulance pulled up, the police finally made their way over to the two "agitators." They asked which hospital they wanted to go to, and Salter told them St. Dominic, the Catholic hospital where his daughter had been born. The two men were put into the ambulance. On the way to the hospital, King began to come to and started talking incoherently.

The ambulance, without explanation, took them not to St. Dominic but to Baptist Hospital, which was farther away. There, the two were put on stretchers and left out in the rain while the ambulance driver told the hospital staff who they were. At first, the hospital refused to treat them. But, fortunately, Dr.

Beittel had heard about the accident, shown up at the hospital, and insisted that they be admitted.

Salter's eyelid was slashed, but the eye was not damaged. Nearly all the bones on the right side of his face were broken, however, and he had several broken ribs. Despite these injuries, there was no significant damage to his internal organs. He was going to be fine, the nurses told him. When he was placed on a gurney in a separate room, some policemen came in and began walking around, making the semiconscious Salter feel like he was on a funeral bier, witnessing his own wake. One of the policemen said, "I want to see your driver's license, son." Not one to allow the cops to have the last laugh, Salter obliged defiantly. "Even though I could hardly move, I reached in and took out my damned billfold."

A little later, both Salter and King were wheeled into a pre-op room, where Salter found a phone and called his brother in Arizona to tell him about the accident before someone came in and took the phone away. Just before he went under the anesthesia, Salter remembered, he looked at the white doctor and said, "You'd like to kill me, wouldn't you?" The doctor shook his head no, and the activist descended into a deep, drugged sleep.[86]

Ed King fared much worse than Salter, though he retold his hospital experience with an unexpected degree of humor. Prior to being anesthetized for what would be the first of many operations on his severely damaged face, King recounted that he was "determined not to die with John getting a traffic ticket for the accident." He swore he told the doctors and nurses in the emergency room all about the incident, but then admitted that "I didn't have head enough or face enough" to tell them anything. He was dreaming perhaps, but even unconsciously, was trying to stand up for his friend.[87]

More than thirty-five years after the accident, both men remained convinced that the collision was intentional. Prat Pyle was the son of a prominent judge and Citizens' Council member who lived near the neighborhood where the wreck occurred. Both were certain that they were set up as retribution for their perceived role in the demonstration after the Evers funeral, and that their absence from the scene during this crucial phase of the Jackson Movement helped secure the deal between the Kennedy administration, the Thompson government, and the local black ministers. To argue the other side—that it simply was an accident—was unthinkable to them. Reporter Bill Minor, however, scoffed at their suspicions. "That's a stretch," he said, "really a stretch. . . . I don't think there was enough good evidence to show" what really happened.[88]

The truth may never be fully known. Prat Pyle's explanation was that his brakes had failed. The police did not contest his claim, nor did they check his brakes. Years later, during an insurance trial to determine who should pay for the damages, Pyle's father asked the defending insurance company to settle the claim after seeing photographs of the wreck and hearing a doctor's detailed description of Salter's and King's injuries.[89]

The *Jackson Daily News* provided same-day coverage of the car wreck, complete with a large Freddie Blackwell photograph of the totaled car. The paper reserved its lead story, however, for the president's phone call to Mayor Thompson the day before. The story also said that Robert Kennedy had called prior to the president to insist that demonstrators be released from the fairgrounds and that those under the age of eighteen have their arrest records expunged. The attorney general also insisted that some real progress on the desegregation front had to be made for the negotiations to be viable. The paper announced that a meeting of the black ministers was scheduled with the mayor for 3:30 Tuesday afternoon, only a few hours after King and Salter's car crash.[90]

Just prior to the meeting with the ministers, the mayor called President Kennedy to go over the agreement he was about to offer to ensure it would meet with White House approval. After a few niceties, Thompson told Kennedy that "we have an explosive situation here." He admitted that the ministers are "doing their best" to negotiate, but complained that the young people "have just gone wild!" "They have it in their system," Thompson said, "and the people can't control them." Thompson then went over the specifics of the deal, but cautioned that "we have to do it our way. . . . I have to maintain my image with the white and colored people, with the police, with my employees, with everybody."[91]

Kennedy pressed for a specific date for the settlement to go into effect, then suggested that the black ministers were also "out on a limb." "They have to look like . . . when they call off these demonstrations . . . that they're getting someplace," Kennedy insisted. Correctly anticipating that the ministers would have a hard sell to the black community, he told Thompson, "Now it should be possible . . . to work out some language which would save your situation and at the same time not make it look like they've all quit." Before the president turned the call over to his brother to work out the details, Thompson made a final plea that he try to control the attorney general, who was pressing for more than the mayor wanted to give. In his final words to Thompson, President Kennedy said, "I think the problem is to see what it is we can get the Negro community to accept . . . without any of these riots."

The deal ended up being not much more than what the mayor had been offering all along and fell far short of the demands articulated by the ministers and business leaders when they walked out of Thompson's office the day before the Woolworth's sit-in. There would be no biracial committee, no voluntary desegregation of eating establishments, no voluntary desegregation of schools and other public facilities. The mayor agreed only to hire six black policemen within the next sixty days to patrol the black areas of the city; to hire eight black crossing guards to help black children cross the street on their way to black schools; to promote one black garbage truck driver to a supervisory position; and to allow seven black municipal workers to operate heavy machinery.[92]

That was it. That was what the black leadership settled on for all of the turmoil, for the demonstrators who had risked their lives, for the more than one thousand arrests, and for the life of Medgar Evers. It seemed then, and seems now, such a small, small advance for all of the effort. But it was progress, and that's how the ministers presented it.

At a mass meeting Tuesday evening—exactly three weeks after that jubilant, unified gathering following the demonstration at Woolworth's when there seemed no end to where the Jackson Movement might lead—a battle-scarred and fragmented group of three hundred listened as Reverend Haughton described the mayor's concessions, which this time the ministers had gotten in writing. Besides meeting three of the eight specified demands of the movement, the mayor had also agreed—at Robert Kennedy's insistence—to release seventy-eight juveniles into the custody of their parents without charging them so that there would be no record of their arrests. Mayor Thompson also said that although he wouldn't establish a biracial committee, he would continue to meet with black ministers and business leaders, as would his cabinet, to resolve any grievances. What Thompson had asked for in return was that there be no more mass demonstrations and that the racial agitation that had disrupted the city during the past three weeks be curtailed. Although the ministers had openly wondered at the time about the constitutionality of such an agreement, they had verbally given their consent, subject to the approval of the community.[93]

As predicted, Reverend Haughton and Reverend Jones had a hard time selling the plan to the assembly. There were questions and challenges from the floor. Parliamentary procedure was invoked many times, but just as many times was ignored. The two ministers pleaded with those assembled to accept the agreement, explaining that "this is the best the mayor can do" under the circumstances. Haughton, in frustration, finally asked the negotiating committee to stand, and one by one, asked the audience to point out who among the group was "a rascal that would betray you." "If you believe I'm an Uncle Tom, raise your hand!" Haughton shouted. "If you believe I'm a fool, raise your hand!" The audience rustled but raised no serious objection. Then Reverend Jones invoked Evers's memory by reminding the crowd of their slain leader's words. "It appears from every indication," Jones began, "that some people do not regard what Medgar Evers said at the beginning of the Jackson Movement. Medgar said we did not want a Birmingham. And you agreed. I think if we want freedom for Medgar's sake, we still don't want a Birmingham."[94]

A young Hedrick Smith, who had replaced Claude Sitton as the *New York Times* correspondent in Jackson, reported that the crowd "reluctantly accepted the mayor's proposals . . . at the recommendation of their leaders." Bill Minor was more pointed, saying the group had "begrudgingly accepted the mayor's terms," but questioned the requirement to end the demonstrations. Dorie Ladner, who was at the meeting, believed there was nowhere else to turn. "We were infuriated at the agreement," she said. "But it was clear the mayor was not willing to negotiate in good faith. We accepted it under duress. Otherwise, there would have been all out war and likely more loss of life."

No matter how chaotic or frustrating the meeting was, the crowd voted by a ten-to-one margin to accept the negotiated settlement. That final vote officially ended the direct action demonstration phase of the Jackson Movement.[95]

MEDGAR EVERS WAS BURIED IN ARLINGTON CEMETERY, JUST ACROSS THE POtomac River from Washington, D.C., on Wednesday, June 19. Six hundred cars participated in the funeral cortege as it made its way through the city, past the Lincoln Memorial, where it stopped momentarily to pay tribute to another fallen civil rights hero, and then crossed Memorial Bridge. Myrlie Evers recalled seeing "block after block" of "people standing, many with heads bowed, many making the sign of the cross as we passed. Most of them were white."[96]

There was a small funeral service at the Fort Myer Chapel: it was the kind that Myrlie had wanted, the kind that Medgar had asked for. "I remember how thankful I was that Medgar had this quiet, simple service before being laid to rest," she later wrote.[97]

An estimated two thousand people were on hand for the graveside ceremonies, the largest funeral in the nation's capital since that of renowned Secretary of State John Foster Dulles in 1959. Myrlie cried quietly as a lone bugler sounded out taps. Mickey Levine of the American Veterans Committee spoke: "No soldier in the field has fought more courageously, more heroically than Medgar Evers. We pledge that this fight is not ended." Roy Wilkins delivered the final eulogy. His eyes brimming with tears, Wilkins said of the slain Evers: "Every morning he went forth. He was offering his life for the things he believed in. That offering was finally accepted. He believed in his country. It now remains to be seen whether his country believes in him." Overcome with emotion, Wilkins ended his remarks and walked away from the microphone.[98]

Myrlie jumped nervously when a volley of shots were fired by an integrated honor guard in Medgar's honor. Then she broke down and sobbed uncontrollably as Clarence Mitchell's son spontaneously started singing her late husband's favorite freedom anthem, "We Shall Overcome." The entire throng joined in.[99]

It was a gallant gesture, the singing, but the truth was far more bitter. The Jackson Movement, like its leader, had suffered a fatal blow. Unlike Evers, the movement would continue, primarily in the form of a voter registration drive and an economic boycott. But never again would it spark the kind of grassroots spirit and attention to nonviolent social change that had embodied its finest moments. For all practical purposes, it was over.

CHAPTER 10

NEXT STEPS

ALTHOUGH THE DIRECT ACTION PHASE OF THE JACKSON MOVEMENT ENDED with the Evers funeral march and the resulting negotiated settlement, much was left to be done during what might be called the movement's implementation phase. Charles Evers and the activist black ministers led the charge to hold the city accountable for its promises while also pushing for additional concessions. Progress was slow, however, and not at all like the kind of full-frontal push that Jackson had witnessed during the four weeks after the Woolworth's sit-in. As a result, many of the activists began to move in different directions that summer and fall, disappointed that their efforts had not brought about more immediate and tangible results.

On Friday morning, June 21, John Salter left Baptist Hospital. This was just two days after Medgar Evers's burial at Arlington Cemetery and one day after the Jackson ministers met with the mayor to give final approval to the settlement. Despite his doctor's reluctance to release him, Salter felt able to walk, and he didn't like being stuck in a place where everyone, including his enemies, could find him. Always a master of surprise, Salter announced his release to the city police by standing on the corner of Lynch Street near the NAACP offices. Two patrolmen driving by responded as the activist had hoped. "Their mouths just opened," he said, "and they came to a screeching halt." They stared and then hurried back to their downtown headquarters to report that Salter was back on the streets.[1]

Still, the brazenness of Salter's personal actions couldn't mask the obvious halt of the Jackson Movement's momentum. According to Salter, it "was destroyed. The ministers had sold the thing down the river." Even if he had wanted to try and pick up the pieces and continue to push for a resolution granting more rights to the city's black citizens, many of his supporters had already begun to leave. "Our best workers went off with SNCC and CORE, [to] Canton and the Delta," Salter said. "It was sad."[2]

Eldri Salter had flown back from Minnesota to be with her husband after the automobile crash, leaving little Maria with her parents. Professor Salter, facing increasing criticism from other Tougaloo faculty members, was unsure what his professional future held. He was also suffering aftershocks from the stress of the previous month. During this period, he says, he would wake up every night in a sweat, smelling blood—an experience he continued to have, though with less frequency, for the rest of his life. Though Salter was in shock, he was still functioning, and wondering what his next move should be.

He decided to first take care of his immediate needs. After a brief recovery period, he and Eldri bought a new car to replace the one destroyed in the wreck and took a short vacation. They headed north, first stopping in Kentucky to visit Anne and Carl Braden of the Southern Conference Educational Fund (SCEF). Salter let on that he might be looking for a new challenge. The family then headed to Minnesota to pick up Maria and on to Kansas to visit John's grandparents. While there, a call came from Jim Dombrowski, the head of SCEF, offering him a job as a field secretary—organizing grassroots communities around civil rights and economic issues and speaking at fund-raisers and educational events around the country. It seemed like the perfect opportunity, and he accepted. After a summer of travels, which included a trip back to Mississippi to resign from Tougaloo and pack the family's belongings, the Salters headed to Raleigh, North Carolina, where the SCEF job would be based.[3]

"'Mustard Man' Joins Braden" the front page *Jackson Daily News* photo caption announced. "Tougaloo Prof. Joins Pro-Red Organization" claimed the accompanying article. The white Mississippi establishment was delighted to be rid of this troublesome outside agitator, and Salter, who had both influenced and been profoundly influenced by Mississippi, never lived or worked in the state again. The other Woolworth's demonstrators, however, stayed—though they also shifted their efforts into the movement's next steps.[4]

Up in the hard-core racist town of Canton, where whites—outnumbered by blacks three to one—held on to power through a particularly vicious reign of terror, one of the Woolworth's veterans was facing a harsh reception. George Raymond had headed to Canton in early June to begin CORE's first independent voter registration project in Mississippi. During the same week as Medgar Evers's graveside ceremony in Arlington, Raymond was already being harassed by local police and segregationists in Madison County's seat of government.[5]

Raymond had just begun to organize the young people of Canton to help him canvass homes for a voter registration drive when the trouble started. First, his CORE office was broken into; then, shots were fired at volunteers who had driven up from Jackson. Raymond was being targeted so quickly because of his success: in just ten days he had already encouraged about sixty blacks to attempt to register to vote, and fourteen of them had been admitted to take the required state constitution literacy test.[6]

Among Raymond's helpers in Canton were two of the Jackson Movement's strongest foot soldiers, Bettye Ann Poole and Annie Moody. Moody had grown so tired of the bickering among Jackson groups that she said she was "ready to go almost anywhere, even Madison County, where Negroes frequently turned up dead." The two women worked on voter registration and organized high school students, hoping the youth would then convince the adults that voter registration was essential in the fight for civil rights.[7]

CORE's leadership had seriously underestimated what it would cost to run the Canton project. As a result, the Canton workers were getting only twenty dollars a week and even that didn't arrive regularly, so they were living off bread and water or, on a good day, grits and gravy. Despite these hardships, Raymond, Moody, Poole, and others worked diligently that summer to organize those young people who did show up, while attempting to attract willing adults as well.[8]

While struggling in Canton, Annie Moody was invited by Jackson NAACP leader Doris Allison to participate in what Allison designated a "Women's Leadership Rally" back in the state capital. Having been less than impressed with the men's conduct in the negotiations with the mayor, and frustrated over the outcome, Allison wanted to have a program where only women spoke and gave instruction, prayer, and encouragement. Ed King's wife, Jeannette, participated, as did a number of other leading women in the Jackson NAACP.[9]

Moody, who arrived late for the rally and looked a wreck, was asked to make some inspirational remarks. Though she'd only been in Canton for a month, she had lost fifteen pounds working under such Spartan conditions. She had also been receiving letters from her mother again, pleading with her to stop her movement activity. Toosweet also reported rumors that whites from Centreville were plotting to kill Annie. Reeling under all these pressures, the twenty-two-year-old was perhaps the last person who could provide inspiration at that time. In fact, she broke down while describing the constant threats, compounded by the subsistence rations, under which the CORE workers were living daily. At one point, when Moody began shaking and crying, Ed King— one of the few men present—walked up and escorted her from the dais. "You touched them, Annie. I think you got your message across," he assured her. Moody later said that she feared she was "cracking up." Nevertheless, she returned to Canton a few days later.[10]

Back in Jackson, Charlie Newell, D. C. Sullivan's friend, was preparing for his future career in the military and wasn't focused much on the civil rights struggle that summer. Newell had gone to Central High because it was the only school in Jackson with an ROTC program. He knew he liked the regimentation of the military and had committed to give two years to the Army National Guard upon graduation. As his final semester drew to a close, Newell was working at the guard's Jackson headquarters but was angry that he wasn't allowed to participate in any real military activities. "The only thing they let me do was wax jeeps and sweep the floor," Newell said. "Hell, I need[ed] to be making important military decisions!" he joked. Frustrated, he decided to join the marines.[11]

When he went to the recruiter's office to enlist, Newell ran into D. C. Sullivan's father. Admiring the young man's determination, Sullivan asked him to suggest that D. C. follow his example. When Newell did, the younger Sullivan agreed and urged his friend Snoogy Meiers to enlist as well. Together they hatched what Sullivan later called "the buddy plan." By the end of the week, the three dreamed of fighting side by side.

There was only one snag in their plan: Newell had to get released from his prior commitment to the National Guard. But the guard wouldn't let him off the hook until he served his entire two years, so Sullivan and Meiers left for marine boot camp on the Fourth of July, with Newell waving good-bye at the station, promising to find a way to join them.

Memphis Norman, Lois Chaffee, and Tom Beard continued to be involved in the civil rights movement, though each went in a different direction. Norman turned down an invitation to join an international goodwill mission called Crossroads Africa because of his prior commitments at Tougaloo, but he spoke to the group's members at Rutgers University about the situation in the South before they left for Africa. That summer, Norman also stood in for Dr. Borinski at the social science lab, handling much of the esteemed professor's correspondence and setting up speakers for the coming school year's lecture series.

Throughout this time, Norman was struggling to deal with his newfound celebrity, which he later said "was unwelcome." Although he was still uncomfortable with being in the spotlight and emphasized that he did not seek to make a name for himself as a result of the Woolworth's sit-in, he reluctantly accepted the fact that many wanted to hear his story. He thus accepted invitations to speak to civil rights groups and to participate in seminars at Millsaps College in Jackson and at Xavier University in New Orleans that fall. As a result of his speaking engagements, he often received fan mail. Many people wrote expressing support for his nonviolent behavior at the lunch counter and some even enclosed checks to assist with the movement; Norman turned those usually small sums over to Tougaloo's treasurer.[12]

Lois Chaffee's commitment to the civil rights movement deepened as a result of her Woolworth's experience. "After the Jackson Movement, I kind of knew that I had to get involved," she recalled, though "I wasn't any more clear than I had been in the beginning." But she was convinced she was becoming part of something that might help turn America in a new direction. "Inequality was one of the primary things that was ruining our country," she reflected, "making it impossible [for it to be] the land of the free and the home of the brave." After Medgar Evers's death, Chaffee joined the CORE staff and was first assigned by Dave Dennis to a rural Louisiana parish to work with poor black sharecroppers on voter registration and community-organizing campaigns.

Dennis said he sent her there to provide a place for her beloved Irish setter to roam, but Chaffee remembered little of the experience other than feeling completely unprepared for that type of work. Although being there was "eye-opening," she said the work "was certainly over my head and beyond my understanding." After a few months, she was transferred back to Jackson to help staff the CORE office and help with voter registration in the city.[13]

Tom Beard began to pull inward after Medgar Evers's death: "I just didn't want to be involved with a lot of people after that. You learn to start looking out for yourself and protecting yourself, and I had got to that point." He felt that deceit and hypocrisy had entered the Jackson Movement once Evers, with his charisma and integrity, was no longer on the scene. Nevertheless, he remained involved in the cause. "After Medgar, I was determined not to be stopped," he said. "We had gotten to be more or less like soldiers." Beard worked with Charles Evers in the months after Medgar's murder, supporting the boycott efforts by leafleting the black community and monitoring Capitol Street to identify those not complying.[14]

In fact, movement activities continued in Jackson, though at a significantly reduced level. Within two weeks after the ministers approved the agreement with Mayor Thompson, Reverend Haughton was threatening demonstrations. He and seven other black leaders met with the mayor on June 29 and pushed for further advances toward desegregation, including opening up the parks and golf course to black citizens. When Thompson refused, the group set the Fourth of July as the next date for direct action initiatives to force integration of these public facilities.[15]

Although the demonstrations were delayed for another two weeks, twelve youths were arrested on Wednesday, July 17, as they attempted to integrate two of Jackson's seven whites-only parks. The next day, another dozen were arrested at another park. On Friday afternoon, four young people were arrested for trying to join the white YMCA, and that evening tempers flared at a mass meeting at the Masonic Temple. More than three hundred demonstrators marched down Lynch Street in the first nighttime march of the Jackson Movement. Led by the increasingly activist Reverend R. L. T. Smith, the group sang freedom songs and walked peacefully toward the downtown area. After five blocks, they were met by about thirty policemen with rifles. Charles Evers urged the group to halt their protest and return to the temple, which they did. No arrests were made.[16]

At about the same time, Charles Evers and the group of ministers complained that their voter registration drive was being thwarted by the Hinds County circuit clerk who was turning away qualified applicants and slowing the registration process. John Doar and the U.S. Justice Department began investigating the clerk's practices after he closed his office for voter registration, claiming that he couldn't register voters and prepare for the upcoming guber- natorial primary at the same time. It was becoming clear that even federally sanctioned civil rights activities would not be ceded without a fight.[17]

While the Jackson Movement was having a temporary resurgence, Myr- lie Evers was preparing to accept on her husband's behalf the highest honor given by the NAACP. The Spingarn Medal, established in 1914 by an NAACP founder, Joel Spingarn, was presented annually for "the highest achievement of an American Negro." Before Medgar Evers's death, the award committee, which included the U.N.'s Ralph Bunche and author Ralph Ellison, were considering such nominees as James Baldwin, Dick Gregory, and Fred Shuttlesworth, the father of the Birmingham Movement. But the day after the Evers assassination, Roy Wilkins sent a telegram to the committee suggesting that the honor go to the fallen Jackson Movement leader. The nine committee members unani- mously agreed. Thus, Medgar Evers became the forty-eighth recipient of the Spingarn Medal, joining a select group that included Dr. Martin Luther King, Jr., Thurgood Marshall, Marian Anderson, and Langston Hughes. On July 4, 1963, Myrlie Evers accepted the award for her slain husband in Chicago—her first public appearance since the funeral.[18]

The most significant event on the national civil rights stage that year was the enormous March on Washington for Jobs and Freedom. Many of the Jack- son Movement activists participated.

One of these was Pearlena Lewis, who had taken a leave of absence from Tougaloo in the spring of 1963 to focus on her role as president of the North Jackson Youth Council and later as cochair of the Jackson Movement strategy committee. Although she had intended to return to school the following fall, the loss of Evers and other events of early summer convinced Lewis that ac- tivism should take precedence over education for a time. She dropped out of Tougaloo and took John Salter's place as advisor to the youth council, working mostly on the boycott and voter registration.[19]

In her last serious discussion with Evers—the one in which he foreshad- owed his death—Lewis recalled that he expressed interest in making sure that Mississippi's youth took part in the March on Washington. Lewis was instru- mental in ensuring that Evers's last wish was carried out, and four buses left downtown Jackson on Tuesday morning, August 27, headed for Washington. Lewis, her brother Alphonzo, and Doris Allison all participated, as did many of the Jackson ministers and members of the youth council.[20]

Allison recalled that the white bus drivers gave their passengers trouble all the way to Washington. The driver of her bus slowed down more and more as they came closer to the nation's capital, until Allison got up her nerve to challenge him. "Damn you!" she shouted. "We don't care if we don't get there, but let me tell you something: neither you nor nobody's going to put out this fire!" Because of the delay, the Mississippi group arrived later than expected, and even the NAACP's Roy Wilkins expressed concern when they didn't show up on schedule.[21]

Finally, as the march was getting under way, one of the speakers at the podium called out, "Mississippi, are you out there? Let me hear you!" Allison recalled with glee how the nearly 250 Mississippians, just arriving, responded with a shout that rang out across the mall. The crowd cheered, their relief palpable that members of the nation's most closed society had, if only briefly, found their way out.

Annie Moody traveled to the march with Ed and Jeannette King, and despite the integrated group in the car, they arrived without incident. Joan Trumpauer was also on hand. In fact, she had been working that summer in the march's press office, assisting with preparations for the historic event. She was still working when the march itself began and had to be bused to the front, where a special section had been set aside for march workers. Her late arrival was noted by a Scripps-Howard reporter under the small headline "Marched 50 Times, Misses Big One."[22]

Moody and Trumpauer had similar reactions to Dr. King's famous "I Have a Dream" speech that day. Both felt he was talking about pie in the sky. "Certainly at this point, looking back on it and reading the speech and hearing it again, I can see the majesty of it," Trumpauer later admitted. "But our reaction as young radicals was, 'He's in his own dream world.'" Moody's recollection was even more pointed: "I sat on the grass and listened to the speakers, to discover we had 'dreamers' instead of leaders.... Martin Luther King went on and on talking about his dream.... In Canton we never had time to sleep, much less dream."[23]

After the march, Trumpauer caught a ride back to Tougaloo with Moody and the Kings, and she and Moody were subjected to some name-calling when they integrated a shower stall at a federal campground in Tennessee.[24]

The rest of the Jackson contingent were assaulted with more than words on their return trip. As their buses rolled into Meridian near midnight, they discovered a crowd of about twenty-five whites who had gathered to taunt them. It seems the bus drivers had radioed ahead and arranged for the welcoming party just inside Mississippi's border. When some riders went into the bus station to use the facilities and get coffee, at least three of them were attacked inside, and another was assaulted as he returned to the bus. Although police witnessed the attacks from their headquarters across the street, their only action was to urge the riders to get back on the bus and leave town. Doris Allison reported that as the bus drove off, she saw "carloads of white men coming from all directions" aiming to harm the riders. It was a harsh welcome home after such an uplifting time away. The message was clear: no matter what you saw up there in Washington, nothing has changed down here in Mississippi.[25]

An even stronger message in reaction to the march was delivered two weeks later when a bomb exploded in the basement of the Sixteenth Street Baptist Church in downtown Birmingham, Alabama. It was Sunday morning, September 15, just before services were to begin. The explosion killed four young girls and injured at least twenty additional church-goers, many of them also children. The bombing had a devastating impact on some of the Woolworth's demonstrators. Annie Moody said that it caused her to reevaluate not only her commitment to nonviolence but also her belief in a loving God. "If Martin Luther King thinks nonviolence is really going to work for the South . . . then he is out of his mind," she told George Raymond. Raymond couldn't believe his ears. "Hold it—is that Miss Woolworth, the Nonviolent Miss Woolworth talking like that?" he asked. Moody spent the better part of the day by herself in the woods trying to come to terms with the new realities of the civil rights struggle and with a God who had seemingly deserted them.[26]

An integrated group from Tougaloo, including Ed King and Joan Trumpauer, drove to Birmingham to attend the girls' funerals. When they were stopped by Birmingham police, King wondered aloud why the police were spending their time stopping them instead of looking for those who caused the girls' deaths. "That's why we stopped you," the policeman told him.[27]

Years later, Trumpauer contrasted the experiences of Washington and Birmingham. "It was just shattering," she said, "to go from the euphoria of having this huge, huge [nonviolent] march in Washington to those kids being killed. We'd felt the nation had reached a new high of civility with the March on Washington, and then to be brought down so hard. No matter how good it felt in Washington, the reality of the South was still there. That ugliness and violence hadn't gone anywhere." To memorialize those low moments, Trumpauer walked around the church before the funeral, picking up shards of stained glass shattered in the blast and bullet casings from police shots fired during demonstrations that followed the bombing.[28]

A more public image of Trumpauer lives on from this occasion in an arresting scene in the *Eyes on the Prize* documentary series. At the end of the segment on the Birmingham bombing incident, as the girls' small coffins are being carried out of the blast-scarred church, the camera zooms in on a lone white mourner in a sea of black ones and the grief-stricken face of Joan Trumpauer fills the frame. The image holds for a long moment, then fades to black.[29]

ALTHOUGH THE JACKSON MOVEMENT'S DIRECT ACTION CAMPAIGN HAD MOSTly ended, the Tougaloo chapter of SNCC continued to focus its efforts on integration once the new school year got under way. Visits to white churches became a weekly activity, and Ed King, who led this initiative, invited Methodist ministers from the North to join black students in these integration attempts.[30] Both Memphis Norman and Joan Trumpauer participated in the church visit campaign. Trumpauer wrote an essay explaining the rationale for the change in strategy:

> The church visits have proved meaningful on two counts: they have provided a way (the only way to date) of reaching white Jackson, and they have awakened the Protestant North to the plight of the church in the South. On the steps of a church, a Negro can communicate with the "backbone" of the white community as he cannot hope to do at a lunch counter. People come to church with entirely different attitudes and motives than the ones which make them join a mob behind a Woolworth sit-in. They must face the issue and discuss it, for there is no place for them to hide.[31]

The church visits continued throughout the fall of 1963 and into the spring of 1964 as an ongoing way of pricking the conscience of white Jackson. Eventually, the police began arresting the visitors, but the visits had an impact as white congregations had to openly discuss their feelings about whether blacks should be turned away from Christian services.

Another initiative launched that summer was the Freedom Vote (or Vote for Freedom, as it was initially called)—an innovative exercise in political jockeying that would ultimately pay huge dividends. The plan was developed as an attempt to get around the voter registration roadblocks that SNCC and CORE workers had been encountering for more than two years. The effort was designed both to gain publicity and to change the psychology of local blacks who had a hard time conceiving of themselves actually voting in an election. If black citizens could simply experience what it was like to vote, the thinking went, perhaps it would demystify the process and empower them to fight harder to overcome the barriers to the ballot. Holding a mock election would educate blacks about the voting process and demonstrate that the black population would indeed vote if they had something to vote for, thus disproving the popular southern myth that African Americans had no interest in the political process. From these premises, the Freedom Vote was born.

SNCC and CORE representatives, under the banner of the Council of Federated Organizations (COFO), set up voting precincts in all counties in which they had a presence and encouraged black citizens to register to vote in the mock elections. SNCC's Bob Moses asked NAACP state president Aaron Henry to run for governor and, since COFO wanted an integrated ticket, asked Ed King to run for lieutenant governor. Both men accepted and began giving speeches across the state. Because King's face had not yet healed from the car wreck, he wore a big bandage across his right cheek.

Nearly all civil rights workers in the state threw themselves into the project, including George Raymond in Canton and Lois Chaffee and Joan Trumpauer in Jackson. On "election" day in early November, more than eighty thousand voted for the Henry-King ticket. Despite hopes for a larger turnout, organizers judged the experiment to have been a success.[32]

In the fall of 1963, some of the Woolworth's participants along with Tougaloo's SNCC contingent attempted to integrate the new coliseum the city had built to attract nationally recognized entertainers to the area. When those attempts failed, Tougaloo students wrote to entertainers booked to perform there and asked them to break their contracts because of segregation at the venue. Among entertainers who decided not to perform were opera singer Birgit Nilsson, New Orleans trumpeter Al Hirt, and Dan Blocker, who played Hoss on the hit television series *Bonanza*. When Blocker refused to appear, the entire cast of the show followed suit.

In an effort to compensate for the reduction of entertainment available locally, Tougaloo's SNCC contingent invited Joan Baez to perform at Woodworth Chapel on campus and sold tickets at the low price of two dollars per seat. The concert drew an audience of five hundred or so—three hundred of them white, Joan Trumpauer estimated, since Tougaloo was on spring break. Trumpauer was thrilled with the turnout, particularly since many of the whites in attendance were from local schools. The day after the concert, when the folk singer wanted to go shopping, Trumpauer was chosen to escort Baez. "The deal was," she said, "that if she [Baez] was spotted and if somebody took offense to her in a violent way, I would know how to get her out of there." The shopping trip, which did not include any Capitol Street stores, went off without incident.[33]

During her last year at Tougaloo, Trumpauer, along with roommate Joyce Ladner, spearheaded the campus civil rights activities, including bringing Martin Luther King in for a speech. Ladner recalled with irony how Mississippi's only true student movement wasn't given a seat on the SNCC Executive Committee until she and Trumpauer pressed the point. As a result, both were given seats on SNCC's governing board for the 1963–64 school term.[34]

Things were not going so well for the other Woolworth's demonstrators at this time. Lois Chaffee had been charged with making what the prosecution claimed was a false statement under oath, saying that she saw police beating marchers on Rose Street the day John Salter's head was cracked open with a billy club. In early December 1963, Chaffee was tried and convicted of perjury and was forced to spend three weeks in the Hinds County jail while her case was appealed. Her bond was set at the extraordinary sum of five thousand dollars, and neither the NAACP nor any other group was willing to bail her out. The only visits she received during her incarceration were from Ed King, who brought her a copy of Thoreau's writings on civil disobedience. "I read that and played the radio," she recalled. "That was about it."

Chaffee also noted the impact her arrest and participation in demonstrations had on her family. Her father never quite got over some of the things she did during her civil rights days and some family members continued to speak in hushed tones about her jail time thirty years later. But she said that during her incarceration, her father did attempt to raise a fuss: "He was calling congressmen and stuff like that. The Idaho governor was calling the Mississippi governor, and the Idaho senator was calling the Mississippi senator." The response he received was that his eldest daughter "was no damned good!"[35]

Up in Canton during the late summer and fall of 1963, Annie Moody and George Raymond were continuing to endure hardship, rejection, and harassment from the police and others. Moody suffered bouts of anxiety, was unable to sleep in the Freedom House without sleeping pills, and worried constantly about whether she would live to see the next day. The last straw for Moody, however, was when she visited a friend in Jackson in early October and was shown a handbill produced by the Klan that had been mistakenly delivered to a black home. It was a crude hit list on which she was pictured, as were Joan Trumpauer, John Salter, Ed King, Bob Moses, Medgar Evers, James Meredith, and Emmett Till. The faces of those already killed had been x-ed out. Moody was stunned and decided to leave Canton a few weeks later.[36]

After the March on Washington, Pearlena Lewis threw herself into her work with the NAACP and the implementation phase of the Jackson Movement. She assisted Charles Evers in continuing the boycott, which made its most dramatic comeback during the Christmas season of 1963, exactly one year after the Jackson Movement's original demonstrations had begun. Nationally, the NAACP, SCLC, and other civil rights organizations declared that Christmas 1963 would be a "Black Christmas" to emphasize the terrible losses the black community had suffered during the year—primarily the deaths of Medgar Evers and the four little girls from Birmingham—as well as to commemorate the assassination of President Kennedy, which occurred in November of that year. No lights were to be hung, no decorations purchased, no Christmas trees brought home. December was declared a month of mourning. Lewis described how in Jackson, phone trees were used to inform the entire black community just as they had been used with the boycott a year earlier, and volunteers were sent around to ensure compliance. The Jackson NAACP printed a brochure with photographs of Medgar Evers and President Kennedy on the cover and text that read, "Sure, children enjoy lots of toys and gifts, but they will appreciate first class citizenship more."[37]

The Black Christmas project was a huge success, forcing additional hardships on the Capitol Street businesses that still refused to compromise with the black community and causing the first of those stores to close its doors. Herman's Jewelry Store, just up the block from Woolworth's, along with O.P.O. Men's Wear and King the Tailor had liquidation sales during December. A modest amount of picketing also occurred to emphasize the boycott's message. Six mothers were arrested for parading without a permit on Friday, December 6—almost exactly a year from when the first Jackson Movement pickets appeared in front of Woolworth's. By February, when two more Capitol Street stores went out of business, Pearlena Lewis was working on voter registration activities and providing monthly progress reports to Doris Allison, who continued to serve as president of the Jackson NAACP.[38]

The Jackson Movement had national implications for its sponsoring organization, as well. In January 1964, the NAACP announced that for the first time its membership exceeded the half-million mark—an increase of nearly 30 percent over the prior year. The movement—and particularly the death of Medgar Evers—had put the association back on the map and revitalized, for a time, its outdated image.[39]

AS THE NEW YEAR OF 1964 DAWNED, JACKSON'S FOCUS TURNED TO THE TRIAL of the man accused of assassinating Medgar Evers. Byron De La Beckwith, an oddball southern aristocrat, had been arrested within ten days of the shooting and held without bond, much of the time in the Hinds County jail in Jackson.[40]

Beckwith's trial, which began in late January, proved an interesting exercise for Mississippi. Most believed the outcome was a foregone conclusion and that Beckwith would be acquitted. But an earnest district attorney named Bill Waller put together a strong case against Beckwith. Though the activists railed at the occasional racist characterizations of Medgar Evers, most reports indicate that Waller—who would later become governor of Mississippi—did a good job of presenting the evidence. Nonetheless, the district attorney was hamstrung by state tradition, under which a white person had never been convicted of killing a black. The all-white male jury didn't help matters, either. The politically charged nature of the trial was heightened when Ross Barnett, who had just ended his term as governor, entered the courtroom on more than one occasion, shook hands with Beckwith, and held extended conversations with him in the presence of the jurors.[41]

The trial was unprecedented for other reasons, as well. In an attempt to avoid racial conflicts, the legislature allowed the courtroom to be integrated. As a result, many local activists, including groups from Tougaloo, made it a point to show up daily. Joan Trumpauer chronicled the trial in one of her weekly updates to friends:

> [At] the Beckwith trial, it was hard to tell the prosecution from the defense. There was evidence that should have been investigated which [was] not. The prosecution, during the choosing of the jury, consistently referred to Beckwith as "courteous gentleman" and brought out that he was a Mason, churchman, etc. Medgar was that "obnoxious nigger," "repulsive," etc. People were frisked going in, and you couldn't wear freedom buttons in. One day it was announced they would have to tighten up on security measures because of the left wing types and outsiders who were going. That means integrationists and exchange students

from Tougaloo. One day they arrested a Negro lady in court. We did our best to get students in to the trial. Usually two or three car loads a day.[42]

On Friday, February 6, when the jury recessed to deliberate Beckwith's fate, Trumpauer claimed that "Jackson was a police state." Ed King was driving Trumpauer and another Tougaloo student into town for the trial that day, and Trumpauer recalled that their car was followed from the time they left campus until they reached the downtown area. Then the police stopped the car and charged King with failing to signal when he turned off State Street. All three riders were taken to the basement where policemen with German shepherds on slack leashes held their prisoners in check. "They brought out the dogs and let them work themselves into a frenzy and leap at us," Trumpauer reported. "The closest they came was within a foot and a half of me." "I have decided," she concluded, "that that is one way I don't want to go."[43]

To the surprise of nearly all of Jackson, the trial ended in a hung jury rather than acquittal—with six jurors voting guilty—leaving the door open for another trial. Waller tried again two months later with the same result, although this time the jury split eight to four in Beckwith's favor. By mid-April, Beckwith was a free man, given a hero's welcome when he returned to his hometown of Greenwood in the Mississippi Delta.[44]

Aside from the diversions of the Beckwith trial, voter registration efforts continued to be the primary civil rights activities across Mississippi. George Raymond continued to doggedly pursue the ballot for the mostly rural Madison County black residents, with some startling successes. Raymond organized events known as Freedom Days at the county courthouse.

A Freedom Day was part media event, part grassroots political organizing, part scare tactic. On that day, all black adults were asked to go en masse to the courthouse to register to vote, rather than going a few at a time. By making voter registration an event rather than an everyday occurrence, Freedom Days could attract media attention. Because the event was scheduled rather than spontaneous, the Justice Department could be on hand to witness how the county clerks treated the registrants. Freedom Days also bolstered the spirits of the wary black citizens who were reluctant to attempt to register in small groups for fear of violent reprisals.[45]

Raymond organized three Freedom Days during the late winter and spring of 1964, with strong turnout each time. Raymond's supervisor Dave Dennis marveled at his tenacity. "He would spend morning, noon, and night talking to people, working in those rural areas," recalled Dave Dennis. "He did a hell of a job." Dennis remembered rural people coming into Canton in horse-drawn buggies, and when the media asked them why they were there, they would respond, "We coming to vote for George Raymond!" They may not have fully understood the process, but they showed up as a tribute to their new friend.[46]

Raymond scheduled the third Freedom Day just a few days before Tougaloo's 1964 graduation exercises. Annie Moody, who had left Canton the prior November and moved to New Orleans, hastily returned to Mississippi when she found out that she'd be able to graduate with the rest of her class. Tougaloo had finally accepted her transfer credits from Natchez College. Moody decided to make the day trip to Canton when she heard about the Freedom Day in late May and was amazed at the transformation that had occurred there. Hundreds of adults were ready to march on the courthouse to register to vote; hundreds more teens planned to march around the town square in support. Events quickly turned violent, however, when local law enforcement showed up and began to harass the youths. One young man was beaten so brutally that he was feared dead. Fifty-five individuals were arrested when a cohort of adults and teens decided to march in defiance of police prohibitions.[47]

After witnessing the day's events, Moody returned to Tougaloo with a warning to Ed and Jeannette King, Joan Trumpauer, and others who were planning to attend a mass meeting in Canton that night. Against Moody's advice, however, the group went to the meeting and were returning to Jackson when their car was suddenly run off the road by two cars and a truck, all full of angry, armed white men. Trumpauer remembered the scene: "A dozen men. Armed. Clubs. Tire [irons]. Wrenches. Set to do us in."[48]

Tougaloo social science professor Hamid Kizilbash of Pakistan, who was driving, thoughtlessly opened his window, and some of the men unlocked his door, pulled him out, and began beating him on the head with a billy club. Ed King recalled that the day before, on the first anniversary of the Woolworth's sit-in, an international incident had flared in Jackson when a dignitary from India had been taken into police custody for staging an impromptu sit-in at a Capitol Street restaurant. The story had been front-page news that morning. Thinking quickly, King pleaded with the assailants to let their captive go, asserting that Kizilbash also was Indian and that the attackers would call down the wrath of the State Department and the rest of the federal government if their victim were seriously harmed. The story convinced the men to release Kizilbash, and the carful of Tougaloo activists sped back to Jackson. There, they attempted to complain directly to Governor Johnson, but after being rebuffed at the governor's mansion on Capitol Street, they returned to campus and called the Justice Department and the FBI.[49]

Trumpauer later told Moody, "If I have ever been close to death, it was tonight." More than thirty years later, Trumpauer still felt a tremor when she thought about that night. "That's probably the closest I came to dying in Mississippi," she said. "We just all figured we were goners. All of us. We sort of made our peace with the Lord since we knew we were going to die."[50]

ON SUNDAY, MAY 31, MEMPHIS NORMAN, JOAN TRUMPAUER, AND ANNIE MOODY graduated along with ninety-five other Tougaloo students. Moody received a bachelor of science in biology; Norman, a cum laude bachelor of arts in sociology; and Trumpauer, a magna cum laude bachelor of arts in history. Ed King delivered the opening prayer, and Dr. Beittel presented the diplomas.[51]

It would be the college president's last Tougaloo commencement. Beittel had made a surprise announcement the prior month, telling faculty in a hastily arranged staff meeting that he would be stepping down before the beginning of fall term. The news came as a shock to many present since Beittel had come to Tougaloo on the promise that he would stay until he was seventy. Back in January, however, the board had insisted on his departure, pointing out disingenuously that he had reached the typical retirement age of sixty-five the month before.[52]

Stories abound as to the reasons for Beittel's forced resignation. Some, particularly those who attended Tougaloo at the time, point to student unrest on campus as a cause. Joan Trumpauer, in fact, claimed that students referred to the college president as "Hitler" because of his diminutive stature, his heavy mustache, and his forceful personality. At the time, some students were protesting to demand higher hourly wages for on-campus jobs.[53]

Others suggest that the American Missionary Association was making way for a stronger, more fiscally responsible administrator. The college was struggling financially, and the board of trustees was looking for a more aggressive approach to fund-raising. "His [Beittel's] experience was had in another era when the American Missionary Association picked up the deficit," wrote Tougaloo board member and AMA executive Wes Hotchkiss. "He just hasn't been able to operate in the contemporary scene of academic administration."[54]

Ed King believed that "Beittel was a direct casualty of Woolworth's," and cited the timing of his ouster as proof. It was less than a month after Beittel was photographed with his students making their stand at Woolworth's that a select group of board members began the discussions about Tougaloo's future that led to Beittel's resignation.[55]

Even the head of the Mississippi State Sovereignty Commission, Erle Johnston, took credit for Beittel's release. He and others from the Commission had visited the AMA brass asking for Beittel's (and King's) removal just days before the announcement of Beittel's retirement. In return, they promised favorable treatment for Tougaloo by the state legislature, which was once again threatening to shut down the college because of its role in the Jackson Movement.[56]

In an interview with historian John Dittmer, Beittel pleaded ignorance as to the reasons for his removal.[57] Dittmer's further investigation, however, uncovered political and academic treachery that, though somewhat common for the period, still seems shocking. Tougaloo's board had initiated a cooperative relationship with Brown University, hoping to gain access to foundation and grant funding to put the college onto better financial footing. Brown's president, Barnaby Keeney—later discovered to be a CIA operative—took an active interest in Tougaloo, but not in its storied civil rights support. Dittmer posits that Beittel's dismissal was part of Keeney's (and by suggestion, the U.S. government's) effort to steer the college away from activism. Though Tougaloo gained the financial support it needed, "the college would never again be at the center of civil rights activity," Dittmer wrote.[58]

Upon hearing of the forced resignation (which the Associated Press reported was due to health concerns), poet and literary scholar Elizabeth Sewell, who was spending the school year at Tougaloo as a visiting professor, wrote a poem in Beittel's honor. "*This has been quite a year for heads falling,*" she began. Then she referred to the horrible report that the head of one of the little girls killed in Birmingham had been severed in the bomb blast and mentioned the bullets that pierced President Kennedy's skull. She went on to describe Beittel with

> *. . . old, old words*
> *And I think of two for you,*
> *Integrity and valour,*
> *Because they came to me when I first met you*
> *That hot September*
> *Half a year, or a lifetime, ago,*
> *And nothing since to make me change my mind.*[59]

As Tougaloo's 1964 commencement exercises ended, Ed King invited Annie Moody, Joan Trumpauer, and Memphis Norman—the "three Woolworth's orphans," as Trumpauer tagged them—to dinner on graduation night, since none of the graduates' families had shown up. Ed and Jeannette King took the three to Steven's Kitchen on Farish Street in the black business district for a steak dinner. It was the last time this many of the Woolworth's demonstrators would be together in Jackson—a moment to celebrate before moving on.[60]

AS THE ONE-YEAR ANNIVERSARY OF THE ASSASSINATION OF MEDGAR EVERS approached, the NAACP attempted to use the commemoration as a way to increase its membership ranks even further. Indicating that the organization had successfully defended more than six hundred Jackson Movement demonstrators in the courts, Roy Wilkins urged all of the association's branches to hold a "Medgar Evers Memorial event on or about June 12" and crassly called for "100,000 new Medgar Evers memberships." The letter to branches went on: "Let not Medgar Evers' death have been in vain." Indeed, not when it could add to the NAACP's coffers.[61]

As a more fitting memorial, the Civil Rights Act of 1964 was passed by the U.S. Congress that same June. The act, which had been suggested by President Kennedy in his speech the night of Evers's murder, was signed into law by Kennedy's successor, Lyndon Johnson, on July 2, 1964. The act guaranteed equal treatment of all people nationwide in public accommodations, employment, and education.[62] Charles Evers and the Mississippi NAACP decided to test compliance with the act. To the surprise of all—and despite the objections of local and state lawmakers—the Jackson Chamber of Commerce came out in favor of the new law and recommended that their businesses comply. On July 5, a delegation of national NAACP officials, along with Evers and local NAACP volunteers, successfully checked into hotels and ate in restaurants on and around Capitol Street. Groups of NAACP representatives, including Pearlena Lewis, then went around the state testing the larger cities for compliance with the new law; in almost every one, they met with success. By the end of the month, Evers was suggesting that the Capitol Street boycott be called off, subject to a period of testing for compliance with the demands of the Jackson Movement. Jackson's *Clarion-Ledger* heralded the end of the boycott with the headline "Jackson Movement Lifts Embargo on Purchasing," reporting that twenty-three stores had gone out of business on Capitol Street since the protest had begun fourteen months earlier.[63]

THUS, THE JACKSON MOVEMENT QUIETLY CAME TO AN END MORE THAN A year and a half after that first picketing occurred on Capitol Street in December 1962. Though the strategy committee continued, with Pearlena Lewis serving as its secretary throughout 1964, it essentially was absorbed by Charles Evers's state NAACP apparatus, becoming an arm for pushing for a variety of social changes, such as the integration of Jackson's schools and the ever-present goal of voter registration.[64]

It is difficult to assess the true impact of the Jackson Movement, since its real goal was to end the apartheid system that had so vigorously been enforced in Jackson, and to gain for blacks equal access to the city's economic, political, and social power structures. Putting stores out of business wasn't really the point. As it turned out, many businesses pulled up stakes on Capitol Street only to reappear at suburban malls, where more whites tended to live than blacks, and far removed from the easy access of inner city populations. It would be unfair to assume, however, that because of such shifting demographics, the Jackson Movement's impact was blunted. After all, much of America went suburban at about this time.

John Salter, the Jackson Movement's radical heart, believed the movement had a substantial impact not only on Jackson, but on Mississippi as a whole. "[The Jackson Movement] cracked the establishment in Jackson once and for

all. It certainly destroyed once and forever the self-serving myth [of] Missis-
sippi black satisfaction. It played a major role in mobilizing black Mississippi.
And it played a major role in securing the eventual passage of the 1964 Civil
Rights Act."[65]

Salter also accurately suggested that because of the Jackson Movement's
strident stance, when the Civil Rights Act was passed, "a majority of Jackson
merchants decided to comply with it, even though the Citizens' Council attempted to pressure them against it. Their compliance can be traced directly
to the movement a year before."

Certainly the Civil Rights Act of 1964 and the Voting Rights Act of 1965
were the keys that opened the doors for America's black citizens to fully grasp
the freedoms that their white counterparts enjoyed. And the Jackson Movement, as part of the overall civil rights movement in this country, contributed
to the securing of those freedoms.

Salter made one final observation about the Jackson Movement, which
historians and even fellow activists may dispute, but which seems worthy of
note. "The Jackson Movement was the most massive grassroots upheaval that
Mississippi has ever had," he said. "It's never had anything like that again."[66]

Pearlena Lewis, Salter's cochair of the strategy committee, had a less sweeping but equally relevant take on the Jackson Movement's accomplishments.
Looking back on her days as a student leader with pride, Lewis suggested that
her example at Woolworth's—and that of those who followed her into the Jackson Movement—changed the psychology of the beaten-down black masses
in Mississippi. "That sense of hopelessness just didn't seem as hopeless after
the Jackson Movement," she said. "[People] saw that we had enough belief in
ourselves and it gave them the courage to sit there and say, 'I want this to be
changed!'" Lewis truly believed that, as a result of her determined, principled
protest at Woolworth's, she—and all those who participated in Jackson's upheaval of 1963—witnessed firsthand "the beginning of change in Mississippi."[67]

CHAPTER 11

VETERANS OF DOMESTIC WARS

†

Medgar W.
Evers

Mississippi
TEC 5
QMC
WORLD WAR II

JUL 2 1925
JUN 12 1963

MEDGAR EVERS IS BURIED ON THE EDGE OF A SMALL OAK GROVE, JUST INSIDE the north gate of Arlington Cemetery, the one directly opposite the Lincoln Memorial. The solitary grave site is easy to find. Visitors entering the north gate need go only about a hundred paces up a slight hill, past a tall ivy-covered arbor on the right, to a flight of concrete stairs. There, down about two dozen steps and to the right is where the fallen hero was laid to rest.[1]

In this quiet spot, the general of the nonviolent Jackson Movement was buried after his shockingly violent death. Three rounds of gun blasts and the sorrowful sound of taps sent his spirit on while his wife, children, and brother just stared into the emptiness that had been shot through their lives.[2] It was a veteran's funeral, one that Evers had earned on the battlefields of France in World War II. But he deserved this honor just as much for his heroic efforts in another conflict as well: America's domestic war of freedom by and for its own citizens.

In an interview shortly before his murder, Evers told a Washington-based reporter, "I've been fighting for America just as much as the soldiers in Viet Nam."[3] The same could be said of all of the Woolworth's demonstrators. They are veterans of that same domestic war. And like any group of veterans, some emerged in better shape than others from the harrowing stress of daily facing the shadow of death. Some got out intact, stronger for the ordeal. Others lost too much along the way and had to retreat to recover some measure of stability. Still others stayed too long at the front and became so battle-scarred that they died soon after or were so wounded that their lives were irreparably damaged. The rest of their story, like the most intensive and memorable period of their lives, is filled with both hope and sadness. For some, it has not yet reached an end.

Anne Moody

ANNE MOODY'S *COMING OF AGE IN MISSISSIPPI* ENDS WITH HER BOARDING A bus to Washington, D.C., in June 1964 to participate in the COFO hearings, designed to bring more attention to conditions in Mississippi. On that trip, she hooked up with twelve-year-old Gene Young, an inspirational speaker and Jackson Movement participant who was also set to testify.[4] After the hearings—which were moderately successful, at best—Moody stayed in Washington with Young and together they began to speak at CORE fund-raisers. At one of those events, a United Auto Workers convention in Atlantic City, Anne was scheduled to speak for thirty-five minutes. She went on, she claimed, for two and a half hours. Afterwards, they passed the hat and twenty thousand dollars was raised.[5]

When Anne Moody—who had come to prefer the more formal version of her name—became a hit on the speaking circuit, baseball phenomenon Jackie Robinson and his wife joined a UAW official and others in encouraging her to write a book about her experiences. After a year living in New York and working as the civil rights project coordinator at Cornell University's School of Labor Relations, Moody quit her job and began to write. When she gave a hundred pages to Robinson's editor, she was offered a contract on the spot. Fearing that the editor was only doing her a favor because of her connection to Robinson, she took the manuscript to a second editor for another opinion. That editor happened to be the now-celebrated author E. L. Doctorow, then working for Dial Press. When Dial offered Moody a contract with a big advance, she took it and spent the next year writing and enjoying her first taste of economic freedom.

There is some speculation among Moody's civil rights associates that she didn't really write her memoir. Rumors have circulated for years that Lois Chaffee, who had also moved to New York and was close to Moody, had a lot to do with the manuscript. Chaffee, however, adamantly denied such speculation, saying that whenever she tried to give Moody editorial advice, she was sharply dissuaded from changing even a comma. Moody apparently talked through her earlier chapters with Chaffee and asked her to proofread parts and help with the typing, but that was the extent of Chaffee's involvement.[6]

When Doctorow first read Moody's manuscript, "we all realized its accomplishment immediately," he said.[7] For editing, he assigned it to Joyce Johnson, who had just joined Dial. Like Doctorow, Johnson was an accomplished editor and would go on to become a best-selling author. She had been Jack Kerouac's lover at the time his *On the Road* was published in 1957; her memoir of that period, *Minor Characters*, would later win the National Book Critics Circle Award. Johnson would make her editorial reputation in the late 1960s, working with such authors as LeRoi Jones (aka Amiri Baraka), H. Rap Brown, and Abbie Hoffman, and even at this point she was strongly committed to bringing into print accounts of civil rights activists.

"Anne was a natural storyteller," Johnson recalled, "and her material was very powerful and important. But . . . the book was in a raw state. It needed structure, it needed a selective eye, it needed transitions and rewrites. . . . I did what was called 'a very heavy edit,' asking Anne to write some additional material to fill in certain gaps." Moody reportedly was furious with the changes and the delay the editing process caused, but finally accepted Johnson's remarkable job in turning the fledgling work of a first-time author into a masterpiece. Johnson also suggested the title—a reference to Margaret Mead's *Coming of Age in Samoa*—as an indication of just how foreign and ritualistic were the mores and culture of Mississippi.[8]

The book was released in December 1968 to rave reviews, including one by Senator Edward Kennedy in the *New York Times*.[9] Moody was interviewed on the *Today* show, and the book, an alternate selection of the Book-of-the-Month Club, ultimately became a best seller. After a time, however, Moody found that the constant attention was a distraction from the writing she wanted to do, so she and her husband—"a Jewish guy from Brooklyn," whom she had married in 1967—moved to Europe.[10] But there, she discovered that she and her book were also amazingly popular. The book was translated into seven languages and was embraced as an American classic in Germany. So taken were German publishers with her work that future Nobel Prize–winning author Heinrich Böll wrote a foreword to the German edition and his wife, Annemarie, handled the translation. Böll titled his piece "Farewell to Uncle Tom," the accommodating slave hero of Harriet Beecher Stowe's novel *Uncle Tom's Cabin*. In it, Böll described Moody's style as "purely documentary . . . everything is addressed with a striking combination of common sense and sensibility." He saw Moody's coming of age as a metaphor for what was then happening globally—a questioning of all the established order. "The farewell to Uncle Tom is international," Böll concluded.[11]

As a result of the Bölls' patronage, Moody moved with her husband from France, where they had first settled, to Germany. Because of citizenship issues, she returned to the United States briefly to give birth to a son, then returned with him to Berlin in 1972, where the city had awarded her a one-year fellowship. When her residency ended, she moved to a small town outside of Frankfurt and there vigorously pursued her writing career.

In 1975, Harper & Row published a collection of Moody's stories titled *Mr. Death*, which were marketed as children's literature but which seem far more appropriate for adults. In a way reminiscent of the southern gothic style of Flannery O'Connor, each of the four stories describes a bizarre encounter with death by a young boy or girl. The stories confirm Moody's talent and are similar in subject matter to parts of *Coming of Age*, but the book was not a success.[12]

Moody divorced her husband in 1977 and remained in Europe until 1984 with her son. Upon their return to the States, she wandered cross continent, seeking to solidify her hard-won celebrity status, but having a rough go of it. Moody is said to have written other manuscripts—including a sequel to *Coming of Age* called *Farewell to Toosweet* about the death of her mother and her own subsequent life—but nothing additional has been published at this point. Nevertheless, *Coming of Age in Mississippi*, which has never gone out of print, is read in history, literature, and women's studies courses in high schools, colleges, and universities across the globe.

In the late 1990s, Moody inherited some property in her native Wilkinson County—the place she believed she'd never return to—and settled there at the turn of the century. It is, perhaps, an apt conclusion to her story that she finally found a modicum of peace where her mother, her siblings, and she had scratched so fiercely to find sustenance in that once impossible place.

Joan Trumpauer

AFTER GRADUATING FROM TOUGALOO, JOAN TRUMPAUER RETURNED TO HER home turf in Washington, D.C., and never returned to work in Mississippi. Despite a letter from Ed King inviting her to participate in the project that would come to be known as Freedom Summer, Trumpauer felt that there was a time and place for everything and, once she had graduated, it was time to leave Mississippi and the student movement.[13]

In Washington, she worked in a clerical job with the Smithsonian Institution for a year. Eventually she landed a role in the newly created Community Relations Service of the Justice Department, headed by Roy Wilkins's nephew Roger. Here she helped handle the government's response to civil rights crises. Through that job, she met the man who became her second husband, changing her name once again, this time to Joan Mulholland. After some travel abroad, the Mulhollands settled in Arlington, Virginia, and had five sons—fulfilling for a time Joan's long-held intention to live a traditional family life. The marriage broke up, however, in 1975 and she became a single parent, though her husband helped raise and support the children as did her parents, with whom she had reconciled after returning from Mississippi.

Following the divorce, Mulholland took a job as a teacher's assistant in the Arlington County (VA) elementary school system because her hours would accommodate the boys' schedules. Her love of the social sciences led her to develop a novel approach to multicultural studies long before the term gained popularity. She continued to delight in learning about vastly different cultures, primarily those of indigenous peoples, and in translating their customs into educational projects for her students. She felt that her work connected to her earlier work in civil rights. "I have a long-term interest in human relations and equal treatment of people," she said. "[This] has been expressed in the way I've worked with special education and second language students . . . to see that they get an equal chance." Calling her approach "the justice of status," Mulholland remained determined to change how the disadvantaged are treated in American society. She retired from full-time teaching in 2008.

Mulholland kept in touch with her movement friends and would often attend civil rights reunions and other events honoring heroes of that struggle. Until recently, she seldom talked about her own heroism, believing that what she did was not exceptional. In the last few years, however, she has begun to take her experiences and archival materials into high school and college classrooms to give students a first-person account of a movement that changed the course of American history. She has appeared in a variety of books and documentaries about the civil rights movement, including the Stanley Nelson film *Freedom Riders*, commemorating the fiftieth anniversary of the historic Freedom Rides.

D. C. Sullivan

D. C. SULLIVAN'S FRIEND CHARLIE NEWELL NEVER DID JOIN SULLIVAN AND Snoogy Meiers in the marines.[14] "I showed up at Fort Polk," Newell recalled, "and when I was exposed to army basic training . . . it suddenly got military enough for me." By that time the other friends in the "buddy plan" had seen more military maneuvers than they had ever hoped to as well. Years later, Sullivan admitted that he had been foolish to sign up for an optional fourth year when he could have enlisted for only three.

Sullivan and Meiers went through basic training at Parris Island, South Carolina, then moved on for additional training in North Carolina. Sullivan was shipped off to Guantánamo, Cuba, just a year after the Cuban missile crisis. A year later, he was sent to another hot spot—Santo Domingo, capital of the Dominican Republic, where in April 1965 U.S. troops were sent in under suspicious circumstances, ostensibly to keep communists at bay after a popular revolt against an authoritarian military regime. When Sullivan returned from the Caribbean, the twenty-one-year-old became an expert in a new weapon—a portable, disposable rocket launcher. Thanks to his perfect aim, the young rebel was asked to train Marine Corps leaders in its usage, and he spent six months at the U.S. Marine base in Quantico, Virginia.

When that stint ended, Sullivan exhibited the kind of heroism that so often surfaces in wartime. He had received orders to report to Norfolk, Virginia, while a friend of his who had recently married and had a baby on the way was assigned to duty in Vietnam. Immediately, Sullivan offered to swap assignments with him. The exchange was hastily arranged, and within a few weeks D. C. Sullivan was on his way to Southeast Asia.

North of Da Nang, just four months after his arrival, Sullivan was leaving mail call when a volley of mortars exploded around him. He was near the ammo bunker, so he grabbed his gun and started shooting back, but his attackers were too quick. He caught one bullet in the chest, and as he spun around, another in the back. Seeing blood spurting from his chest and thinking that he had been hit in the heart, Sullivan "took off running." He was tackled by a fellow corpsman, who ripped the cellophane off his packet of cigarettes and held it over the hole in Sullivan's chest until a medevac helicopter arrived. By that time, one of Sullivan's lungs had collapsed and the other was filling with blood. He blacked out when he was laid on the floor of the chopper and only woke up when the medical team began siphoning blood from his one good lung.

In an uncanny twist of fate, on the very day he was shot, D. C. Sullivan had received a letter from the woman whose husband he had traded places with. She told him they had named the baby Dorman Carroll after him. Unhappily, however, the father of the new little D.C. had been sent to Vietnam a few months after the swap took place and had been killed. Sullivan kept the letter, stained with his own blood, that brought him this strange and sorrowful news.

When he was sent to recover at a military hospital in Tennessee, Sullivan had an unlikely reunion with some of his Central High graduating class who had preceded him there as war veterans. Sullivan had received the kind of wounds that cause lifelong damage. Some of the shell that punctured his lungs lodged in the muscle around the heart and was never removed. He also lost feeling in two fingers and had chronic pain in one arm. When his four-year stint was up, Sullivan was more than ready to move on. He was honorably discharged and awarded a medical disability.

When he returned home in midsummer 1967, Sullivan knew that college would be a waste of time for him. As he acknowledged, "I loved to party too much. There wasn't no use spending my parents' money to go to college." Instead, he went to work to learn a trade. First he took a job blowing insulation into newly built homes. When that work didn't suit him, he joined the Local

406 of the Sheetmetal Workers Union and loved it. He made a career of sheet-metal work and never looked back.

The same year that he got out of the service, Sullivan met his wife-to-be while working at the Mississippi State Fair. Wanda was a student at Belhaven College in Jackson; D.C., with his new LeMans, infectious smile, and good-natured wit, won her over in an instant. They were married in 1968. Three years later, they moved to Wanda's hometown of Laurel, Mississippi, and their first child, Chad, was born in 1972. Sullivan eventually went into business for himself, having tired of union politics and what to him seemed illogical rules. The Sullivans had their second child, Tina, whom D. C. caddishly named after a former girlfriend.

Sullivan turned into the "good ole boy" he always knew he was: friendly, likable, still a bit of the class clown. He would never miss a Central High reunion, but as he looked over some old yearbooks, he counted an inordinate number of classmates who had either met untimely deaths or lived miserable lives. Sullivan, it turned out, was one of the lucky ones.

Not one to mince words, Sullivan continued to believe that integration was the wrong path for the South to take. He admitted to having black acquaintances, who he swore were genuinely good people, but none with whom he would choose to socialize. Even though his children went to integrated schools, he couldn't fathom a completely integrated society.

Sullivan fondly remembered the role he played that day in Woolworth's and relished the fact that his image in Fred Blackwell's photograph would out-live him. Wanda would spot the photo every so often and point it out to her husband; they had a few versions of it lying around the house. He continued to wear his defiance of the move toward integration as a badge of honor and his best friends continued to feel likewise, he claimed. They were among the remaining defenders of old Dixie, waiting patiently for a third Civil War, which he felt certain they would win.

John Salter

JOHN SALTER'S YEARS OF EXPERIENCE IN SOCIAL MOVEMENTS LED TO HIS PHI-losophy of how to survive as an activist. He came to believe that the answer is to keep moving: "You just simply recognize that danger lurk[s] everywhere," he said. "You [don't] respond to it by rushing recklessly ahead, or freezing, or retreating. You simply move step by step ... like walking through a swamp full of snakes and alligators."[15]

When Salter left Mississippi and joined the staff of the Southern Confer-ence Educational Fund, he set up a regional office in Raleigh, North Carolina.

His work for SCEF included joint speaking tours with the legendary Ella Baker, SCEF's then-Atlanta-based field representative, but he focused primarily on organizing voter registration and desegregation drives in northeastern North Carolina, an area he claimed was "showing signs of be[coming] the 'Klan Capital of the South.'" He entered one police station to find the poster "Be a Man, Join the Klan" hanging on the wall, and he said that dues for the organization were collected at police headquarters. Again with Bill Kuntsler, Salter initiated federal lawsuits against discriminatory voter registration practices and for the rights of black teachers to participate in civil rights activities. He also joined numerous demonstrations, was arrested frequently, and received death threats—just like Jackson all over again. Salter's work also extended into areas of economic enfranchisement, which was becoming a focus for many civil rights workers at that time.[16]

After ending up on the losing end of a power struggle over SCEF's future, Salter took a teaching position at Goddard College in Vermont in 1965. He was enticed back to North Carolina in June 1966 to work in Lyndon Johnson's War on Poverty as director of training for the North Carolina Fund, an antipoverty program headquartered in Durham and supported by the state and federal governments. His job was to train young black, Native American, and white community action technicians how to organize grassroots groups, but on weekends he would head east to help his old movement groups organize around economic issues. Once his arrangement with the North Carolina Fund ended in the summer of 1967, Salter and family, including new son, John III, moved to Seattle, where Salter took graduate courses in the sociology of education at the University of Washington. He referred to this period as the family's "emergence" from the South's second Civil War and believed that they fared about as well as anyone who had spent significant time there during that period: "For the better part of six years, we had been immersed in combat zones. Unlike many, I didn't crack up."

Salter continued his pattern of alternating between working for social causes he believed in and teaching. In the fall of 1968 he spent a year teaching sociology at Coe College in Cedar Rapids, Iowa and, on the side, helped organize maintenance workers into Local 1162 of the State, County, and Municipal Workers Union. Salter and his family next spent four years in Chicago, where he directed community organization activities in neighborhoods on the city's depressed South Side. Salter also began at this time to increase his involvement in the struggle for the rights of Native Americans, a cause that became his passion in later life.

In the summer of 1978, after three years teaching urban planning at the University of Iowa and two years as the first director of social justice for the Catholic Diocese of Rochester, New York, Salter returned home to northern Arizona, where he taught education and social sciences for the next three years at the Navajo Community College—an institution established for the Navajo peoples by one of his father's students. Salter became an important part of the fledgling experimental college, heading its academic standards and curriculum committees, founding the student court system, serving as president of its chapter of the American Association of University Professors, and helping lobby for additional funding. Also during this time, Salter wrote his memoir, *Jackson, Mississippi: An American Chronicle of Struggle and Schism.*

From Arizona, Salter accepted a professorship at the University of North Dakota in Grand Forks and, from 1981 through 1994, taught in the Indian Studies program, receiving tenure in 1983 and serving as chair of the department for four years. Salter continued his traditional pattern of community activism and was involved in a variety of committees to improve police relations with the community and to enhance the lives of North Dakota's indigenous people. Perhaps most significantly, Salter organized the legal defense for a celebrated religious freedom case involving the use of peyote in native religious ceremonies. Known as the Warner case for its two main defendants, the case was won in federal court on appeal.

While on a trip with his elder son to Mississippi in 1988, Salter had one of the strangest experiences of his life. Both he and his son recount, independently, that while traveling on a backwoods highway in Wisconsin, they were diverted onto a rough side road and up into some woods. There they claim to have been taken on board a small, landed alien spacecraft, medically tested, treated with potent healing agents, then returned to their vehicle. Salter said that "the atmosphere throughout was very friendly," but at first neither he nor his son could remember anything about it. Only later did they start to piece together what had occurred. Salter swears by this story and points to many improvements in his body chemistry and health to support the point. As a result, he became a staunch believer in friendly extraterrestrial life and lectured extensively on the subject.

Salter also continued to be a strong defender of human rights and stayed active in causes that he considered to be important. As one who viewed nonviolence more as a tactic than as a way of life, Salter continued to be an avid gun collector throughout his life, was a life member of the National Rifle Association and an active member of the American Civil Liberties Union. In 1989, in recognition of Salter's many community service and civil rights activities, the governor of North Dakota presented him with the state's Martin Luther King, Jr., Social Justice Award. It was just one of many awards John Salter received during this period for his activism.

Always the optimist, Salter sought to forgive past wrongs while searching for the deeper humanity within the heart of his enemies. Long after his Mississippi sojourn, he became an unlikely acquaintance, then friend, of Erle Johnston, once the head of the Mississippi State Sovereignty Commission.

Even more telling, in May 1970, during a civil trial attempting to force the Pyle family's insurance company to pay for the damages he and Ed King had suffered in their 1963 auto wreck, Salter engaged in a rare form of closure. After viewing horrific photographs of Salter and King taken just after the crash, the Pyle family patriarch abruptly halted the proceedings and asked the insurance company to negotiate a settlement. It was a stunning victory for both activists. But Salter wasn't interested in winning alone. He looked across the courtroom to the family, one of whom he believed had tried to kill them. What he saw was the father and mother—"just two scared old people"—of the boy who'd been the driver of the car. The "boy" was by that point in medical school, and his older brother was a Jackson attorney with a reputation for being a moderate on race relations.

Salter's eyes locked on those of the older brother, and suddenly they were walking toward each other, extending their hands. "Tell your brother that we wish him well in his career as a physician," Salter said. The older brother shook Salter's hand with great emotion and thanked him for his graciousness. Salter admitted that he had allowed himself to hate that family for seven years. "I'm so glad that I was able to grow up a little bit more at that point and realize that we had to end something," he said. "The real settlement was a reconciliation."

In 1994, Salter retired from teaching. His father had died some years earlier, and Salter decided to honor his life and legacy and connect more explicitly to his ancestors by changing his name to John Hunter Gray. His father's birth name was Frank Gray, and the name Hunter was from his mother's family.

After surviving the Grand Forks flood in the spring of 1997, the Salters, then in their sixties, moved farther west to Pocatello, Idaho, where they live high above the Pontneuf River, surrounded by mountains and close to the Fort Hall Indian Reservation. Salter continued to agitate for social justice and to believe that there are still many social causes that need a champion. Though well into his seventies, he was as ready as ever to fight a good fight. "Our rights come from the Creator," he said, quoting his native cousin Alex Gray. "And I would add to that, in order to secure those rights, we have to organize."

Memphis Norman

AFTER GRADUATING FROM TOUGALOO IN 1964, MEMPHIS NORMAN STARTED down the track that his mentor Ernst Borinski had initiated when Norman applied for and received a scholarship to the University of Pittsburgh to study toward a master's degree in public administration. The experience was an education for him beyond book learning, as his time there exposed him to a style of life and a circle of friends unimaginable to the child from the Turpentine Quarters of Wiggins, Mississippi. He described vividly how a whole new world opened up to him when he took what he referred to as "my journey north." He went to synagogues, cathedrals, museums, and musicals; he attended classes with men and women of all nationalities and excelled at schoolwork. He could hardly get over the difference in his life. "There was this sudden freedom to do things," he said, as if a prisoner were suddenly set free. "It was totally new."[17]

When he left Pittsburgh in the late spring of 1965, he took a job as a management intern at the Atomic Energy Commission (AEC) in Washington, D.C., but was there only a year when a different reality interrupted. Norman was drafted into the army and, after a year of training, was sent to Vietnam. He didn't agree with the premise of the war and even tried to get a deferment because of the work he was doing for the government, but nothing worked. Because he was looking forward to a government career and felt a nagging sense of duty toward his country, he decided he had no choice but to serve.

Talking about his Vietnam experience thirty years later could still draw Norman's emotions to the surface. He remembered living through the Tet Offensive of early 1968 while serving as a personnel specialist at the base camp at Cu Chi, where the enemy had burrowed tunnels deep into the earth below the American base to protect themselves from the bombs. Norman recalled how his camp was attacked by rockets, killing a favorite sergeant. But despite the hardships, he insisted that nothing he survived in Vietnam could compare with the sheer terror he felt while being escorted from the Jackson Woolworth's on that stifling day in 1963.

In the summer of 1968, Norman returned to his civilian job. After three years at the AEC, primarily providing budget analysis and management oversight for the building of nuclear reactors, he was told by a friend about a job opening for a budget examiner at the Office of Management and Budget. Still struggling to escape a poor sharecropper's mentality, Norman was awed as he entered the Old Executive Office Building next to the White House for an interview. He was stunned when he got the job. For the next twenty-eight years, Norman served as a program examiner for some of the most prominent agencies of the U.S. government, including the National Aeronautics and Space Administration, the Smithsonian Institution, the National Gallery of Art, and the John F. Kennedy Center for the Performing Arts. Meanwhile, he completed his master's degree and earned a doctorate in public administration from the University of Southern California. After retiring from federal service in 1999, Norman taught management and social science at Catholic University's Metropolitan College and at Northern Virginia Community College. In some of his classes, he presented his own unique blend of personal experience while discussing the history of the civil rights movement.

Despite all of his professional achievements, Norman's personal life was somewhat less successful, including two failed interracial marriages and a child put up for adoption after the first marriage ended because of the stigma of mixed-race children at the time. His later life seemed happy enough, though. He stayed active up to the end, keeping in close contact with Joan (Trumpauer) Mulholland, his Woolworth's partner, who lived only a few miles away.

In later life, Norman would often visit his mother and sister who lived together in Ocean Springs, Mississippi, a small resort town along the Gulf Coast. Sometimes he would take a drive with his mother to the area of the Turpentine Quarters, which have long since been torn down, and to some of the places they sharecropped in Alabama. He said he went there searching for something intangible: a piece of his past to help him measure the distance he had traveled. "What happened back then," he wondered, "that made it possible for me to come this far?" Despite his many accomplishments, this gentle, soft-spoken soul seemed to still be searching for answers about his life. In 2005, Memphis Norman unexpectedly passed away in his sleep at the age of sixty-two at his home in an integrated neighborhood in Falls Church, Virginia.[18]

Pearlena Lewis

PEARLENA LEWIS CONTINUED WORKING FOR THE NAACP EVEN AFTER THE boycott of Capitol Street was called off in July 1964. She served as secretary of the strategy committee, which persisted and moved into new areas of the struggle, including school integration issues. She also became for the next year the Mississippi NAACP Youth Conference president, with responsibility for coordinating the activities of all of the youth councils in the state. In the fall of 1965, Lewis finally returned to Tougaloo, graduating in 1967 with a bachelor of arts in social science. After that, she continued her NAACP work, while also becoming involved with the Mississippi Young Democrats, an integrated group of moderates formed as an alternative to the more activist Mississippi Freedom Democratic Party established by SNCC and CORE. Both groups worked to wrest control of the party from the entrenched and segregated Democratic Party. Lewis helped plan annual conferences for the Mississippi Young Democrats and worked to establish the upstart group as a significant political force within the state.[19]

In 1968, Lewis moved to Hattiesburg with her family when her father finally was offered his lifelong dream of pastoring a church full-time. She initially remained active in the NAACP in her new home, becoming the youngest person to serve on a statewide branch's Executive Committee, but when she married, she began to pull back from her nearly full-time commitment of so many years to the NAACP. "I felt I had done my part," she said. However, the move surprised her longtime friends from the organization, prompting Ruby Hurley to ask, "Pearlena, what has happened?" But Lewis was determined to put more of her energies into her marriage and her two children.

In 1982, Lewis's husband was diagnosed with cancer and died just ten years into the marriage, and she became a single mother at the age of thirty-nine. She went to work as a community organizer and social worker in Hattiesburg; as always, she also had the support of her large family and found strength and sustenance in her strong religious faith. In 1986, nearly all of the remaining Lewis family moved to Ann Arbor, Michigan, where Reverend Lewis started the New Progressive Missionary Baptist Church—"A Church Where Everybody Is Somebody and Christ Is All." Lewis remained deeply engaged in her family's church activities and continued as a social worker in Ann Arbor.

In 2001, Pearlena Lewis was diagnosed with skin cancer and died a year later.

Lois Chaffee

IN MAY 1965, AFTER WORKING FOR CORE FOR NEARLY TWO YEARS, ASSISTING with Freedom Summer, and participating in the Mississippi Freedom Democratic Party's challenge at the 1964 Democratic National Convention, Lois Chaffee began to look for new challenges. Once the 1965 Voting Rights Act was passed, civil rights activities began to focus more on local politics and economics, areas in which Chaffee had little interest because she felt no personal connection to the issues. In addition, with the movement's shift in focus and mood, the real point, she said, "was no longer to [achieve] an integrated society in the South . . . but to develop a black identity, and the most important things had to be done by black people. I didn't see anywhere to go there."[20]

In June 1965, Chaffee was given a fellowship to study Gandhian techniques of nonviolence in India, but at the last moment accepted instead an invitation to visit the family of a Freedom Summer contact in New York City. She has lived there ever since.

After earning a graduate degree in early childhood education from Bank Street College, she worked for ten years in day care centers and nursery schools in the city. During that time, she was involved in the antiwar movement and was on hand when activists took on the Chicago police at the 1968 Democratic National Convention. As with the Mississippi movement, Chaffee felt the antiwar movement was again pulling her into issues that were nationally important but didn't speak directly to her own life. At last, after the 1968 convention, Chaffee discovered the just-emerging women's movement and felt she'd finally found her own cause: "That was the first time I ever felt like this was a movement where I was not a supporter. The women's movement was my longest and most serious commitment."

Chaffee served on the board of a women's center in Chelsea for nearly twenty years and continued to believe that involvement in social causes was important. "What I get out of it is just the opportunity to serve," she said, "to keep the motion going, to feel that you [are] committing your energies to something that makes a difference."

Her career also took some interesting turns. In the mid-1970s, when funding dried up in her chosen field of early childhood education, Chaffee shifted gears and took over a project funded by the federal Comprehensive Employment and Training Act (CETA) to provide job training and placement services primarily for women and minority populations. In 1979, just after she turned forty, she was hired by New York City's Department of Employment to administer CETA programs throughout the city; she worked for the same agency until she retired in 2009. Although she has few illusions about overhauling such a bureaucracy, she saw hope in the movement toward a customer-focused environment—what she calls "a revolution in social relationships"—and believed that this might ultimately solidify the kind of cultural revolution she had worked for most of her life.

Of her time in Mississippi, Chaffee commented, "Every now and then history sort of gives you a little boost. And that kind of experience only has to happen to you once. I was very thankful that it happened to me while I was young. It sticks to the ribs for a very long time."

In a touching note of optimism, Chaffee joined Joan (Trumpauer) Mulholland on the National Mall on January 21, 2008, to witness the inauguration of the first African American president of the United States, Barack Obama. Together they gloried in the distance both they and the country had traveled since that searing day at Woolworth's in 1963. "It was all worth it," Chaffee exclaimed. "It was all worth it."

George Raymond

GEORGE RAYMOND'S LEGACY BECAME THE MASS MOVEMENT HE LED IN CANton, one of the most repressive cities in the state of Mississippi. But he suffered severely for his devotion and his convictions.[21] From 1963 through 1965, Raymond had police on constant lookout for him. They would stop his car without even pretending to have a reason, simply attempting to slow his progress and hoping to scare him out of Canton. In just some of many examples, a cocked shotgun was pointed at him while he was taken in a squad car to jail and arrested for "reckless driving" because he had transported CORE workers to a voter registration drive; he was pistol-whipped by a Canton constable, then charged with intimidating a police officer; he was stopped while driving a group of people home after a mass meeting, taken behind the squad car, and severely beaten; he was hit with an ax handle by the local marshal while leading some teens in integrating a little cafe and then shot at as the group fled.[22]

This and much more happened to this young, committed activist, still only in his early twenties.

Despite his exposure to this sort of extreme brutality, Raymond managed to have fun with his tormentors every now and then. Billy Nobles, Canton's vicious deputy sheriff, had a running joke going with the civil rights worker. He had said if he ever saw Raymond in the town square, he would come across the street and "kick his ass." Raymond, partly jokingly, partly to shield himself, would put all sorts of protective clothing and even pots and pans inside his overalls to soften the blow that inevitably would come. Dave Dennis, who witnessed this ritual, couldn't believe what he was seeing. "Don't worry about it," Raymond would tell him. "I'm OK."[23]

George Raymond participated in every significant civil rights project that came along during those years. He helped organize the Mississippi Freedom Democratic Party in Madison and surrounding counties; he was a major participant in the Freedom Summer activities within his district; and he became part of the Child Development Group of Mississippi when that organization proposed its radical approach to fighting poverty within the state during Lyndon Johnson's War on Poverty campaign.[24]

As tireless and courageous as he was as a freedom fighter, however, Raymond often seemed to have trouble with those who worked with and for him. At one point, his coworkers asked Dave Dennis to reassign Raymond to another project somewhere else in the state; Dennis refused, believing Raymond's contacts with the local people were much too valuable to lose for internal staff reasons.[25]

Throughout those challenging times, Raymond was also trying to maintain the respect of his family, which was especially important to him because, unlike many movement participants who saw their commitment as temporary, Raymond seems to have viewed his as lifelong. On a trip to New York City in January 1964, when Raymond and his friend Jerome Smith stayed with James Baldwin in his Greenwich Village apartment, Raymond wrote a letter to his parents on Baldwin's stationery, asking for their prayers and understanding. "My dearest mother and father," he wrote, "just a few lines to let you and the children know that I am doing well and that I still love all of you. My belief[s] may seem strange to you all some time, but all I ask of you all is to trust in me and believe in me. My goal is my people and everything that will make them progress. . . . Please always love me, mom and pop, because I need love very much. . . . the world do[es] not offer it and I really need it from you all always."[26]

A significant part of George Raymond's life fell into place in June 1964 when he knocked on the door of the Evans family home in Sandhill, Mississippi, during a voter registration drive, and eighteen-year-old Myrtis Evans answered. Evans was immediately taken with Raymond, and he with her.

Within a few months she was on her way with him to Canton—a trip she also remembered for the random harassment Raymond received from the Madison County sheriffs. Evans moved in with Raymond at the Freedom House in Canton in the late summer of 1964, and the next year they married and had a son, Jomo Kenyatta Raymond. Though happy with her new family, Myrtis Raymond became exposed to the shocking brutality her husband encountered daily. She told of acid being thrown on him in one demonstration; of how police would stop them and take their money; of how she would regularly visit the police station to bail George out for one trumped-up charge after another.[27]

In 1965, George Raymond was appointed CORE's Mississippi field secretary, taking Dave Dennis's old post after Dennis was reassigned to New Orleans as CORE's southern regional director and after Dennis's first replacement stayed only six months. The following year, the Raymonds helped organize the James Meredith March Against Fear when it came through Canton on its way to Jackson. Myrtis Raymond was pleased to have hosted Martin Luther King for lunch on that occasion. The march, however, turned brutally hostile as it moved through Madison County, with police using tear gas on the marchers for simply attempting to set up tents on public property. The federal and state government's lack of response to the abuse pushed the movement in a radically new direction. It was during this march that Stokely Carmichael, then the head of SNCC, articulated his militant "black power" manifesto. Soon thereafter, CORE also adopted a black power stance. Raymond could not accept the organization's shift in philosophy and resigned.[28]

To make ends meet, Raymond next took a job in Michigan with Foundation Cooperative Housing, which managed low-income housing projects. After a few months, the job turned sour, and he returned to Canton. Other disappointments followed. Raymond ran unsuccessfully for the Mississippi legislature in the 1967 elections under the Mississippi Freedom Democratic Party banner. He also tried getting jobs in and around Canton, but inevitably word would spread about his movement work and he would be fired. Raymond began borrowing heavily from a supportive Ohio-based organization called Operation Freedom, including a business loan to open a restaurant and bar called Club Desire. When it folded after less than a year, Myrtis Raymond got a job with Head Start and became the primary wage earner of the family.[29]

Myrtis begged her husband to consider relocating with her and their son to New Orleans, where with the strong support of his tight-knit family, they might be able to succeed. Raymond wouldn't hear of it. "He was just too dedicated," she said, "and he loved the people [of Canton]." Raymond's friend and fellow CORE worker Mat Suarez summed up Raymond's predicament. "George felt that he could not walk away from that community," Suarez said, and likened Raymond to a combatant abandoned in enemy territory: "The movement pulled out and left George behind."[30]

Raymond eventually became bitter over what he saw as the movement's failure to effect real change in the lives of the people for whom he had worked so hard. He also scorned the poverty programs and the welfare initiatives that were being created because he thought they fostered dependency upon the government. The constant economic hardships and his growing frustrations became too much for Raymond, and he began to smoke and drink heavily. This was especially dangerous for him because this lion of an activist, who had lived all his life with a heart full of courage, suffered from an enlarged heart—a congenital condition of which few in the movement were aware.[31]

The situation gradually became too much for Myrtis Raymond. In November 1969, after regularly pleading with her husband to break away and make a new start, a pregnant Myrtis took Jomo and moved to her sister's home in Jackson. Two months later, Shindina Raymond was born; a year after that, Myrtis filed for divorce.[32]

Raymond continued to live and work in Canton, at times taking odd jobs in Jackson at nightclubs or factories, but by the end of 1971, he was so sick that he could hardly walk. Someone called his family in New Orleans, and his brother John came to take him home. Dave Dennis, who had just graduated from law school and was living in New Orleans, remembered Raymond visiting him, though his heart was clearly in bad shape. "I lived in an apartment . . . just one flight of stairs up, but he couldn't make it. He'd make a few steps, then he'd have to sit."[33]

Raymond's sister Lois remembered doctors telling her that her brother, still under thirty, had the heart of a seventy-year-old. His family said he'd changed in other ways too. "He was very quiet," Lois said. Raymond's nephew Robert believed his uncle "was in a state of constant grief." "He would sit around and talk about his people being free," Lois continued, "and how he was not able to really accomplish all that he wanted to accomplish. He was not the same active George that we knew. . . . [It] seem[ed] like he had just given up."[34]

Myrtis Raymond was aware that her ex-husband was in terrible shape. She visited him in New Orleans and asked him to come back and remarry her so she could care for him in Jackson. She felt he'd get better care at the University of Mississippi Medical Center, and she had a job with medical benefits, but Raymond refused. He had little time left at that point. On March 8, 1973, at the age of thirty, George Raymond died of congestive heart failure.[35]

Dave Dennis spoke at Raymond's funeral service in New Orleans. "Dave cried through that eulogy," remembered George's brother John. A week later, when a memorial service was held in Canton, his family was stunned to see the outpouring of emotion and support. The Raymond family had had no idea of George's impact on this small community in a neighboring state.[36]

Raymond's siblings remained at a loss to understand their brother's fate. During the intervening years, they tended to idealize his complex character while appropriately honoring his contributions. "He believed in freedom," said his sister Verna, "not only for himself but for everyone. And he was willing to make the sacrifice—the ultimate sacrifice—to give his life to see everyone free."[37]

Tom Beard

LIKE PEARLENA LEWIS, TOM BEARD REMAINED ACTIVE WITH THE NAACP AF-ter the direct action phase of the Jackson Movement ended, working primarily in NAACP-sponsored voter registration drives. "I started feeling like we accomplished more registering people to vote than [being] out there on the street," he said. "That became more important to me."[38]

Beard recalled how for a year or so after Medgar Evers's death, he was followed home frequently by the police wherever he went. Such attention might strike some as disconcerting, but Beard credited this constant surveillance with having saved his life on more than one occasion when angry whites tried to assault him because of his civil rights work.

In March 1964, Beard dropped out of Jim Hill High School and married his sweetheart. A year later, he received his first draft notice and began wandering the country to avoid enlistment, going first to Memphis, then to Baltimore, where for about six months he was involved in the civil rights movement there. He visited Jackson every now and then to check on his growing family—five children over the next five years. At times, the draft board would require his return, but surprisingly they never actually came after him. If they had, Beard said he wasn't about to go to Vietnam and would probably have been sent to jail if they had forced the issue. He came to believe that the draft notices were meant to dissuade him from participating in civil rights activities—a claim voiced by other activists as well.

Beard continued to drift to places like Chicago, California, and Ohio before settling back in Jackson in 1972, just after he passed the draftable age limit. By then his focus had shifted entirely from movement to money and struggling to make a living, which he has continued trying to do, more or less successfully, ever since. Though his constant wandering put an end to his marriage, he stayed in regular contact with his children and continued to be involved in their lives.

For all of his movement work, Beard became one of the many underclass of blacks who offered their lives for freedom but were not in a position to take advantage, particularly economic advantage, of opportunities as society began to open up. During his entire career, Beard worked long days in the housing construction business and seemed skeptical about the gains he and others worked so hard to ensure. "I think young people's as bad off now as they were [back then] as far as opportunities are concerned," he said. "When I look back at it now, I think it just went in a circle."

Despite this view, Beard was proud of his involvement in the movement, and he made sure his kids were aware of the part their father played to secure their rights. He had no regrets about his role and believed it was his generation's duty to take the risks they did: "Somebody had to make a change."

Ed King

ED KING, LIKE GEORGE RAYMOND, STAYED IN MISSISSIPPI AND DEVOTED HIS life to ensuring that lasting change came to his native state.[39] He participated in Freedom Summer and was a founding member of the Mississippi Freedom Democratic Party (MFDP), which challenged the segregated Democratic Party for the right to represent all of Mississippi's voting population within the national party structure. In fact, King was one of only three MFDP aspiring delegates to testify before the Democratic Party's Rules Committee in 1964 when the fledgling party challenged the credentials of Mississippi's segregationist party members at their Atlantic City convention.[40]

King returned to Mississippi after the convention and continued to play a significant role in the state's civil rights movement, including the ongoing operations of the MFDP. He also continued to serve as chaplain and dean of students at Tougaloo and became a founder and board member of the Delta Ministry, a creation of the National Council of Churches. Throughout this period, he continued to have regular, painful surgeries—about a dozen in all—to attempt to reconstruct his face.

In the spring of 1966, as the movement shifted toward black power and away from a focus that had been nonviolent, integrated, and deeply Christian, King threw his energy into the primary elections for MFDP candidates for Congress. King himself ran for the Fifth District, which included Jackson, against incumbent and future governor John Bell Williams. King earned a respectable 22 percent of the vote, the best of any MFDP candidate that season.[41]

A year later, King resigned from Tougaloo and devoted his energies to the Delta Ministry. Initially created to support the Freedom Summer initiative, the Delta Ministry eventually grew into a longer-term project to promote economic and community development in the Mississippi Delta region.[42] In 1968, after just a year with the Delta Ministry, King moved his family to New Orleans, where, with the help of a grant from the Southern Regional Council, he worked on a manuscript about his time in the movement. Despite his efforts, King never got his work-in-progress to a point where he felt comfortable publishing it. Life just seemed to keep getting in the way.

In 1970, King was awarded a fellowship from the Center for the Development of Social Change to study nonviolence at the Gandhi Peace Foundation in India. He brought back from that experience a firm belief that programs like affirmative action would not work and would ultimately cause further bitterness between the races. When he returned from India, he took another job with the Delta Ministry, this time attempting to convince white parents in Mississippi to keep their children in public schools and not to flee integration. After two years at this thankless task, he began teaching religion and sociology part-time at Millsaps College. He also started teaching about the human side of health care, death and dying issues, and the ethics of medicine at the University of Mississippi's medical school in Jackson. Additionally, he served as a recruiter of underprivileged, mostly black, students for the medical school.

In his personal life, Ed had two daughters with his wife, Jeannette, but the marriage began to falter in the 1980s, and the couple separated and later divorced. King blamed the women's movement for the breakup, citing the fact that every couple in their social circle separated and divorced at that time.[43]

As Mississippi's political realities also continued to shift, this white patriarch found himself rather out of fashion. King became a staunch right-to-life advocate, which put him outside most liberal circles. His financial resources also became strained, largely due to the divorce settlement and an ongoing battle with the Internal Revenue Service—a battle King characterized as tax harassment for political purposes. As a result of his broken heart, his strained finances, and his tax woes, he lived alone for a time in a run-down rented house in a racially changing neighborhood in north Jackson and often wore secondhand clothes. He became one of the poor, or close to it, and learned to identify even more completely with their struggles.

Along with John Salter, King also fought the proposition that the Mississippi State Sovereignty Commission's papers—those spy sheets filled with rumor as well as personal facts about people in the movement—should be released to the public without protections for individuals similar to those afforded under the Freedom of Information Act. Salter and King had earlier teamed up to obtain the release of those archives, until it became clear that the method of release would jeopardize individuals' privacy. The two battle-scarred freedom fighters won a partial settlement in 1989. However, they had hoped for a system like that administered by the FBI, in which names of all individuals other than the requester are blacked out entirely. Instead, the Mississippi settlement only allowed for individuals to request that their names be excised from their records. Otherwise, all names would be revealed.[44]

Salter decided that, with this judgment, individuals would maintain at least some control over whether their names would show up in the record, and he removed himself from any further objections. Like a modern-day Don Quixote, however, King decided to fight on. As a result, he was decried as an obstructionist, and his old enemies, as well as his friends, wondered publicly whether he himself had something grievous to hide. King, nevertheless, battled on, though he lost his final challenge when the U.S. Supreme Court refused to hear the case in early 1997. At that point, the Mississippi Department of Archives and History began to issue public notices that the papers were to be released and asked individuals who suspected they had been spied upon to contact the department for a prior review copy of their file.

Approximately eighty-seven thousand names are indexed in the Sovereignty Commission documents, including those of every single Woolworth's demonstrator. About a thousand people wrote to request the information packet explaining the procedure for obtaining their files, should one exist. Only seven hundred of those asked to see their files, and of those only three hundred sixty actually had their names in the spy papers. After seeing their files, only thirty-two requested privacy, including King himself.[45]

After the release of the Sovereignty Commission papers, King worked with the black and white clergy of Jackson to begin a racial reconciliation project in Mississippi, similar to what occurred in South Africa after the end of apartheid. King also initiated a historical preservation project to renovate and preserve the COFO headquarters in Jackson that served as the strategic center of the Freedom Summer Project.

Professionally, King became a professor at the University Medical Center, teaching death and dying to the medical staff. He continues his work on staff there while laboring to complete his memoirs, which no doubt will feature his unique perspective of this tumultuous period in the history of his native state.

Dan Beittel

DR. BEITTEL AND HIS WIFE, RUTH, STAYED IN JACKSON AFTER HE WAS PUSHED out of the presidency of Tougaloo College. He soon accepted a new job as director of the American Friends Service Committee's Mississippi project and continued to do volunteer work as well, including serving on the Advisory Committee of the U.S. Commission on Civil Rights and as a director of the Southern Regional Council, a group established in the 1940s to foster racial harmony. Thanks to his lifelong affiliation with the National Council of Churches, Beittel was invited in late 1964 to become a founding member of the Delta Ministry, the same group that Ed King later joined.[46]

In addition, Beittel began to apply his significant organizational talent toward dealing with educational and economic issues facing poor blacks, both in rural and urban settings. In the spring of 1965, he became a lead sponsor of the first Jackson Head Start project, which set up a dozen preschool centers in the city and served twelve hundred poor children. Also in 1965, he became a founder and first chairman of the board of the Child Development Group of Mississippi, a pioneering regiment of President Johnson's War on Poverty that during its two years of existence established 125 Head Start centers and served fifteen thousand children across the state.[47]

During the last week of March 1968, Beittel marched with Dr. Martin Luther King, Jr., in Memphis to support the rights of black sanitation workers to equal treatment. Violence broke out during the march, challenging King's image as the world's leading proponent of nonviolence, and Beittel participated afterwards in a discussion with King and others about how to recover the momentum. The group recommended that King return to Memphis a week later to lead another march that could be better controlled. On Thursday, April 4, 1968, while in Memphis preparing for that follow-up march, King was assassinated.[48]

In 1969, Dan and Ruth Beittel finally left Mississippi and retired to San Rafael, California. Beittel continued his social activism in his new surroundings, serving, for example, as chairman of the board of Pilgrim Park, a low-cost housing project sponsored by the United Church of Christ. One of his last wishes was to have the stamina to view the speeches of Senator Ted Kennedy and Reverend Jesse Jackson at the 1988 Democratic National Convention. That wish fulfilled, he died a few days later on July 26, 1988, at the age of eighty-nine.[49]

Other NAACP Workers

DORIS ALLISON NEVER QUITE GOT OVER THE LOSS OF MEDGAR EVERS. SHE served out her two-year term as president of the NAACP's Jackson branch through November 1964, though she never learned to like Medgar's successor, his brother, Charles. "It was so hard for us to get used to working with Charles Evers," she said. "It's hard for me to conceive that a woman could give birth to two kids so different. So, so different!"[50] Like many, she was enraged by many of the elder brother's tactics and decisions, including his calling off the boycott of the Capitol Street stores in July 1964 without consulting her or the local NAACP board. She insisted, after the fact, that the strategy committee of local ministers be reinstituted to oversee the transition to integration of public accommodations and school desegregation. Allison decided to stick with the NAACP, even though she knew the national office had struck a less than favorable deal with the Kennedy administration and local authorities to relieve the pressure that the Jackson Movement had created. Fannie Lou Hamer, aware of Allison's radical heart, invited her to join SNCC, but Allison wouldn't hear of it. "Fannie Lou, I can't do that," Allison told her. "I'd feel like I'm letting [Medgar] down."[51]

Allison finally resigned from the board of the Jackson NAACP in 1967. In the years that followed, she spoke at many freedom events and tried in her own way to keep the memory of Medgar Evers alive. She lived out her life in Jackson with her husband, Ben, and lost neither her fiery edge nor any of her incredible memory for detail. She also retained a wicked sense of humor. When she heard, for instance, that Bennie Oliver—the former police officer who assaulted Memphis Norman and others at Woolworth's—had been killed in a bar brawl, Allison called Pearlena Lewis and told her, "Pearlena, your boyfriend's gone."[52]

Allison has never been adequately recognized for the role she played in assisting Medgar Evers as he became more outspoken in his views about race and politics. Her love for him was complete, and her association with him was the highlight of her life. "I'd have walked through hell with Medgar," she once said. Indeed, she did—and then some. After a life full of commitment and struggle, Doris Allison died in 2004 at the age of eighty-six.[53]

After **Charles Evers** completed his controversial service with the NAACP, he became Mississippi's first black mayor of a racially mixed town since Reconstruction when in 1969 he was elected in the small city of Fayette in the state's southwestern corner. Although he attempted to use that victory as a springboard to higher political office, he was never successful. He penned several books about his civil rights year. Unfortunately they all come off as overly self-serving, and his attempts to claim credit for his assassinated brother's character and early leadership role seem unfounded. In retirement, Evers hosted a blues and jazz radio show in Jackson well into his eighties.[54]

Lillian Louie continued to work for the NAACP's Jackson office for the next twenty-five years, serving as executive secretary to Charles Evers and every subsequent NAACP field representative for Mississippi until she was pushed out when a new group took over in 1988. Doris Allison felt that the organization's treatment of Lillian was abominable, but Louie seemed philosophical about the matter, if a little bitter.

She went to work as the receptionist for the Catholic Archdiocese of Jackson and rarely granted interviews about her life and times as the assistant to both Evers brothers. (She confided that she actually liked the take-charge attitude of Charles Evers and enjoyed working for someone who wasn't afraid to challenge the NAACP's national office brass.) When asked about her role as the glue that held the NAACP's Mississippi office together, she seemed satisfied that she did her best in a job that few envied. She stayed well connected to a large network of former NAACP "family" and remained particularly close to Pearlena Lewis throughout her life.[55]

Alphonzo Lewis joined the U.S. Air Force after high school, then went to the University of Southern Mississippi in Hattiesburg, which by then was admitting blacks. He is the only member of the Lewis family who stayed in

Mississippi when the others moved to Michigan in 1986. He did, however, become a Baptist minister like his father and entered the "family business," serving as pastor of Mt. Elam Baptist Church in Pearl, Mississippi, just east of Jackson. More recently, Lewis moved to Meridian to become senior pastor at Mount Olive Missionary Baptist Church, "a church where everybody is somebody." He continues to have a strong commitment to civil rights issues and remembers fondly his youthful days demonstrating for freedom on the streets of Jackson.[56]

Willie Ludden continued his work for the NAACP but never fully recovered from what he witnessed in Jackson. He felt the national office had squelched the Jackson Movement, and he was bitter at having been pushed aside during Medgar Evers's funeral, where he had hoped to say a few words to honor the slain Jackson Movement leader. He also thought more focus should have been put on the youth, who had been the fuel that drove the movement to its greatest accomplishments.

Ludden ended up having substantive disagreements with his immediate NAACP supervisor, Ruby Hurley, and resigned in May 1964, a year after his heroic involvement in Jackson. He later moved to California and then to Texas, where he wrote his memoir, *Anatomy of a Civil Rights Worker*, which was self-published in 2002. Ludden resides in Grand Prairie, Texas.[57]

Laplois Ashford outlasted Ludden at the NAACP, but just barely. He, too, became disenchanted with the organization, particularly after what he witnessed firsthand of its top-down bureaucratic approach in Jackson. He was horrified at Evers's murder and believed the national office top brass—particularly Roy Wilkins and Gloster Current—had not done everything in their power to prevent it. He also lamented the inability of the NAACP to collaborate with other civil rights organizations, which, he admitted, caused the most talented youth to leave the NAACP for SNCC and CORE. He took some pride, however, in the fact that the NAACP's youth ranks swelled during his tenure— from sixteen thousand in 1962 when he took over as national youth coordinator to forty-eight thousand in 1965 when he resigned. After leaving the employ of the NAACP, Ashford took a variety of public service administrative jobs in urban settings, in Rochester, Chicago, and Washington, D.C. He retired in 1997 and died in 2004.[58]

Gloster Current continued to play a major role at the NAACP, eventually becoming its administrator and deputy executive director. Even after he retired in 1978, he was brought back by Roy Wilkins's successor, Benjamin Hooks, to serve on the association's board of directors from 1978 through 1983. In retirement, Current also became a pastor of a community church in the Bronx. An accomplished jazz musician, he additionally served as organist at another church in Queens from 1985 through 1995. Current died in 1997 in New York City at the age of eighty-four.[59]

Roy Wilkins stayed on as executive secretary of the NAACP for another fifteen years after the Jackson Movement's exhilarating and tragic rise and fall. Wilkins was forced to beat back several attempts to oust him in the early 1970s when his detractors claimed he had outlived his usefulness and that he was out of step with the times—charges easily foreseen by his handling of the Jackson crisis. Failing health caused Wilkins to retire in 1977 on his own terms, however, at the age of seventy-six. He died of kidney failure in 1981.[60]

Myrlie Evers went on to a successful career of her own. She became a spokesperson and fund-raiser for the NAACP after her husband's assassination; then in 1964 she moved with her three children to California where she completed her college education, ran unsuccessfully for political office, and became involved in local Los Angeles politics. By 1987, when Mayor Tom Bradley appointed her to the Los Angeles Board of Public Works, she had married longshoreman and union activist Walter Williams. In the early 1990s, she and her husband relocated to Oregon. In 1995, she was part of a group that challenged the troubled NAACP national leadership, which by then was facing severe financial and management problems. By a narrow margin, Myrlie Evers-Williams was elected chairman of the board, and she successfully led the effort to get the esteemed civil rights organization back on track. She resigned as chairman in early 1998, but continued to work tirelessly in the racial struggle that Medgar taught her to embrace. In tribute to her commitment to reviving the organization, the NAACP awarded Myrlie Evers-Williams her own Spingarn Medal in July 1998, exactly thirty-five years after she had accepted it posthumously for her slain husband.[61]

Her greatest personal triumph had come a few years earlier, however, when she partnered with the Mississippi district attorney's office to bring to trial for the third time the man most people believed had killed Medgar Evers. A guilty conviction against Byron De La Beckwith was finally handed down by an integrated jury in 1994. The story of how Beckwith was finally brought to justice was the subject of several popular books and of the film *Ghosts of Mississippi.*[62]

The acknowledgment of the contribution that **Medgar Evers** made to Mississippi's freedom struggle continues to grow with each passing year. The city of Jackson itself began to thaw in its attitude toward the civil rights leader. In 1992 Jackson's central federal post office was named in his honor, and a statue of Evers was erected nearby. A major thoroughfare that ran past his old neighborhood was also renamed for the slain Mississippi hero, as was the neighborhood itself. A nearby library has also been dedicated in his honor. In a bitter irony, Myrlie Evers-Williams was on hand in March 2003—forty years after Medgar's death—when the Mississippi state legislature honored the pair's contributions to the people of Mississippi. Three months later, during the exact anniversary of Evers's death, the U.S. Congress declared June 9–16 "Medgar Evers Week."

In an additional tribute, U.S. Secretary of the Navy and former Mississippi governor Ray Mabus announced in 2009 that he would name a newly commissioned naval ship after Evers. The ship will transport food, fuel, ammunition, and other supplies to U.S. military installations worldwide, much like Evers and his fellow Red Ball Express veterans did during World War II.

Perhaps the most unusual irony is that the airport that Allen Thompson worked so hard to develop was named for Evers and the city they both served. The Jackson-Evers International Airport sits on Thompson Field. The airport boasts a Medgar Wiley Evers pavilion, which houses museum-quality photos and a comprehensive narrative about the slain civil rights leader's life and times. Fred Blackwell's photo of the sit-in features prominently in one of the displays. In another part of the pavilion, statues of two smiling young girls—one white and one black—stand together in a show of unity. The caption reads: "Reconciliation: A Work in Progress," which aptly describes the state of Jackson's current race relations.

Many books and articles have been written about the life and times of Medgar Evers, and Myrlie Evers-Williams has contributed mightily to keeping his legacy alive through the Medgar Evers Foundation. She has written several memoirs and she commissioned a serious work of research into his writings and speeches. *The Autobiography of Medgar Evers*, published in 2005, is a striking work of nonfiction that captures the man's courage and commitment as it unfolded with each new challenge.

Myrlie Evers-Williams was a special guest at the 2008 inauguration of Barack Obama as president of the United States.

Representatives of the Law

JIM BLACK, THE UNDERCOVER ARRESTING OFFICER AT WOOLWORTH'S, HAD A long and distinguished career on the Jackson police force, where he worked for a total of thirty-one years, eight of those as chief of police. After retirement from the police force, he became a private consultant on legal and police issues. Jim Black died in 2007.[63]

Charlie Newell, D. C. Sullivan's "buddy" in the military plan that didn't quite come off, replaced Jim Black as Jackson's chief of police in 1990, a post he held until May 1991. Newell then served as chief of police in Ridgeland, a suburb north of Jackson. Newell seemed apologetic about what happened in Jackson during his adolescence and believed that times had changed for the better. Appalled at the lack of police protection given the demonstrators at Woolworth's, Newell commented that the police department had come a long way since then.[64]

Both Black and Newell gave their highest praise to **Deputy Chief John L. Ray**, who handled most police coordination during the demonstrations of the Jackson Movement. They spoke in nearly reverential tones of Ray's dedication and his desire not to see anyone get hurt. "He was my idol," Black said simply, "my hero." "He was a very kind, good man," Newell added. "He never encouraged policemen to be cruel. He never encouraged policemen to use any more force than was necessary. He said the right things and did the right things. I think we were lucky that he was here." Deputy Chief Ray died in 1969 at the age of forty-nine after a long battle with cancer.[65]

The U.S. Justice Department's **John Doar** went on to further prominence after his important work in the South during the civil rights era. Frank Schwelb, another department attorney working in Mississippi, recalled a phrase in civil rights circles that black freedom was in the hands of "SNCC, CORE, and Big John Doar." Doar later became chief prosecuting counsel for the Senate Judiciary Committee during the Watergate investigation, which led to the resignation of President Richard Nixon. He later opened a law practice in New York. In July 2012, he received the Presidential Medal of Freedom from President Barack Obama.[66]

Thelton Henderson, the black Justice Department attorney who was nearly arrested on the day Medgar Evers and Roy Wilkins were booked, had an unfortunate setback to his career in November 1963, when Alabama Governor George Wallace accused him of assisting Martin Luther King by driving him from Birmingham to Selma. Henderson denied the charge. In fact, he had not driven King anywhere, but he had loaned King and the SCLC his government-paid rental car. The situation got the Kennedy administration into such difficulty with southern politicians that Henderson resigned just days before President Kennedy was assassinated. Henderson's career recovered, however, and in 1969 he became associate dean of the Stanford University Law School and later received an appointment from President Jimmy Carter in 1980 to the Federal District Court in San Francisco, where he continues to serve with distinction.[67]

Representatives of the Media

BILL MINOR CONTINUED TO COVER MISSISSIPPI'S "RACE BEAT" FOR THE NEW Orleans *Times-Picayune*, as well as every other socially and politically significant development in the state until the paper did away with its Jackson bureau in 1976. Rather than return to Louisiana at that time or take another job offer outside the state, Minor decided to retire from the *Times-Picayune* and start his own weekly investigative journal about Mississippi politics, *The Capital Reporter*. That venture ended in 1981. Minor then found his niche as a syndicated columnist, whose "Eyes on Mississippi" now finds its way into nearly forty newspapers across the South.

Minor is the recipient of numerous journalism honors, including the Louis Lyons Award (given by the Nieman Foundation at Harvard University) for "conscience and integrity in journalism," as well as the John Chancellor Award for Excellence in Journalism (presented by the Annenberg School Public Policy Center of the University of Pennsylvania). Asked once why he decided to stay in Mississippi, the veteran newsman said, "I had seen Mississippi come this far, and I wanted to see how it all came out."[68]

Ken Toler met an untimely death at the age of sixty-two when he suffered a massive heart attack in 1966. By then he had covered the Mississippi political scene for thirty-four years and was regularly "consulted by governors, senators and other public figures," according to his *New York Times* obituary. As a testament to the high regard that Mississippi politicians accorded him, Toler had for more than thirty years performed the duty of gaveling the official adjournment of the Mississippi state legislature. (An arcane Mississippi custom called for no legislators to be on hand at the formal conclusion of the legislative session.)[69]

Cliff Sessions went on to a varied and eventful career, shifting in and out of news, government, and corporate positions with ease. In 1964 he moved to Washington, D.C., where he continued to work for UPI, covering the political beat for two years. He was then appointed deputy director of public information at the U.S. Justice Department, and later promoted to director of public information under Attorney General Ramsey Clark. It was by this route that he became the chief spokesperson for the department in the wake of the assassination of Martin Luther King. In 1969 Sessions left government to help start the *National Journal*, a weekly nonpartisan magazine about politics and emerging political trends. He later worked for the American Bankers Association and corporate giant General Foods, and also served as the assistant secretary for public affairs for the U.S. Department of Health, Education, and Welfare. Sessions returned to Biloxi, Mississippi, when he retired in 1990; he died in 2005.[70]

Dub Shoemaker, the segregationist reporter for the *Jackson Daily News*, continued writing for the paper until it folded in the 1980s, the victim of the economic realities of being the second-ranked paper in a one-paper town. Shoemaker eventually came to see that the cause for which Medgar Evers devoted his life was a just one. "Medgar's program was destined to win," Shoemaker later admitted. "He was right. . . . But it was a turbulent time in the birthing."[71]

The City of Jackson

JACKSON'S **CENTRAL HIGH SCHOOL**—THE SCHOOL ATTENDED BY MOST OF the white students who tormented the young men and women sitting-in at Woolworth's in 1963—first opened its doors to black students in 1966. At that time, many white parents pulled their kids out of the public schools and enrolled them in the Citizens' Council academies, private all-white educational units created to keep white children from attending school with blacks. Central High ultimately closed in 1977 as attendance fell—a victim of white flight. After being acquired by the state in 1979, the building was used temporarily as the state capitol while the new capitol building underwent renovations. After sitting idle for many years thereafter, the school underwent extensive renovations of its own and reopened in 1998 as the state's department of education headquarters, a fitting use for such a stately edifice.[72]

Capitol Street, the commercial heart of the city in the postwar era, entered a period of decline after the boycott—a situation from which it has only recently begun to recover. The boycott hastened the flight of many prominent stores into the more affluent areas north and west of Jackson. For a period of about twenty-five years, the street where all of Mississippi used to shop had few stores of any worth. Beginning in the year 2000, the city began to refurbish and rebuild, thanks largely to the influx of major banking, insurance, and telecommunications institutions. In 2003, Union Station, the train station that anchors the western edge of Capitol Street, was renovated and now houses both the city's train and bus stations. The King Edward Hotel, which had also lain vacant and dilapidated for years, has now been renewed by the Hilton Hotel chain and reopened in 2009. In 2010, a new 330,000-square-foot convention center opened within view of Capitol Street. The city now seems poised to take advantage of the kinds of business and entertainment revenue that eluded it during its years of racial turmoil.

The Woolworth's store on Capitol Street was torn down in the 1980s to make way for an office building, business supply shops, and a six-story parking garage. Right next to where the building once stood is a landscaped field of grass, just the sort of space that could someday accommodate a memorial to Jackson's civil rights struggles.

The black shopping district just around the corner on North Farish Street and two blocks up from the old Woolworth's is severely blighted. As elsewhere, integration in Jackson was not kind to many black business districts. Once the Jackson Chamber of Commerce approved mass integration in accordance with the Civil Rights Act of 1964, black shoppers—eager for the lower prices of national chains—abandoned the establishments that had served them for years. The street is now peppered with honky-tonks and bars, although there are still remnants of the street's former glory. Chief among them is the Collins Funeral Home, looking much as it did the day of Medgar Evers's funeral march. It is one of the few remaining landmarks that has not lost its 1950s charm. In 2005, Hurricane Katrina swept through Jackson and left low-lying areas in shambles. There are rows of shotgun houses on North Farish Street that still lie abandoned, an unfortunate symbol of the city's continuing legacy of economic disenfranchisement.[73]

The city of Jackson's leadership, however, underwent a dramatic change in the late 1990s when a black man, Harvey Johnson, Jr., was elected mayor in 1997. Johnson became the first black to occupy the city hall built by slaves, from which Allen Thompson fought to uphold segregation's worn-out customs.[74] The city council itself is now an integrated group—a biracial committee, if you will, much like what the Jackson Movement was demonstrating for—that makes policy and passes ordinances on behalf of all of Jackson's citizens.

Allen Thompson himself served as mayor for one more term after "the troubles" his administration suffered through during the civil rights crises of 1963 and 1964. He never did change his mind on segregation. In February of 1964, he testified against the Civil Rights Act, claiming that the bill was "the most destructive bill that has ever been presented to [this] august body." Thompson stepped down as mayor in 1969 but did not go quietly. Just after his retirement, he addressed the Jackson Chamber of Commerce and publicly castigated the U.S. Supreme Court over school desegregation, saying they had "anointed themselves as the Super School Board of the Southern States." Soon after that speech, Thompson accepted a position with a group called Freedom of Choice in the U.S. (FOCUS), which was devoted to "asserting the freedom of people to maintain control over their schools." Thus, Thompson helped to continue the movement of whites away from integrated schools and into their own private academies, a situation that continues to this day. Thompson died of a heart attack in 1980.[75]

Tougaloo College

TEN MILES NORTH OF DOWNTOWN JACKSON, TOUGALOO COLLEGE STILL stands. Its days as the heart of the Jackson Movement have long since passed into the school's collective memory, though a mural on the old gym wall, which included a lone white female student with long blonde hair helping to lead a march, kept that history alive until a major renovation of the campus swept through in the early 2000s. As part of that renewal, Woodworth Chapel was lovingly restored and upgraded, thanks in large part to the steering of federal funds to the project by U.S. Representative Bennie Thompson, a Tougaloo graduate and Mississippi's second black congressman since Reconstruction.

A less visible memorial can be found near the old entrance to the college. **Dr. Ernst Borinski**, who taught at the college until his death in 1983, is buried in a small cemetery on the campus. His beloved Beard Hall was demolished in 1999 to make way for a state-of-the-art academic and civil rights research center, complete with a floor-to-ceiling photo mural of Fred Blackwell's iconic Woolworth's sit-in image—a fitting representation of one of Tougaloo's finest moments.[76]

Other Activists

THE **LADNER** SISTERS, **JOYCE AND DORIE**, WHO, ALONG WITH JOAN TRUMP-auer were Tougaloo's primary student radicals, eventually migrated to Washington, D.C. Joyce Ladner earned her doctorate in sociology from Washington University in St. Louis, Missouri, thanks in large part to Dr. Borinski's encouragement. She went on to a distinguished career in academics, including becoming the first woman to head Howard University, where she served as acting president from 1994 to 1995. In 1996, President Clinton appointed her to Washington, D.C.'s first financial control board, a post she held until 1998. She then became a senior fellow at the Brookings Institution, a liberal Washington think tank, from which she retired in 2003. A noted author and scholar, Dr. Ladner now resides in Sarasota, Florida.[77]

Joyce Ladner's older sister, Dorie, who is credited with starting the singing at the Evers funeral march, went to work for SNCC in the Delta after the Jackson Movement crumbled. A year later, she was one of the first women to head a COFO project when she started the first freedom center in Adams County in the southwest corner of the state. She later headed up a Mississippi Freedom Democratic Party voter registration drive. When she moved to the nation's capital, Ladner decided to continue in public service. She received her master's of social work from Howard University and went to work for the city's only public health institution, D.C. General Hospital, where she worked until the facility was closed as a result of budget difficulties in 2001. She continued to serve as a social worker for the D.C. government until she retired in 2006. Dorie Ladner still lives in Washington, D.C.[78]

A few miles from the Tougaloo campus, **Myrtis Raymond**, George Raymond's widow, lived out her days in a single-family home off Interstate 55, the most direct route to her old Canton digs. She remarried after George Raymond's death, had two more children, and then divorced again. Her eldest son, Jomo Raymond, was the picture of his father, with the same stocky build and quiet manner. The younger Raymond served in the air force, married a white woman, and had three children of his own. Unfortunately, Raymond knew little of his father's legacy. "I guess I was kind of scared to look into it," he said.

His wife encouraged him to learn more, however, and he began to locate rich source material about the lasting contributions his father made to the Mississippi Movement.[79]

Jerome Smith, George Raymond's friend from New Orleans, spent a number of years in Mississippi as CORE's project director in Holly Springs. He then returned to his native city, where he served as a long-time project director for a New Orleans community center. Nearly every Saturday, he could be seen accompanying his young students to the Martin Luther King Memorial in the shadow of the Superdome, where he would give lessons about his movement days and teach that the youth of America still have the power to change the world.[80]

Dave Dennis opened a successful law practice in New Orleans and was content there for many years until, in 1989, he ran into Bob Moses at a civil rights conference and his old friend suggested that Dennis open a southern office for the Algebra Project, which Moses had founded to teach basic math skills to economically disenfranchised youth to better prepare them for the challenges of the modern, math-based computer economy. Dennis considered the offer and decided to continue his law practice while running the project on a part-time basis.

Then, on a trip back to New Orleans one evening, Dennis was struck by the reminders all around him of his Mississippi past. "I was coming through the Delta and I could see faces," he said. "Mrs. Hamer, Aaron [Henry]. It was like I'd left a part of me here. There was a lot of stuff that was unfinished."

He resolved then and there to return to Mississippi to complete the work he felt he had left undone so many years ago. He became the head of Positive Innovations, the southern branch of the Algebra Project. Headquartered in Jackson, Dennis and a small staff worked to improve the economic future of the same citizens he worked to free politically.

His return gave Dennis a sense of spiritual closing and an assurance that he was back on track with his lifelong mission. "I have really found myself," he said. "I'm very happy. It's just this freedom inside and reuniting with the spirits that exist here, both people dead and people alive. . . . There were some good friends of mine whose spirits are here. Even George Raymond—although he died in New Orleans, I think he really died here. . . . [There are] parts of me scattered all over this dirt, this soil. . . . A part of Mrs. Hamer is with me; a part of Amzie Moore; Medgar. Because we really did things together that helped to reshape our lives."

Their lives and the lives of many, many others.[81]

PERHAPS THE LAST WORD SHOULD BE PROVIDED BY SOMEONE WHO STAYED with the Jackson Movement through all its ups and downs and kept on pushing after all seemed lost. **Mercedes Wright**, the veteran Savannah Movement leader, came to Jackson in April 1963 at the request of the NAACP, along with Willie Ludden and Laplois Ashford. She participated in most of the strategy sessions and was at Woolworth's when the movement came to life. She was also on hand when it all fell apart, through Medgar's murder and the negotiated settlement. She kept faith in the movement and was employed by the NAACP to lead the continuing boycott under the direction of Charles Evers. Wright remained with the NAACP for at least the next ten years, eventually becoming the association's acting director of education.

On the one-year anniversary of the Evers assassination, while she was temporarily assigned to lead an NAACP membership drive in Detroit in Medgar's honor, Mercedes Wright penned a message to the members of the Jackson Movement. Her words reach across the decades and eloquently summarize what the movement, despite its setbacks and shortcomings, had come to mean for Jackson's black citizens.

My dear friends, though I am physically in Detroit tonight, my heart, mind and soul are with you in Jackson, Mississippi. The occurrence of June 12, 1963 will cause me to pause, reflect and think of you on that date wherever I may be as long as life shall last. Although my thoughts will bring sadness because we lost MEDGAR, there will also be a ray of light heralding the fact that from this unbearable loss came unity and determination among you to free yourselves from the shackling chains of segregation and discrimination that bind you. Your achievements of the past year in Jackson and your diligence in the future collectively and individually will say to our oppressors, "MEDGAR did not die in vain." The program started by you and Medgar Evers in Jackson, Mississippi must not be abandoned until victory is OURS. Continue to abide by the rules of the JACKSON MOVEMENT, for there could be no greater monument to Medgar....

After this assignment is complete and I visit with my family, I expect to come to Jackson to be with you. I am eagerly looking forward to strengthening our program in Jackson and re-iterating our determination. WE SHALL NOT BE MOVED.[82]

EPILOGUE

One Moment in Time

WHEN HE TOOK THE PHOTOGRAPH THAT WOULD PROPEL HIM INTO THE HIS-
tory books, Fred Blackwell was just twenty-two years old, the same age as some
of the demonstrators at the counter, but he had already worked for the *Jackson
Daily News* for more than a year. The newspaper's editor, Jimmy Ward, had
offered young Blackwell a job when at age fourteen he was named "Paper Boy
of the Year." "When you finish high school," Ward told him, "come on back and
we'll put you to work." The idea stuck in the teen's imagination, and he would
eventually take Ward up on his offer after pursuing another boyhood dream—
serving in the U.S. National Guard.[1]

Just as Charlie Newell would do several years later, Fred Blackwell transferred to Central High School during his junior year (1958–1959) in order to
enroll in Central's ROTC program. He therefore knew many of the kids who
showed up at Woolworth's to heckle the demonstrators—he had gone to school
with their older siblings. A native of south Jackson, Blackwell in fact lived just
a few doors down from D.C. Sullivan's family and was friends with D.C.'s older
brother.

After one year at Central, Blackwell transferred back to Provine High for
his senior year. As soon as he finished school, he joined the guard and spent
the next year completing his basic training and serving on active duty. It was
during his tour of duty that Blackwell received his initial apprenticeship in
photography. "They made a photographer out of me," Blackwell acknowledged.
He was captivated by the process of taking and printing photographs. "There's
just something magical about watching a photo come to life in the [chemical]
tray," he would later say.[2]

In 1962, with his National Guard service behind him, Blackwell marched
into the *Jackson Daily News* offices just across the street from city hall and
reminded its editor of his offer. "Put him to work," Ward commanded. At first
Blackwell started off as a copy boy, doing whatever odd jobs needed to be
done around the office. He soon honed in on a dynamo named Jack Thornell,
the paper's primary photographer, and started to shadow Thornell to see how

news photography was done. When the paper's other photographer unexpectedly moved on late in 1962, Blackwell asked Thornell to put in a good word for him with the boss. "Give him a camera and let him try," Ward declared. Thus, Freddie Blackwell, at the age of twenty-two, became an apprentice to his hero, Jack Thornell, and the newspaper's backup camera man.[3]

Thornell had some impressive credits to his name even prior to coming to Jackson. He had begun studying photography as an enlisted man when he made a wrong turn on an army base and ended up at photography rather than radio school. Not one to question destiny, Thornell stayed and became a respected army photographer. His most high-profile assignment during this period was serving as the corps photographer of the just-enlisted Elvis Presley when the King conquered Europe as a GI. After his army service, Thornell became the *Jackson Daily News*'s chief photographer and covered every significant civil rights activity in Mississippi from 1960 until 1964. Later, when he was an Associated Press photographer, his picture of James Meredith lying on the ground howling in pain after being shot during his March Against Fear in 1966 won Thornell the Pulitzer Prize.[4]

Blackwell, therefore, had the opportunity to learn his craft from a seasoned perfectionist who knew how to cover all the angles. Within a few months of his apprenticeship, Blackwell was being sent out regularly on assignments alone. He typically used the square-format RoloFlex 120, the industry standard of the time, which provided handsome, high-quality images on a 2¼-inch squared negative.

When the sit-in at Woolworth's began, Blackwell was the only *Jackson Daily News* photographer on hand. Thornell was up the street covering the picketing until arrests were made; then he, like Joan Trumpauer and Lois Chaffee, moved down to Woolworth's to see what was up.

Blackwell captured the early moments of the sit-in: Memphis Norman, Annie Moody, and Pearlena Lewis sitting peacefully at the counter while journalists hover and a few customers depart. Then Thornell swooped in and caught on film Bennie Oliver's dramatic assault on Memphis Norman. Eager to make the afternoon deadline, Thornell picked up Blackwell's early film canisters and headed back to the office to print what he and Blackwell had already shot.

It was left to the novice Blackwell to stay and cover the rest of the afternoon's traumatic events. He framed and shot his now-iconic photograph of the sit-in, as well as an array of other arresting images: Walter Williams lying unconscious on the floor; Lois Chaffee and Pearlena Lewis huddling together in self-defense; a white youth spraying mustard into the air toward the demonstrators.

Since he knew many of the high school kids causing the ruckus, Blackwell found it somewhat strange being on the other side of the camera, shooting images of his neighbors during this surreal event. Despite his inexperience and youth, Blackwell did his job that day and came away with one of the most memorable photographs of the civil rights era.

It was not immediately recognized as a classic. Thornell's photo of Oliver brutalizing Norman appeared on the front page of the *Jackson Daily News* that afternoon, as it did in many newspapers across the country the next day, including the *New York Times*. Blackwell's photos were mostly an afterthought. Although one of his early sit-in pictures appeared on the *Daily News*'s front page, below the fold, his most striking images do not show up until the next day, and they took second stage to his mentor's action shots.

But the seasoned judgment of history transcends the immediacy of a daily deadline's rush and ultimately selects an image that captures the essence of an era. What Fred Blackwell came away with from Woolworth's that day turned out to be the quintessential sit-in photograph. His composition had every-thing: the shiny counter, the tortured demonstrators, the rowdy crowd, the gazing FBI, the weary press, even the standard Woolworth's sign and middle-America ambiance, right down to the churning lemonade dispenser. It had movement as well as a focal point; it had intense human drama and pathos; it had heart and it had soul. It has endured while other images from that day have faded from the national consciousness.

Blackwell's first indication that his sit-in photographs were more than just passing news shots came when the international large-format news magazine *Paris Match* offered him five thousand dollars to borrow his negatives for a feature on the sit-in. They colorized the photos and ran them full-page a few weeks after the event.[5] Many more requests followed.

The iconic sit-in shot now shows up wherever a sit-in photo is called for. Although it came late in the student movement era, the image conveys fully, without need of a caption, what it must have been like to brave a vicious mob for the sake of freedom. Every major civil rights museum has it hanging some-where within its displays. The Martin Luther King Center in Atlanta shows it, as does the Birmingham Civil Rights Institute. The JFK Library in Boston displayed it for many years, until the museum space was reorganized for ad-ditional family artifacts. The Smithsonian Institution's National Museum of American History, which in the early 1990s acquired the actual Woolworth's counter where the very first sit-in took place, has displayed Blackwell's photo alongside one of that first Greensboro, North Carolina, sit-in.

The most dramatic use of the photograph appears at the Memphis Civil Rights Museum, housed within the historic Lorraine Motel where Martin Lu-ther King was assassinated. Inside this elaborate museum are interactive dis-plays and photo montages of all phases of the civil rights movement, and there, overlooking the sit-in section, hangs a life-size cut-out print of Fred Blackwell's photo, commanding attention amid an entire room full of sit-in memorabilia.

In the center of that room is an actual lunch counter, with red plastic-topped stools. On the far side of the counter, four life-size statues—two whites and two blacks—sit eternally demonstrating while two white thugs jeer from the side. The model for one of the white demonstrators is a direct copy from Blackwell's photo: Joan Trumpauer, right down to her fifties-style hair bun. The other is a loose interpretation of a slimmed-down John Salter, with short-cropped hair and a determined look. The menacing thugs could be taken for an older D.C. Sullivan, cigarette in hand, and one of his friends.

Blackwell's picture also shows up whenever a single image is needed to portray the look and feel of the era. It appears in the *Eyes on the Prize* video and print documentaries and among the history-making images reproduced in the *New York Times* Sunday magazine's one-hundredth anniversary edition of April 14, 1996. It also was chosen by Steven Spielberg for inclusion in his five-minute film summarizing the most important images of the twentieth century and consistently shows up in the various editions of *Life* magazine's "100 Photographs that Changed the World." The photograph has traveled around the globe in a variety of exhibits and showcases, and Blackwell continues to get requests for reprints of the unforgettable image.

It may seem surprising that this famous photograph, certainly of Pulitzer quality, did not win the prize that year. It was, in retrospect, a year of amazing, horrifying images. Those that made it to the final judging included one of a man being attacked by a police dog in Birmingham and several related to President Kennedy's assassination. Robert Jackson's split-second picture of Jack Ruby shooting Lee Harvey Oswald was the winner that year.[6] It may be even more startling to learn that, although Blackwell himself thought the picture was in contention, his photograph was never even submitted for consideration to the Pulitzer committee. In the early 1960s, the newspaper—not the photographer—submitted work to the committee for consideration. Undoubtedly, the editors of the *Jackson Daily News* must have viewed the work as a disgrace to the South—not the sort of image a white southern newspaper would recommend for America's top photojournalism prize.

Like his mentor, Blackwell was offered a job with the Associated Press, but travel didn't appeal to him. "I was a homebody," he admitted. Blackwell chose to remain in Jackson, hoping to stay at the forefront of his field as civil rights history unfolded all around him. "Those were very exciting times," he recalled. "I expected it to go on forever." Although he stayed with the *Jackson Daily News* for seventeen years, when the country moved on to other issues, Blackwell's passion for his career faltered. "After civil rights," he said, "everything else was boring."

Blackwell left the paper in 1979 and after a two-year sabbatical began work as a medical photographer for the McMillan Eye Clinic in Jackson. Ophthalmology requires skilled photographers because the eyes cannot be X-rayed:

they must be photographed for diagnosis and treatment. Blackwell applied the same commitment to excellence and attention to detail to his new profession as he had to his news photography. He retired from the clinic in 2007.

Blackwell's civil rights days are never far from his mind, though he admitted that the things he photographed at that time troubled him greatly. "I hated seeing people hurt," he said. He used the camera to create some emotional distance. "I imagined that when I looked through the camera I was looking at a picture on the wall," he admitted. "By thinking that way, it didn't hurt so much."

His most famous photograph hangs in his home office. Below it is a caption written in his own hand: "A Tragic Moment for Mississippi." In one of the only interviews he has ever granted about his experience that day, after many hesitations and second thoughts, Blackwell told with choked emotion of how not only his professional life but his entire world view changed as he covered the Woolworth's sit-in.

"I wasn't on either side," he stated emphatically. "I was strictly doing my job." But being "a Jackson boy" he admitted that his sentiments, at least early on that day, were with the crowd. He was expecting that the standoff would result in the demonstrators' arrest or early retreat. As the drama unfolded before his lens, however, and as the taunts turned to violence, Blackwell's perspective changed. Somehow, while watching the demonstrators display quiet moral courage against such vicious intolerance—some of it perpetrated by his friends and neighbors—the balance of power shifted in Fred Blackwell's heart.

"It hit me when I was photographing," he said, in a voice barely audible, eyes close to tears, "that they were right and we were wrong."

ACKNOWLEDGMENTS

YOU MIGHT SAY THAT THIS BOOK BEGAN DURING THE SUMMER OF 1977 WHEN I first encountered Joan Mulholland's five boys careening across an open field, kicking up dust as they made their way from their house to the neighborhood playground two blocks away. I happened to be working as a playground counselor and was struck by this force of nature heading my way. Those phenomenal children with unusual names—Bino, Django, Jomo, Loki, and Geronimo—drew me into Joan's orbit and I have never left. A quiet, self-effacing woman, Joan rarely discussed her earlier "movement" days. But gradually, over the course of those first few years, she began to let on that her life had not always been one of suburban child rearing, school socials, and purple Volkswagon minibus trips to the movies. During her late teens and early twenties, in fact, her life had been more dramatic than any movie I had ever seen. When she began inviting me to family gatherings where her movement friends were present and they would passionately discuss their years in Mississippi, I realized I was witnessing something rare, something unbelievably precious, something that needed to be recorded and preserved.

This book started gradually, with the sole objective of telling Joan's story—the story of this singular white southern woman who risked everything to ensure that the region she lived in would become more just, equitable, and humane. As Joan began to reveal more and more of her experiences in the South, particularly in Jackson, and as I began to delve into the history of the period, I realized there was much more to this story than Joan's intersection with it. Through Joan, I began to branch out and talk to others who had been part of this remarkable transformation, who had lived through some of the darkest days of the Mississippi Movement, and who had instigated some of the most outrageous demonstrations the Magnolia State had ever witnessed.

The demonstration that stuck in my mind, aided by an iconic photograph taken by a young news photographer named Fred Blackwell, is the centerpiece of this book. Joan is at the Jackson Woolworth's counter staging a sit-in with John Salter and Anne Moody, each taking their share of abuse as a mob of mostly young teens offers the equivalent of a rebel yell against the nonviolent suggestion that their way of looking at the world might need some adjustment. Times were ripe for change. Sam Cooke began writing his signature song, "A Change Is Gonna Come" in May 1963, the same month as this groundbreaking demonstration. Another demonstrator present that day, Pearlena Lewis, called this moment "the beginning of change in Mississippi."

My vision for this book expanded as I spoke to these and other luminaries of what came to be known as the Jackson Movement until the book encompassed the entire scope of what that movement accomplished. I am fortunate enough to have caught the recollections of many of the leaders of the movement before they and their memories have slipped away. Above all others, I have these brave souls to thank for allowing me into their lives and sharing with me some of the most intimate and hair-raising tales of their young and not-so-young lives.

Through Joan I met Memphis Norman, John Salter, Ed King, and Lois Chaffee. Through them I was introduced to Anne Moody and Doris Allison, who led me to Lillian Louie, who put me in touch with Pearlena Lewis and her brother Alphonzo. I called Dave Dennis out of the blue, and he put me in touch with Jerome Smith, who helped me find the family of George Raymond. I found Tom Beard and Walter Williams in the Jackson phone book. I was lucky enough to converse with every single living individual who had sat in at the Woolworth's counter on that day. The memories of these individuals form the core of this book, and I cannot thank them enough for sharing their stories with me.

Even then I was not satisfied. I wanted to talk to others who were on the scene that day—the police, the rowdy kids, the newsmen who recorded the event. Small towns are fascinating because they often will cough up their secrets if you poke around and are brash enough to ask out loud what others might only whisper. What was astonishing to me, a big-city northerner, was how many of the people who had some involvement in the events of that day had stayed in Jackson. Photographer Fred Blackwell, though reluctant at first to talk to me, eventually relented and slowly unraveled his remembrances of a day that changed his life. He also hinted at knowing some of the kids in the photo and suggested I try to find them. It was through studying the 1963 Central High School yearbook that I discovered several individuals who looked like they might have been in the photo. That's how I ended up talking to Charlie Newell. Charlie hadn't been at Woolworth's that day, but one of his best friends, D. C. Sullivan, had. He gave me D.C.'s number and also put me in touch with Jim Black, the police officer on undercover duty during the sit-in. Both D.C. and Jim invited me into their homes and spent hours going over their memories of the event and their roles in it. I can't recall how I stumbled upon Bill Minor, but Bill also opened his home and shared with me his reporter's recollections as if it all had happened just yesterday. To all of these men I owe a deep debt of gratitude.

This book would not have been written had my wife, Allyson, not put me in touch with a friend of hers, Lynn Whittaker, who was just starting her own publishing adventure—Charles River Press. Lynn was the first to offer encouragement and, more importantly, a book contract. I would never have invested the enormous amount of time and energy in this project without some form of certainty that it would eventually see the light of day. Ironically, when the book was nearing completion, Lynn shuttered CRP due to the ever-present struggles of small presses and her need to move in a different direction. She served as my agent for a time, trying to sell the story to larger for-profit presses, but nothing stuck. We eventually parted ways as friends, but no one was more of an advisor, editor, and supporter of my work than was Lynn Whittaker.

It was through Lynn that I met Julian Bond. Lynn had interned in a nearby congressional office when Julian was in the Georgia legislature. Julian became a champion of this project after I had the opportunity to present the story of the Jackson Movement to his classes at the University of Virginia and at American University in Washington, D.C.—one of my own alma maters. Julian's encouragement during the darkest days of the book's gestation helped me move forward when there seemed no hope of getting the story published. I am humbled and so very grateful for this lion of the movement's foreword, but more so for his friendship.

I am also grateful to my one-time editing professor Shirley Rosenberg, who read an early draft of the manuscript and gave me helpful and reassuring advice.

It was Joan who put me in touch with a graduate student at the University of Mississippi who was researching an aspect of the movement that this story touched upon—the church visits in the days after the Woolworth's sit-in. He encouraged me to resubmit the manuscript to the University Press of Mississippi. UPM seemed like an obvious choice, but early in 2000 when I submitted my proposal, it was rejected. A "new crew" was there now, he told me. So I sheepishly tried again. What a turnaround! Within a week I got a call from UPM's energetic new director, Leila Salisbury, who was enthusiastic about the book's possibilities and supportive of recommending it to her board of reviewers. The rest, for me, has been a magical alignment of vision and focus. Leila sent the manuscript to an anonymous reader whose observations and recommendations have served to strengthen and deepen the book's conclusions. The staff at UPM have also been enormously helpful, particularly Anne Stascavage for guiding the project through the production process, Pete Halverson for his dramatic cover design, Shane Gong Stewart for her production oversight, and Valerie Jones for her overall editorial assistance. I also appreciate Carol Cox's copyediting of the manuscript. University presses nationwide are keeping the spirit of accessible scholarly writing alive, and nowhere is that trend more evident than at UPM. My heartfelt thanks, Leila, for taking me on.

There are many others who participated in this project who deserve recognition. Jerry Thornbery was encouraging from the early stages and even shared some of his own research with me on George Raymond and Operation Freedom. John Dittmer, author of *Local People: The Struggle for Civil Rights in*

Mississippi, was extremely encouraging and shared with me his interview with Dr. Dan Beittel, the president of Tougaloo who ended up at the Woolworth's counter and whose remonstrations with the police and the Woolworth's management helped bring an end to the three-hour-long demonstration. Charles Marsh, author of *God's Long Summer: Stories of Faith and Civil Rights* and whose grandfather Ken Toler was present at the Woolworth's demonstration, was also supportive of my efforts to bring this story to light. This triumvirate of Thornbery, Dittmer, and Marsh offered me the collegial recognition that sustained me during the more than fifteen years that this book was in development. The various libraries I worked in deserve special appreciation: the U.S. Library of Congress, which houses the national NAACP Papers; the NAACP Henry Moon Library in Baltimore, which houses the Mississippi chapter and branch papers; the Amistad Research Center at Tulane University; Howard University's Moorland-Springarn Collection; the Mississippi Department of Archives and History, which houses the John Salter papers as well as the Mississippi State Sovereignty Commission collection; and even the Jackson city libraries, which (at the time of my research) carried microfilmed copies of the *Jackson Daily News* and the *Clarion-Ledger*. All of the librarians without fail were helpful to a fault and dedicated to their mission of preserving and sharing the national treasures they curate. They are the keepers of the flame.

I had the unique honor of corresponding with Annemarie Böll, wife of Nobel Prize winner Heinrich Böll, who had praised Anne Moody's *Coming of Age in Mississippi* and written the foreword for the German translation. Mrs. Böll connected me with Breon Mitchell, who translated that foreword, from which I quoted in the final chapter. In addition, I was further supported in this work through the correspondence with E. L. Doctorow and Joyce Johnson, who provided me with invaluable information about the publication of Anne Moody's exemplary work. In addition, prior to her death, Lena Horne corresponded with me about her involvement in the Jackson Movement, which was a thrill from which I may never recover.

Finally, I must acknowledge the contribution of my wife, Allyson, and our children, Erica, Tevin, and Raymond. As noted earlier, it was my wife's introduction to a publisher that started me on this journey, and her solid anchoring helped me persevere when all seemed lost. My children provided regular reminders of why this story was essential to the nation's consciousness. We are a transracial family, something utterly new and a direct by-product of the civil rights revolution. May we always remember Dr. King's admonition to judge not by the color of one's skin but by the content of one's character. I am forever in debt to my family for giving me their love. I return it to them through this work.

NOTES

List of Abbreviations Used in Notes

AI	Author's Interview
AP	Associated Press
ARC	Amistad Research Center, Tulane University, New Orleans, Louisiana
Beittel Papers	Dan Beittel Papers, L. Zenobia Coleman Library, Tougaloo College, Tougaloo, Mississippi
CA	*Commercial Appeal*, Memphis, Tennessee
CDN	*Chicago Daily News*
C-L	*Clarion-Ledger*, Jackson, Mississippi
COJPDA	City of Jackson Police Department Archives
CORE Papers	Congress of Racial Equality Archives, 1941–1967, on microfilm, Library of Congress, Washington, D.C.
CORE Addendum	CORE Archives, 1944–1968, on microfilm, Library of Congress, Washington, D.C.
CT	*Chicago Tribune*, Chicago, Illinois
Dent Collection	Oral history interviews conducted by Tom Dent, not transcribed, Amistad Research Center, Tulane University. Copies of tapes also available at the L. Zenobia Coleman Library, Tougaloo College, Tougaloo, Mississippi.
ES	*Evening Star*, Washington, D.C. Generally provided Associated Press (AP) wire service reports from Jackson.
FBI Files	Obtained from FBI by author through Freedom of Information Act request.
Howard CRDP	Civil Rights Documentation Project, Moorland-Spingarn Research Center, Howard University, Washington, D.C.
JDN	*Jackson Daily News*, Jackson, Mississippi
JFK	John F. Kennedy Presidential Library, Boston, Massachusetts
(Ed) King Papers	Papers of R. Edwin King, Jr., L. Zenobia Coleman Library, Tougaloo College, Tougaloo, Mississippi
MDAH	Mississippi Department of Archives and History, Jackson, Mississippi
MFP	*Mississippi Free Press*, Jackson, Mississippi
MSC Files	Mississippi Sovereignty Commission Files, Mississippi Department of Archives and History
NAACP Papers	National Association for the Advancement of Colored People Papers, Manuscript Division, Library of Congress, Washington, D.C.
NAACP MS Papers	National Association for the Advancement of Colored People Mississippi Papers, Henry Moon Library, NAACP Headquarters, Baltimore, Maryland. (Papers were not yet catalogued.)

NJA	*North Jackson Action*: the official bulletin of the North Jackson Youth Council (NAACP), Jackson, Mississippi
NYT	*New York Times*
PC	*Pittsburgh Courier*
Pacifica Radio	Pacifica Radio Archive, Los Angeles, California
Salter Papers	Papers of John R. Salter, Jr. (John Hunter Gray), Mississippi Department of Archives and History, Jackson, Mississippi. Also available at the State Historical Society of Wisconsin Library, Madison, Wisconsin.
SHSW	State Historical Society of Wisconsin Library, Madison, Wisconsin
SNCC Papers	Student Nonviolent Coordinating Committee Papers, on microfilm, Library of Congress, Washington, D.C.
TA	Tougaloo Archives, Tougaloo College, Tougaloo, Mississippi
TC	Thornbery Collection. Private collection of civil rights documentation from various sources. Jerry Thornbery, Baltimore, Maryland.
T-P	*Times-Picayune*, New Orleans, Louisiana
UPI	United Press International
WP	*Washington Post*, Washington, D.C. Generally provided United Press International (UPI) reports from Jackson.
WSJ	*Wall Street Journal*, New York, New York

CHAPTER 1

1. Evers's date of birth recorded in Evers (Mrs. Medgar), *For Us, the Living*, p. 18; characterization of Mississippi primarily derived from Loewen and Sallis, *Mississippi: Conflict and Change*.

2. This brief biographical sketch of Medgar Evers was developed from materials included in Evers (Mrs. Medgar), *For Us, the Living*; Evers (Charles), *Evers*; Evers (Charles) and Szanton, *Have No Fear*; Evers-Williams, *Watch Me Fly*; and Evers-Williams and Marable, *The Autobiography of Medgar Evers*.

3. Evers and Szanton, *Have No Fear*, p. 5.

4. Ibid., pp. 12–13.

5. Aspects of this oft-recounted family story are taken from Evers (Mrs. Medgar), *For Us, the Living*, p. 16; Evers (Charles), *Evers*, pp. 27–28; and Evers and Szanton, *Have No Fear*, p. 16.

6. Medgar Evers, "Why I Live in Mississippi."

7. As told to reporter Ben Bagdikian and recorded in Mendelsohn, *The Marytrs*, p. 65.

8. Evers, *Evers*, p. 25.

9. Evers and Szanton, *Have No Fear*, p. 43.

10. Evers, *For Us, the Living*, p. 30.

11. Ibid., p. 24.

12. Evers and Szanton, *Have No Fear*, p. 61.

13. Evers, "Why I Live in Mississippi," op. cit.

14. Evers and Szanton, *Have No Fear*, p. 58.

15. Evers-Williams, *Watch Me Fly*, p. 51.

16. Ibid., p. 52.

17. Ibid., p. 61.

18. Summary of NAACP historical information was gleaned from Harris, *History and Achievement of the NAACP.*

19. James Farmer, a founder and later executive director of the Congress of Racial Equality (CORE), worked for the NAACP from 1959 to 1960. He provided a rather derisive assessment of the NAACP's organizational structure that would later be trumpeted by members of the Jackson Movement: "The association's more than fourteen hundred branches were all too often mere collection agencies, signing up members once a year, collecting dues, and holding annual freedom fund banquets. . . ." Farmer, *Lay Bare the Heart*, p. 191.

20. Evers, *For Us, the Living*, p. 92.

21. Ibid., p. 101.

22. Ibid., p. 104.

23. Evers and Szanton, *Have No Fear*, p. 78. Also see Evers, "Why I Live in Mississippi."

24. Evers, *Evers*, p. 99.

25. Evers-Williams, *Watch Me Fly*, p. 68.

26. Evers, *For Us, the Living*, p. 112; also see Loewen and Sallis, *Mississippi: Conflict and Change*, p. 254.

27. 1955 Annual Report, Mississippi State Office, NAACP Papers, II:C346, Medgar Evers, 1954–1955.

28. Evers and Szanton, *Have No Fear*, p. 78.

29. Mendelsohn, *The Martyrs*, p. 67.

30. Evers, "Why I Live in Mississippi."

31. Mendelsohn, *The Martyrs*, p. 67.

32. Information on Jackson's history and background derived from various sources, including: Loewen and Sallis, *Mississippi: Conflict and Change*; Williams, *Eyes on the Prize*; Dittmer, *Local People*; *Collier's Encyclopedia*, and various travel guides. The Old State Capitol went through a number of renovations, including one completed in 1961 that removed the stucco and exposed the brick, creating a Federalist look. In 2009, the building was restored to its original stucco and limestone front exterior. mdah.state .ms.us/oldcap/restorationphp.

33. Evers, *For Us, the Living*, p. 194.

34. Evers and Szanton, *Have No Fear*, p. 86.

35. Evers-Williams and Marable, *Autobiography*, pp. 52, 66.

36. *NYT*, 11/10/57.

37. AI, Calhoun.

38. Evers, *For Us, the Living*, pp. 210–211.

39. The bus incident is recounted in two secondary sources: Evers and Szanton, *Have No Fear*, p. 106, and Mendelsohn, *The Martyrs*, p. 70. Evers also provided a firsthand account of the incident and issued a press release about it. NAACP Worker Attacked on Bus in Mississippi, March 13, 1958; Report (via phone) from Medgar Evers, March 13, 1958; and Personal Statement, all included in NAACP Papers, III:A114, Medgar Evers Correspondence, 1957–1962.

40. Thompson biographical sketch derived from various newspaper accounts, including *C-L*, 8/1/48, 1/1/61, 1/3/69, and 10/19/80. Jackson population data derived from U.S. Department of Commerce, Bureau of the Census, 1960 Census Report.

41. *JDN*, 10/13/60.

42. *JDN*, 5/30/61. Thompson appeared on NBC's *Dave Garroway Show*, a forerunner to *Today*.

43. For a summary of the NAACP's approach to the bail issue, see Memorandum from Gloster B. Current, February 9, 1961, "NAACP Position on Jail, No Bail," NAACP Papers, III:A290, Sit-Ins, NAACP Instructions for 1960–1961.

44. For a view of Evers's early attitude toward the student movement, see "Special Report, Mississippi Field Secretary," October 12, 1961, NAACP Papers, III:A115, Mississippi Field Reports, 1960–1962.

45. Ibid.

46. For more on the creation of COFO, see Dittmer, *Local People*, pp. 118–119. Also see Meier and Rudwick, *CORE*, pp. 178–179.

47. History of Tougaloo College is derived from Campbell and Rodgers, *Mississippi: The View from Tougaloo;* from the Murray Resource Directory to the Nation's Historically Black Colleges and Universities; and from interviews with students enrolled at the college in the early 1960s.

48. Borinski biographical sketch derived from Edgcomb, *From Swastika to Jim Crow*, chapter 8.

49. AI, Memphis Norman.

50. Clifton A. Johnson interview with Beittel, ARC; John Dittmer interview with Beittel, May 25, 1981.

51. Report, NAACP Field Secretary, January 27–February 28, 1955, NAACP Papers, II:C346, Evers, Medgar, 1954–1955.

52. Medgar Evers letter to Robert Carter, March 15, 1961, NAACP Papers, III:A290, Sit-ins, States A–N, 1960–1965.

53. Tougaloo Nine library sit-in and related actions derived from Dittmer, *Local People*, pp. 87–89 and from various NAACP memoranda and reports of the period.

54. As reported in Dittmer, *Local People*, p. 89.

55. Report, Mississippi Field Secretary (received via telephone), November 29, 1960, NAACP Papers, III:A115; Monthly Report, Mississippi Field Secretary, January 5, 1962, NAACP Papers, III:A115; Salter, *Jackson, Mississippi*, p. 28.

56. Evers-Williams, *Watch Me Fly*, p. 73.

CHAPTER 2

1. Brief summary of Anne Moody's early life is derived from her *Coming of Age in Mississippi*.

2. Moody, *Coming of Age*, p. 33.

3. Ibid., 34.

4. Ibid., 39.

5. Ibid., 45.

6. Ibid., 50.

7. Ibid., 125.

8. Ibid., 242.

9. Ibid., 249.

10. AI, Trumpauer.

11. Notes from author's phone conversation with Moody, May 1996.

12. AI, Salter.

13. Author's phone conversation with Moody, May 1996.

14. Brief biographical sketch of Joan Trumpauer is derived from author's interviews with Trumpauer, October 1992 to November 1995. Unless otherwise noted, all quotations from this section come from these interviews.

15. Incidents occurred Friday, May 6, 1960, and Wednesday, May 11, 1960. See *(Durham) Morning Herald*, 5/6/60, 5/7/60, 5/11/60, and 5/12/60; *Raleigh News and Observer*, 5/7/60; *Charlotte Observer*, 5/7/60, 5/12/60.

16. *Avent et al. v. North Carolina*, United States Reports, Volume 373: Cases adjudged in the Supreme Court at October Term, 1962 (April through June 1963), p. 375.

17. Trumpauer's claim is overstated. The overwhelming majority of riders from this period (immediately following the cessation of the original Freedom Ride) came from Nashville, followed distantly by those from Washington, D.C., New Orleans, and Atlanta. Four prominent NAG members, all friends of Trumpauer, joined or rejoined the ride at this time: Paul Dietrich, Dion Diamond, Hank Thomas, and John Moody. See Arsenault, *Freedom Riders*, p. 255 and pp. 537–541.

18. MDAH, Newsfilm Collection, 1954–1971.

19. Joan (Trumpauer) Mulholland Private Collection, Hinds County Jail citation. For a more complete summary of the Freedom Ride experience, particularly for those whose final destination was Jackson, see Etheridge, *Breach of Peace*. Trumpauer's profile and youthful photograph can be found on pp. 86–89.

20. Ibid., Mulholland Collection. Diary transcribed by author.

21. AI, Trumpauer.

22. Charlotte Phillips, a white student from Swarthmore College, visited Tougaloo for the fall 1961 semester, joining Trumpauer on campus. Trumpauer, however, holds the distinction of being the first full-time white student (other than children of faculty) to enroll at the historically black institution.

23. *Jet*: story and photo, "Miss. Sheriff Probes White Coeds' Entry at Negro School," 10/5/61; *Jet*: photo and caption, "Mississippi Melting Pot," 10/19/61; *Jet*: photo and caption, "Reverse Integration," 12/29/62; *Ebony*, article and photographs, "Reverse Integration in Mississippi," January 1963. Trumpauer also wrote articles about her decision to enter Tougaloo. These appeared in *The Southern Patriot*, "White Student Finds an Oasis at Negro College," September 1962; and *Horizons (Church of the Brethren)* "Integration in Reverse," 3/17/63. Mainstream media mentions of Trumpauer's enrollment and experience at Tougaloo appeared in *NYT*, "Negro School Takes Two White Women," 9/15/61; *WP*, "Two White Girls Enter Mississippi Negro College," 9/17/61; *NYT*, "2 White Coeds at Negro College Living Their Integration Ideals," 11/13/61.

24. For a thorough review of the Nashville students' effect on Jackson from June 1961 through May 1962, see Halberstam, *The Children*, and Dittmer, *Local People*.

25. Some copies of this mimeographed newsletter are still extant in the Joan (Trumpauer) Mulholland Private Collection. See also SNCC Papers, LOC.

26. Braden correspondence to Jim Dombrowski, 5/15/62, Anne Braden Papers, SHSW. Braden tempers her assessment of Trumpauer's state of mind nearly a year later in a letter to "Horace" dated 3/19/63. Acknowledging that she initially thought Trumpauer was in "an impossible situation" and "on the verge of a nervous breakdown," Braden acknowledges that "I believe . . . she *is* coming through [her ordeal] in good shape." Anne Braden Papers, SHSW. Trumpauer began to contribute articles to a number of news outlets, including *The (Baltimore) Afro-American*, 6/26/62; *The Militant*, 6/6/62; and *The National Guardian*, 6/18/62.

27. AI, Trumpauer.

28. Brief biographical sketch of D. C. Sullivan derived from author's interview, November 1996. Unless otherwise noted, all quotations are taken from that interview.

29. AI, Newell.

30. Ibid.

31. The 1962 *Cotton Boll*, Central High School Yearbook, p. 77.

32. AI, Newell.

33. Brief biographical sketch of John Salter derived from author's interviews, December 1995. Unless otherwise noted, all quotations are taken from those interviews.

34. Confirmation of Salter's involvement provided in 11/17/81 letter from IRA Associate Editor Lisa Klopfer to John R. Salter, Salter/Gray Private Collection.

35. For more about Salter's role, see Radest, *Toward Common Ground*.

36. "A Lincoln Emancipation Conference: To Discuss Means for Securing Political and Civil Equality for the Negro," known as "The Call," William English Walling Papers, Manuscript Division, LOC.

37. For more on the William James connection, see Lewis, *The Jameses*, p. 414.

38. Josephine Heath's legacy derived from author's interview with Salter, supplemented by obituaries of Thomas Hunter Heath and article by Reed Hoffman, "Teller Tales," The Dickinson County (KS) Bank, June 1990, Salter/Gray Private Collection.

39. Quoted from Salter's FBI files, released to him under FOIA: Salter/Gray Private Collection.

40. AI, Salter. A version of this story is included in Vollers, *Ghosts of Mississippi*, p. 97.

41. Salter, *Jackson, Mississippi*, p. 7.

42. Ibid., p. 14.

43. Ibid., pp. 4, 15. For further documentation about Lidell's civil rights involvement, see Halberstam, *The Children*.

44. Ibid., p. 20.

45. This fact is verified by various individuals close to Evers. See Hurley interview in Raines, *My Soul Is Rested*, p. 271.

46. AI, Salter; also see Salter letter to Polly Greenberg, 9/27/66, Box 1, Folder 6, Salter Papers, MDAH.

47. Salter, *Jackson, Mississippi*, p. 21.

48. AI, Salter.

49. *Exploratory Report Re Economic Destitution of Rural and Urban Negro Families in the Delta Region of the State of Mississippi*, NAACP Papers, III:A 229.

50. *Eaglet*, the Tougaloo yearbook, 1963, p.144, TA.

51. Salter, *Jackson, Mississippi*, p. 134.

CHAPTER 3

1. Brief biographical sketch of Memphis Norman is derived from author's interviews, October/November 1995. All quotations in this section are taken from those interviews.

2. Brief biographical sketch of Pearlena Lewis is derived from author's interviews, March 1996 and September 1998. Unless otherwise noted, all quotations in this section are taken from those interviews.

3. Lewis earned an academic scholarship to Tougaloo. AI, Lewis (Alphonzo).

4. Brief biographical sketch of Lillian Louie and her quotes are derived from author's interview, November 1996.

5. AI, Salter.

6. Brief biographical sketch of Lois Chaffee is derived from author's interviews, March 1996. All quotations in this section are taken from those interviews.

7. Brief biographical sketch of George Raymond is derived from author's interviews with family members and CORE associates.

8. AI, Lois Blakes et al., January 1997.

9. Ibid.

10. Ibid.

11. AI, John Raymond, January 1997.

12. AI, Lois Blakes et al.

13. AI, John Raymond.

14. AI, Lois Blakes et al.

15. Summary of Jerome Smith's early life is derived from author's interview, January 1997, and from Meier and Rudwick, *CORE*, pp. 115–116.

16. AI, Smith.

17. Robert Wright interview of George Raymond, September 1968, Howard CRDP.

18. AI, John Raymond.

19. Wright interview, Howard CRDP.

20. *NYT*, 11/30/61 and 12/1/61.

21. Undated handwritten letter courtesy of Verna Polk.

22. Brief Dennis biographical sketch is derived from AI, Dennis, as well as from Meier and Rudwick, *CORE*, pp. 115–116.

23. AI, Dennis.

24. Ibid.

25. Brief biographical sketch of Tom Beard is derived from author's interviews, May/ November 1997.

CHAPTER 4

1. Biographical sketch of Jim Black is derived from author's interview, November 1996.

2. Biographical sketch of John Ray is derived from his obituary, *C-L*, 1/16/69, and from a *Clarion-Ledger* editorial, *C-L*, 1/17/69.

3. Shoemaker confirmed Black's role, AI, Shoemaker.

4. *WP*, 5/16/97.

5. Biographical sketch of Bill Minor is derived from author's interview, November 1996, as well as from Roberts and Klibanoff, *The Race Beat*, p. 343.

6. Biographical sketch of Ken Toler is derived from his obituary, *CA*, 10/18/66, a *CA* editorial, 10/18/66, and *NYT*, 10/19/66.

7. AI, Minor.

8. *CA*, 10/18/66.

9. Ibid.

10. Roberts and Klibanoff, *The Race Beat*, pp. 200–203; *WP*, 12/29/2005.

11. AI, Shoemaker.

12. AI, Minor.

13. Biographical sketch of Ed King is derived from author's interviews, February 1996. Another summary of King's life and civil rights activities can be found in Marsh, *God's Long Summer*. All quotations in this section from AI, King unless otherwise noted.

14. Moody, *Coming of Age*, p. 379. Joan Trumpauer confirmed the suspicion with which King was initially greeted. Apparently, even though there were many white professors like Salter and Borinski and even white administrators like Beitel, the thought of having a white minister—and a native Mississippian at that—serve as chaplain felt like a step backwards for most students. The prior chaplain had been black.

CHAPTER 5

1. AI, Louie.

2. Dittmer, *Local People*, p. 157.

3. AI, Salter.

4. AI, King.

5. Summary of Meredith showdown is taken from Dittmer, *Local People*; Branch, *Parting the Waters;* and Williams, *Eyes on the Prize*, as well as from *WP* and *NYT* accounts. For more on the Meredith crisis, also see Cohodas, *The Band Played Dixie*, and Meredith, *Three Years in Mississippi*.

6. Letter from Joan Trumpauer to Anne Braden, 9/25/62. Handwritten draft in Trumpauer (Mulholland) personal archives; handwritten final in Braden Papers, Box 39, Folder 1, SHSW.

7. Meredith was a transfer student from Jackson State and had only one year left to graduate when he entered the University of Mississippi. He graduated on August 18, 1963.

8. First edition (Vol. I, No. 1, 9/22/62) found in Joan Trumpauer's personal archives. All subsequent editions (Vol. I, Nos. 2–17, 9/29/62 through 4/15/63), as well as occasional special "Newsletter Reports" are part of Salter Papers, MDAH.

9. Salter, *Jackson, Mississippi*, p. 52.

10. Summary of the first NJYC meeting with Salter as adult leader is summarized from *NJA*, Vol. 1, No. 4: 10/11/62, as well as from AI, Salter, AI, Lewis, and Salter, *Jackson, Mississippi*, p. 48.

11. AI, Allison.

12. Summary of Youth Council activities derived primarily from complete archive of *North Jackson Action* newsletters, as noted above.

13. *NJA*, Vol. I, No. 4: 10/11/62.

14. Ibid.

15. "Dear Friend" letter dated 10/30/62 included in Salter *NJA* file, MDAH.

16. As reported in *NJA*, Vol. I, No. 9: 11/9/62.

17. An extensive search turned up no copies of *NJA* in the NAACP files at the LOC, although Vol. I, No. 1 of the newsletter was discovered in the NAACP MS Papers in Baltimore.

18. *NJA*, Vol. I, No. 9: 11/9/62.

19. Salter, *Jackson, Mississippi*, p. 53.

20. Ibid., p. 54.

21. Kunstler, *Deep in My Heart*, p. 135.

22. AI, Allison. Allison's recollection of this event was inaccurate in that she believed Roy Wilkins was on hand to make the announcement. Wilkins's schedule records that he was in New York on this day. In all likelihood it was Gloster Current who was on hand to make the announcement. Photographs of this period show Current with Evers in the new NAACP office space.

23. The story of Evers's recruitment of Allison for the post is taken entirely from AI, Allison.

24. *NJA*, Vol. I, No. 10: 11/16/62.

25. *NJA*, Vol. I, No. 11: 11/30/62.

26. Salter, *Jackson, Mississippi*, p. 54.

27. Ibid.

28. *NJA*, Vol. I, No. 10: 11/16/62.

29. Salter, *Jackson, Mississippi*, p. 57.

30. Ibid., pp. 57–58.

31. Story of first Jackson Movement picketing and resulting press coverage derived from Salter, *Jackson, Mississippi*, pp. 58–65, as well as from AI, Salter, and *JDN*, 12/13/62–12/16/62.

32. Signs are clearly visible in photograph that ran the next day: *JDN*, 12/13/62.

33. Ibid.

34. Salter, of mixed-race heritage, consistently claimed his Native American ancestry as equal to that of his Caucasian ancestry. He bristled at any reference to being "white."

35. AI, Salter.

36. Ibid.

37. Salter, *Jackson, Mississippi*, p. 60.

38. AI, King; AI, Salter.

39. AI, Moses.

40. AI, Lewis.

41. AI, Ashford.

42. This designation, as well as the following biographical sketch of Wilkins, is taken from his obituary, *NYT*, 9/9/81, as well as from Wilkins, *Standing Fast*.

43. Ibid., *NYT*, 9/9/81.

44. AI, Allison.

45. AI, Salter (Eldri).

46. AI, Lewis (Alphonzo).

47. *NJA*, Vol. I, No. 13: 12/29/62; Salter, *Jackson, Mississippi*, pp. 66–68; AI, Salter; *JDN*, 12/21/62.

48. "Boycott Tougaloo," *MFP*, 1/5/63; also see *NHA*, Vol. I, No. 13: 12/29/62, and *The (Baltimore) Afro-American*, 1/12/63.

49. *NJA*, Vol. I, No. 13: 12/29/62; Salter, *Jackson, Mississippi*, p. 69; AI, Salter. In his book, Salter indicates that Joan Trumpauer was at his home when the shot came through the window, but *NJA* does not report this, nor does Trumpauer remember being there.

50. Salter, *Jackson, Mississippi*, p. 69.

51. Monthly Report, Mississippi Field Secretary, December 1962. NAACP Papers, III:A115, Reports.

52. *NJA*, Vol. I, No. 13: 12/29/62; Salter, *Jackson, Mississippi*, pp. 69–70.

53. Monthly Report, Mississippi Field Secretary, December 1962. NAACP Papers, III:A115, Reports.

54. *NJA*, Vol. I, No. 15: 2/9/63; Salter, *Jackson, Mississippi*, pp. 72, 80.

55. Salter, *Jackson, Mississippi*, pp. 73–74; *NJA*, Vol. I, No. 14: 1/24/63.

56. *NJA*: Vol. I, No. 15: 2/9/63. Also see letter from North Jackson NAACP Youth Council, 1/28/63, NAACP Papers, III:A230, Mississippi Pressures, Jackson, MS, 1956–1965.

57. Letters to Current and Ashford from John R. Salter, 1/28/63, NAACP Papers, III:A230, Mississippi Pressures, Jackson, MS, 1957–1965. Also see Salter, *Jackson, Mississippi*, p. 82.

58. Memorandum to Messrs. Wilkins, Carter, Morsell, Moon, and Ashford from Gloster B. Current, 1/31/63, NAACP Papers, III:A230, Mississippi Pressures, Jackson, MS, 1957–1965.

59. Current background from his obituary, *NYT*, 7/9/97.

60. Memorandum to Committtee on Branches from Gloster B. Current, 1/31/63, NAACP Papers, III:A230, Mississippi Pressures, Jackson, MS, 1957–1965.

61. Minutes, NAACP Executive Committee Meeting, 2/11/63, p. 3, NAACP Papers, III:A26.

62. NAACP Executive Committee Meeting, 3/11/63, pp. 3–4, NAACP Papers, III:A26. The secretary of the association was also advised to send a letter to all NAACP branches asking them to participate in the boycott of the seventeen stores recommended by Salter.

63. Letter from "The Jackson Area Boycott Movement," January 1963, with handwritten annotation, "Sent with a leaflet to all white businessmen involved in the boycott, in early January"; NAACP Papers, III:A230, Mississippi Pressures, Jackson, MS, 1957–1965; also included in Salter Papers and NAACP MS papers (without notation). Also see Salter, *Jackson, Mississippi*, pp. 72–73.

64. Jackson Boycott Movement Information Bulletin, February 1963, NAACP MS Papers.

65. AI, Salter, p. 32. Also see *NJA*, Vol. I, No. 16: 3/26/63.

66. Allison's call to ministers taken from AI, Allison.

67. Salter, *Jackson, Mississippi*, pp. 90–91.

68. AI, Moses.

69. *Sing for Freedom*, Track 24, "Medgar Evers Speaking."

70. Monthly Report, Mississippi Field Secretary, 3/6/63, NAACP Papers, III:A115, Reports.

71. Salter, *Jackson, Mississippi*, p. 98.

72. Letter to Kunstler, 3/17/63, Salter Papers: "Medgar is with us. . . ." Also see Salter, *Jackson, Mississippi*, p. 91.

73. Monthly Report, Mississippi Field Secretary, 2/7/63 and 3/6/63, NAACP Papers, III:A115, Reports.

74. Ibid.

75. C-L, 4/5/63; JDN, 4/5/63; NJA, Vol. I, No. 17, 4/15/62; Salter, *Jackson, Mississippi*, pp. 93–94.

76. Letter "To the Businessmen of Jackson" from The Jackson Boycott Movement, spring 1963, with handwritten annotation, "Sent with a leaflet to all white businessmen involved in the boycott, in late March," NAACP Papers, III:A230, Mississippi Pressures, Jackson, MS, 1957–1965. Also see Salter, *Jackson, Mississippi*, pp. 91–92.

77. James Farmer letter to John R. Salter, Jr., 2/6/63, Salter Papers; Julian Bond letter excerpted in NJA, Vol. I, No. 17: 4/15/63.

78. "Dear Friend" letter from The Jackson Boycott Movement, spring 1963, with handwritten annotation: "Sent with a leaflet, to all Negro businessmen & clergy in Jackson area, on April 5"; NAACP Papers, III:A230, MS Pressures, Jackson, MS, 1957–1965. File also contains similar "Dear Friend" letter with handwritten annotation "Negro teachers in Jackson area." Also see Salter, *Jackson, Mississippi*, p. 94.

79. Letter to Laplois Ashford from John R. Salter, 3/30/63, Salter Papers. Also see Salter, *Jackson, Mississippi*, p. 93.

80. Regarding Ashford's call, see response letter to Laplois Ashford from John R. Salter, Jr., 4/9/63, Salter Papers. Also see Salter, *Jackson, Mississippi*, p. 94. Regarding Ashford letter, see Letter to John R. Salter from Laplois Ashford, 4/15/63, Salter Papers. Regarding Wilkins encouragement, see Letter to John R. Salter from Roy Wilkins, 4/15/63, NAACP Papers, III:E9, Tougaloo College, Tougaloo, 1963.

81. Ibid.

82. Summary of Birmingham campaign relies primarily on Branch, *Parting the Waters*, and Williams, *Eyes on the Prize*.

83. Salter, *Jackson, Mississippi*, p. 94.

84. Wilkins, *Standing Fast*, p. 287.

85. Historian John Dittmer comes to a similar conclusion regarding the reason for the NAACP's decision to back the Jackson Movement. He points, however, to a later memorandum from Gloster Current to regional and field secretaries on May 13. See Dittmer, *Local People*, p. 160. See also endnote 103 below.

86. Salter, *Jackson, Mississippi*, p. 97; also see Letter from Laplois Ashford to John R. Salter, 4/15/63, NAACP MS Papers, and Letter to Laplois Ashford from John R. Salter, Jr., 4/19/63, confirming date of visit. NAACP Papers, III:E9, Tougaloo College, 1963.

87. Biographical sketch of Laplois Ashford is derived from author's interview, April 1999.

88. Biographical sketch of Willie Ludden is derived from Ludden, *Anatomy of a Civil Rights Worker*.

89. Ludden, *Anatomy of a Civil Rights Worker*, p. 120.

90. AI, Ashford; Ludden, *Anatomy of a Civil Rights Worker*, p. 121.

91. Salter, *Jackson, Mississippi*, p. 99.

92. Ibid., p. 100. Also see Ashford Memoranda of 5/9/63 and 5/10/63 to Current, Wilkins, Moon, Ludden, Evers, and Hurley, NAACP Papers, III:A230, Mississippi Pressures, Jackson, MS, 1957–1965. In them, Ashford details his visit to Jackson the prior month and specifically says that the demonstrations were postponed for ten days to give high school students an opportunity to finish out the school year, as well as to let the media spotlight on Birmingham cool.

93. Letter to Laplois Ashford from John R. Salter, Jr., 5/8/63, NAACP Papers, III:E9 Youth File, 1956–1965, Mississippi, Jackson. Carbon copy of letter can also be found in Salter Papers.

94. AI, Ashford.

95. Salter, *Jackson, Mississippi*, pp. 97–99. Also see *NJA*, Newsletter Report to Out-of-State Friends, 5/19/63, p. 2.

96. Jackson Boycott Movement, For Immediate Release, 4/25/63, NAACP MS Papers.

97. Memorandum to Current et al. from Ashford, 5/9/63, NAACP Papers, III:A230, Mississippi Pressures, Jackson, MS, 1957–1965. Besides Kunstler's involvement, the NAACP was also squeamish about SCEF's participation, as Ashford references in his memo: "It was made very clear to Mr. Salter, Advisor to the North Jackson Youth Council, that the NAACP has the resources and facilities to handle all facets of the campaign and that all future efforts would be directed by and through the NAACP; and that no further support in any form should be accepted from the Southern Conference Educational Fund."

98. Memorandum to Gloster Current from Roy Wilkins, 5/2/63, NAACP Papers, III:E9, Youth File, 1956–1965, Mississippi, Jackson.

99. Salter, *Jackson, Mississippi*, p. 105. Also see final resolution of Mississippi State NAACP Board of Directors, May 12, 1963, in which they "go on official record as supporting an intensive and massive campaign in the city of Jackson." NAACP MS Papers.

100. Salter, *Jackson, Mississippi*, pp. 105–106.

101. Ibid., pp. 106–107. Also see letters to the Downtown Jackson Association and Mississippi Bankers Association, 5/12/63, NAACP MS Papers. In addition, see draft of same letter to Hon. Alan [*sic*] Thompson et al., 5/13/63. NAACP Papers, III:A230, Mississippi Pressures, 1957–1965. Includes Lillian Louie's note "Taken on phone from Medgar Evers."

102. Salter, *Jackson, Mississippi*, p. 107.

103. Memorandum from Gloster B. Current to various regional and field secretaries, 5/13/63, NAACP Papers, III:A237, Current, Gloster B., Correspondence, Memoranda 1963, Jan.–Jun.

104. Salter, *Jackson, Mississippi*, p. 109. Full text of Thompson's remarks can be found in NAACP Papers, III:A290, Speakers—Evers, Medgar, W. Also see NAACP's "Background Information on New Desegregation Drive in Jackson, Miss.," 5/28/63, NAACP MS Papers (original) or NAACP Papers (copy), III:A230, MS Pressures, Jackson, MS, 1957–1965.

105. Salter, *Jackson, Mississippi*, p. 100. Also AI, Salter; AI, Lewis (Pearlena).

106. NAACP Executive Committee Meeting Minutes, May 13, 1963, NAACP Papers, III:A26, Minutes, 1956–1965.

107. Salter, *Jackson, Mississippi*, p. 113. See also NAACP's "Background Information on New Desegregation Drive in Jackson, Miss.," 5/28/63, NAACP Papers, III:A230, MS Pressures, Jackson, MS, 1956–1965.

108. *JDN*, 5/15/63; Salter, *Jackson, Mississippi*, p. 114; NAACP's "Background Information" 5/28/63, NAACP Papers, III:A230, MS Pressures, Jackson, MS, 1956–1965.

109. *JDN*, 5/18/63. Also see Salter, *Jackson, Mississippi*, p. 116.

110. Salter, *Jackson, Mississippi*, p. 117.

111. *JDN*, 5/27/63, and AI, King.

112. *JDN*, 5/14/63.

113. *C-L*, 5/19/63.

114. *JDN*, 5/21/63.

115. Ibid., 5/15/63.

116. "Remarks of Mr. Medgar Evers, Field Secretary, NAACP, Monday, May 20, 1963, 8:00 p.m. For Delivery over WLBT and WJTV," NAACP Papers, III:A290, Speakers— Evers, Medgar, 1963. Excerpts of Evers's speech can be found in Evers-Williams and Marable, *Autobiography*, pp. 280–283.

117. As an example of blacks becoming more emboldened, the Baptist Ministers Union of Jackson issued a statement to the Associated Press later that week, noting that they had "voted unanimously to commend Mr. Medgar W. Evers for his stand taken in his reply to the News Cast made by Mayor Thompson . . . ," NAACP MS Papers.

118. All cases as reported in United States Reports, Volume 373: Cases Adjudged in The Supreme Court at October Term, 1962 (April 29 through June 3, 1963), U.S. Government Printing Office, Washington, D.C., 1963.

119. AP wire story, dateline Atlanta, as it appeared in *JDN*, 5/21/63.

120. FBI Files: #157-896, Vol. 1, 5/29/63 Teletype, "Desegregation of Jackson, Mississippi."

121. MSC Files: #2-55-10-76-4-1-1, "Contacting Informants in an attempt to ascertain if negro agitators plan to come to Jackson, Mississippi . . ."

122. Salter, *Jackson, Mississippi*, p. 122; *JDN*, 5/22/63, "Negroes Threaten Jackson Outburst." Also see *MFP*, 5/25/63.

123. Salter, *Jackson, Mississippi*, p. 122; *JDN*, 5/22/63, *MFP*, 5/25/63, and *PC*, 6/1/63.

124. Salter, *Jackson, Mississippi*, p. 123; *JDN*, 5/22/63, and *MFP*, 5/25/63. Also see *C-L*, 5/28/63; *MFP*, 6/1/63; *PC*, 6/8/63; *WP*, 6/1/63.

125. Salter, *Jackson, Mississippi*, pp. 123–124. Text of telegrams also found in NAACP MS Papers. The national NAACP also sent telegrams to the national chain stores. See NAACP telegram, "NAACP National Office Fully Supports its Jackson, Miss. Branch," 5/23/63, NAACP Papers, III:H42, Telegrams, Jan.–Aug. 1963.

126. Salter, *Jackson, Mississippi*, p. 124; *JDN*, 5/22/63, and *MFP*, 5/25/63. Also see NAACP press release, "Showdown on Civil Rights Imminent in Jackson, Miss.," 5/25/63, NAACP Papers, III:A230, Mississippi Pressures, Jackson, MS, 1957–1965.

127. Salter, *Jackson, Mississippi*, pp. 124–125; *JDN*, 5/22/63, and *MFP*, 5/25/63. Also see NAACP "Background Information," 5/28/63, NAACP Papers, III:A230, MS Pressures, Jackson, MS, 1956–1965. Regarding the "paid spy," see also NAACP "Background Information," 5/28/63; and Evers (Myrlie), *For Us, the Living*, p. 270.

128. *JDN*, 5/22/63 and 5/24/63; Salter, *Jackson, Mississippi*, pp. 125–126. Also see NAACP "Background Information," 5/28/63, Ibid.

129. Salter, *Jackson, Mississippi*, p. 126. Also see *JDN*, 5/27/63 and 5/29/63, as well as *C-L*, 5/29/63.

130. Ibid., p. 128.

131. AI, Salter.

132. AI, King.

133. AI, Salter.

134. AI, King.

135. **Lewis chosen**: AI, Lewis, I-24 (Salter, however, says that he asked Lewis); **Moody chosen**: AI, Salter, II-43; Moody, *Coming of Age*, p. 263; **Norman chosen**: AI, Norman, II-20.

136. AI, Salter. Salter says Steve Rutledge was in the room during this heated discussion. Rutledge, however, did not remember the conversation. AI, Rutledge.

137. Tougaloo Commencement brochure, Trumpauer personal archives; also see Salter, *Jackson, Mississippi*, p.129.

138. Salter, *Jackson, Mississippi*, p. 130; *NYT*, 5/28/63 (dateline May 27).

139. Full text on Thompson's statement reproduced in *C-L*, 5/28/63. Also see *JDN*, 5/27/63 and 5/28/63.

140. Ibid. See also Salter, *Jackson, Mississippi*, p. 131, as well as video footage of meeting, MDAH film archives.

141. FBI Files: #157-896, Vol. 1,"Desegregation of Jackson, Miss. Business Establishments and Public Facilities," 5/27/63.

142. AI, King, II-53.

143. Salter, *Jackson, Mississippi*, p. 131.

CHAPTER 6

1. Much of the detail in this chapter was gleaned from press reports of eyewitnesses who covered the sit-in, as well as from interviews with those who were on the scene in various capacities. Press reports include the following: *JDN*, 5/28/63; *C-L*, *JDN*, *T-P*, *CA*, *NYT*, *WP*, *ES*, *WSJ*, *CT*, UPI, and AP, 5/29/63. Also, eyewitness accounts appeared in *Newsweek*, 6/10/63; *Look*, 7/16/63; *MFP*, 6/1/63; *PC*, 6/8/63; and the *Daily Telegraph* (Australia), 5/29/63. The chapter also draws from published first-person accounts by Moody in *Coming of Age* and Salter, *Jackson, Mississippi*, and from the chapter titled "Bacchanal at Woolworth's" from Ed King's unpublished memoir, Ed King Personal Archives. A version of "Bacchanal" was published in *Freedom Is a Constant Struggle: An Anthology of the Mississippi Civil Rights Movement*, ed. Susie Erenrich (Black Belt Press, 1999).

2. AI, Lewis (Pearlena).

3. Weather report, *C-L*, 5/28/63.

4. AI, Lewis (Pearlena).

5. Moody, *Coming of Age*, p. 264; AI, Norman.

6. AI, Salter; also see Salter, *Jackson, Mississippi*, p. 132.

7. AI, Salter; Salter, *Jackson, Mississippi*, p. 132; Moody, *Coming of Age*, p. 264. Moody places the time that Evers contacted the media at "around 10 o'clock." Press reports suggest it was closer to 10:45 a.m. See *JDN*, 5/28/63. That same morning, the NAACP New York office alerted the AP and UPI wire services that "mass action appears imminent." NAACP Papers, III:H42, Telegrams, April–June 1963.

8. AI, Wells; AI, Norman.

9. *JDN*, 5/28/63; also King, "Bacchanal," p. 3.

10. AI, Norman; *JDN*, 5/28/63.

11. Extant film footage of the early part of the sit-in is available through MDAH, Audio-Visual Collection. AI, Norman; *JDN*, 5/28/63.

12. AI, Norman; Moody, *Coming of Age*, p. 264.

13. *JDN*, 5/28/63; Moody, *Coming of Age*, p. 264; King, "Bacchanal," p. 4; AI, Lewis (Pearlena).

14. Though Braun "refused to be identified" (*C-L*, 5/29/63), Ken Toler reported the manager's name (*CA*, 5/39/63).

15. Moody, *Coming of Age*, p. 265; *JDN*, 5/28/63; AI, Lewis (Pearlena).

16. AI, Lewis (Pearlena); AI, Norman; busboy seen in MDAH film footage; Moody, *Coming of Age*, p. 265.

17. AI, Wells; AI, Salter.

18. AI, King.

19. Ibid.

20. King, "Bacchanal," p. 5.

21. AI, King; also King, "Bacchanal," p. 5; *JDN*, 5/28/63; *JDN*, 5/29/63. Also *C-L*, *T-P*, *CA*, and *JDN*, 5/29/63.

22. AI, Black.

23. MDAH footage; Blackwell photograph appeared on front page of *NYT*, 5/29/63.

24. *JDN*, 5/28/63; also see Moody, *Coming of Age*, p. 265, and King, "Bacchanal," p. 6. On Hydrick, see also Vollers, *The Ghosts of Mississippi*. On Citizens' Council, see AI, Salter.

25. *Newsweek*, 6/10/63, p.28; also see King, "Bacchanal," p. 8.

26. *JDN*, 5/28/63; Moody, *Coming of Age*, p. 265. Also see AI, Lewis, and *PC*, 6/8/63.

27. AI, Lewis (Pearlena); Moody, *Coming of Age*, p. 265; AI, Norman.

28. AI, Black. Oliver height and weight taken from police arrest report, COJPDA.

29. AI, Black.

30. *Newsweek*, 6/10/63, p. 28; AI, Black.

31. AI, Norman; *Newsweek*, 6/10/63, p. 28; *JDN*, 5/28/63; *T-P*, 5/29/63; *CA*, 5/29/63.

32. The best surviving footage of the attack on Norman is included (briefly) in *Time Was–1960s* (Bruce Cohn Productions). Also see MSNBC's *Time and Again* and WNET's *Lena Horne*.

33. *JDN, WP, NYT*, and many other papers ran the more violent photograph of Oliver kicking Norman in the face; *C-L* ran the more benign photo of Oliver pulling Norman up from the floor.

34. King, "Bacchanal," pp. 7–15.

35. *C-L*, 5/29/63.

36. AI, Norman.

37. Ibid.

38. *Newsweek*, 6/10/63; AI, Black; also see film footage, MSNBC's *Time and Again* series. Black's police report substantiates this sequence of events. "Benny Oliver knocked [Norman] out of the chair with his fist. He then started to kicking this subject in the head and in the stomach. I then ran over to them and got between them and broke the fight up." Serial #O5304, 5/28/63, COJPDA.

39. AI, Norman.

40. Ibid.

41. Moody, *Coming of Age*, p. 265; King, "Bacchanal," p. 6. Also see *MFP*, 6/1/63; *JDN*, 5/29/63; *ES*, 5/29/63; *PC*, 6/8/63.

42. AI, Lewis (Pearlena).

43. Ibid.

44. *C-L*, 5/29/63; *JDN*, 5/28/63; *MFP*, 6/1/63; *PC*, 6/8/63.

45. AI, Trumpauer.

46. AI, Chaffee.

47. AI, Lewis (Pearlena); King, "Bacchanal," p. 8. Also see *C-L*, 5/29/63.

48. AI, Chaffee; King, "Bacchanal," p. 8.

49. *Look*, "Five Days in Mississippi," 7/16/63.

50. King, "Bacchanal," p. 8; *Newsweek*, 6/10/63. Also see *NYT*, 5/29/63.

51. AI, Trumpauer.

52. Ibid.; Moody, *Coming of Age*, p. 266.

53. As reported on Sparkman arrest citation, Arrest #284-6, 5/28/63, COJPDA.

54. Ibid. Sparkman's arrest record cites Black as the arresting officer.

55. Moody, *Coming of Age*, p. 266.

56. *JDN*, 5/28/63. Also AI, Trumpauer (follow-up phone interview), and Moody, *Coming of Age*, p. 266.

57. AI, Chaffee.

58. JDN, 5/28/63; Moody, *Coming of Age*, p. 266; King, "Bacchanal," p. 14.

59. AI, Wells.

60. AI, Norman.

61. AI, Wells; also see AI, Salter; Salter, *Jackson, Mississippi*, p. 133. In his written account, Salter reported that Wells informed them of the violence. In his interview, Salter said King reported the violence just after Wells called to say that a hostile crowd was gathering; AI, King.

62. AI, Salter; Salter, *Jackson, Mississippi*, p. 133.

63. AI, King; King, "Bacchanal," pp. 9–11.

64. Ibid.

65. AI, King; AI, Louie; *Newsweek*, 6/10/63.

66. Story and biographical sketch of Bullock derived from AI, Bullock.

67. AI, Minor.

68. MDAH video archives.

69. AI, Lewis (Pearlena and Margaret).

70. AI, Salter (Eldri and John).

71. AI, Salter; reporter W. C. Shoemaker wrote that Salter entered the store at 1:20 p.m., *JDN*, 5/28/63; he also reported that Moody and Trumpauer were pulled from their stools "shortly after 1:00 p.m.," *JDN*, 5/29/63. FBI Files, 157–896, Vol. 1, 5/28/63, teletype to director, FBI, "RE: F. W. Woolworth Store, Capitol St., Jackson, Miss."

72. FBI files refute this claim, indicating that no still or motion pictures were taken on this occasion. FBI Files, #157-896, Vol. 1, 5/28/63. None have been discovered by author.

73. AI, Salter, II–52. Also Salter, *Jackson, Mississippi*, pp. 133–134; *JDN*, 5/28/63; also *PC*, 6/8/63.

74. AI, Salter; Salter, *Jackson, Mississippi*, pp. 134–135.

75. AI, Salter; Salter, *Jackson, Mississippi*, pp. 134–135; *Time*, 6/7/63.

76. AI, Salter.

77. Ibid.

78. AI, Lewis (Pearlena), Chaffee, Trumpauer.

79. *Newsweek*, 6/10/63; film footage also records the youth standing on the counter, MDAH video archives.

80. AI, Sullivan.

81. Ibid.; Roger Scott identified through corresponding photo in 1963 Central High School Yearbook; FBI agents noted in *JDN*, 5/28/63; *PC*, 6/8/63; AI, Salter; King, "Bacchanal," p. 7; Red Hydrick identified by Vollers, *Ghosts of Mississippi*, p. 110; also identified by Sullivan and Newell. AI, Smitty, phone interview, Smitty's Spuds, Jackson, MS.

82. FBI reports indicate that Salter was "observed to be struck on the back of the head and back by an unknown white male described as about 20 years of age, 5' 10", 145 pounds, light brown hair combed straight back, wearing a white sport shirt." The description nearly fits the description of D.C. Sullivan that day, although Sullivan was shorter. FBI Files, #157-896, Vol. 2, "Desegregation of Jackson, Mississippi Business Establishments," June 6, 1963.

83. AI, Sullivan; AI, Salter.

84. King, "Bacchanal," p. 14; Salter, *Jackson, Mississippi*, p. 134; Moody, *Coming of Age*, pp. 267–268; AI, Lewis (Pearlena); AI, Trumpauer.

85. For the most graphic footage, see *Time and Again* and *Time Was*; *Look*, "Five Days in Mississippi," 7/16/63; Bill Peart identified by Bill Minor, AI, Minor.

86. *CT (UPI)*, 5/29/63; *JDN*, 5/28/63; *Daily Telegraph* (Australia), 5/30/63; *PC*, 6/8/63; *MFP*, 6/1/63.

87. *Newsweek*, 6/10/63; also see the *Daily Telegraph* (Australia), 5/30/63.

88. This scene is captured both in MSNBC footage and in the Spike Lee movie *Malcolm X*.

89. AI, Ashford.

90. AI, Salter; Salter, *Jackson, Mississippi*, p. 135.

91. Salter, *Jackson, Mississippi*, p. 135. Also AI, Trumpauer and AI, Salter; *Time*, 6/7/63; *Newsweek, 6/10/63*. Author visually confirmed lasting evidence of scarring on back of Salter's neck from cigarette burns and glass cuts.

92. AI, Salter.

93. AI, Trumpauer.

94. Ibid.

95. AI, Dennis.

96. AI, Beard.

97. King, "Bacchanal," p. 10; also see AI, King, II–54 and *JDN*, 5/28/63.

98. Dittmer interview of Beittel, 5/25/81.

99. Ibid.; also see Moody, *Coming of Age*, p. 267.

100. NAACP telegram, 5/23/63, NAACP Papers, III:H42, Telegrams, April–June 1963.

101. F. W. Woolworth's letter from E. F. Harrigan to Roy Wilkins, 5/28/63, NAACP Papers, III:A289, Sit Ins, General, 1961–1974.

102. King, "Bacchanal," p. 15.

103. Ibid. Also see Salter, *Jackson, Mississippi*, p. 135, and Moody, *Coming of Age*, p. 267. The FBI puts the closing of the store closer to 2:00 p.m. FBI Files, op. cit., as does *JDN*, 5/29/63.

104. Dittmer interview of Beittel. Also see Salter, *Jackson, Mississippi*, p. 135. AI, Trumpauer (with King) and AI, King.

105. The cropped Blackwell photo ran in *JDN* on 5/29/63. "Pete" identified by J. L. Black, AI, Black.

106. Dittmer interview of Beittel.

107. Ibid.; also King, "Bacchanal," p. 15.

108. AI, Salter.

109. Salter later found out that the woman in the limousine was the mother of Bobby Ezelle, who in 1979 had become president of the Jackson Chamber of Commerce. Ezelle told Salter that upon seeing the sight of the demonstrators on Capitol Street his mother had wondered, "What has become of Mississippi?" She said it was "the worst thing" she had ever seen. AI, Salter.

110. From various author interviews, as well as Salter, *Jackson, Mississippi*, p. 136, and Moody, *Coming of Age*, pp. 267–268; King, "Bacchanal," p. 16.

111. FBI Files, #157-896, Vol. 2, "Desegregation of Jackson, Mississippi Business Establishments," June 6, 1963.

112. AI, Lewis (Pearlena and Alphonzo).

113. Quotes and story derived from AI, Norman.

114. AI, Norman. Although Salter reports that Tougaloo's public relations director drove Norman back to campus (Salter, *Jackson, Mississippi*, p. 137), Ken Toler reported that Norman "walked away [from the police station] with Dr. A. D. Beittel" (*CA*, 5/29/63).

115. AI, Louie. *C-L*, 5/29/63, estimates five hundred; *MFP*, 6/1/63, estimates more than six hundred; *WP (UPI)*, 5/29/63, estimates one thousand; Salter, *Jackson, Mississippi*, p. 138, estimates "almost a thousand"; AI, Lewis.

116. AI, Salter.

117. Salter Papers.

118. The original program for the service was also preserved in the NAACP MS Archives in Baltimore. Interestingly, another one turned up in the Sovereignty Commission files that were released in 1998. The accompanying report indicates that an informant provided the commission with the document the next day along with an update on what happened at the meeting. MSC Files: #3-74-1-44-1-1-1.

119. *JDN*, 5/29/63.

120. *C-L*, 5/29/63.

121. FBI Files, #157-896, Vol. 2, "Desegregation of Jackson, Mississippi, Business Establishments," June 6, 1963.

122. *Arizona Republic* (UPI), 5/29/63.

123. AI, Lewis.

124. AI, Salter. Also *JDN*, 5/29/63.

125. AI, Lewis.

126. Salter, *Jackson, Mississippi*, p. 139. Also AI, Salter.

127. *C-L, CA, JDN, T-P, NYT*, 5/29/63; *MFP*, 6/1/63; *PC*, 6/8/63.

128. Salter, *Jackson, Mississippi*, p. 139.

129. FBI Files, #157-896, Vol. 1, "Desegregation of Jackson," Memorandum from C. L. McGowan, May 29, 1963.

130. *JDN, ES (AP), CA*, 5/29/63; *PC*, 6/8/63; Evers (Myrlie), *For Us, the Living*, p. 273–277.

CHAPTER 7

1. Much of the detail in this chapter was gleaned from daily press reports from the following newspapers: *JDN, C-L, NYT, TP, CA, WP,* and *ES*; also, the weekly *PC, MFP,* and *Newsweek*. All reports provided firsthand accounts of the activities described. In addition, Salter's *Jackson, Mississippi* and Moody's *Coming of Age* offer essential first-person accounts, as do various author interviews.*C-L*, 5/29/63.

2. *WSJ*, 5/29/63.

3. AI, Allison.

4. Ibid.

5. Ibid.

6. *ES*, 5/30/63; Moody, *Coming of Age*, p. 270; AI, Dennis; *NYT*, 5/30/63 and 5/31/63.

7. AI, Allison; *JDN*, 5/29/63; *NYT* and *C-L*, 5/30/63. Tom Beard claimed that earlier that morning, he entered Central High School and asked to be admitted as a full-time student. The principal called his mother, who came and retrieved her son. The incident, apparently, was not reported to the press.

8. *JDN*, 5/29/63; *C-L* and *NYT*, 5/30/63.

9. *NYT*, 5/30/63.

10. Ibid.; *C-L* and *JDN*, 5/30/63.

11. This is speculation based on *JDN*, 5/29/63: "For 30 minutes before the pickets arived a lone CORE worker clad in sports shirt and new overalls, strolled back and forth along Capitol Street." Dave Dennis suggested that this must have been Raymond: "That was his 'm. o.'" AI, Dennis.

12. AI, Allison.

13. Ibid.; *JDN*, 5/29/63.

14. *JDN*, 5/29/63; *C-L, ES, WP, CA, T-P,* and *NYT*, 5/30/63.

15. *JDN*, 5/29/63.

16. *JDN*, 5/29/63; *C-L, ES, WP, CA, T-P,* and *NYT*, 5/30/63.

17. *C-L*, 5/30/63.

18. *MFP*, 6/1/63.

19. AI, Black.

20. AI, Lewis (Pearlena); AI, Lewis (Alphonzo).

21. AI, Norman.

22. Moody, *Coming of Age*, p. 269.

23. *JDN*, 5/29/63; *C-L*, 5/30/63; AI, Trumpauer; AI, Chaffee.

24. *Arizona Republic* (Phoenix), 5/29/63; *Arizona Daily Sun* (Flagstaff), 5/29/63; AI, Salter.

25. Salter, *Jackson, Mississippi*, pp. 143–144; AI, Salter, King. Also see "NAACP Position on Jail, No Bail," 2/9/61. NAACP Papers, III:A-290, Sit-Ins, NAACP Instructions for 1960–1961.

26. "This happened Tuesday, May 28, 1963, in Jackson, Mississippi in a F. W. Woolworth store." NAACP untitled press release w/photo, NAACP Papers, III:A230, MS Pressures, Jackson, MS, 1956–1965. Also see Wilkins telegram "To All NAACP Branch Presidents," Tuesday, 5/28/63, 3:55 p.m. NY time. NAACP Papers, III:A230, MS Pressures, Jackson, MS, 1956–1965. Wilkins asked branches to "rush contribution from your branch to help us meet bail money requirements, medical bills and other costs. The need is urgent."

27. *JDN*, 5/29/63.

28. Ibid.

29. *T-P*, 5/29/63.

30. Film footage, Jackson Movement activities, MDAH.

31. *JDN*, 5/30/63 and 5/31/63.

32. Ludden, *Anatomy*, p. 125; Moody, *Coming of Age*, p. 273; *T-P*, *NYT*, and *CA*, 5/31/63.

33. What happened next is not clear. See Moody, *Coming of Age*, pp. 273–274; *T-P*, *NYT*, *CA*, and *C-L*, 5/31/63. Also see *JDN*, 5/30/63.

34. One report suggests that the woman kicked a police officer. *C-L*, *JDN*, *T-P*, *NYT*, and *CA*, 5/31/63.

35. Salter, *Jackson, Mississippi*, p. 146; AI, King; AI, Salter.

36. AI, Trumpauer.

37. *WP*, *CA*, *NYT*, *T-P*, *JDN*, and *C-L*, 5/31/63.

38. *WP*, *ES*, *T-P*, *C-L*, 5/31/63. See also Salter, *Jackson, Mississippi*, p. 147, and Moody, *Coming of Age*, p. 271.

39. *NYT*, 5/31/63.

40. AI, Trumpauer (w/King).

41. *C-L*, 5/31/63.

42. *ES*, 5/31/63.

43. *WP*, 6/1/63; AI, King.

44. *NYT*, 6/1/63.

45. *JDN*, 5/30/63.

46. Letter to Mr. T. M. Hederman, Jr., Editor, *Clarion-Ledger*, and Letter to Mr. James M. Ward, Editor, *Jackson Daily News*, 5/31/63. NAACP MS Papers.

47. Ibid.

48. Salter, *Jackson, Mississippi*, p. 148; Moody, *Coming of Age*, p. 273.

49. FBI Files 157-896, Vol. 2.

50. AI, Lewis. See also Ludden, *Anatomy*, pp. 125–129.

51. AI, Lewis (Alphonzo).

52. Ibid.

53. *JDN*, 6/1/63; AI, Lewis (Alphonzo).

54. *Newsweek*, 6/10/63. Also see Salter, *Jackson, Mississippi*, p. 149.

55. *NYT*, *C-L*, *JDN*, *T-P*, and *WP*, 6/1/63.

56. Ludden, *Anatomy*, pp. 133–135.

57. Ibid.

58. Ibid. Also see AI, Salter, *T-P* and *WP*, 6/1/63. A later NAACP complaint of police brutality to both the Justice Department and the FBI suggests that police huddled around Ludden before beating him so as to obscure the view of reporters. Ludden himself said he was "jabbed in the groin with a billy club." One week after the incident, his doctor reported that Ludden was "still passing blood" and would not be released from his care for another two weeks. See FBI File #157-896, Vol. 2; Ludden, *Anatomy*, pp. 133–135.

59. AI, Beard.

60. *NYT* and *C-L*, 6/1/63. On 6/2/63, the *New York Times* quoted a parent who had just retrieved a child from the fairgrounds that children as young as "five or six" were being housed there. The FBI reports confirm that the children were singing "We Shall Not Be Moved." FBI File #157-896, Vol. 2.

61. Salter, *Jackson, Mississippi*, p. 149. Also see *T-P*, 6/1/63.

62. AI, King.

63. Ludden, *Anatomy*, p. 135.

64. Salter, *Jackson, Mississippi*, p. 150; *NYT*, 6/1/63.

65. AI, King.

66. The story of King's hearing was run on the front pages of the *Jackson Daily News* (5/31/63) and the *Clarion-Ledger* (6/1/63).

67. AI, King.

68. *C-L*, 6/1/63.

69. For a description of the NAACP's attempted shift in focus from legal to direct action, see "NAACP Shifts Its Policy to Direct Rights Action," *WP*, 6/1/63.

70. Evers, *For Us, the Living*, p. 253.

71. Memorandum from Roy Wilkins to Branch, Youth Council, College Chapter and State Conference Presidents, May 31, 1963. NAACP Papers, III:A230, MS Pressures, Jackson, MS, 1956–1965.

72. NAACP News Release, "Nazism Rules Jackson, NAACP Leader Charges," 6/1/63, Ibid. Also see "Background Information on New Desegregation Drive in Jackson, Miss.," Addendum, p. 8, Ibid.

73. Salter, *Jackson, Mississippi*, p. 152.

74. King, "Jackson Movement: Wilkins and Control of Medgar Evers," unpublished manuscript, Ed King Personal Archives.

75. *JDN*, 6/1/63. Also see Salter, *Jackson, Mississippi*, pp. 152–153. *MFP* reported that one woman came to reclaim her arrested child and the child protested that she wanted to remain at the fairgrounds. When the mother conceded, the police beat her until she agreed to remove her child from the compound. *MFP*, 6/8/63.

76. AI, Salter, III-3; Salter, *Jackson, Mississippi*, pp. 152–153.

77. AI, Norman.

78. AI, Lewis, II-25. Tom Beard said that he and Pearlena Lewis stayed at the fairgrounds compound the first night and were transferred to the Hinds County jail the next day. AI, Beard.

79. *NYT*, "Negro Leads a Training School for Racial Protests in Jackson," 5/31/63; AI, Dennis.

80. FBI Files, 157-896, Vol. 2.

81. Dittmer interview with Henderson; AI, Chaffee.

82. Ludden, *Anatomy*, pp. 141–142.

83. Salter, *Jackson, Mississippi*, p. 154; *T-P*, 6/2/63.

84. Various photos of the arrest appeared in *NYT*, *WP*, and *ES* on 6/2/63.

85. *CA*, "Negro Leader Says Marches Have Just Begun," 6/2/63. Also see *ES* and *T-P*, 6/2/63.

86. *NYT*, 6/2/63; *C-L*, 6/2/63. Also see Dittmer interview with Henderson.

87. *CA*, 6/2/63; *T-P*, 6/3/63.

88. Salter, *Jackson, Mississippi*, p. 156.

89. Ibid; AI, Salter.

90. Estimates for this march range from two hundred (*CA*, 6/2/63) to one hundred (AP as reported in *WP*, *ES*, and *C-L*, 6/2/63). Salter also estimated about a hundred. See Salter, *Jackson, Mississippi*, p. 157.

91. Moody, *Coming of Age*, p. 275.

92. Salter, *Jackson, Mississippi*, p. 157.

93. Ibid., pp. 158–159.

94. Ibid. Also see AI, King.

95. Evers, *For Us, the Living*, p. 252.

96. AI, Wells.

97. Branch, *Parting the Waters*, p. 816. Wilkins, in fact, had been arrested in 1934 while picketing the U.S. attorney general's office for antilynching laws. See Wilkins, *Standing Fast*, pp. 126–136.

98. AI, Dennis, Wells, Louie, Allison. Houston Wells was the next-door neighbor to Evers; James Wells was one of the drivers of the demonstrators on the day of the Woolworth's demonstration. Both were confidantes of Evers.

99. Evers, *For Us, the Living*, p. 279.

100. *T-P*, 6/3/63.

101. AI, Salter; *NYT*, "Quiet Integrationist: Medgar Wiley Evers," 6/1/63.

102. *CA*, 6/3/63. Also see *MFP*, 6/8/63.

103. Salter, *Jackson, Mississippi*, p. 165.

104. Ibid., pp. 164–166; AI, Salter, King. Historian John Dittmer concurs, noting that as a result of these changes to strategy, "the Jackson movement lost momentum" and "[a]ttendance at nightly mass meetings declined drastically." Dittmer, *Local People*, p. 164.

105. AI, Lewis.

106. AI, Allison.

107. Ludden, *Anatomy*, pp. 119–121.

108. Ibid.

109. In a fascinating letter to Roy Wilkins a few days later, Clarence Mitchell describes the back-door discussions being held with the mayor by a mutual acquaintance of both parties. Brooks Hays, former eight-term congressman from Arkansas, who knew both Mitchell and Thompson, indicated that Thompson was willing to negotiate on areas under his control "such as the police department, city services and the like but would try not to assert any influence with store owners." Hays vouched for Thompson as "a person who would not want to operate in the manner of Ross Barnett" and who understood that "there must be a realistic facing up to the need to desegregate."

Mitchell suggests that Thompson would have an easier time politically if he were seen negotiating with local ministers and business people rather that "with civil rights advocates" such as the NAACP. Mitchell concludes by stating his opinion—mirroring that of the NAACP—that "the general gains in the deep South which have come about through mass demonstrations are, for the most part, symbolic and subject to being wiped out when merchants or city officials have a change of heart. The only lasting gains are those which are won by court and legislative action. I believe this will be the case in Mississippi." See Mitchell letter to Wilkins, 6/5/63, NAACP Papers, III:A322, Washington Bureau Correspondence, Mitchell, Clarence, 1963.

110. *JDN*, 6/4/63; *CA*, 6/3/63; Gregory, *Nigger*, p. 182.

111. Moody, *Coming of Age*, p. 274.

112. AI, King; *JDN*, 6/4/63; *NYT*, 6/4/63. Other papers had Thompson stating more bluntly, "It's all over." *JDN*, 6/3/63; *C-L*, 6/4/63. Also see Salter, *Jackson, Mississippi*, p. 170.

113. Ludden, *Anatomy*, p. 138. Also see AI, Ludden.

114. *C-L*, 6/4/63. Also see *NYT*, 5/4/63, and *JDN*, 6/5/63.

115. *T-P*, 6/5/63. FBI Files, #157-896, Vol. 2.

116. *NYT*, 6/5/63; FBI Files, #157-896, Vol. 2.

117. *JDN*, 6/4/63, *NYT*, *C-L*, and *T-P*, 6/5/63. Also see FBI Files, #157-896, Vol. 2.

118. *NYT*, 6/4/63.

119. *NYT* and *C-L*, 6/4/63; *JDN*, 6/5/63.

120. AI, Trumpauer; Salter, *Jackson, Mississippi*, p. 168.

CHAPTER 8

1. AI, Louie.

2. Evers, *Watch Me Fly*, p. 73.

3. Ibid., p. 76.

4. Ibid., p. 77; AI, Ashford.

5. Evers, *Watch Me Fly*, p. 77.

6. AI, Lewis, King, Louie, Salter.

7. AI, Salter, Lewis, Allison.

8. "Remarks of Medgar Evers, NAACP Field Secretary, Jackson, Miss., at Mass Meeting, June 4, 1963, at Pearl Street AME Church," NAACP MS Papers.

9. AI, Lewis (Alphonzo). Also see *MFP*, 6/8/63; Evers, *For Us, the Living*, pp. 256–257; *JDN*, 6/5/63.

10. *NYT*, "Beater of Negro Named Political Campaign Aide," 6/5/63.

11. See Ludden, *Anatomy*, p. 127.

12. *C-L*, 6/6/63.

13. Salter, *Jackson, Mississippi*, p. 173.

14. Moody, *Coming of Age*, pp. 274–275.

15. *NYT*, *C-L*, and *T-P*, 6/6/63.

16. Salter, *Jackson, Mississippi*, p. 174. A hilarious account of how Ed King tried to avoid being served with the injunction is included in his unpublished manuscript in the chapter "Injunction in Jackson." "The City of Jackson Municipal Corporation vs. John

R. Salter, Jr., et al.": full text of injunction cited in Salter, *Jackson, Mississippi*, pp. 174–175. Also see FBI File #157-896, Vol. 3. AI, Salter.

17. King, "Injunction in Jackson," from unpublished manuscript.

18. Roy Wilkins Bulletin to NAACP Branch Officers, "In Jackson, Mississippi," 6/6/63, NAACP Papers, III:A230, MS Pressures, Jackson, MS, 1956–1965.

19. *C-L*, 6/7/63. Also see "Statement by Medgar Evers in response to June 6, 1963 Injunction against demonstrators" (hand dated 6/10/63), Ibid.

20. *JDN, C-L*, 6/7/63. AI, Sullivan.

21. *NYT, T-P, CA, JDN, C-L*, 6/8/63. For full text of Carter's statement, see "Press Conference with Robert L. Carter, June 7, 1963," NAACP Papers, III:230, MS Pressures, Jackson, MS, 1956–1965. Also included in NAACP MS Papers.

22. Affidavits and court filings discovered in FBI Files, #157-896, Vol. 3.

23. *T-P, JDN*, 6/8/63. Also see *NYT*, 6/8/63 (only cites forty-two arrested).

24. *T-P*, 6/8/63.

25. Salter, *Jackson, Mississippi*, p. 179. AI, Salter (Eldri).

26. AI, Allison.

27. AI, Allison; AI, Lewis; AI, Louie. Also see Vollers, *Ghosts*, p. 118, and Evers, *For Us, the Living*, pp. 288–289.

28. AI, Allison.

29. AI, Black.

30. AI, King. For a detailed description of the meeting with Kennedy, see Branch, *Parting the Waters*, pp. 809–813. Also see *NYT*, 5/25/63; Horne and Schickel, *Lena*, pp. 275–281; and Gavin, *Stormy Weather*, pp. 312–314.

31. "Excerpts from remarks by Miss Lena Horne," NAACP Papers, III:E9, Mississippi, Jackson, 1956, 1961–65. Also see *PC*, 6/15/63.

32. *PC*, 6/15/63. Vollers, *Ghosts*, p. 118.

33. Evers, *For Us, the Living*, p. 284.

34. Ibid. AI, Chaffee; AI, King.

35. AI, Norman.

36. Salter, *Jackson, Mississippi*, p. 179. Memorandum, John Doar to Burke Marshall, "Demonstrations in Jackson, Mississippi," 6/10/63, Mississippi File, Burke Marshall Papers, JFK.

37. *WP*, 6/9/63. Memorandum, John Doar to Burke Marshall, "Demonstrations in Jackson, Mississippi," 6/10/63, Mississippi File, Burke Marshall Papers, JFK. Gregory, *Nigger*, p. 188.

38. Evers, *For Us, the Living*, p. 297. AI, Dennis. Also see Vollers, *Ghosts*, pp. 119–120. *WP*, "Evers Was Used to Threats," 6/13/63. I chose to use this eyewitness account rather than the one reported by Myrlie Evers, who said that it was the police who put their car into reverse in an attempt to run over her husband: Evers, *For Us, the Living*, p. 290. John Salter also said it was the police who had tried to swerve into Evers: Salter, *Jackson, Mississippi*, p. 182. It is possible, however, that the "two white men" cited in Wallace Terry's *WP* report were undercover policemen.

39. Evers, *For Us, the Living*, p. 291. In a later memoir, written nearly thirty years after these events had transpired, Myrlie Evers admitted that she was, in fact, pregnant with their fourth child. She would miscarry, however, in the stressful days ahead. Evers, *Watch Me Fly*, pp. 76–78.

40. Evers, *For Us, the Living*, p. 293.

41. *C-L* and *JDN*, 6/10/63. Selah's defection became national news: *WP* and *NYT*, 6/10/63.

42. AI, Norman; *C-L*, 6/10/63; *C-L/JDN, T-P*, 6/9/63.

43. AI, Lewis (Pearlena); AI, Allison. Alphonzo Lewis's view of Salter is much more sympathetic and appreciative, recognizing that Salter "didn't have to do [what he did]." Lewis also commented on Salter's "genuineness," something that the NAACP leadership seemed to question. AI, Lewis (Alphonzo).

44. AI, Salter, King. Ludden, *Anatomy*, pp. 138–139.

45. *C-L*, 6/11/63.

46. Letter to Gloster Current from Clarence Mitchell, 6/10/63. NAACP Papers.

47. Salter, *Jackson, Mississippi*, p. 181; Branch, *Parting the Waters*, p. 816 and related footnote. Also see Branch, *Pillar of Fire*, pp. 101–102 and related footnote.

48. Evers, *For Us, the Living*, p. 298.

49. AI, Allison; King, "Wilkins and Control of Medgar Evers" and "Final Conversation with Medgar Evers," unpublished chapters in a work about the Jackson Movement. Also see Salter/King interview with John Jones, MDAH, pp. 99–100. Salter disagreed with King on this point and did not believe Evers's job was in jeopardy.

50. AI, Allison.

51. *C-L*, 6/12/63.

52. Salter, *Jackson, Mississippi*, p. 181. AI, Lewis (Alphonzo).

53. AI, Lewis (Alphonzo).

54. AI, Salter; Salter, *Jackson, Mississippi*, p. 182.

55. AI, Salter.

56. Evers, *For Us, the Living*, pp. 298–299.

57. *ES*, 6/15/63.

58. *NYT*, 6/13/63.

59. Excerpts from Kennedy's speech from *NYT*, 6/12/63.

60. AI, Salter; AI, Shoemaker; AI, Lewis (Alphonzo).

61. AI, Allison.

62. AI, Black; AI, Trumpauer (with King); Salter, *Jackson, Mississippi*, p. 183.

63. AI, Lewis (Pearlena); AI, Louie; AI, Lewis (Alphonzo); AI, Ludden; Ludden, *Anatomy*, p. 151.

64. Salter, *Jackson, Mississippi*, pp. 183–184; AI, King, Trumpauer (with King) and Salter. Also see King's "Death of Medgar Evers," a chapter from his unpublished memoir on the Jackson Movement.

65. *CA*, "Evers' Busy Night Ended in Death," 6/13/63. Also see Vollers, *Ghosts*, pp. 124–125. King believed Evers got involved in a card game on one of his visits, which is why he returned so late to his home; AI, King. Gloster Current, who was staying at the home of attorney Jack Young, always maintained that he was the last person to talk to Evers before he was shot. See Current obituary, *NYT* 7/9/97.

66. Evers, *For Us, the Living*, pp. 299, 302.

67. *CA*, 6/13/63. Also see Vollers, *Ghosts*, p. 128.

68. Evers, *For Us, the Living*, p. 305.

69. AI, Wells.

70. AI, Lewis; AI, Louie; AI, Beard; AI, Salter. Also see Salter, *Jackson, Mississippi*, pp. 184–185.

71. Moody, *Coming of Age*, p. 276; AI, Dennis.

72. AI, Allison.

73. AI, Allison; Evers, *For Us, the Living*, p. 307.

74. AI, Black.

75. FBI Files, #157-896, Vol. 4.

76. AI, Bullock.

77. Wilkins, *Standing Fast*, p. 290; NAACP Papers, III:H42, Telegrams, April–June 1963.

78. Horne and Schickel, *Lena*, pp. 284–285.

79. AI, Sullivan.

80. AI, Trumpauer; AI, Chaffee.

81. AI, Allison.

82. AI, Salter; AI, Lewis.

83. AI, Allison; AI, King; *NYT*, 6/13/63; *JDN*, 6/12/63.

84. Ludden, *Anatomy*, p. 152; *JDN*, 6/12/63; *WP*, 6/13/63; *NYT*, 6/13/63.

85. *NYT*, 6/13/63; Branch, *Parting the Waters*, p. 828; Garrow, *Bearing the Cross*, p. 269.

86. *JDN*, 6/12/63.

87. Salter, *Jackson, Mississippi*, p. 189.

88. *T-P*, 6/13/63; AI, Salter; Salter, *Jackson, Mississippi*, pp. 189–190; AI, King; FBI Files, #157–896, Vol. 4.

89. Salter, *Jackson, Mississippi*, p. 190; FBI Files, #157-896, Vol. 4.

90. AI, Dennis; *ES*, 6/13/63.

91. Myrlie Evers's remarks have been pieced together here from a number of firsthand accounts, including those appearing in Evers, *For Us, the Living*, p. 310; Salter, *Jackson, Mississippi*, p. 192; *WP*, 6/14/63; *ES*, 6/13/63; *MFP*, 6/22/63; and *NYT*, 6/13/63.

92. *WP*, 6/14/63.

93. Salter, *Jackson, Mississippi*, p. 193.

CHAPTER 9

1. Salter, *Jackson, Missssippi*, pp. 186–187; Moody, *Coming of Age*, p. 277.

2. Salter, *Jackson, Mississippi*, p. 194; *NYT*, 6/14/63.

3. Ibid. Accounts from the FBI and from Thelton Henderson of the Justice Department are taken from FBI files made available to John Salter through an FOIA request. File #44-1804 (6/20/63) and #144-41-552 (7/23/63). Also see FBI File: #158-896, Vol. 4. *NYT*, 6/14/63.

4. Ibid. Also see *MFP*, 6/22/63.

5. *T-P*, *NYT*, and CA, 6/14/63. See also Burke Marshall Papers, Box 31, Demonstrations, JFK: "Subject: Jackson Demonstrations; Telephone Call from Thelton Henderson; June 13, 4:05 p.m." AI, Chaffee; AI, King.

6. Salter, *Jackson, Mississippi*, p. 195; AI, Salter; *MFP*, "Police Power Meets Protesters During Days of Demonstrations," 6/22/63.

7. MDAH Audio-Visual Collection. *T-P, C-L, NYT,* and *CA,* 6/14/63. Also see Moody, *Coming of Age,* p. 279.

8. *NYT,* 6/14/63; *MFP,* 6/22/63; *CDN,* 6/14/63; AI, Trumpauer (with King).

9. AI, Chaffee; *NYT,* 6/14/63.

10. Burke Marshall Papers, Box 31, Demonstrations, JFK: "Subject: Jackson Demonstrations; Telephone Call from Thelton Henderson; June 13, 4:05 p.m." AI, Minor.

11. Moody, *Coming of Age,* pp. 279–280. Moody's original estimate of time in the truck was one hour, as reported in *MFP,* 6/22/63. She also reported that one woman fainted and that the prisoners were given hot water to drink while the police drank ice water.

12. AI, Lewis (Alphonzo).

13. Salter, *Jackson, Mississippi,* p. 196. Moody, *Coming of Age,* p. 281.

14. *ES,* 6/14/63.

15. *T-P, CA,* and *WP,* 6/14/63.

16. AI, Salter. Salter, *Jackson, Mississippi,* p. 201; AP wire report, as run in the *Evening Telegram,* Superior, Wisconsin, 6/14/63.

17. *NYT,* 6/14/63. Kunstler, *Deep in My Heart,* p. 204. Salter, *Jackson, Mississippi,* p. 201.

18. *CA,* 6/14/63.

19. Salter, *Jackson, Mississippi,* p. 203.

20. *NYT,* 6/14/63.

21. Salter, *Jackson, Mississippi,* p. 204; *JDN,* 6/15/63.

22. *JDN,* 6/14/63; *NYT, CA, C-L,* and *T-P,* 6/15/63.

23. Evers, *For Us, the Living,* pp. 322, 314–315; AP report, as recorded in the *Evening Telegram,* Superior, Wisconsin, 6/14/63; Schulke, *He Had a Dream,* pp. 56–58.

24. *PC,* 6/22/63.

25. *CA,* 6/15/63; *NYT,* 6/15/63; *C-L,* 6/15/63.

26. *JDN,* 6/14/63; *NYT, ES,* and *C-L,* 6/15/63.

27. Salter, *Jackson, Mississippi,* pp. 206–208.

28. *NYT,* 6/15/63.

29. Ibid.

30. Salter, *Jackson, Mississippi,* p. 206; AI, Ladner (Dorie).

31. *PC,* 6/22/63.

32. Estimates vary on the number in attendance from 4,000 to 5,000. *JDN* and *C-L* both cite 4,000. *T-P* and *CA* record "more than 4,000." *ES* staff reporter estimates 5,000. UPI (as run in WP) cites "more than 5,000." Record-breaking heat: *C-L,* 6/14/63; *T-P* cites 101 degree heat.

33. Evers, *For Us, the Living,* p. 315.

34. Salter, *Jackson, Mississippi,* pp. 208–209; *T-P,* 6/16/63; Dittmer interview with Beittel. A photo of the stage participants, including Wilkins, Diggs, Bunche, Clarence Mitchell, and Beittel ran in the *New York Times,* 6/16/63.

35. AI, various participants.

36. *NYT,* 6/16/63.

37. AI, Chaffee.

38. AI, Dennis.

39. Partial content of Howard's remarks is included in "Where Do We Go From Here?," Pacifica Radio.

40. Wilkins's remarks were widely quoted in the national media. A transcript of his entire eulogy is included in the NAACP Papers, LOC. An audio version is included in "Where Do We Go From Here?," Pacifica Radio.

41. The entire text of the mayor's march permit can be found in *C-L* and *JDN*, 6/16/63.

42. Evers, *For Us, the Living*, pp. 317–318; *ES*, 6/16/63. Other estimates of marchers range from 1,500 (*MFP*, 6/22/63) to 4,000 (*C-L* and *JDN*, 6/16/63) to more than 5,000 (*PC*, 6/62/63).

43. *NYT*, 6/16/63. Gregory, *Nigger*, p. 190.

44. Evers, *For Us, the Living*, p. 318.

45. Salter, *Jackson, Mississippi*, p. 212.

46. *NYT*, *T-P*, and *CA*, 6/16/63.

47. Eleanor Holmes Norton, who was at the funeral, often joked with Ladner: "You started that mess down in Jackson. It was you, Ladner." Ladner herself did not remember singing "Oh, Freedom," but vividly remembered starting "This Little Light of Mine." Ladner said she was furious that the march had not been allowed to pass the state capitol and that she could not keep silent. AI, Ladner (Dorie). A photograph of the ensuing march toward Capitol Street clearly shows a young, determined Dorie Ladner in the lead. See Holland, *From the Mississippi Delta*, photo section, photo uncredited.

48. AI, King; King's assertion is supported by the report of the melee in *MFP*, 6/22/63. This eyewitness report specifically uses the word "spontaneously" to describe how the march began.

49. AI, Salter.

50. Kunstler, *Deep in My Heart*, p. 207; AI, Rutledge; Salter, *Jackson, Mississippi*, p. 213.

51. Salter, *Jackson, Mississippi*, p. 215; AI, Salter; AI, King. Also see *T-P*, *C-L* and *JDN*, 6/16/63.

52. *T-P*, *C-L*, and *JDN*, 6/16/63. See also Ed King's unpublished manuscript "Funeral of Medgar Evers—Prison."

53. *NYT*, 6/16/63; *T-P*, 6/16/63. MDAH Audio–Visual Collection; a thorough audio recording of the showdown is included in "Where Do We Go From Here?," Pacifica Radio.

54. *NYT*, 6/16/63.

55. "Where Do We Go From Here?," Pacifica Radio; also see T-P 6/16/63; *NYT*, *C-L*, and *JDN*, 6/16/63.

56. *NYT*, 6/16/63.

57. *WP*, 6/16/63; AI, Minor.

58. *T-P*, 6/16/63; *NYT*, 6/16/63.

59. AI, Dennis; Vollers, *Ghosts*, p. 144.

60. *NYT*, 6/16/63; "Where Do We Go From Here?," Pacifica Radio; Kunstler, *Deep in My Heart*, p. 209; Ludden, *Anatomy*, p. 152; *C-L* and *JDN*, 6/16/63.

61. Salter, *Jackson, Mississippi*, p. 216.

62. Ibid.; Kunstler, *Deep in My Heart*, pp. 208–209.

63. *NYT*, 6/16/63. *JDN*, 6/18/63.

64. AI, Newell; AI, Sullivan.

65. AI, Salter; Salter, *Jackson, Mississippi*, pp. 222–223.

66. *JDN*, *CA*, *T-P*, *NYT*, 6/16/63.

67. Salter, *Jackson, Mississippi*, p. 221.

68. *Coming of Age*, pp. 283–285; *NYT*, 6/17/63.

69. *NYT*, 6/17/63.

70. *ES*, *WP*, and *NYT*, 6/17/63. Wilkins singled out CORE for his scorn and indirectly Dave Dennis and George Raymond. "Do you know how many members CORE had in Jackson?" Wilkins asked. "Not 200. Not 20. Two!" *ES*, 6/17/63.

71. *C-L*, 6/17/63; *NYT*, 6/18/63; *JDN*, 6/18/63. In a memorandum to Wilkins months later, Current describes a telephone call with a "one of the leading ministers in Jackson" who had been in touch with Myrlie Evers. "Mrs. Evers had some reservations about Charles' appointment. . . . She was concerned lest his appointment mar the record made by her husband. . . . Her reservations about her brother-in-law grew out of some of his past impulsive activities and attitudes." Current, however, seems willing to give Evers the benefit of the doubt. "He is not as well prepared and grounded in our movement as we would like. On the other hand, I have been impressed by his aggressiveness and willingness to move out in several directions and not wait to find out what he should do." Current also seems to imply that Myrlie Evers herself may have been interested in the job, though he does not mention her by name. "There is also a doubt in my mind about what a woman could do in that job at the present time, especially if she has children to care for." See Current memo to Wilkins RE: Charles Evers, 9/9/63. NAACP Papers, III:C236, Current, Gloster B., Correspondence and Memoranda, 1963, July–Dec.

72. Kunstler, *Deep in My Heart*, p. 204.

73. AI, King; AI, Salter; Salter, *Jackson, Mississippi*, p. 225.

74. AI, Salter; also see Salter, *Jackson, Mississippi*, pp. 228–229. Salter's suspicions, though accurate, are a bit behind the curve. By early June, Clarence Mitchell had determined that the Justice Department's John Doar had already been in direct contact with Mayor Thompson. A settlement was under discussion a full week prior to the Evers assassination. See Wilkins letter to Wilkins, 6/5/63, NAACP Papers, III:A332, Washington Bureau Correspondence, Mitchell, Clarence, 1963.

75. Burke Marshall Papers, May–June, 1963, JFK. Also available in Salter Papers, Box 10, MDAH.

76. Salter, *Jackson, Mississippi*, pp. 227–230; *JDN* and *T-P*, 6/18/63.

77. *JDN*, 6/18/63.

78. Papers of John F. Kennedy, Presidential Papers, President's Office Files, Presidential Recordings, Logs and Transcripts, Civil Rights, 1963, JFK.

79. *WP* and *ES*, 6/18/63.

80. AI, Trumpauer.

81. For Myrlie Evers's further remarks, see *WP*, 6/19/63, and *ES*, 6/19/63; *WP*, 6/18/63.

82. The complete story of the car wreck that put Salter and King in the hospital at this critical time is included in its entirety in Salter, *Jackson, Mississippi*, pp. 230–239. Also see AI, Salter; AI, King.

83. Ibid.

84. *JDN*, 6/18/63; *C-L*, 6/19/63.

85. AI, Salter. Also see Salter, *Jackson, Mississippi*, p. 232.

86. AI, Salter; Salter, *Jackson, Mississippi*, p. 236.

87. AI, King.

88. AI, Salter; AI, King; AI, Minor.

89. AI, Salter; AI, King.

90. *JDN*, 6/18/63.

91. The excerpts of the Thompson/Kennedy interchange are taken from the Presidential Recordings, Logs and Transcripts, Civil Rights, 1963, JFK.

92. *C-L*, *JDN*, *T-P*, and *NYT*, 6/19/63.

93. Segments of this mass meeting are included in "Where Do We Go From Here?," Pacifica Radio. Also see *T-P*, *JDN*, *C-L*, and *NYT*, 6/19/63.

94. "Where Do We Go From Here?," Pacifica Radio.

95. *NYT* and *T-P*, 6/19/63; Salter, *Jackson, Mississippi*, p. 238; AI, Ladner (Dorie).

96. *WP*, 6/20/63; Evers, *For Us, the Living*, p. 324.

97. Ibid., pp. 324–325.

98. *NYT*, 6/20/63; *PC*, 6/29/63. Other news accounts estimated 1,000 people at the gravesite, including *WP*,6/20/63; *ES*, 6/19/63.

99. Evers, *For Us, the Living*, p. 325; *WP*, 6/20/63.

CHAPTER 10

1. AI, Salter.

2. Ibid.

3. Ibid. Also see Salter, *Jackson, Mississippi*, p. 240.

4. *JDN*, 9/63.

5. Moody, *Coming of Age*, p. 288.

6. Dittmer, *Local People*, pp. 186–188; Dave Dennis to Jim McCain, 8/8/63, CORE Addendum, Reel 22.

7. Moody, *Coming of Age*, p. 288.

8. Dennis to McCain, 8/8/63, Core Addendum, Reel 22: "The situation at hand now is that we are working off of bread and water." Dennis to Core Groups and Members, Detroit, Michigan, 8/19/63: "These people are now presently sleeping in sleeping bags on floors. . . . Grits and gravy has become their standard meal. . . ." Also see Moody, *Coming of Age*, p. 297. Moody reported that "we sometimes went for days without a meal."

9. AI, Allison. Allison kept a program from that evening, July 11, 1963. Annie Moody is listed last as providing "Inspiration." Doris Allison personal papers.

10. Moody, *Coming of Age*, p. 297.

11. This story was told by both Newell and Sullivan. AI Newell; AI, Sullivan.

12. AI, Norman.

13. AI, Chaffee; AI, Dennis.

14. AI, Beard.

15. *C-L*, 6/29/63; *MFP*, 7/6/63.

16. *MFP*, 7/27/63.

17. *MFP*, 7/20/63.

18. Spingarn Medal, Purpose and Conditions Statements, Spingarn Medal Awards Program; "To the Members of the Spingarn Medal Award Committee" from Roy Wilkins, 6/4/63, 6/13/63, NAACP Papers, III:A40, General Office File, Awards, Spingarn Medal, Evers, Medgar Wiley, 1963.

19. *MFP*, 5/11/63; *Tougaloo Southern News*, 6/63.

20. AI, Lewis (Pearlena).

21. AI, Allison.

22. Moody, *Coming of Age*, p. 306. "Marched 50 Times": Scripps-Howard Newspapers undated clipping in Joan Trumpauer (Mulholland)'s personal archives.

23. AI, Trumpauer; Moody, *Coming of Age*, p. 307.

24. Moody, *Coming of Age*, p. 309; AI, Trumpauer.

25. *MFP*, 9/27/63; AI, Allison; affidavit by R. L. T. Smith, 9/13/63, NAACP MS Papers; handwritten summary of events by Mrs. Doris Allison, 8/24/63, NAACP MS Papers.

26. Moody, *Coming of Age*, p. 319.

27. AI, Trumpauer (with King).

28. Ibid. Nearly fifty years later, Trumpauer still had the glass shards in her civil rights memorabilia collection and showed them during civil rights presentations.

29. *Eyes on the Prize: America's Civil Rights Years*, Vol. 2, "No Easy Walk (1961–1963)."

30. For a complete description of Ed King's involvement in the church visitation project, see Marsh, *God's Long Summer*, chapter 4, "Inside Agitator, Ed King's Church Visits."

31. "'On Our Knees': The Story of the Jackson Church Visits," November 18, 1963, Joan Trumpauer (Mulholland) personal archives. This document can also be found in the Anne Braden Papers, SHSW.

32. *MFP*, 8/24/63, 8/31/63, 9/21/63, 10/5/63, 10/19/63, 10/26/63, 11/2/63, and 11/9/63. For more on the Freedom Vote, see Dittmer, *Local People*, pp. 200–207; Branch, *Parting the Waters*, 920–921.

33. AI, Trumpauer; *MFP*, 11/9/63, 2/1/63; "Greetings," letters from Joan Trumpauer, 2/18/64, 3/11/64, and 4/29/64, Joan Trumpauer (Mulholland) personal archives (also available in Anne Braden Papers, SHSW, and Ed King Papers, Tougaloo Archives). Trumpauer called this the "Cultural and Artistic Agitation Committee." Also see Dittmer, *Local People*, pp. 226–228.

34. AI, Ladner (Joyce).

35. "Greetings," letter from Joan Trumpauer, 12/12/63, Joan Trumpauer (Mulholland) personal archives; AI, Chaffee.

36. Moody, *Coming of Age*, pp. 328–329, 339.

37. *MFP*, 12/14/63, 12/21/63; AI, Lewis; the national black Christmas effort is referenced in the Spike Lee documentary "4 Little Girls"; the Jackson Movement Information Bulletin, "MURDER INC.," NAACP MS Papers. In addition to the cover photos of Kennedy and Evers, the bulletin features a photograph of Memphis Norman being assaulted by Bennie Oliver at the Woolworth's sit-in.

38. *MFP*, 12/14/63; *MFP*, 2/22/64. Some of Pearlena Lewis's reports are preserved in the NAACP MS Papers.

39. NAACP Press Release, "NAACP 1963 Membership Tops Half-Million Mark," January 10, 1964, NAACP Papers. III:A231, MS Press Releases, 1956–1965.

40. For a detailed description of the three trials of Byron De La Beckwith, see Vollers, *Ghosts of Mississippi*, and Nossiter, *Of Long Memory*.

41. Vollers, *Ghosts*, p. 164.

42. "Greetings," letter from Joan Trumpauer, 2/18/64, Joan Trumpauer personal archives.

43. Ibid.

44. Vollers, *Ghosts*, pp. 201, 208; Nossiter, *Of Long Memory*, pp. 108–109. Years later, it was revealed that the Mississippi State Sovereignty Commission had profiled potential jurors and fed that information to Beckwith's defense team prior to jury selection for the second trial. Although the Commission's actions were judged to be legal and did not meet the technical definition of jury tampering, release of this information in 1989 helped create public interest in holding a third trial of Beckwith for the murder of Medgar Evers. See Nossiter, *Of Long Memory*, pp. 233–242.

45. For more on the Freedom Day strategy, see Dittmer, *Local People*, chapter 10, "Freedom Days."

46. AI, Dennis.

47. Moody, *Coming of Age*, pp. 369–375. See also Meier and Rudwick, *CORE*, pp. 274–275.

48. AI, Trumpauer.

49. Moody, *Coming of Age*, p. 376; *MFP*, 6/6/64; AI, Trumpauer.

50. Moody, *Coming of Age*, p. 377; AI, Trumpauer.

51. Tougaloo Southern Christian College 1964 Commencement Program, Joan Trumpauer personal archives.

52. "Dr. A. D. Beittel, President of Tougaloo College, Tougaloo, Mississippi, announced today that he will retire. . . ." Tougaloo College News, For Release, Public Relations Office, 4/25/64, TA.

53. AI, Rutledge; AI, Trumpauer. A summary of student unrest can be found in *The Student Voice*, Tougaloo College, Tougaloo, Mississippi, Edition #9, 2/14/64, TA (also available in Salter Papers, MDAH). Similar unrest cropped up during Beittel's tenure at Talladega College. See chapter 7, "Irreconcilable Differences," in Jones and Richardson, *Talladega College*.

54. Letter from Wesly A. Hotchkiss to Dr. Robert W. Spike, Commission on Religion and Race, National Council of Churches, 6/24/64, A. D. Beittel Papers, TA. For a further airing of the Beittel matter, see Dittmer, *Local People*, pp. 234–236.

55. AI, King.

56. Johnston, *Mississippi's Defiant Years*, pp. 301–302; Memorandum from Erle Johnston, Jr., to Dr. W. A. Hotchkiss, 4/17/64, A. D. Beittel Papers, TA. Apparently Beittel even charged into Johnston's office saying, "I heard you had something to do with my getting fired." Johnston, *Mississippi's Defiant* Years, p. 302.

57. Dittmer interview with Beittel, May 25, 1981. Dittmer personal archives.

58. See Dittmer, *Local People*, pp. 234–236.

59. "For A. D. Beittel, President, 1960–1964, Tougaloo College, Mississippi" by Elizabeth Sewell, May 20, 1964, A. D. Beittel Papers, TA.

60. Moody, *Coming of Age*, p. 378.

61. Urgent—All Branch Officers, "Dear Co-Worker," May 22, 1964, NAACP Papers, III:A229, Mississippi Pressures, General, 1956–65.

62. Carson, *Civil Rights Chronicle*, p. 271.

63. *MFP*, 7/11/64; Dittmer, *Local People*, pp. 275–277; *C-L*, 7/29/64; *JDN* carried a similar UPI story. It is interesting that neither local paper chose to have its own reporters cover the story or provide a synopsis of the Jackson Movement and its impact.

64. Pearlena Lewis's notepad on which she transcribed notes of 1964 strategy committee meeting minutes survives in the NAACP MS Papers.

65. AI, Salter.

66. Ibid.

67. AI, Lewis (Pearlena).

CHAPTER 11

1. The *Washington Post* reported that "Evers served in the Army from 1943 to 1946 and received two battle stars for his part in the Normandy invasion and the campaign in France. He was a technician 5th class [TEC5] at the time of his discharge from the famed 'Red Ball Express' unit of the Quartermaster Corps [QMC]." *WP*, 6/20/63. Other sources report that the honors he won for his Normandy invasion bravery were bronze stars. See Peters, *Arlington National Cemetery*, p. 86.

2. Evers, *For Us, the Living*, p. 325.

3. *ES*, 6/12/63.

4. The COFO hearings were not hearings in the formal congressional sense. They were something of a publicity stunt devised by Bob Moses to bring the story of what was happening in Mississippi within earshot of the Capitol and the White House. A day-long session of testimony by Mississippi grassroots activists was held at Washington's National Theatre before a panel of such noted figures as psychiatrist Robert Coles, author Joseph Heller, and educator Dr. Harold Taylor. *WP*, 6/9/64. Excerpts from the testimony were entered into the Congressional Record by Representative Ryan (D-NY) on June 16, 1964, pp. 13996–14013. Although it appears that Gene Young testified, there is no record of Anne Moody's testimony.

5. The following section on Anne Moody relies heavily on her recollections, as recorded on videotape during a class she presented to the students of Tougaloo College in 1984, titled "My Life Since *Coming of Age*." Ms. Moody presented a copy of that videotape to the Tougaloo College Archives in the autumn of 1996.

6. AI, Chaffee.

7. E. L. Doctorow letter to author, 3/4/97.

8. Joyce Johnson letters to author, 4/29/97 and 11/29/98.

9. Senator Edward Kennedy wrote a glowing review for the *New York Times*, 1/5/69.

10. Moody, "My Life Since *Coming of Age*," TA.

11. The German edition of the book was released in 1970 by S. Fischer Verlag as *Erwachen in Mississippi: Eine Autobiographie*. Böll's *Vorwort* can also be found, in German, in the second volume of his essays, *Essayistische Shcriften und Reden*. Translation of the foreword was generously provided to the author by German scholar Breon Mitchell, Indiana University.

12. See tape cover and printed matter, "Anne Moody reads her *Mr. Death* and *Bobo*," Caedmon, CDL5 1642, 1980, Broadway, New York, New York. LOC #79-740804.

13. All of the material for this section was derived from author's interviews with Joan Trumpauer (Mulholland).

14. All of the material for this section was derived from author's interviews with D. C. Sullivan and Charlie Newell.

15. All of the material in this section was derived from author's interviews with John Salter (Hunter Gray). Salter's epilogue to his book *Jackson, Mississippi*, titled "Reflections on an Odyssey" also reviews many of these aspects of his life after his time in Mississippi.

16. Salter's SCEF involvement is confirmed in various SCEF newsletters of the period.

17. All of the material for this section was derived from author's interviews with Memphis Norman.

18. *WP*, 2/6/05.

19. Most of the material for this section was derived from author's interviews with Pearlena Lewis. Information about Lewis's further NAACP involvement can be found in the NAACP MS Archives in Baltimore. For more information about the Young Democrats and the Mississippi Freedom Democratic Party, see Dittmer, *Local People*, pp. 348–349.

20. All of the material in this section was derived from author's interviews with Lois Chaffee.

21. Material for this section was pieced together from various sources, including interviews with his surviving family members and with his best friends from CORE, Jerome Smith and Dave Dennis. Additional information was found in the CORE Addendum.

22. **a cocked shotgun:** George Raymond's "Report," 10/21/63, Reel 23, Item #253, CORE Addendum. **pistol-whipped:** Report of Edward S. Hollander, CORE Field Secretary, 2/26/64, "Report on Canton, Madison County, Mississippi," p. 2. CORE Addendum. "In January [1964], Raymond was pistol-whipped by [Constable] Evans. After the beating, Raymond was charged with intimidating an officer and resisting arrest." **severely beaten:** Ibid., p. 5. "On Monday, January 27 [1964], George Raymond was told to get out of town by plainclothes policeman John Chance. He did not leave. On Wednesday, January 29, about 11:30 p.m., Raymond was driving from Canton to Jackson following a community meeting in the Pleasant Green Church. He was stopped by the state highway patrol on Highway 51 just outside Canton. He was taken behind the patrol car and found Constable Herbie Evans waiting there. Evans challenged Raymond to a fist fight. . . . When Raymond remained passive, Evans kicked him several times, knocking him against the back of the patrol car. Evans then let him go. The passengers in Raymond's car could not see the incident; the only possible witness was a highway patrolman who turned his back during the incident." This same incident is recounted by Mat Suarez in "O, Freedom Over Me," produced by Minnesota Public Radio and narrated by Julian Bond. **beaten with an ax handle:** AI, Myrtis Raymond; CORE Press Release, 11/2/65, "CORE Worker Sues Mississippi Mayor, Police Chief For $100,000," CORE Addendum. Also see Robert Wright interview of George Raymond, 9/28/68, Howard CRDP.

23. AI, Dennis.

24. For a complete description of the Child Development Group of Mississippi, see Greenberg, *The Devil*.

25. Field Report, Canton, Miss., 1/11/64, by Carole E. Merritt. "There have been some staff changes: . . . George Raymond will be away from Canton for at least a month and will return as a regular staff member, not as project director." Also see letter from Roger Phenix to Jack McKart, coordinator, Operation Freedom, 4/29/64, Operation Freedom

File, TC. "After two days of meeting which included shouting, harsh accusations, people stamping out in anger, and the like, it was decided that George Raymond should leave and be reassigned somewhere else. . . ."

26. Undated letter from George Raymond to "Mr. & Mrs. G. Raymond." Verna Polk, personal collection. 27. AI, Myrtis Raymond.

28. Letter from Richard Haley to George Raymond, 8/10/65, CORE Addendum. It states, in part, that "you have been designated to act as the CORE field secretary in Missisisippi."

29. **George ran unsuccessfully**: See "To Get That Power," a campaign brochure that includes not only Raymond, but Fannie Lou Hamer, Unita Blackwell, and others running for various state political posts. Box 1, Folder 7, Amzie Moore Papers, SHSW. **began to borrow heavily**: The author is indebted to Jerry Thornbery for generously sharing his extensive files on Operation Freedom, which include handwritten letters from Operation Freedom administrators about Raymond's condition at the time, as well as loan applications from Raymond and others.

30. AI, Raymond (Myrtis). Although Myrtis Raymond never mentioned it, Mat Suarez said that George Raymond once made an exploratory trip to New Orleans to see if there was any chance that his movement contacts there—many of whom had come and gone from the Mississippi scene—might have a job for him. Sadly, Suarez noted, no one was in a position to offer him a job. Both Suarez and Dave Dennis express sorrow over not being able to have helped Raymond at this time. See Dent interview with Matteo Suarez, Dent Collection. Also see AI, Dennis.

31. AI, Raymond (Myrtis); AI, Blakes et al.

32. AI, Raymond (Myrtis).

33. AI, Dennis.

34. AI, Blakes et al.

35. AI, Raymond (Myrtis).

36. AI, Raymond (John); AI, Blakes et al.

37. Ibid.

38. Information from this section was derived from author's interview with Tom Beard.

39. Much of the material from this section was derived from author's interviews with Ed King.

40. For more on the 1964 Democratic Convention and the MFDP challenge, see Dittmer, *Local People*, pp. 272–302.

41. King likes to point out that the MFDP ticket that year was an integrated group that included Rev. Clifton Whitley, the black Methodist chaplain of Rust College, who ran against Senator James O. Eastland. Also see Dittmer, *Local People*, p. 394.

42. For more on the NCC's Delta Ministry, see Dittmer, *Local People*, pp. 336–337.

43. Jeannette King made her own significant contributions to the Mississippi freedom fight, particularly as one of the trailblazers in the creation of the Child Development Group of Mississippi, where she served as field social services director. Jeannette, who had a master's degree in social work from Boston University, also taught social science at Tougaloo during the years she and Ed were there. See Greenberg, *The Devil*, p. 205. As an interesting aside, in a fictional account of the dissolution of a civil rights marriage,

author Rosellen Brown offers a more complicated view of the Kings' breakup. Although Brown said the individuals in her novel *Civil Wars* "began in memory" but have been "transformed into fiction," it is clear that she based her two main characters, Ted and Jessie Carll, primarily on Ed and Jeannette King. Brown worked with the Kings while she and her husband taught at Tougaloo in the mid-1960s, and she and Jeannette grew particularly close. See Brown, *Civil Wars*. For more on Jeannette King, see *Hands on the Freedom Plow: Personal Accounts by Women in SNCC*.

44. AI, King; AI, Salter. Also see "State Secrets," by Calvin Trillin, *The New Yorker*, 5/29/95. See *American Civil Liberties Union of Mississippi, Inc. et al. v. State of Mississippi et al.* (Edwin King and John Salter, Plaintiffs) No. 89-4647, U. S. Court of Appeals, Fifth Circuit, 9/14/90.

45. Although there are eighty-seven thousand "indexed names," this does not mean that a total of eighty-seven thousand individuals were spied on. Each variation of a name constitutes a separate entry. Joan Trumpauer, for instance, shows up as Joan Trumpauer and Joan Trumpower, etc. See "Unsealing Mississippi's Past," *Washington Post Magazine*, 5/9/99. Also see "State Secrets," *The New Yorker*, 5/29/95.

46. Obituary, Adam D. Beittel, 7/28/88, *Marin Independent Journal*; Greenberg, *The Devil*, pp. 212–213.

47. John Q. Adams interview with Dr. Beittel, Millsaps College; Greenberg, *The Devil*, p. 31.

48. Dittmer interview with Beittel.

49. Beittel obituary, 7/28/88, *Marin Independent Journal*.

50. AI, Allison.

51. Ibid.

52. Ibid.; also AI, Lewis.

53. Ibid.

54. Charles Evers has written two autobiographical accounts of his efforts in Mississippi: *Evers* and *Have No Fear*. In addition, see Berry, *Amazing Grace*, an account of Evers's run for governor of Mississippi.

55. AI, Louie; AI, Allison.

56. AI, Lewis.

57. Various correspondence in NAACP Papers, III:C276. Also see Ludden, *Anatomy*, p. 180. The memoir was a product solely of Ludden's memory and as such is substantially unreliable. However, I have used excerpts from it when it directly involves Ludden's recollections of his own actions or when it confirms the actions of others that are documented elsewhere. Also see AI, Ashford.

58. AI, Ashford; Ashford obituary as reported on the website Rochester A.B.O.V.E.

59. Current obituary, *NYT*, 7/9/97.

60. Wilkins obituary, *NYT*, 9/9/81.

61. Evers has written several memoirs of her life with and after Medgar Evers. See Evers, *For Us, the Living*, and Evers, *Watch Me Fly*. Also see *NYT*, 2/22/98, for information on her stepping down as chairman of the NAACP. See the NAACP's *Crisis* magazine, 9/98, for a description of her receipt of the Spingarn Medal. The medal was awarded to her for her roles as "civil rights activist, risk taker, mother, true believer."

62. See Vollers, *Ghosts of Mississippi*, and Nossiter, *Of Long Memory*.

63. AI, Blackwell.

64. AI, Newell.

65. AI, Black; AI, Newell.

66. AI, Schwelb; Doar biographical sketch on website of his law firm, Doar Rieck Kaley & Mack, www.doarlaw.com.

67. John Dittmer interview of Thelton Henderson; also see AI, Schwelb.

68. AI, Minor; "State of the Heart Journalism," *WP*, 5/16/97. Also see Minor biographical sketch on Mississippi Writers and Musicians website: www.mswritersandmusicians .com. For a complete overview of Minor's career and writing, see Minor's own *Eyes on Mississippi: A Fifty-Year Chronicle of Change* (Jackson, Mississippi: J. Prichard Morris Books, 2001).

69. Toler obituary, *NYT*, 10/19/66, and *CA*, 10/18/66. See also *CA* editorial "Kenneth Toler—Newspaperman," 10/18/66, and "Leaders Toler Wrote About Voice Their Grief, Respect," *CA*, 10/18/66.

70. Sessions obituary, *WP*, 12/29/05.

71. AI, Shoemaker.

72. *Central High School Yearbook*, 1966–1967; *Central High School Yearbook*, 1976–1977. Also see plaque outside of Central High School building, which provides a brief yet complete history of the school's building and usage.

73. Author's observations during various visits to Jackson from 1997 to 2012.

74. Plaque in front of city hall.

75. Information on Allen Thompson is derived from various news reports and his obituary. *C-L*, 12/3/69, 1/31/70, 10/19/80. Opposition to Civil Rights Act of 1964 taken from Thompson's testimony before the Senate Judiciary Committee, 2/20/64, as found in Thompson's file at MDAH.

76. Author's observations during several visits from 1997 to 2012.

77. AI, Ladner (Joyce).

78. AI, Ladner (Dorie). It may be of interest to some readers that Ladner was briefly romantically involved with the poet/singer Bob Dylan in the mid–1960s. His song "Outlaw Blues" on the album *Bringing It All Back Home* (Columbia Records, 3/65) references the liaison.

79. AI, Raymond (Myrtis and family).

80. AI, Smith.

81. AI, Dennis. For more on the Algebra Project, see the *New York Times Magazine*, "Mississippi Learning," 2/21/93; *Reader's Digest*, "Bob Moses's Crusade," 3/95.

82. Telegram from Mercedes A. Wright to the Jackson Movement (undated). NAACP MS Papers. For Wright's tenure at the NAACP, see *The Crisis*, March 1974.

EPILOGUE

1. The descriptions of Blackwell's and Thornell's backgrounds and professional experiences are derived from author's interviews with both men.

2. AI, Blackwell.

3. Ibid.

4. AI, Thornell.

5. Both Fred Blackwell and Joan Trumpauer heard from friends about the colorized photos of the sit-in that were published in *Paris Match*. An extensive search of the Library of Congress archival editions of the magazine turned up only full-page black and white images of the sit-in. "Dans Le Sud, C'est Pire Que La Violence," *Paris Match*, 9/63.

6. Report of the Photographic Jury, 1964 Pulitzer Prize (for calendar year 1963). Pulitzer Prize archives, Columbia University Graduate School of Journalism.

BIBLIOGRAPHY

AUTHOR'S INTERVIEWS

Allison, Doris. November 15, 1996. Jackson, Mississippi.

Ashford, Laplois. April 25, 1999. Washington, D.C.

Beard, Tom. May 1997 (I) (telephone); November 1997 (II). Jackson, Mississippi.

Black, James (Jim) L. November 14, 1996. Jackson, Mississippi.

Blackwell, Fred. February 7, 1996 (I); October 16, 2010 (II). Jackson, Mississippi.

Blakes, Lois, Verna Polk, and Robert Blakes, Jr. (with Jerome Smith). January 16, 1997. New Orleans, Louisiana.

Bullock, Bob. November 14, 1996. Jackson, Mississippi.

Calhoun, Robert. March 16, 1996 (telephone).

Chaffee, Lois. March 16, 1996 (I); March 16, 1996 (II).

Dennis, Dave. May 7, 1996 (I) (telephone); November 13, 1996 (II); February 1997 (III) (telephone). Jackson, Mississippi.

Donald, Cleveland. Spring 1997 (telephone).

King, Ed. February 9, 1996 (I); February 10, 1996 (II); February 11, 1996 (III). Jackson, Mississippi.

Ladner, Dorie (Churnett). July 1998 (telephone). Washington, D.C.

Ladner, Joyce. September 1997 (telephone). Washington, D.C.

Lewis, Alphonzo. March 1997 (telephone). Pearl, Mississippi.

Lewis, Pearlena (London). March 10, 1996 (I), Ann Arbor, Michigan; March 10, 1996 (II), Ypsilanti, Michigan; September 8, 1998 (III), Ypsilanti, Michigan.

Louie, Lillian. November 13, 1996. Jackson, Mississippi.

Ludden, Willie. June 1999 (telephone).

Lyons, Jerry. September 8, 1998. Jackson, Mississippi.

Minor, Bill. November 15, 1996. Jackson, Mississippi.

Moody, Anne. Various dates, April through July, 1996 (telephone).

Moses, Bob. July 3, 1997. Cambridge, Massachusetts.

Newell, Charlie. November 12, 1996. Ridgeland, Mississippi.

Norman, Memphis. October 8, 1995 (I); October 22, 1995 (II); November 12, 1995 (III). Falls Church, Virginia.

Raymond, John. January 20, 1997 (telephone). Slidell, Louisiana.

Raymond, Jomo. October 4, 1997. Jackson, Mississippi.

Raymond, Myrtis. October 4, 1997. Jackson, Mississippi.

Rutledge, Steve. June 1998 (telephone). Friars Hill, West Virginia.

Salter, Eldri. July 1997 (telephone). Grand Forks, North Dakota.

Salter, John. (Hunter Gray). December 27, 1995 (I); December 28, 1995 (II); December 29, 1995 (III). Grand Forks, North Dakota.

Schwelb, Frank. July 1997. Washington, D.C.

Shoemaker, W. C. (Dub). November 1996 (telephone). Jackson, Mississippi.

Smith, Jerome. June 3, 1996 (I) (telephone); January 16, 1997 (II); December 1, 1998 (III). New Orleans, Louisiana.

Sullivan, D. C. November 14, 1996. Laurel, Mississippi.

Thornell, Jack. March 1996 (telephone).

Trumpauer, Joan (Mulholland). October 17, 1992 (I); November 22, 1992 (II); March 7, 1993 (III); March 28, 1993, with Ed King (IV); September 9, 1995 (V); November 5, 1995 (VI). Arlington, Virginia.

Wells, James. November 12, 1996 (telephone). Jackson, Mississippi.

BOOKS

Arsenault, Raymond. *Freedom Riders: 1961 and the Struggle for Racial Justice*. New York: Oxford University Press, 2006.

Beecher, John. *To Live and Die in Dixie*. Birmingham, Alabama: Red Mountain Editions, 1966.

Berry, Jason. *Amazing Grace: With Charles Evers in Mississippi*. New York: Saturday Review Press, 1973.

Böll, Heinrich. *Essayistische Schriften und Reden. Vol 2*. Koln: Verlag Kiepenheuer & Witsch, 1979.

Branch, Taylor. *Parting the Waters: America in the King Years, 1954–63*. New York: Simon & Schuster, 1988.

———. *Pillar of Fire: America in the King Years, 1963–65*. New York: Simon & Schuster, 1998.

Brown, Rosellen, *Civil Wars*. New York: Dell Publishing, 1984.

Buckley, Gail Lumet. *The Hornes: An American Family*. New York: Alfred A. Knopf, Inc., 1986.

Cagin, Seth, and Philip Dray. *We Are Not Afraid: The Story of Goodman, Schwerner and Chaney and the Civil Rights Campaign for Mississippi*. New York: Macmillan Publishing Company, 1988.

Campbell, Clarice T. *Civil Rights Chronicle: Letters from the South*. Jackson, Mississippi: University Press of Mississippi, 1997.

Campbell, Clarice T., and Oscar Allan Rodgers, Jr. *Mississippi: The View From Tougaloo*. Jackson, Mississippi: University Press of Mississippi, 1979.

Carson, Clayborne et al. *Civil Rights Chronicle: The African-American Struggle for Freedom*. Chicago: Publications International, Ltd., 2003.

Cohodas, Nadine. *The Band Played Dixie: Race and the Liberal Conscience at Ole Miss*. New York: The Free Press, a division of Simon & Schuster, 1997.

Dittmer, John. *Local People: The Struggle for Civil Rights in Mississippi*. Urbana and Chicago: University of Illinois Press, 1994.

Edgcomb, Gabrielle Simon. *From Swastika to Jim Crow: Refugee Scholars at Black Colleges*. Malabar, Florida: Krieger Publishing Company, 1993.

Erenrich, Susie, ed. *Freedom Is a Constant Struggle: An Anthology of the Mississippi Civil Rights Movement*. Montgomery, Alabama: Black Belt Press, 1999.

Etheridge, Eric. *Breach of Peace.* New York: Atlas & Co., 2008.

Evers, Charles. *Evers.* New York: The World Publishing Company, 1971.

Evers, Charles, and Andrew Szanton. *Have No Fear: The Charles Evers Story.* New York: John Wiley & Sons, 1997.

Evers, Mrs. Medgar, with William Peters. *For Us, the Living.* Garden City, New York: Doubleday & Company, Inc., 1967.

Evers-Williams, Myrlie, and Melinda Blau. *Watch Me Fly.* New York: Little, Brown & Company, 1999.

Evers-Williams, Myrlie, and Manning Marable, eds.*The Autobiography of Medgar Evers.* New York: Basic Civitas Books, 2005.

Farmer, James. *Lay Bare the Heart: An Autobiography of the Civil Rights Movement.* New York: New American Library, Plume Books, 1986.

Garrow, David J. *Bearing the Cross: Martin Luther King, Jr., and the Southern Christian Leadership Conference.* New York: William Morrow, 1986.

Greenberg, Polly. *The Devil Has Slippery Shoes: A Biased Biography of the Child Development Group of Mississippi.* Toronto: The MacMillan Company, 1969.

Gregory, Dick, and Robert Lipsyte. *Nigger: An Autobiography.* New York: E. P. Dutton & Co., Inc., 1964.

Halberstam, David. *The Children.* New York: Random House, 1998

Harris, Jacqueline L. *History and Achievement of the NAACP.* New York: Franklin Watts Publishing Co., 1992.

Haskins, James. *Lena Horne.* New York: Coward-McCann, Inc., 1983.

Holland, Endesha Ida Mae. *From the Mississippi Delta.* New York: Simon & Schuster, 1997.

Horne, Lena, and Richard Schickel. *Lena.* Garden City, New York: Doubleday & Company, Inc., 1965.

Hunter-Gault, Charlayne. *In My Place.* New York: Farrar Straus Giroux, 1992.

Johnston, Erle. *Mississippi's Defiant Years, 1953–1973: An Interpretive Documentary with Personal Experiences.* Forest, Mississippi: Lake Harbor Publishers, 1990.

Jones, Maxine E., and Joe M. Richardson. *Talladega College: The First Century.* Tuscaloosa, Alabama: University of Alabama Press, 1990.

Kunstler, William M. *Deep in My Heart.* New York: William Morrow & Company, 1966.

Lawson, Steven F. *Black Ballots: Voting Rights in the South, 1944–1969.* New York: Columbia University Press, 1976.

Leekley, Sheryle, and John Leekley. *Moments: The Pulitzer Prize Photographs.* New York: Crown Publishers, Inc., 1978.

Lewis, Anthony, and the *New York Times. Portrait of a Decade: The Second American Revolution.* New York: Bantam Books, 1965.

Lewis, R. W. B. *The Jameses: A Family Narrative.* New York: Farrar, Straus, and Giroux, 1991.

Loewen, James W., and Charles Sallis. *Mississippi: Conflict and Change.* New York: Pantheon Books (a division of Random House), 1974.

Ludden, Willie B., Jr. (with Leon Turner). *Anatomy of a Civil Rights Worker.* Baltimore: Publish America, 2002.

Marsh, Charles. *God's Long Summer: Stories of Faith and Civil Rights.* Princeton, New Jersey: Princeton University Press, 1997.

McMillen, Neil R. *Dark Journey: Black Mississippians in the Age of Jim Crow.* Urbana and Chicago: University of Illinois Press, 1989.

Meier, August, and Elliott Rudwick. *CORE: A Study in the Civil Rights Movement, 1942–1968.* New York: Oxford University Press, 1973.

Mendelsohn, Jack. *The Martyrs.* New York: Harper & Row, 1966.

Meredith, James. *Three Years in Mississippi.* Bloomington, Indiana: Indiana University Press, 1966.

Moody, Anne. *Coming of Age in Mississippi: An Autobiography.* New York: The Dial Press, 1968. All citations from paperback edition, New York: Bantam Doubleday Dell Publishing Group, Inc., 1976.

———. *Erwachen in Mississippi: Eine Autobiographie.* Frankfurt am Main: S. Fischer Verlag GmbH, 1970.

———. *Mr. Death: Four Stories.* New York: Harper & Row, 1975.

Moore, Charles, and Michael S. Durham. *Powerful Days: The Civil Rights Photography of Charles Moore.* New York: Stewart, Tabori & Chang and the Professional Photography Division of Eastman Kodak Company, 1991.

Nichols, John P. *Skyline Queen and the Merchant Prince: The Woolworth Story.* New York: Simon & Schuster, 1973.

Nossiter, Adam. *Of Long Memory: Mississippi and the Murder of Medgar Evers.* Reading, Massachusetts: Addison-Wesley Publishing Company, 1994.

Oshinsky, David M. *Worse Than Slavery: Parchman Farm and the Ordeal of Jim Crow Justice.* New York: The Free Press, 1996.

Payne, Charles M. *I've Got the Light of Freedom: The Organizing Tradition and the Mississippi Freedom Struggle.* Berkeley and Los Angeles: University of California Press, 1995.

Peters, James Edward. *Arlington National Cemetery: Shrine to America's Heroes.* Kensington, Maryland: Woodbine House, 1986.

Radest, Howard B. *Toward Common Ground: The Story of the Ethical Societies in the United States.* New York: Frederick Ungar Publishing Company, 1969.

Raines, Howell. *My Soul Is Rested: Movement Days in the Deep South Remembered.* New York: G. P. Putnam's Sons, 1977.

Roberts, Gene, and Hank Klibanoff. *The Race Beat: The Press, The Civil Rights Struggle, and the Awakening of a Nation.* New York: Vintage Books, 2006.

Salter, John R., Jr. *Jackson, Mississippi: An American Chronicle of Struggle and Schism.* Hicksville, New York: Exposition Press, 1979. All citations from paperback edition, Malabar, Florida: Robert E. Krieger Publishing Company, 1987.

Schlesinger, Arthur M., Jr., *Robert Kennedy and His Times.* New York: Houghton Mifflin Company, 1978.

Schulke, Flip. *He Had a Dream: Martin Luther King, Jr., and the Civil Rights Movement.* New York: W. W. Norton & Company, 1995.

Silver, James W. *Mississippi: The Closed Society.* New York: Harcourt, Brace & World, Inc., 1966 (enlarged edition).

Silverman, Jerry. *Songs of Protest and Civil Rights.* New York: Chelsea House Publishers, 1992.

Viorst, Milton. *Fire in the Streets: America in the 1960s.* New York: Simon and Schuster, 1979.

Vollers, Maryanne. *Ghosts of Mississippi: The Murder of Medgar Evers, The Trials of Byron De La Beckwith, and the Haunting of the New South.* Boston: Little Brown & Company, 1995.

Watson, Denton, L. *Lion in the Lobby: Clarence Mitchell, Jr.'s Struggle for the Passage of Civil Rights Laws.* New York: William Morrow & Company, Inc., 1990.

Wilkins, Roger. *A Man's Life: An Autobiography.* New York: Simon and Schuster, 1982.

Wilkins, Roy, with Tom Mathews. *Standing Fast: The Autobiography of Roy Wilkins.* New York: Viking Press, 1982.

Williams, Juan. *Eyes on the Prize.* New York: Viking Penguin, Inc., 1987.

ARTICLES, PAMPHLETS, AND REPORTS

"Are You Curious About Mississippi?" New York: The National Association for the Advancement of Colored People, January 20, 1961.

Handbook of Historically Black Colleges and Universities, 1995–1997. Wilmington, Delaware: Jireh and Associates, Inc., 1995.

"M Is for Mississippi and Murder." New York: The National Association for the Advancement of Colored People, December 1955.

The Murray Resource Directory to the Nation's Historically Black Colleges and Universities. Washington, D.C.: Daniel A. P. Murray Associates, 1993.

"Why I Live in Mississippi." Medgar Evers (as told to Francis H. Mitchell), *Ebony*, November 1958.

FILM AND VIDEO MATERIALS

Anne Moody: My Life Since Coming of Age: A ninety-minute class presented by Anne Moody at Tougaloo College in 1984. Courtesy of Tougaloo Archives.

Eyes on the Prize: America's Civil Rights Years. Blackside Inc., Boston, MA, 1987.

Lena Horne: The Lady and Her Music. Thirteen/WNET, An *American Masters* Special. Includes a brief clip of the Jackson Woolworth's sit-in, as well as footage of Horne's appearance in Jackson on June 4, 1963. Also includes footage of the Evers funeral march.

MDAH Audio-Visual Collection. Includes substantial footage of the Jackson Movement events, including the sit-in (early stages) and the march after Medgar Evers's funeral.

Time and Again. An MSNBC series. The segment broadcast on 9/5/96 includes the most extensive footage of the Jackson Woolworth's sit-in, which was culled from an NBC *Special Report on Civil Rights*, originally broadcast 9/2/63.

Time Was—1960s. Dick Cavett narrates key events of the 1960s. Bruce Cohn Productions for Home Box Office, 1979. Includes a brief clip of the most violent part of the Jackson Woolworth's sit-in.

Malcolm X. A Spike Lee film. 40 Acres and a Mule Filmworks, Inc., 1993. Includes brief clip of the Jackson Woolworth's sit-in.

AUDIOTAPED/TRANSCRIBED ARCHIVES

Anne Moody Reads Her *Mr. Death* and *Bobo*. New York: Caedmon, 1980.

Interview of John R. Salter, with Rev. Edwin King, by John Jones, MDAH, 1/6/81.

Interview of John R. Salter, Jr., by Betsy Nash, John C. Stennis Oral History Project, Department of History, Mississippi State University, 12/26/90.

Interview of Dr. A. D. Beittel by John Dittmer, Dittmer Archives, 5/25/81.

Interview of Dr. A. D. Beittel and Ruth Beittel by Clifton A. Johnson, Amistad Research Center, Tulane University (undated).

Interview of Dr. A. D. Beittel by Gordon Henderson, Millsaps Oral History of Contemporary Mississippi Life and Viewpoint, Millsaps College, 6/2/65.

Interviews of Charlie Cobb, Mat Suarez, Annie Devine, and C. O. Chinn by Tom Dent, Tom Dent Collection, Amistad Research Center, Tulane University.

Interview of Thelton Henderson by John Dittmer, Dittmer Archives, 12/30/83.

"Where Do We Go From Here?," a synopsis of Medgar Evers's funeral, the demonstration afterward, and the Jackson Movement's negotiated settlement, Pacifica Radio Archives, Los Angeles, California.

Discussions between President John F. Kennedy, Attorney General Robert F. Kennedy, and Mayor Allen C. Thompson of Jackson, John F. Kennedy Presidential Library.

SOUND RECORDINGS

Sing for Freedom: The Story of the Civil Rights Movement through Its Songs. Smithsonian/Folkways Records, Washington, D.C., 1990.

INDEX